*Factory and Production
Management*

Factory and Production Management

K G Lockyer

Professor of Operations Management
University of Bradford

Third Edition of *Factory Management*

PITMAN

PITMAN BOOKS LIMITED
39 Parker Street, London WC2B 5PB

PITMAN PUBLISHING INC
1020 Plain Street, Marshfield, Massachusetts

Associated Companies
Pitman Publishing Pty Ltd, Melbourne
Pitman Publishing New Zealand Ltd, Wellington
Copp Clark Pitman, Toronto

© K. G. Lockyer 1962, 1969, 1974

Third edition published in Great Britain 1974

Reprinted 1976, 1977, 1979, 1981 (twice)

Printed and bound in Great Britain
at The Pitman Press, Bath

ISBN 0 273 00465 4

To Doris
my life—my love

Preface to the Third Edition

'As all experienced factory managers know, there are but two simple devices necessary to run a factory—a crystal ball and a magic wand. In the absence of these, the present volume is offered to those engaged in that peculiar form of juggling known as Factory Management, in the hope that it will indicate some areas of knowledge which it may be of use to study. The text is not encyclopedic, nor is it intended to be a training manual for any of the specialist disciplines: illumination is intended to be general, rather than intense.'

The above paragraph opened the Preface to both the first and second editions and as a statement of purpose it will serve to introduce this third edition, now re-titled *Factory and Production Management*. This edition has been re-structured to present the contents in a more logical form. It is in six sections; the first gives a perspective view over the whole of the production function. Section Two deals with the product, its choice and its qualities, and Section Three discusses the location, design, layout, equipping and maintaining of a production unit to make the product, and concludes with a discussion on the use of the budget as an organizational tool and as a summary of policy. Section Four assumes that a product is available for manufacture and a fully equipped plant to hand, and it then deals with some of the problems of manufacture and the various methods used to identify the costs incurred. No factory can operate without a timetable of some sort and this is discussed in Section Five. This is largely concerned with production and material control; buying and storekeeping are also discussed.

In the final analysis all factories, whether automated or not, operate through people, and the final section of this book deals with some of the organizational and administrative tasks which arise when employing people. No attempt is made to enter the realms of industrial sociology and psychology as these are comprehensively dealt with elsewhere, but the work of the Personnel Department, the operation of incentive schemes and the safety of the employee are discussed at some length.

A number of techniques are used in Production Management in a variety of situations; these are gathered together in the Appendices. Each chapter concludes with some suggestions for Further Reading; these do not pretend to be comprehensive but list some of the books which the author has found useful in his work as a Manager, Consultant and Teacher. Appendix 6 ('Representative Examination Questions') is considerably enlarged, and now contains over 360 questions from a wide variety of sources. The author had intended to discontinue this Appendix, but a study of examination papers obtained from most Polytechnics and Universities concerned with the teaching of 'Production Management' indicated that teachers were finding this section extremely useful, and it has accordingly been retained and amplified. Some of the questions are of considerable age, but perhaps good examination questions, like good jokes, never die.

This edition includes a number of treatments not found in the previous editions, notably: The Choice of Product (Chapter 2), The Workplace (Chapter 16), Group Technology (Chapter 18), Line of Balance (Chapter 25), Safety (Chapter 32). In addition, all other chapters have been considerably amplified to match the ever increasing ability of practising managers and students to deal with quantitative analyses. This has resulted in a general widening of subject matter and hence the change in the title of the book.

When the book was first published in 1962 it was possible to identify with some precision the examinations whose syllabuses had helped determine the form of the volume. The enormous increase in the teaching of 'management', in various forms and in diverse establishments, now makes this quite impossible. As previously, the text covers most of the 'production' work in the Diploma in Management Studies, together with parts of the examinations of various professional bodies, including the Institution of Production Engineers, the Institute of Cost and Management Accountants, and the Institute of Chartered Accountants in England and Wales (Diploma in Management Information). Undergraduates taking 'management' or 'administration' in their degree studies and M.Sc. or M.Tech. students who are taking 'conversion' type administration courses will also find much helpful material in the present text. No serious student, however, whether seeking for success in examinations, or at employment, should confine his reading to any single book, and attention is again directed to the suggestions for further reading which appear at the end of most chapters.

My thanks are due to my wife for her help and forbearance and to my good friend Jack Prichard for his many helpful comments. I would also like to thank my friends and colleagues at the Polytechnic of Central London and at the Universities of Technology at Bradford and Loughborough. Further, I have been most fortunate in that my readers have been concerned enough to write to me pointing out where the book required amplification and/or amendment; to these and all other persons who have been of such assistance my most heartfelt thanks. Any mistakes in the book clearly I am privileged to claim as my own.

December 1973
K. G. Lockyer

Contents

Contents

Section III The Factory

Section IV Manufacture

Contents

Section One   Perspective

1. Introduction to the Production Function

Chapter 1
Introduction to the
Production Function

THE FACTORY WITHIN THE CORPORATION

A factory is '... any premises in which ... persons are employed ... for ... the ... purposes of making ... altering, repairing, ornamenting, finishing, cleaning, washing, breaking up ... demolishing, or ... , adapting for sale ... any article'. Thus the Factories Act, and thus long ago, the essential features of the production function—the bringing together of people, plant and material to provide goods or services for sale—were set down. The jurists here recognize clearly that which too many managers forget, that is, that the factory is *necessarily* part of a larger entity. This being so, the successful factory manager must, therefore, plan, execute and control his work within the framework of the corporate plan. Indeed, unless the factory plan is *part* of the corporate plan, the *total* enterprise can only be a failure, or at best a sub-success. In a brilliant and perceptive paper, Moran expresses the resultant dilemma: 'The optimization of the total enterprise frequently requires the sub-optimization of its component divisions, but it is always difficult to get divisions graciously to accept such restraints on their objectives.'[1]

Too often the factory is regarded as a self-contained, self-sufficient body, and its dependence upon integration with the rest of the system is recognized only when other parts of the enterprise change. The dangers of this tunnel-vision are great; for example, government legislation may force a marketing change which requires a design modification: in turn, this can alter production processes in such a way that operators are displaced, with consequent redundancy and retraining problems. Had the factory manager looked outside the four walls of his own production unit, these problems could well have been foreseen and their effects mitigated. Similarly, a Board decision to change from a selling policy, where orders are *accepted*, to a marketing policy, where orders are *sought*, will inevitably demand major changes in the whole system of factory management; again, these can be foreseen if the factory manager looks outwards as well as inwards.

---

[1] Moran's paper appears as one of the appendices to Starr's *Production Management Systems & Syntheses*.

It is only when the factory is understood to be part of a whole—a sub-system within a system—that its management can be truly successful. All organizations 'maintain themselves only by carrying on active transactions with their environment', and the factory stands within two identifiable—but not independent—environments, the community at large and the parent corporation; therefore the effects of either or both must always be considered. Furthermore, *the factory itself* provides the environment for its own constituent departments, and again the interaction of the parts with themselves and with the host environment must be realized. These interdependencies produce two important consequences of high practical value—

(a) changes in the environment impose changes on the organization;

(b) changes within the organization affect the environment.

To survive, therefore, organizations must be prepared to *respond to change*, and no manager should ever believe that any decision is eternal. To construct an organization to be so rigid that it cannot accept change is to invite disaster, particularly since technological change is now accelerating at such a rate that continuous adaptation is essential for any sustained success. Clearly 'change for the sake of change' is wasteful, and piecemeal change, 'tinkering with the parts', likely to be unproductive, even counter-productive. All too often the installation of a new 'efficient' machine or system has produced no effect on the *organization as a whole*, since the necessary accompanying changes elsewhere have not been put into effect.

One of the most potentially powerful change-agents of today is the computer, which can permit the consideration of problems which are more complex than any which can be dealt with by unaided thought. It is now technically possible to construct a model of a complete organizational system, and to examine the way in which this system behaves. Whilst the cost of such model-making is high—in many cases prohibitive—the analysis which precedes this is often in itself extremely valuable, as it may disclose something of the underlying structure of the system. This ability of the computer is probably of greater fundamental importance to the manager than the data-processing facility, and nowhere is this more true than in the production area. Here many of the very varied sub-systems can be effectively modelled and analysed, and the rewards which can thence be obtained in improved effectiveness can be very great. No computer, or computer program, can in itself 'solve' anything without the co-operation of management, however, and this co-operation must inevitably spring from understanding.

Whilst recognizing that the factory is a structure within a structure, it is worth pointing out that it has characteristics which distinguish it from the rest of the organization. It generally employs the bulk of the manpower, utilizes the bulk of the physical assets, requires the bulk of the financial resources and is made up of many sub-systems. This is not to suggest that the production function is more important than, say, the marketing function, but to indicate that its planning is likely to be *of a different kind* from that of other functions. In particular, the weight and size of the resources involved are such that the planning must enable operating decisions to be made rapidly. The scale of resources deployed will often permit analyses within the factory of a type which cannot be carried out elsewhere—but with this condition goes the danger that these analyses are carried out *for their own sake* and not for the results which flow from them.

PLANNING AND CONTROL

Objectives and Policies

Management at all levels is constantly required to take decisions, and in order that these will stand the test of time and advance the organization as a whole it is necessary that they should be taken logically, not arbitrarily. This is as true of the decisions taken by the most junior chargehand as of those taken by the managing director, and each in his own way requires to know—

1. *The objectives* of the organization, that is, the purpose for which the undertaking is in being.
2. *The policies* of the organization, that is, the means whereby the objectives are to be achieved.

In the absence of such knowledge decisions can only be taken capriciously, and a short-term decision may determine some long-term action which is undesirable but inescapable. Without a clear understanding of objectives and policies a manager cannot, for example, embark upon a rational training programme, or a maintenance programme or a plant replacement scheme: in fact, no decisions can be sensibly taken which are of anything but immediate value.

Planning

Taken together, the objectives and policies form a *plan* for the operation of the organization. Planning occupies a considerable portion of the factory manager's time, and it is worth while to try to identify those characteristics which should be found in a useful plan. Such a plan is—

(*a*) *Explicit.* Lack of clarity usually indicates a lack of understanding, of knowledge or of purpose.

(*b*) *Understood.* The recipients of a plan may not have the same technical skills as the originator of the plan, so that although it is expressed quite explicitly, there is a barrier to understanding. This is most often found in plans drawn up by specialists for non-specialist colleagues.

(*c*) *Accepted.* Any plan should be accepted by all concerned in its execution—indeed, it is often felt that a plan should be drawn up by all those who will be held responsible for its execution. Inevitably, there will need to be tactical modifications to any plan, and if it has not been both understood and accepted, then there is a very real danger that these modifications may seriously affect the ultimate achievement of the purpose of the plan.

(*d*) *Capable of accepting change*. As mentioned above, circumstances may arise which require changes to be made. Any plan which is made or presented in an unnecessarily rigid form will be of limited value in times of change.

(*e*) *Compatible with the internal and external constraints*. Cognizance must be taken of the internal limitations (men, materials, machines, money) and of the environment within which the company is operating.

(*f*) *Capable of being monitored*. In order to check on the execution of a plan, it should be cast in such a form that it can be monitored. This will usually involve expressing the plan in numerical terms—in itself a useful discipline.

(*g*) *A spur to action*. Any plan which is not a very real stimulus to action is of limited value.

Is the *time scale* correct?

Has the *external environment* been considered?

Are the *internal resources* adequate?

Can it *accept change*?

Is it *explicit*?

Is it *understood*?

Is it *accepted*?

Can it be *monitored*?

Is the plan a *spur to action*?

Characteristics of an Effective Plan

The factory manager, then, to be successful, requires an unequivocal statement of the purpose of his factory and the means of achieving that purpose, which statement should be explicit and in writing. The act of preparation of such a statement must start from the top—the board of directors—and must spread downwards to each executive level, gaining in detail as each succeeding managerial level is reached. Thus a board will, after discussion, issue a broad directive to the factory manager indicating the objectives of the factory and the general policies to be carried out—

> The factory will be required to produce.................................... and ...., and associated equipment, to be sold in the .... price range for use in the .... market. Wherever possible .... labour will be used, ..., ... and .... classes of work being subcontracted. The OUTPUT will be expected to increase by at least .... per cent for the next .... years and labour will be trained accordingly.

From this the factory manager with his senior executives will derive his departmental requirements, and the following further directive will be issued—

To implement the board's decisions, the factory will be organized as follows—

Department I will be headed by Mr. A, and will be required to . . . .

Department II will be headed by Mr. B., and will be required to . . . .

Department III will . . . .

and these will be discussed between the appropriate department managers and their subordinates. This procedure will be carried out at each level, so that all concerned should know what is required and how it is expected that it will be achieved.

The most succinct expression of objectives is the *sales forecast*, which can be considered as the quantitative statement of the corporate objectives of the company. In turn this forecast is translated into policy by a *factory budget*, the quantitative representation of corporate policy. Clearly there is a very real interdependence between objectives, policies, forecasts and budgets, and it is difficult—and possibly unnecessary—to try to decide where one ends and another begins. The important requirement is that they should all be self-consistent and this may mean that the examination, of a forecast may require a re-examination of either objectives or policies as the derived budget may demonstrate the impracticability of that forecast. The planning process is essentially an iterative one, and the planner will frequently need to travel up and down the chain—

$$\text{Objectives} \rightleftharpoons \text{policies} \rightleftharpoons \text{forecasts} \rightleftharpoons \text{budgets}$$

before a stable plan is achieved.

Forecasts

To the factory manager there are two basic forecasts without which he can only take arbitrary decisions. These are—

1. The long-term market forecast, covering the expectations of the marketing department for the next five (or more) years.
2. The short-term sales forecast, covering the requirements of the marketing department for the next twelve months.

The Long-term Market Forecast

The detail of the preparation of a long-term forecast is outside the scope of the present text, since the factory manager has little responsibility for it. It is carried out by the marketing department, backed by economic, statistical, political and technical advisers, and will be based upon information on such matters as—

1. Levels of industrial production both national and international.
2. Government expenditure.
3. Labour availability.
4. Possible changes in price structure.
5. Variations in living standards.
6. Competition, both national and international.
7. Possible new products.

8. Market potentials.
9. Technological changes.
10. Company resources.
11. Company history.
12. Long-term company objectives, policies and plans.

This forecast may take the form of a statement of anticipated output in monetary terms for the next five years, with notes on each year as amplification (see Fig. 1.1). A long-term forecast is particularly necessary when

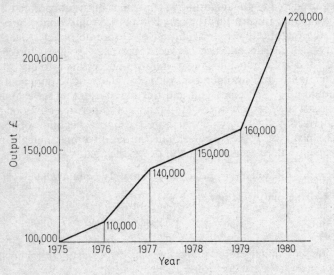

Fig. 1.1. Long-term Forecast

1976   Expected output £110,000. During this year new products A and B will be developed to be ready for marketing in 1977.

1977   Expected output £140,000. Products A and B will be marketed. Staff increase of 10 per cent anticipated to cope with expected increase in sales. Inauguration of work-study department.

1978   Expected output £150,000. Consolidation of sales targets. No increase in staff. Plans for move to new premises in 1979 to be completed.

1979   Expected output £160,000. Move to new plant completed. Increase in space available permits increase in development department.

1980   Expected output £220,000. No productive-staff increases expected: increase in development and production planning staff to permit increase in productivity and range of products.

considerable expansion is required and when heavy capital expenditure is contemplated. In exceptional cases—for example, the building of a new oil refinery or the construction of a new steel rolling mill—forecasts of up to twenty years are made, although some authorities believe that in view of political uncertainties there can be little usefulness in forecasts of any kind over periods of longer than five years.

The Short-term Sales Forecast

The short-term forecast is the basis from which all factory activity stems. It is a prediction covering the next budget period, usually twelve months, of—

1. The products to be sold;
2. The price of the products;
3. The quantity of each product;
4. The dates by which the products are to be available;

and will be in agreement with general company policy as laid down by the board and the long-term forecasts previously made. Where a company is making items for stock the statement of the short-term forecast is quite straightforward. However, a difficulty might appear to arise in the case of a company manufacturing to customers' designs, or a company offering a service rather than a product—for example plating, painting, repairing, packaging. In these cases it is necessary to assume that the work done is of a foreseeable nature—should it be purely random no forecast is possible. Accepting this reservation it is then necessary to determine the Product or Service Groups offered, defining a Group as work offered having a stable and similar cost pattern. The short-term forecast will then detail—

(*a*) The product/service groups offered.

(*b*) The volume of business measured financially to be derived from each group.

(*c*) The distribution of this business throughout the year.

(Typical sales forecasts are given on p. 397 *et seq.*).

The procedure for setting up a forecast may be as follows—

1. A target figure for profit and/or volume for the forthcoming year is received from the board.

2. The marketing department, using information on such matters as past sales, knowledge of present trends and market research information, will set up a tentative forecast, which is submitted to the production and costing departments.

3. The production department will consider the feasibility of meeting the tentative forecast, having regard to the production facilities available and obtainable. As a result of this scrutiny it might be found that one or more sections of the works is overloaded whilst others are underloaded. Modification to the draft forecast will then be suggested.

4. The costing department will then examine the amended forecast to see if it will satisfactorily meet the company's policy on earnings and investment. This might reveal, for example, that the most readily sold product has the lowest profit margin and that the marketing department, by requiring a substantial increase in the sales of this product, has seriously affected the total profit yield. From considerations of this kind the costing department may propose further modifications to the forecast.

5. With the comments of the production and costing departments available, the sales department will produce another sales forecast which again is scrutinized. Eventually, after a series of trials, a forecast is produced which is acceptable to all concerned.

6. The final sales forecast is then submitted to the board to be approved or rejected.

The above procedure, although apparently cumbersome, must be carried out effectively if the forecast is to be stable and useful. The sales forecast *must* have the support of the marketing, production and costing departments, and *must not* be produced by any one department in the absence of either of the other two.

The Use of Linear Programming

In some circumstances the above procedure can be carried out analytically using the technique known as Linear Programming (L.P.). When using this method it is necessary to know—

(*a*) The objective function, that is, that which the organization wishes to optimize. This is frequently total contribution, although it may be plant utilization or output measured in terms other than financial.

(*b*) The constraints within which the forecast must operate: these are usually the capacities in each work-unit and the maximum/minimum quantities acceptable to the marketing department.

The basic assumption which must be made when using L.P. is that all parameters vary linearly with volume. Accepting this assumption and given the data above, it is then possible to set up a series of first-order equations expressing the objective function in terms of the constraints and the volume of each product. From this set of equations a solution can be derived giving the 'mix' of products, in absolute terms, which will optimize the objective function.

The solution to an L.P. problem when there are more than a few variables and constraints is tedious in the extreme. There are, however, many existing computer programs which will enable solutions to be very rapidly obtained. A much more difficult task is to express in quantitative terms all the constraints, and it is this difficulty which prevents L.P. being used more extensively in this area. However, this should not be allowed to prevent the manager from examining the method and judging for himself its appropriateness in his own circumstances.

The Budget

When preparing and finalizing the sales forecasts, it will have been necessary to examine the various constraints upon the organization to ensure that the forecast lies within these constraints. In so doing, all the data necessary for drawing up a budget will have been assembled—although possibly not in the form most appropriate to budgetary control. When this crude data is broken down into responsibility areas, then a *budget* will have been created, and the basis for budgetary control laid down. Similarly, if the information is grouped together in cost centres around products or services, then a *cost control* system can follow. This subject is more fully discussed in Chapter 12.

Control

Together the sales forecast and the factory budget express a *plan* for the organization, and this having been agreed, *control* must be exerted. The word 'control'[2] is here used in the sense of ' . . . the ensuring that all that takes place is in accordance with the rules established and the instruction issued'. It is *not* used in the sense of direct supervision of labour.

A control department is in the position of a navigator who, being given a destination, carries out the following tasks—

1. Sets a course, having knowledge of the limitations of his vessel.
2. Informs the helmsman of the course to be taken.
3. Observes the position of the vessel in its journey at such intervals as are considered necessary.
4. Checks the actual position against the planned position.
5. Reports any deviations to his commanding officer.

At no time can the navigator be said to be responsible for the ship, since this responsibility is always in the hands of the captain, who may require the navigator to re-plot a course to accommodate variations in circumstances. Obviously a navigator may recommend changes, but he may not demand that such changes be implemented.

The Six Features of Control Activity

All control activities have the following features in common—

1. *Planning.* A plan must be laid down in conformity with the policies of the company. In the case of Budgetary Control, this involves the drawing up of the factory budgets, whilst Quality Control (i.e. inspection) plans take the form of quality and inspection standards or specifications. Production Control plans cover the use of material, labour and machines; and Cost Control plans involve setting cost standards for production. All these are guides to future action, and all should have the characteristics previously discussed.

2. *Publishing.* Once a plan has been agreed it must be recorded and distributed to all interested parties, in order that they may know what is expected of them. This is often neglected, with disastrous results.

3. *Measuring.* The plan being in operation, performance must be measured. The frequency of measurement will depend entirely on circumstances, but should not be more frequent than necessary to give a reliable representation of behaviour. Thus, slowly changing circumstances require observations much less frequently than rapidly changing ones. The obtaining of this information is, in the case of production and budgetary control, most difficult, the difficulties arising from two main causes—

[2] The first time this meaning was given to 'control' in industry appears to have been in 1916 when Henri Fayol published his *Administration Industrielle et Générale*, which was translated into English in 1929.

(*a*) the difficulty in measuring the amount of work in a partly completed assembly or process;

(*b*) the difficulty of dealing with a very large volume of information. Even in a small workshop there will need to be a very large number of observations taken and analysed to give a comprehensive representation of the production situation. In some circumstances the rate of change of values can be a more significant indicator than the values themselves.

4. *Comparing*. The observations above must be compared with the plans made, and significant divergencies noted. Clearly, when such comparisons are made, conformance will be seen as well as divergence, but it is only the variations from plan which excite interest: this principle is, of course, the principle of management by exception. Consider an activity-time plan (Fig. 1.2) represented graphically by the line OA. While

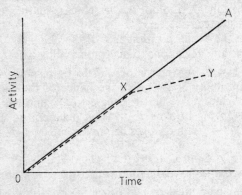

Fig. 1.2. Activity-time graph

performance falls along this line no action on the part of the control department is required—thus OX is a satisfactory, quiescent stage. Should performance then deviate from this line—for example, along XY—action is needed to restore the performance back along OA. The deviation XY thus excites action, but the knowledge that there was an agreement with plan before X is clearly of importance also, since it demonstrates that the plan was, for some time at least, a practicable one.

5. *Reporting*. The results of the observations and the subsequent comparisons need to be presented to those responsible for the activity under examination, although the actions subsequently taken are the responsibility of the supervisor, not of the controller. In presenting these reports, care should be taken to make them brief and intelligible. It is often useful to present only the significant deviations so that the supervisor concerned can 'Manage by Exception'.

6. *Correcting*. Deviations from the plan must clearly be corrected, *or the plan itself modified to accept the deviations*. It may well be that the deviations arise from circumstances which are outside the knowledge of the controller, but the responsible supervisor should have a comprehensive knowledge of the current situation. Furthermore, to commit a supervisor

to actions over which he has no control is to put him in an invidious position, and a change initiated by a controller without the supervisor's agreement may result in such a committal. No controller can require a supervisor to act in a particular manner: thus, a budgetary controller can report to a production manager that his allowance for training new labour is being exceeded, but he cannot insist that training be discontinued. Clearly, a control supervisor can make suggestions, and experience will often result in these suggestions being framed in such a manner that it would be extremely difficult to ignore them. This advisory role must be clearly understood at all levels, particularly in production control, where a floor 'chaser' (or progress clerk) must not take upon himself the task of a chargehand and instruct an operator to carry out a particular task or function at a particular time. Informal relationships may well be made (or may grow up) where some latitude in this matter is permitted, but the informal nature of this arrangement must always be clearly understood.

An explicitly designed control system will have substantial advantages over the 'wait-and-see-what-happens' methods which are not uncommonly used. These advantages include—

(*a*) the fact that the preparation of a plan requires a detailed consideration of the company organization;

(*b*) prior knowledge of the achievable performance of the company;

(*c*) the ability to take action to correct any malfunctioning of the system;

(*d*) a 'filtering' of information, permitting concentration upon 'trouble' areas;

(*e*) the preparation of the plan and the knowledge that it exists are both powerful stimuli to effective action.

```
Plan
Publish
Measure
Compare
Report
Correct
```

The Six Features of 'Control'

Control and Service Departments

The four most important control departments within a Factory are—

1. The Production Control Department
2. The Inspection (or Quality Control) Department
3. The Budgetary Control Department
4. The Cost Control Department.

All stand in the same relation with regard to the manufacturing departments.

It should be noted that these departments may well incorporate service functions as well as control functions, and there is always a danger that these may swamp the fundamental nature of the department.

Size of Service and Control Departments. In drawing up a budget, the problem of the number of employees must be considered. The 'direct production' staff is reasonably easily calculated from the sales forecast and a knowledge or an estimation of the labour content of each

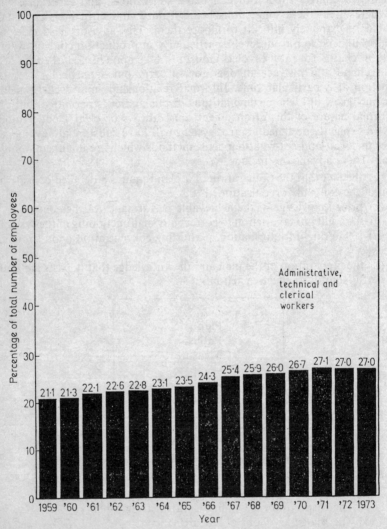

Fig. 1.3. Administrative, technical and clerical workers in manufacturing industry expressed as a percentage of the total number of employees. The figures include managers, superintendents and works foremen, research, experimental, technical and design employees (other than operatives), draughtsmen, tracers and office employees (including works office employees). (Source—Department of Employment Gazette)

product. However, the size of the support staff necessary to uphold this production effort is not so readily determined. Whilst there are many texts dealing specifically with the problems of organization, the author feels that it is impossible to make any recommendations concerning the most appropriate size for any department since this will depend greatly upon local circumstances. It is interesting to note that there has been a steady increase in 'administrative, technical and clerical workers in manufacturing industries' when expressed as a percentage of total number of employees in employment (see Fig. 1.3). Although these figures relate to the U.K., a parallel growth can be seen in the U.S. economy.

Some details of distribution between various trades in July, 1973, are given below—

Table 1.1. Administrative, Technical and Clerical Workers in Manufacturing Industries

Industry	Number of operatives	Number of administrative, technical and clerical staff	Total employees in employment	Administrative, technical and clerical staff as percentage of total employees in employment
Total males and females		(Thousands)		(Per cent)
Food, drink and tobacco	618	194	812	23·9
Coal and petroleum products	33	20	53	38·4
Chemical and allied industries	264	178	441	40·3
Metal manufacture	392	127	520	24·5
Mechanical engineering	686	346	1,031	33·5
Instrument engineering	101	51	152	33·7
Electrical engineering	567	292	858	34·0
Shipbuilding and marine engineering	141	40	181	22·2
Vehicles	571	226	797	28·4
Metal goods not elsewhere specified	446	133	579	23·0
Textiles	478	96	575	16·8
Leather, leather goods and fur	38	9	47	18·8
Clothing and footwear	395	60	455	13·1
Bricks, pottery, glass, cement, etc.	245	70	314	22·2
Timber, furniture, etc	235	63	298	21·3
Paper, printing and publishing	409	185	594	31·1
Other manufacturing industries	259	82	341	23·9
Total, all manufacturing industries	5,876	2,172	8,048	27·0

Note: Because the figures have been rounded independently, rounded totals may differ from the sum of the rounded components.

(*Source—Department of Employment Gazette*, July 1973)

15

THE MAGNITUDE OF THE PRODUCTION FUNCTION

Some indications of the importance of the production function to the U.K. economy is given by Tables 1.2 and 1.3, and Figure 1.4, where it will be seen that it is by far the largest generator within the G.D.P., and the greatest producer of income from exporting. Tables 1.4 and 1.5 give an indication of the number of people employed in factories in the U.K. and the U.S.A., and Table 1.6 shows what percentage of the total employed population of various countries are involved in manufacturing.

Table 1.2. Constituents of Gross Domestic Product 1971

	£m	%
Agriculture, forestry and fishing	1,363	2·9
Mining and quarrying	778	1·7
Manufacturing	15,315	32·0
Construction	2,894	6·0
Gas, electricity and water	1,486	3·1
Transport	2,684	5·6
Communication	1,158	2·4
Distributive trades	4,850	10·0
Insurance, banking and finance (including real estate)	1,948	4·1
Ownership of dwellings	2,425	5·1
Public administration and defence	3,102	6·5
Public health and educational services	2,679	5·6
Other services	6,574	14·0
Residual error	490	1·0
Totals	47,746	100·0

(The Table indicates the contribution of each industry to the G.D.P. before providing for depreciation and stock appreciation)

(*Source—National Income and Expenditure 1972*, CSO, Table II)

Table 1.3. Value of Exports of Produce and Manufactures of the United Kingdom for 1971

Classification		£m	%
0	Food and live animals	280·7	3·0
1	Beverages and tobacco	306·6	3·3
2	Crude materials, inedible	267·5	2·9
3	Mineral fuels, lubricants, etc.	236·0	2·6
4	Animal and vegetable oils and fats	10·6	0·1
5–8	Manufactured goods	7,819·5	85·4
9	Other commodities	254·6	2·7
Total U.K. exports		9,175·5	100·0

(The numbers on the left-hand side of the table refer to the Section and Division numbers of the *Standard International Trade Classification*, Revised)

(*Source—Annual Abstract of Statistics* 1972, H.M.S.O. Table 284)

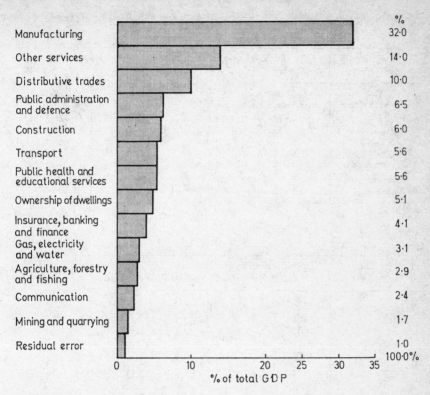

	%
Manufacturing	32·0
Other services	14·0
Distributive trades	10·0
Public administration and defence	6·5
Construction	6·0
Transport	5·6
Public health and educational services	5·6
Ownership of dwellings	5·1
Insurance, banking and finance	4·1
Gas, electricity and water	3·1
Agriculture, forestry and fishing	2·9
Communication	2·4
Mining and quarrying	1·7
Residual error	1·0
	100·0%

% of total GDP

Fig. 1.4

SCOPE OF THE PRESENT TEXT

In order to clarify the scope of the present volume and to simplify reference, an organizational structure is drawn up in Fig. 1.5. The numbers in brackets (see Fig. 1.5) refer to the chapters dealing principally with the department concerned. This structure must only be regarded as one possible suggestion: there are many other possible organizations all equally valid. As with all managerial problems, it is rare to be able to present a unique solution to any problem. Every factory has its own special features—geographical, historical, technical—which cause it to differ from every other factory, so that a structure which is acceptable in one factory is not necessarily so in another, *nor in the same factory at a different time.* It must also be remembered that the majority of factories, both in this country and in the U.S.A., are small (see Tables 1.4 and 1.5), and functions are thus likely to be spread over a limited administrative staff, so that the production controller may, for example, be responsible also for production planning, or the production manager for the maintenance department.

Tables 1.4 and 1.5. Census of Factories According to Size in U.K. and U.S.A.

United Kingdom, June 1961

Size Class (Employees)	Establishments Number	%	Employees Number (000s)	%
* 1– 10	140,000	71·9	700	8·1
11– 24	12,571	6·3	222	4·1
25– 99	27,478	14·1	1,420	16·3
100– 499	12,213	6·2	2,552	26·6
500– 999	1,693	0·9	1,163	13·1
1,000–1,999	777	0·4	1,078	12·1
2,000 or more	429	0·2	1,743	19·7
Totals	195,161	100·0	8,878	100·0

* Estimated figures.   (*Source—Ministry of Labour Gazette*)

U.S.A. 1958

Size Class (Employees)	Establishments Number	%	Employees Number (000s)	%
1– 4	106,000	35·3	218	1·4
5– 9	51,000	17·0	340	2·2
10– 19	47,000	15·7	644	4·2
20– 49	46,000	15·4	1,443	9·4
50– 99	22,000	7·4	1,513	9·9
100– 249	16,000	5·4	2,497	16·2
250– 499	6,000	2·1	2,150	13·9
500– 999	3,000	1·1	1,893	12·3
1,000–2,499	1,000	0·4	2,046	13·2
2,500 and over	W500	0·2	2,649	17·3
Totals	298,500	100·0	15,394	100·0

(*Source—Concentration Ratios in Manufacturing Industry, 1958, U.S. Department of Commerce Bureau of Census*)

Table 1.6. Percentage of Population Employed in Manufacturing, 1971

	%
Hong Kong	41·4
West Germany	36·4
United Kingdom	34·8
Sweden	31·9
Italy	26·5
U.S.A.	26·5
France	26·1
Japan	25·5
India	9·5
Pakistan	9·5

(*Source—Yearbook of Labour Statistics, 1972, I.L.O., Table 2A, Structure of the Economically Active Population*)

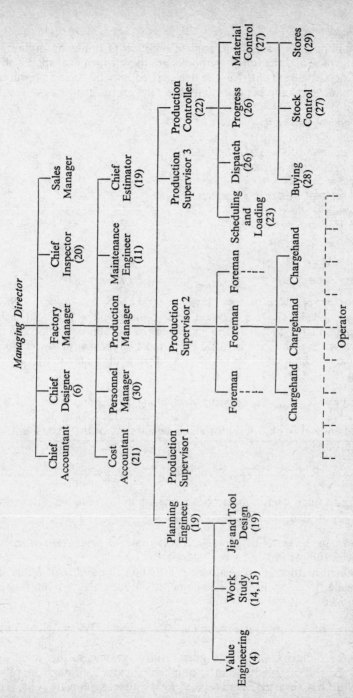

Fig. 1.5. *Possible Factory Organization* (see note – Scope of the Present Text – on p. 17)

Further Reading

It is quite impossible to make a sensible selection of books on organizational principles, and the following books are those which deal specifically with Factory Management. New material is continually being produced and any manager would be well advised to read journals such as—

> *Management Today*
> *Business Management*
> *The Journal of Industrial Engineering*
> *The Production Engineer*
> *Factory*
> *Operational Research Quarterly*
> *Operations Research*
> *The Harvard Business Review*
> *Business Decisions*

Specific text-books are—

1. *Glossary of Management Techniques*, H.M.S.O., London 1967. '. . . compiled . . . to provide a brief outline of the principal techniques, particularly those in the management accounting field.' Some twenty-five main techniques are discussed, most of them with descriptions of subsidiary techniques. There is also a substantial 'Suggested Reading' section at the end of each subject.

2. Antony, R. N., *Management Accounting Principles*, Irwin, Illinois 1970.
A fundamental book, useful for an understanding of the basic financial considerations.

3. Dickey, R. I. (Ed.), *The Accountant's Cost Handbook*, The Ronald Press, New York 1960.
Amongst other useful material this contains a valuable discussion (Section 20) on Budgets and how they are set.

4. Bowman, E. H. and Fetter, R. B., *Analysis for Production Management*, Irwin, Illinois 1967.
Basically a mathematical treatment; it contains a number of examples for the reader to work through and some case study data. A book for the serious worker.

5. Buffa, E. S., *Modern Production Management*, Wiley, New York 1969.
Professor Buffa has covered a great deal of ground in this text, and has used Analytical Methods in a number of cases, although in other instances he has resorted to statement rather than demonstrations. The mathematical level is not too high to distress a practising manager.

6. Buffa, E. S., *Basic Production Management*, Wiley, New York 1971.
Virtually an abridged version of (5) above, but rather '. . . more compact, . . . focused on the application of the most up-to-date concepts'. It contains much material which can be found in works dealing with other disciplines.

7. Wild, R., *The Techniques of Production Management*, Holt, Rinehart and Winston, New York 1971.
'This is a book concerned principally with the techniques of Production Management. It is intended as a teaching text . . . should be used in conjunction with other teaching material.' Dr. Wild concerns himself largely with mathematical treatment.

8. Gedgye, G. R., *Scientific Method in Production Management*, Oxford University Press, London 1965.
A book written primarily for students taking management subjects, it is concerned with a scientific and inductive approach to works management. Illustrated by examples drawn from the author's own experience.

9. Radford, J. D. and Richardson, D. B., *The Management of Production*, Macmillan, London 1972.
An excellent general text covering much the same ground as the present volume.

10. Carson, G. B. (Ed.), *The Production Handbook*, The Ronald Press, New York 1972.
An encyclopaedic tome containing much basic information upon the whole range of problems encountered in production management. Most useful when backed up with more detailed studies.

11. Lowe, P. H., *The Essence of Production*, Pan Books, London 1970.
'The book . . . is a first step to those who wish to acquaint themselves with production.' It is generally descriptive, and employs no mathematics at all.

12. Starr, M. K. (Ed.), *Management of Production*, Penguin Books, Harmondsworth 1970.
A collection of papers, all of which have appeared elsewhere, and 'within each section . . . there is a high variety level of topics and techniques . . .'. It is somewhat difficult, in some cases, to believe that the authors of some of the papers live in the same world as that in which production and production managers exist.

13. Starr, M. K., *Production Management, Systems and Syntheses*, Prentice Hall, London 1972.
'The spirit of this book is embodied in the relationship of systems analysis to systems synthesis. The distinction between analysis and synthesis is neither esoteric nor academic. Analytic behaviour follows . . . principles of disassembly . . . as a set of . . . principles of assembly, involving operations of summation, integration, unification, combination,

amalgamation, and, in general, the Gestalt point of view.' If the above quotation from the author's prefaces does not induce the student to read this book, then the presence within the book of an extremely valuable paper by William T. Moran, 'Marketing-Production Interaction' certainly should. This paper is outstanding and should be read by all serious students.

Section Two   The Product

Chapter 2
Choice of the Product

All production involves a *product* of some sort, and this may be presented to the factory manager either as a completely documented project, or as a new idea which must be translated into a manufacturable product. The design function, therefore, may be without or within the factory, but since the success of the factory starts with the product, it is desirable for the factory manager to understand something of the choice of a new product and of the resulting design process.

THE ORIGINATION OF DESIGN PROJECTS

The systematic seeking out and selection of new products is essentially the responsibility of top management which must actively create a climate in which new projects are brought forward and in which opportunities, however originated, are seized. Opportunities may arise in a number of ways—

(a) *By chance*. It is impossible to ignore the effects of chance. A meeting in a train, the sight of a new device or a technical report, an attendance at a social gathering, all can generate the idea which leads to a successful new project. Luck 'happens' to everybody, but it is the distinguishing feature of the successful manager that he can turn the 'luck' to his own good use. Whilst insight is a personal characteristic, the cultivation of an open mind will assist by creating a climate in which 'luck' can most easily 'take root'.

(b) *By a desire to use idle resources*. Many organizations have idle resources—excess cash, unused machines, unoccupied plant, unextended managerial talent, surplus distribution channels, excess inventory. However these have arisen, they should be used rather than allowed to go to waste. In some cases, the resources may be sold off in order to provide more manageable resources—for example, a factory may be sold in order to produce liquid cash—but the principle is unchanged. The manager must constantly seek to make best use of *all* resources, and in his search he may well discover a valuable new product.

(c) *From a gap in the commercial range*. An existing product and service range may have a gap or gaps which should be filled if a truly competitive service is to be offered.

(*d*) *Need to support existing range.* Even an apparently complete range may be strengthened by the addition of 'adjacent' products. Low profitability may be acceptable here if the additional product gives an enhanced competitive position, provided there is no accompanying 'starving' of higher profit tasks.

(*e*) *By the spreading of risk.* Too narrow a range—one which serves a single client, or consists of a single product—can constitute a real danger, *particularly in a rapidly changing situation.* On the other hand, when demand can be confidently predicted, then a narrow range can give substantial operating economies, and the choice between concentration and spread can be a difficult one. It is vital that this decision should be a conscious one.

(*f*) *To supplement a declining income.* Every product which today provides a high return will eventually decline to a low-return status. Before this happens a new product must be brought to maturity.

(*g*) *From fashion.* A new trend or fashion can provide opportunities for a new development. To produce a new item just because everybody else is doing so is not, in itself, sensible, but to exploit a fashion within an existing range can be very profitable.

(*h*) *In order to exploit special skills.* To seek for uses of special skills is a valid reason for creating new products.

(*i*) *To attract prestige.* Some new products can generate such prestige that they can atttract resources/attention to the originating company.

(*j*) *To exploit special assets.* Where organizations have 'special' or 'unique' assets, they may form the bases for new products.

(*k*) *To repair weaknesses.* There may be organizational/administration weaknesses which need to be repaired, and in so doing, products may be suggested.

Chance
The need to use idle resources
Filling a gap in the product range
Seeking to support existing range
Trying to spread risk
Restoring declining income
Exploiting fashion
Trying to use special skills
Exploiting special assets
Repairing weaknesses

Origination of Design Projects

However conceived, no new design project should be undertaken, nor substantial resources committed to it, until it has been valued as objectively as possible, and a comparison of the project and all recognizable alternatives carried out. Such an evaluation needs to be systematic in order to ensure that some aspects are not ignored and others over-emphasized. It is dangerously easy to be guided by 'hunch', personal preference or immediate excitement.

This evaluation can usefully take the form of a series of enquiries which are made to screen out and test possible new projects. These enquiries are best carried out in a fixed sequence, and an unsatisfactory answer which cannot be overcome at any one stage will render further investigation unnecessary. Clearly, negative thinking must be avoided, and efforts should be made to remove difficulties—the 'no' man is as great a danger to the organization as the 'yes' man. Only when satisfaction at all stages is obtained should the project be considered a serious candidate for further, more detailed, financial assessment.

The most fundamental enquiry which must be made is—

Is the proposed project in keeping with the general corporate objectives?

Here it must be noted that these objectives may derive from a number of sources, personal as well as institutional.

When, and *only* when, this is answered satisfactorily should the screening proceed further. The sequence to be then followed is—

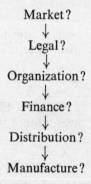

Market?
↓
Legal?
↓
Organization?
↓
Finance?
↓
Distribution?
↓
Manufacture?

Each of these areas is capable of detailed considerations.

Market

What is the potential market?

Reassurance is being sought here that there is a substantial market, either available or capable of being created. This is most usually measured in terms of total income expected, and may include an indication of durability.

What is the state of the existing competition?

To overcome a powerful existing competitor will require considerable effort.

27

Will new competition be created?

Whilst competition may not currently exist, a new product may stimulate other organizations into competitive action. This may not be so costly to overcome as initial competition, but it may indicate that speed in execution is very necessary.

Is there satisfactory growth potential?

Clearly this is associated with the type of product, its development charges, and investment required. A very high initial investment would argue a substantial growth potential, possibly in an allied or complementary field.

Is the timing right?

Many otherwise satisfactory projects have failed because of incorrect timing. A new product can be so far in advance of its time that it is badly received—or so late in the product cycle that demand is decaying.

Is the new product compatible with the existing company image?

A company with a well-established image for, say, producing consumer goods, may have great difficulty in establishing itself as a producer of capital equipment.

What will be the effect on existing products?

A new product, whilst compatible with the company image, may become competitive with, or antipathetic to, an existing product.

Are there any special promotional problems?

Some projects have special cultural, religious, ethical, national or other connotations, which can present extremely difficult promotional problems. An assessment of the ease of penetration is thus required.

What follow-up activities are required?

The 'after-sales' services which are required must be assessed. These are obvious in the case of motor cars but all industries require some 'follow-up' activity. The importance of these activities must never be under-estimated, nor their difficulties dismissed. As service/repair work is often carried out within the factory, the factory manager has a particular interest here.

Legal

Are there any legal prohibitions?

Some materials and processes are prohibited or controlled by law, so that a product involving their use may not be capable of ready manufacture.

Patent protection

Are there any particular patent problems? An existing process may be covered by patents which will then have to be circumvented or purchased—often a costly and time-consuming process.

Are there any problems of foreign exchange?
It is possible that a need for foreign exchange may be created, and this can prove a grave difficulty. This aspect needs to be examined for as far into the future as possible.

Will parts have to be imported from abroad?
As with foreign exchange above, difficulties may arise here, particularly if heavy import duties are levied.

It is worth noting that many legal problems can be circumvented or *avoided altogether* if the constraints are known early enough. Thus, safety can be 'built in' at the design stage if the regulations are known, and import restrictions can be reduced by the setting up of conjoint activities.

Organization

Are adequate managerial resources available?
Whatever the size of the market, and the absence of legal problems, the effective exploitation of the product will depend wholly upon the calibre of the management available. Whilst it may be possible to purchase such talent, it is invariably a slow process to transform a new manager into an effective member of an organization. Probably the manager is the resource which takes longest to become productive—and certainly he is the resource which, if incorrect, can have the greatest long-term effect.

What technical resources are necessary?
Next to the managerial skills, technical resources may present extreme difficulties. Whilst it is easier to purchase technical effort than managerial effort, absence of that effort can be disastrous.

Is the organizational structure adequate?
Here it is important to consider both the 'shape' and the 'size' of the organization. The shape can be changed by an effective manager, particularly if the marketing situation has been clearly defined. Size, however, may not be so easily created. Some projects demand organizations of a certain minimum size, and if this 'critical mass' is not achievable, then the project cannot possibly succeed.

Will existing tasks be affected?
It is not uncommon to find that a new product will attract to itself such resources—managerial, technical, personnel, material—that existing products are starved, and the organization, considered as an entity, suffers. If the scale of the operation is large enough it can be useful to set up a separate, profit-centred, profit-responsible unit, which will then have to

justify all its own resource demands. This will also have the advantage of placing the manager concerned under 'risk'—often a highly stimulating situation.

Finance

Can adequate finance be found?

It is essential to be able to ensure sturdy financial backing. The problems of finance are, in general, subservient to those treated above, since it is usually possible to obtain share or debenture capital if the marketing, legal and organizational problems can be satisfactorily dealt with, whereas financial strength cannot overcome severe weaknesses in the market, the legal situation or the organization. Clearly any financial demands must accord with the long-term financial plans of the organization.

How much cash is generated?

An assessment of the inflow of cash is essential—a small inflow may well indicate that it is undesirable to proceed with the design task.

When will the cash be received?

Not only is the magnitude of the cash return important, the timing of that return can be equally vital, as a large profit in ten years' time may not be as useful as smaller profits each previous year. The financial appraisal of projects is discussed briefly in Chapter 10.

Distribution

Are the channels of distribution open?

Some products with substantial markets may have their distribution channels controlled by competitors.

Are the means of distribution available?

Some products may require special distribution methods—for example, meat must be distributed in refrigerated containers.

Are the distribution staff available?

Special skills may be required on the part of the distributive staffs. This feature, the means of distribution and possibly the channels of distribution, mentioned above, may be dealt with if adequate finance is available.

Manufacture

Are the development resources available?

In this, as in other questions of development, Critical Path Analysis can be invaluable to assist in the assessment of resources needed.

What development costs are involved?
What development time is required?

Assurances on the availability of resources must generate enquiries into the costs and times involved. Since these may be heavy, it is essential that ample consideration is given to their estimation.

Are any special production skills needed?

Absence of such skills can be overcome by adequate finance.

Is a new plant needed?
Is new equipment needed?

Again, shortage here can often be removed by adequate finance, usually more easily and rapidly than shortage of personal skills. An assessment of costs involved and probable delivery times is essential.

Are sources of supply secure?

Is the proposed product likely to involve the supply of materials, equipment, plant, personnel from unreliable sources? Here the reliability of the originating company and the stability of the importing country must be examined.

Will any 'waste' be created?

In the carrying out of design and subsequent manufacture, 'waste' or 'spin off' may be created. This may either be embarrassing or valuable.

Is there existing experience with similar projects?

An existing tradition of production/execution of similar products or processes can be very useful. This is particularly important if quality is a key factor—to try to mix quality levels can be extremely difficult.

PROJECT EVALUATION—A SUMMARY

Evaluate new design projects, comparing them with all possible alternative opportunities as follows—

Market

      (*a*) Potential Market?
      (*b*) Existing Competition?
      (*c*) New Competition?
      (*d*) Growth Potential?
      (*e*) Timing?
      (*f*) Compatibility?
      (*g*) Effect on Existing Products?
      (*h*) Promotional Problems?
      (*i*) Follow-up Activities?

If satisfactory answers are received to the above, consider—

Legal

    (*a*) Prohibitions?
    (*b*) Patent Protection?
    (*c*) Foreign Exchange?
    (*d*) Foreign Importance?

If satisfactory answers are received to the above, consider—

Organization

    (*a*) Managerial Resources?
    (*b*) Technical Resources?
    (*c*) Organizational Structure?
    (*d*) Effect on Existing Tasks?

If satisfactory answers are received to the above, consider—

Finance

    (*a*) Finance Available?
    (*b*) Volume of Cash Generated?
    (*c*) When is the Cash Received?

Further Reading

1. Pessemier, E. A., *New Product Decisions*, McGraw Hill, New York 1966.
A useful text for the serious student.

2. Davidson, J. H., *Offensive Marketing*, Cassell & Co., London 1972.
Although written primarily for the marketing man, this will repay study by the Production Manager.

Chapter 3
Control of Variety

Within any factory, variety is inevitable. There will be variety in the products made, variety in the methods used, variety in the materials employed and variety in organizational and manufacturing techniques. Whilst some variety is desirable, as variety increases, so organizational problems and costs will increase. Thus, for example, an increase in the number of components stored will increase the storage room required, increase the difficulties of stock recording, increase the number of orders placed and so on. Control of variety is essential and the task of *reducing* variety with subsequent control of the remaining variety is one of the most fruitful tasks which can be undertaken by any organization.

VARIETY CONTROL A MANAGERIAL RESPONSIBILITY

In all, it is found that increase of variety is insidious, new parts, plants, materials being introduced for reasons valid only for a short time. Variety control is a matter for management as a whole, and must be accepted as part of the tradition of the company. This is not to imply that no changes should ever take place, but that the widest possible view should be taken of all changes: as has been truly said, change is not necessarily progress.

Carrying out a Variety Reduction Programme

Variety reduction can be undertaken in three ways—

(a) *Simplification*—that is, 'the reduction of unnecessary variety' (*Brisch*);

(b) *Standardization*—that is, 'the control of necessary variety' (*Brisch*);

(c) *Specialization*—that is, the concentration of effort on undertakings where special knowledge is available;

all of which combine to reduce variety. A programme can start in any one place in an organization, or it can proceed on a number of fronts simultaneously. It is a continuing process and, though certain techniques will prevent the spread of variety in some fields, in others there must be a continual awareness of the dangers of uncontrolled diversity: habits must be formed which will build up safeguards.

Benefits of a Variety Reduction Programme

These can be considered under three main headings as follows—

1. *In Marketing*

A wide variety of products reduces the 'selling' which can be done at any one time. Reduction of this variety must not be carried to such extremes that the articles required by the customer are not supplied, but care must be taken to avoid those 'marginal' products which are so often made in small quantities to suit (possibly irrational) customers' tastes and yet are not charged at prices high enough to recover their costs. The argument is often put up that this special product will bring with it a flood of other work, yet all too often the sprat catches no mackerel. A wide diversity of products is often characteristic of a young company, or one which has no need to control costs. Fierce competition brings with it a reduction in the number of products and a consequent intensification of selling effort. During 1959 biscuit production in Britain declined, the rate of increase having fallen during the previous three to four years. To combat this there has been a reduction in the number of varieties of biscuits made, and one manufacturer marketed in 1960 only about a dozen varieties, whereas before 1940 over 400 were marketed.

In cases where an after-sales service must be provided the fewer products the better the service can be and, since the number of spare parts which must be kept is reduced, the less the cost of the service. This can be a very potent selling factor and can often 'clinch' a sale, as well as build up the goodwill which brings with it repeated orders.

2. *In Design*

The fewer the number of piece-parts designed, the greater the productivity of the design and drawing office. It is frequently found that a part will be designed which could be identical to or is replaceable by an existing part. This wastes not only design effort but subsequent production, production control and production engineering effort. Often minor modifications to existing parts will render it useful for a number of functions other than that for which it was first designed. At first this might appear to impose restrictions upon the designer which might inhibit his creative ability, yet in fact it will release him from the drudgery of detailed designing. No designer calls for special screws, nuts, wire diameters, sheet metal thicknesses—standardization is accepted here, yet the variety of products which can be made from these items is infinite.

Concentration upon a limited field allows a designer to build up a body of knowledge which will permit him to answer questions within that field very much more rapidly than if his interests ranged over a wide area. This again does not produce stagnation, since the concentration brings with it a deepening of knowledge and a more fundamental understanding of the problems within that field of limited study. This is generally recognized, so that there are now no individual designers responsible for, say, the complete design of an aeroplane; there are design teams, each member of which specializes upon a few aspects.

3. *In Production*

If one part can be used in place of two, production runs will be longer, and ancillary time (setting, breaking down) will be reduced, both absolutely and when 'spread'. Fewer production aids will be required, and there will be a higher utilization of special plant. Variety reduction generally will reduce stocks by the reduction of the need to hold stocks of so many items, and by the lower minimum (insurance) stocks resulting from the merging of parts, and stores space will be more fully utilized. The cost of stock control and the stock-taking will be correspondingly reduced. The larger quantities and the fewer products produced simplify the production control problem and ease the difficulties of the buyer in that he has fewer orders to place, and those placed are for larger quantities.

---

1. Intensification of selling effect
2. Better after-sales service
3. Greater design productivity
4. Better understanding of design problems
5. Larger productive runs
6. Less ancillary time
7. Fewer production aids
8. Higher plant utilization
9. Reduction in total stocks
10. Greater use of stores space
11. Easier stock control
12. Quicker stock-taking
13. Simplification of production control
14. Reduction in buying effort

Benefits of Variety Reduction

Variety Reduction in the Final Product

When considering variety reduction in the final product, two aspects of the product range must be investigated simultaneously—

(*a*) how much income does each item produce?

(*b*) how much contribution does each item generate [where contribution = selling price − (labour + material costs)]?

To illustrate the need for both aspects to be investigated, consider this simplified and somewhat exaggerated example—

Item	Income Produced	Contribution
A	6210	700
B	2415	607
C	8895	513
D	778	350
E	585	233
F	346	117
G	97	−23
H	391	−47
J	204	−59
K	1142	−82
	21,063	2520−211
		=2309

If these are ranked (see Appendix 3) in order of (*a*) income and (*b*) contribution, the following results will be obtained—

(*a*) *Rank by income—*

			Income
Rank	*Product*	*Unit*	*% of total*
1	C	8895	42·2
2	A	6210	29·5
3	B	2415	11·4
4	K	1142	5·4
5	D	778	3·7
6	E	585	2·8
7	H	391	1·9
8	F	346	1·6
9	J	204	1·0
10	G	97	0·5
		21,063	100·0

See Fig. 3.1

(*b*) *Rank by contribution—*

			Contribution
Rank	*Product*	*Unit*	*% of total*
1	A	700	30·3
2	B	607	26·3
3	C	513	22·2
4	D	350	15·2
5	E	233	10
6	F	117	5
7	G	−23	−1
8	H	−47	−2
9	J	−59	−2·5
10	K	−82	−3·5
		2520−211	100·0
		=2309	

See Fig. 3.2

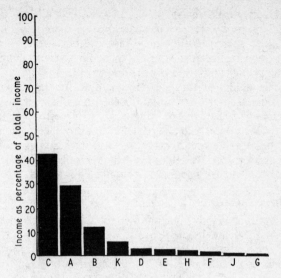

Fig. 3.1. Products Ranked by Income

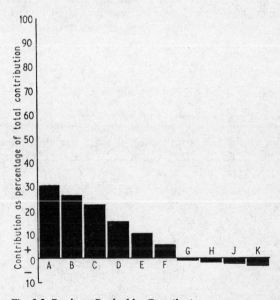

Fig. 3.2. Products Ranked by Contribution

To consider either of these in the absence of the other could readily lead to incorrect conclusions: for example, Product K which is ranked fourth by income actually makes a loss, and Product A, which produces most contribution, does not produce most income.

One common approach to variety reduction at this stage is to consider first the products, ranked by income, and to subject all low-income items to a very close scrutiny. It may be that some of these items have not yet achieved sales maturity, or they may have prestige value. In the absence of any such good commercial reasons these low-income items should be considered as prime candidates for abandonment.

The second analysis—that of contribution for each item—is most usefully considered after the income for each item has been examined. Of the items remaining after the pruning already suggested has been carried out, it may well be found that the contribution provided by some products is either low or negative, and items F, G, H, J, K should again be subjected to a very close scrutiny to determine whether sales can be increased, or whether a cost reduction programme should be initiated.

The Income-Contribution Chart

Another approach, which virtually enables the above two stages to be coalesced, is to plot an income-contribution chart. In this the abscissae are the income-ranks, and the ordinates the contribution-ranks. Thus, product A has an income-rank of 2, and a contribution-rank of 1, and A is represented by the point (2, 1)—see Table 3.1. All the points are plotted on the income-contribution chart (Fig. 3.3): ideally, volume and contribution ranks should correspond, giving a straight line at 45° to either axis. Points lying *above* this line should be tested as follows—

Can costs be reduced?
Can prices be increased?

whilst points lying *below* this line should be tested—

Can sales volume be increased?

Neither of the above approaches in itself can determine the action which must be taken, but they can provide excellent guidance. Both, of course, demand good recording and costing procedures.

Table 3.1. *Income—Contribution Ranks*

	Rank by	
Product	*Income*	*Contribution*
A	2	1
B	3	2
C	1	3
D	5	4
E	6	5
F	8	6
G	10	7
H	7	8
J	9	9
K	4	10

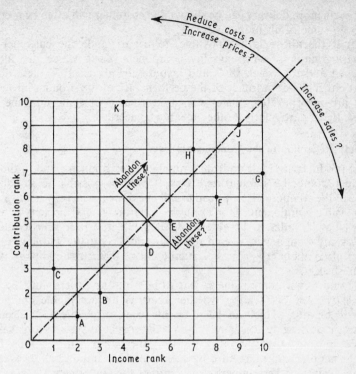

Fig. 3.3. Income—Contribution Chart

One large firm of manufacturing chemists reduced its product range from 1,500 to 221. This was done by—

(*a*) Eliminating all products whose sales were less than £100 a year;

(*b*) Examination of all products whose gross profit was below a certain level;

(*c*) Detailed consideration of the sales trends of each remaining product.

To assist their customers, whose goodwill might have been jeopardized by the abandoning of certain products, they negotiated the transfer of orders for discontinued lines to other firms in the same field who were still making these lines. This drastic reduction of range was accompanied by a reduction in the total number of orders received, but the size of the orders received increased, and there was, in fact, an expansion in total turnover.

The factory making to customer's specification has a much more difficult task, since each customer will require a different product. Here the marketing department can proceed in two ways—

(*a*) Set up a range of stock items which can be offered to the customer in place of the customer's own design. If a substantial saving in price or improvement in delivery can be shown, the customer will often be prepared to forgo some of his individuality.

(*b*) If the above is not possible, to try to guide the customer into preparing designs which employ component parts which are already designed and for which tools and layouts already exist. If these do not affect either the appearance or the performance of the product into which they are incorporated, there is a good chance that the customer will accept them, particularly if other advantages accrue.

Variety Reduction in the Components Used

Most products are built up from a number of components and, if the final product cannot be standardized, then it may be possible to standardize some of the components. This can usually be done most easily in the unseen or invisible components—for example, interlinings and pockets in men's wear—but in order to be able to do it at all it is necessary to identify *readily* any component. Even a relatively small company will have a large range of components—almost certainly over 2,000 if the company is well established.

Should a new component appear to be necessary, there must be some simple way of discovering whether there is an acceptable component already existing. This can be done by using mechanical or electrical/electronic sorting devices, and small needle-sort card systems are available for companies which cannot justify fully mechanized installations. However, a simpler and more effective technique is to number all drawings in such a way that the number itself identifies the component.

A discussion of the desirable properties of an effective coding system appears later (pages 73 to 74) and there is no doubt at all in the author's mind that the long-term benefits of a good coding system will considerably outweigh its installation costs. Care must be taken to ensure that the system is fitted to the user organization: an unnecessarily complex scheme can be expensive, and the simpler the scheme the better. However, *ample provision must be made for expansion*: the costs and inconvenience of changing from one scheme to another can be high.

Variety Reduction in Purchased Items

Wherever goods are purchased from outside manufacturers, they should be bought against definite specifications. These specifications will either be drawings made internally, and covered by a logical numbering system, or specifications laying down the salient factors concerning the item. Such specifications should, wherever possible, be industry-approved specifications—for example, the specification issued by the British Standards Institution. Use of such specifications will not only ensure that items are to a uniform and known standard but also that the goods concerned are most likely to be made in quantity by a number of manufacturers, thus being cheaper and more readily available than specially designed parts. Should any doubt be felt on this score, the reader is advised to purchase first a quantity of screws to a British Standard Specification and then the same quantity of a similar size screw to a special thread form.

Variations in purchased raw material will lead not only to a complexity in the raw material stores itself but also to possible variation in the subsequent product. This in turn will be felt throughout the whole manufacture, causing variations in tools, jigs, and other production aids, and in finishing processes. This is particularly significant in mass-production, where the effects of variation can be very serious, but it must not be ignored in batch production, where variations do not make themselves felt so immediately.

Variety Reduction in Manufacture

Throughout a manufacturing organization there will inevitably be a number of similar processes, or processes which, whilst not being similar in themselves, produce similar results. The work study engineer should examine these and produce defined techniques of optimum efficiency, probably bringing these different processes very close together from a manufacturing methods point of view. This will reduce the variety of methods used, and will result in a greater flexibility of labour, a higher possible utilization of plant, and a simplification of the production control task. Thus, if two different products are made in the same way, the setting-up time of the machines involved can often be substantially reduced. Similarly, if one equipment can be used in place of two, the maintenance problem is considerably eased. The gains in this field are likely to be greater in small quantity productions than in mass productions.

Just as an analysis of finished goods is likely to show that the bulk of income is derived from a comparatively small part of the product range, so an analysis of machining processes is likely to show that, of the total machining capability, an extremely small part produces the bulk of the workload. Thus, Dr. Opitz, in an investigation of manufacturing in twenty-five German companies found that eighty per cent of all turned jobs had diameters of less than 200 mm, despite the fact that the permissible turning diameters of the machine tools were greatly in excess of 200 mm. Similarly, whilst nearly all turning machines have facilities for thread cutting, only twenty-five per cent of the jobs examined used these facilities. Later work by P.E.R.A. (Production Engineering Research Association) in the U.K. has produced similar results, and these *component statistics* indicate that considerable savings can be achieved both by reducing the variety and complexity of machine tools being used and by grouping together components with common technological needs so that groups of components can be produced in one batch, rather than in several separate batches. This gives rise to an organizational system known as 'Group Technology,' which is more fully discussed later (Chapter 18.).

Further Reading
   1. *Variety Reduction*, British Productivity Council, London 1966.

One of the few publications dealing solely with Variety Reduction. Written by two of E. G. Brisch's colleagues, it is, like all B.P.C. seminar papers, down-to-earth.

2. *Variety Reduction—Twelve Case Studies*, British Productivity Council, London 1960.

Illustrates the value of variety reduction in diverse industries.

Chapter 4
Control of Value

Value Analysis is a cost reduction and control technique which operates by attacking the basic design of the product, rather than—as is done in Work Study—by improving the way in which the product is manufactured. The explicit statement of a Value Analysis is comparatively recent, being first put forward by L. D. Miles in the late 1940s and early 1950s. In an ideal world, where all designs were as economical, simple and elegant as possible, value analysis would have no place—or, it could be argued, it had been carried out at the conception and design of the product. In the present, imperfect world in which most factory managers find themselves, Value Analysis can provide a disciplined way of attacking cost.

Value Analysis can be defined as 'an organized procedure for the efficient identification of unnecessary cost . . . by analysis of function . . .' and by *function* is meant 'that property of the product which makes it work or sell'. The essence of value analysis, therefore, is first to identify the function of the product and then to examine alternative ways in which this function can be achieved, finally choosing that which involves least cost. To do this, a routine has been evolved which, if followed, is likely to produce acceptable results.

THE IDENTIFICATION OF FUNCTION

Function has already been defined as 'that property of the product which makes it work or sell', and the first, and most important, step in Value Analysis is to make a formal statement of the function of the product, and in itself this is valuable and often surprisingly difficult. Most investigations of problems start with statements of purpose—

The work study engineer asks:
    'What is the purpose of this operation?'
the marketing manager:
    'What shall we sell?'
and the value analyst:
    'What does it do?'

It is important that the question of function should be answered explicitly and in writing. One authority suggests that the answer should be recorded in two words, a verb and a noun, for example—

'gives light' for a lamp;
'supports weight' for a beam;
'transmits force' for a shaft.

This isolation of function is a 'process of deletion'. For any statement of function the question can be asked—

'What can be discarded without diminishing the statement?'

and steadily, redundant words, ideas, concepts are jettisoned until the most economical statement is obtained.

Rarely is there only one function—there are usually several, and all need to be identified and stated. Of the various functions, one is usually of more importance than the others, and this may be said to be the *primary* function, and it is this function which is examined first.

VALUE

Value may be equated with *price*, which is that which, '. . . must be given, done, sacrificed . . . to obtain a thing', and any product may have several different values—

(*a*) *Exchange value*, which is the price a purchaser will offer for the product. This is the conventional purchase price, and it can be assumed to be the sum of two parts—the value due to the usefulness of the product, and the value which ownership itself bestows upon the purchaser. These are often referred to as:

(*b*) *Use value*, which is the price the purchaser will offer in order to ensure that the purpose (or function) of the product is achieved.

(*c*) *Esteem value*, which is the price which is offered for the product beyond the use value.

So that it can be said that—

$$\text{Exchange value} = \text{use value} + \text{esteem value}$$

The exchange value is set by the marketing situation, and can be influenced by the usefulness and esteem in which the product is held. In purchasing a product it is valuable to try to express these values in monetary terms, in order to assess their acceptability. Thus, consider two products, A and B, both of which can be purchased for the same price (100p). By comparing these products with other products and with the task which has to be carried out, valuations can be made—

'It is worth 60p to get function A completed.'
'It is worth 10p to get function B completed.'

so that the esteem values can be deduced—

	A	B
Exchange value	100	100
Use value	60	10
Esteem value	40	90

Thus, the questions which now can be posed are—

'Is A required so much that 40p must be paid in excess of its use-fulness?'

'Is B required so much that 90p must be paid in excess of its use-fulness?'

Of course, use value is a subjective judgement, but it is one which most people make ('I reckon that is worth . . . ' is a common enough remark) and by setting it down in numerical terms a measure—albeit an imprecise one—is provided. In some cases, when design work is being carried out, the use value is determined effectively by the target cost which should appear as part of the design specification.

When an organization manufactures something for its own use—for example, for incorporation into a marketable product, or for marketing as a complete entity—a fourth value can be recognized—

Cost value (sometimes called the *cost price* or *intrinsic value*), which is the sum of all the costs incurred in providing the product.

The difference between the cost value and the exchange value is the profit, and in most situations it is the profit which must be increased, and the task of the value analyst may be said to be that of decreasing the cost value whilst maintaining or increasing the use and esteem values.

Carrying out a Value Analysis Exercise

Value analysis may be applied to any product or any procedure, but some exercises are likely to be more productive than others. In general, multi-component hardware will generate savings more readily and quickly than single component products or administrative procedures, although startling results have been recorded on the value analysis of a single pin. Clearly, the product to be analysed must be one where worth-while savings are possible.

The Value Analysis Team

Many—possibly most—of the successes of value analysis derive from the fact that a problem is attacked by a number of people simultaneously. Whether these people should constitute a permanent team, or be called together, is open to discussion. Probably the best solution is to have a *small* permanent core of experienced people who co-opt such of their colleagues as seem desirable. Certainly those immediately concerned *must* be present, and where purchased parts are concerned, a representative from the supplier will attend. It will always be found useful to invite intelligent 'laymen' to join, 'laymen' in this context implying those who have no special case to plead or cause to defend. The size of the team is important—too large and it will become unwieldy and impossible to convene, too small and it will be too inward-looking. Between six and ten members appears satisfactory.

Gage's Twelve Steps

In the carrying out of a V.A. exercise, twelve steps have been identified by Gage—

1. *Select the product to be analysed*
   Here the problem is to identify the product which will give the greatest return for the costs incurred in the analysis itself. Rules are obviously impossible to lay down but the following indicate situations likely to produce worth-while results—

   > (*a*) a multiplicity of components
   > (*b*) a large forecast usage
   > (*c*) a small difference between use value and cost value
   > (*d*) considerable market competition
   > (*e*) a long-designed product.

2. *Extract the cost of the product*
   The cost required here is the marginal or out-of-pocket cost. An absorption cost would involve decisions on the apportioning of overheads which could easily distort any apparent cost savings. The calculation of marginal costs is not always easy, and it is here that companies first experience difficulties in value analysis. At this stage details of individual components are not required.

3. *Record the number of components*
   In general, the larger the number of parts, the greater the chance of cost-reduction.

4. *Record all the functions*
   This forces consideration of the purpose of the product. Many products serve more than one purpose and all the functions should be stated here, preferably in verb-noun form.

5. *Record the number required currently, and in the foreseeable future*
   This gives magnitude to the effort which can be expended, and the costs incurred in the analysis.
   These five questions are 'fact-finding'—they firmly establish the bases upon which all further work is created.

6. *Determine the primary function*
   Whilst a number of functions may be present simultaneously, it is not possible to consider them all at the same time—some order of priority must

be established. This is done by reconsidering the list prepared in step 4 and deciding which would be the primary function in the view of the purchaser/user of the product.

7. *List all other ways of achieving the primary function*

It is here that value analysis requires the presence of a number of people, the value analysis team. Ideas are obtained by means of a 'creativity' or 'brainstorming' session at which ideas are generated and advanced by means of a free flow of ideas. It involves a relaxed atmosphere with an absence of criticism and a desire to contribute something by all present. The purpose of the leader is to stimulate these contributions and to create the freedom of thought and behaviour which are essential. Judgements on ideas are withheld until a later date—the more outrageous the idea, the more welcome it should be both for itself and as a stimulant.

Many U.K. managers reject the idea of brainstorming, since the thought of 'making an ass of myself' is such an anathema. Care must be taken therefore in setting up and running the session to see that no criticisms of any ideas are made, and that when the sifting of ideas is carried out later, it is done on objective ground. Follet's Law of the Situation ('. . . accept the orders given by the situation') is as valid in value analysis as in other areas of management.

8. *Assign costs to all the alternatives*

To avoid losing the momentum of the brainstorming session, costs must be assigned to the various alternatives as rapidly as possible, but it is better not to try to assign these costs during brainstorming or the free flow of ideas will be damned. It is probably desirable to adjourn the V.A. meeting and reconvene it later when the costs are available. To avoid too much delay 'order of magnitude' costs are acceptable.

9. *Examine the three cheapest alternatives*

From the list prepared in step 7 and completed in step 8, the three cheapest alternatives are selected and examined for feasibility and performance. The design of the new product will begin to emerge at this stage.

10. *Decide which idea should be developed further*

From step 9 and the examination carried out there, a decision is taken upon which idea should be developed further.

11. *See what other functions need to be incorporated*

Re-examination of step 4 will show which other functions have not already been incorporated in the suggestions in step 10.

The above six steps have produced a complete solution, or it may be that further detailed work requires to be carried out to finalize the design of the product. Here check lists of ideas may usefully be produced. The precise list will depend on the organization, but the common feature in all lists is the question—

'Does its use contribute value?'

Every addition, whether it be an extra component, tolerance, hole, bend . . . should be examined against this question. The inverse—

'Can anything be removed without degrading the product?'

can equally be useful.

Whilst the 'new' product is being developed, the value analysis committee can undertake the final step.

12. *Ensure that the new product is accepted*

Conservatism, the principle of 'worry-minimization' and sheer inertia will all combine to resist new ideas. To forestall this, the V.A. team should consider the ways in which the new idea can be 'sold'. This will almost certainly require—

(*a*) a model

and statements of—

(*b*) anticipated savings
(*c*) anticipated capital expenditure
(*d*) improvements in value

and a proposed plan in terms of—

(*e*) Critical Path Analysis network.

The above twelve steps are incorporated in Gage's twelve questions,

1. What is it?
2. What does it cost?
3. How many parts?
4. What does it do?
5. How many required?
6. Which is the primary function?
7. What else will do?
8. What will *that* cost?
9. Which three of the alternative ways of doing the job shows the difference between 'cost' and 'use value'?
10. Which ideas are to be developed?
11. What other functions and specification features must be incorporated?
12. What is needed to sell the ideas and forestall 'road-blocks'?

Gage's Twelve Value Analysis Questions

Value Engineering

The application of V.A. techniques—and particularly those concerned with the isolation of function—to the design stages of a product or a system is clearly most desirable. Greater savings, though probably less identifiable, can be made, and for 'one-off' and short run tasks, only prior value studies are possible. The term 'value engineering' is often reserved for this 'cost prevention' exercise.

Further Reading

1. Miles, L. D., *Techniques of Value Analysis and Engineering*, McGraw-Hill, New York 1972.

This is the first, and most comprehensive, text on Value Analysis. It is liberally illustrated by examples taken from the U.S.

2. Gage, W. L., *Value Analysis*, McGraw-Hill, London 1967.

This is a British work, intended for practising managers responsible for developing new products and for controlling costs. It sets out possible working documents, and displays the author's considerable experience of installing and applying V.A. in U.K. industry. The present chapter borrows heavily from Gage's work.

3. Raven, A. D., *Profit Improvement by Value Analysis, Value Engineering and Purchase Price Analysis*, Cassell, London 1971.

An excellent book, heavily illustrated from the author's own industrial experience. Contains valuable chapters on the definition of function, and the function-cost matrix, a succinct method of displaying cost information.

4. United States Department of Defense, *Principles and Application of Value Engineering*, U.S. Government Printing Office.

This book was developed by the U.S. Army Management Training Agency in conjunction with other Government departments as a text to be used in teaching. Extremely comprehensive, it covers a great deal of ground, and is very well illustrated. Very useful.

Chapter 5
Quality of the Product

The present chapter discusses the meaning and implications of a statement of policy, particularly as it affects the design of the product. A later chapter (Chapter 20) indicates some of the ways in which the quality statement may be upheld.

THE MEANING OF QUALITY

Quality is not a property which has an absolute meaning: a high quality pair of beach shoes can well be a very low quality pair of walking shoes, a low quality billiard cue can be a very high-quality pea-stick. The quality of an article has meaning only when related to its *function* ('that . . . which makes it work or sell') and the isolation of function is rarely simple.

Essentially it requires that both the needs of the customer *and his belief in his needs* are explored. Frequently a choice of product is made upon apparently irrational grounds; identical products, presented in different ways, will sell in vastly different quantities, and will have different qualities ascribed to them. Similarly, a quality judgement is often related to the price paid without any regard to the discernible properties of the item being purchased. The detergent which sells better in a blue box than a red one, the analgesic which is 'more effective' when sold under a proprietary name than when sold as a B.P. product, are well known. The reasons for the purchase may be difficult to identify, yet their reality must not be denied. 'There is no such thing as a universally better design or function. All wants are utilitarian to their possessors.'[1]

Fundamentally, the quality of a product must stem from a managerial decision, a decision as complex and as important as any which a Board of Directors is called upon to make. It must be based upon consideration of both the external environment and the internal resources: the identification of the customer's perception of function must be matched by the ability to produce a product which he will recognize as satisfying that perception, and in the event of a conflict between these two determinants, the intended market segment may have to be changed, or the internal resources may

[1] Moran 'Marketing-Production Interaction', an appendix to Starr's *Production Management: Systems & Syntheses* (see page 21).

have to be increased. Thus, if a soundly based market investigation reveals that a product requires an accuracy which cannot be economically achieved with existing equipment, the company must either change its intended market or improve its production facilities.

It has been said earlier that no manager should ever believe that any decision is eternal, and nowhere is this more true than in the field of quality. The product which is acclaimed to be 'of high quality' this year may be of unacceptably low quality next year. Not only will the customer's needs change; other products may set new standards which change his perception of his needs. In addition, manufacturing processes and policies may deteriorate so that in total the received appearance of the product has been completely degraded.

A quality policy therefore requires management continuously to—

(*a*) identify the customer's needs and his perception of his needs,

(*b*) assess the total ability of the organization to produce the product economically,

(*c*) ensure that the policy is understood at all levels,

(*d*) obtain feedback of information from the market,

(*e*) monitor performance by the manufacturing unit.

Part of the judgement made of the quality of a product is upon its ability to continue to function satisfactorily, and this property has been given the name *reliability*. Within the literature, therefore, two separate terms are often encountered, quality and reliability, which may be defined as follows—

Quality is fitness for purpose;

Reliability is the ability to continue to function to an accepted quality standard.

Both of these definitions are summaries, but they do serve the need to be able to discuss methods of assessment and control.

THE ACHIEVEMENT OF QUALITY

Accepting with all its implications the above definition of quality, then its achievement must start with an understanding of the purpose of the product, and in turn this derives from a managerial statement of policy. This being available, there are then two distinct, but inter-related aspects to quality—

Quality of Design: the degree of achievement of purpose by the design itself.

Quality of Conformance: the faithfulness with which the product agrees with the design.

Frequently, it is only this latter aspect which is considered when quality is discussed, and this restricted view can lead to excessive costs. Attempts made to achieve conformance to an unnecessarily high design quality ('... we *always* work to 0·001 ...'), or to derive a high total quality from a basically poor design ('... the production department will make it work . . . ') are inevitably expensive and usually unsatisfactory. A poor design can never result in a high quality, unless some re-design takes place, although poor execution can easily debase a good design.

The Cost of Quality

Design quality

If 'precision' is used to indicate the closeness with which a product achieves 'absolute perfection', then the relationships between cost and precision and price and precision are probably substantially as shown in Fig. 5.1—

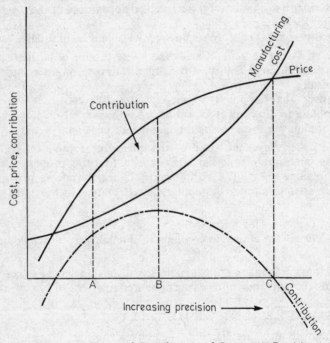

Fig. 5.1. Variation in Cost, Price and Contribution with Increase in Precision

at very low precision, the demand for the product is small and the price which will be paid for it consequently low. As the precision increases, the price obtainable increases, but at a decreasing rate so that increases in precision eventually bring in smaller and smaller increases in price. The opposite tendency, however, is shown in manufacturing cost: as precision increases, manufacturing cost continually and increasingly gets larger. Contribution—the difference between price and manufacturing cost—is shown by the chain-dotted curve: from point A the contribution can be increased by increasing the precision to point B, but further increases beyond point B result in a decreasing contribution to point C, beyond which a loss is made. From a financial point of view, the design quality to be specified should be that represented by B.

Conformance quality

Work done in the U.S.A. by J. M. Juran suggests that the cost of assuring customer satisfaction on quality lies between *four and twelve per cent of total turnover,* and British authorities agree that these figures are probably as true for the U.K. as they are for the U.S.A. Juran defines three main elements in the cost of assuring quality—

(*a*) Failure cost—cost of scrap, rectification, low-price sales of 'second quality' goods, replacement under guarantee, servicing of customer's complaints, after sales service,

(*b*) Appraisal costs—Inspection, test,

(*c*) Prevention costs—Operator training, plant maintenance, design.

The elements which make up, and the sources of, these costs are set out in Tables 5.1, 5.2 and 5.3, which are taken, with permission, from *Quality Costs* a publication jointly of the National Council for Quality and Reliability and the Institute of Cost and Management Accountants.

The relation between these costs and the intrinsic capability of the manufacturing process for a quality acceptable to the customer is likely to be more or less like the relationship shown in Fig. 5.2. below.

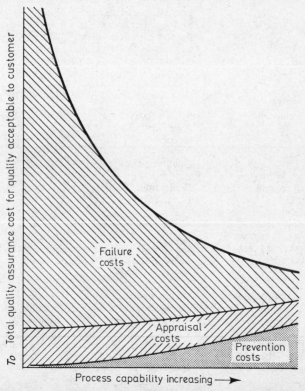

Fig. 5.2. Relation between Process Capability and Total Quality Assurance Costs for any one Customer-perceived Quality Level

Table 5.1. Category (a) Prevention Costs

Activity	Staff and/or Function Involvement	Cost Source
1. Quality Planning		
1.1. Quality investigation within the design specification in respect of 　　Raw materials 　　Methods of manufacture 　　Product characteristics	Quality control and assurance R.D. technologists/design engineers Laboratory Marketing	Salaries
1.2. Proving, sampling or other preproduction trials and tests of prototype and processes	Production Quality control and assurance R. & D. technologists/ design engineers	Wages and salaries Consumable materials Agency costs
Note:	The tests and trials may give rise to specification or design modifications, the cost of which will be a charge to development of the product	
2. Process control		
2.1. Supplier approval	Quality control and assurance Buying	Salaries
2.2. Planning of inspection routines and testing procedures and methods during production processing	Quality control and assurance Production Laboratory	Salaries
2.3. Design and approval of inspection and test equipment	Quality control and assurance Laboratory Instrument engineers	Salaries Sub-contractors
2.4. Training of inspectors	Quality control and assurance courses	Salaries Training aids Courses
2.5. Specifying storage and handling—special conditions	Production Quality control and assurance Stores Transport	Wages and salaries

Table 5.2. Category (b) Appraisal Costs

Activity	Staff and/or Function Involvement	Cost Source
3. Process Appraisal		
3.1. Receiving—raw materials, sub-contract or bought-in finished items	Quality control and assurance Stores	Wages and salaries Purchasing (returns) Consumable materials and samples
3.2. Line inspection at stages of the process	Quality control and assurance Production	Wages and salaries Consumable materials and samples
3.3. Inspection equipment maintenance	Instrument engineers Quality control and assurance Tool and gauge room engineers	Wages and salaries Materials and consumables Outside charges
4. Final appraisal		
4.1. Finished product inspection Certification Tests—destructive Tests—non-destructive Life/reliability Environmental	Quality control and assurance Production Laboratory	Wages and salaries Materials and consumables
4.2. Inspection equipment maintenance	Instrument engineers Quality control and assurance	Wages and salaries Contractor charges Replacement parts Materials and consumables

Thus, where the manufacturing capability is low for a quality acceptable to the customer, the total quality assurance costs are high, the *Failure Costs* predominating. As the manufacturing ability improves (usually by increasing *Appraisal* and—especially—*Prevention Costs*), the *Failure Costs* drop very steeply. When the manufacturing capability is 'matched' to the customer's quality requirements, the total quality assurance costs will be at a minimum. *Failure Costs* (as defined above) will never completely vanish—some after-sales service will be needed, and some complaints will *always* be received—but the necessary increases in Appraisal and Prevention costs are likely to be small compared with the reduction in failure cost. The methods of achieving satisfactory quality conformance are discussed later in Chapter 20.

Table 5.3. Category (c) Failure Costs

Activity	Staff and/or Function Involvement	Cost Source
5. Internal Failure		
5.1. Scrap	Production Inspection Material control	Materials, wages and related overhead
5.2. Rectification	Production Inspection Material control	Wages and salaries Materials, wages and related overhead
5.3. Downgrading	Production Sales Marketing	Wages and salaries Reduced revenue
5.4. Stores—inspection of finished products in stock	Stores Inspection	Wages and salaries Stock losses
6. External failure		
6.1. Complaints		
6.1.1. Return of goods	Product development engineers	Wages and salaries Materials loss/write down
6.1.2. Investigation and analysis	Service engineers Transport	
6.1.3. Corrective action	Stores	Travel costs
6.1.4. Replacement	Quality control and assurance	Allowance costs or compensation costs Consequential costs
6.1.5. Customer liaison and compensation	Sales	
6.2. Warranty		
6.2.1. Replacement	Product development engineers	Wages and salaries Materials for tests
6.2.2. Service fitting	Service engineers	Component cost or reimbursement
6.2.3. Service testing	Sales	Consequential costs
6.2.4. Analysis of service failures	Stores Quality control and assurance	
	Note: Warranty costs should be reviewed in full regardless of any internal accounting problem	

(Tables reproduced by permission of the I.C.M.A.)

RELIABILITY

Quality, as defined above, implies acceptance at a *point in time*. Clearly, there is a need to consider the ability of the product to function *over a period of time*. This aspect of performance has been given the name *reliability*, and defined as 'the probability of a product performing without failure a specified function under given conditions for a specified period of time' in *Reliability of Military Electronic Equipment*, a report by the Advisory Group on Reliability of Electronic Equipment, Office of the Assistant Secretary of Defence (R. & D.) June, 1957. (*Note*—this is often referred to as the AGREE report.)

Clearly, every product will eventually fail, although in some cases the possibility is small enough for the product to be effectively immortal. With the current pressures to reduce cost, and with the needs for increasing complexity, the probability of a piece of equipment failing within the user's anticipation of the working life of the equipment is likely to be finite. Reliability is now an exceedingly important aspect of any product, and there is thus a need to *design reliability into* a product. Unfortunately, the testing of a design to assess its reliability is difficult, sometimes impossible, and the designer must therefore invest in any insurance which is practicable. Some methods of attempting to assure reliability are—

(*a*) use proven designs;

(*b*) use the simplest possible design—the fewer the components and the simpler these designs, the lower the total probability of failure;

(*c*) use components of known or likely high probability of survival. It is usually easier to carry out reliability tests by over-stressing components than by over-stressing a complete equipment;

(*d*) employ redundant parts where there is a likelihood of failure. It may be that a component must be used which has a finite probability of failure. Placing two of these parts in parallel will halve the probability, three will reduce it to a third and so on. Clearly the costs of redundancy must be weighed against the value of reliability;

(*e*) design to 'fail-safe';

(*f*) specify proven manufacturing methods.

Use proven designs
Use simple designs
Use high-reliability components
Use redundancy
Use 'fail-safe' methods
Use proven manufacturing methods

The Designer and Reliability

Measures of Reliability

For the purposes of illustrating some of the commoner measures of reliability in current use, a hypothetical 'life-table' for 150 components operated over 30 units of time has been generated, and set out in Table 5.4. Note that in practice a much larger number of items would be likely to be tested if valid results were required.

Table 5.4

Operating Period in units of time	Number operating at start of period (units)
0– 1	150
1– 2	124
2– 3	107
3– 4	95
4– 5	87
5– 6	80
6– 7	75
7– 8	70
8– 9	66
9–10	62
10–11	59
11–12	56
12–13	53
13–14	50
14–15	47
15–16	44
16–17	42
17–18	40
18–19	38
19–20	36
20–21	34
21–22	32
22–23	29
23–24	26
24–25	24
25–26	22
26–27	20
27–28	17
28–29	15
29–30	13

One indicator of the reliability of the product is the rate at which the units fail—the *failure rate*. This is usually measured by the proportion of units functioning at the beginning of a time interval which fail during that time interval, so that for the unit time period 10–11, where 59 units were functioning at the beginning and 56 were functioning at the end of the period:

$$\text{(Failure rate)}_{10\text{–}11} = \frac{59-56}{59} = \frac{3}{59}/\text{unit time}$$

$$= 0\cdot05/\text{unit time}$$
$$= 5\cdot0\%/\text{unit time}$$

or, in general terms, if—

Q_i = quantity functioning at the beginning of period t_i and Q_{i+1} = quantity functioning at the beginning of period t_{i+1}, then—

$$\text{(failure rate)}_{i,\,i+1} = \frac{Q_i - Q_{i+1}}{Q_i} \cdot \frac{1}{t_{i+1} - t_i}$$

$$= -\frac{1}{Q_i} \frac{Q_{i+1} - Q_i}{t_{i+1} - t_i}$$

and if the time-interval is made as small as possible—

$$\text{(failure rate)}_i = \lambda_i = -\frac{1}{Q_i}\left(\frac{\mathrm{d}Q}{\mathrm{d}t}\right)_i$$

The failure rate for the 30 test periods under consideration is shown in Table 5.5, column 5 and represented graphically by Fig. 5.3. Had the test population been larger and the time-interval finer, the histogram of Fig. 5.3 would tend to the smooth curve of Fig. 5.4, and this 'bath-tub' shape

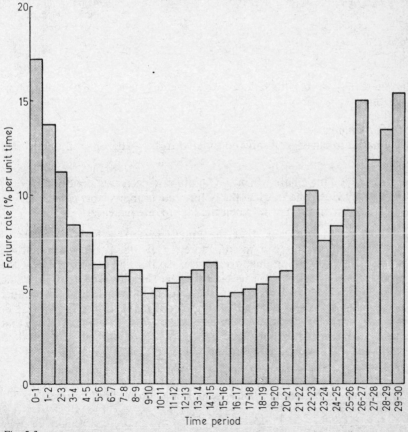

Fig. 5.3

59

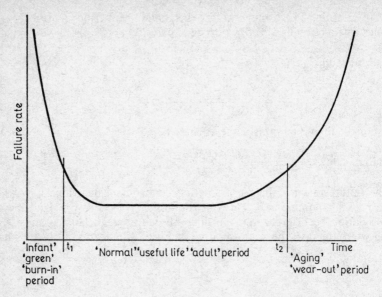

Fig. 5.4

is characteristic of the failure-rate curve of many well-designed components.

The bath-tub curve
The bath-tub curve is usually considered to be made up of three distinct parts—

(*a*) the 'infant' phase, when the failure rate decreases rapidly;
(*b*) the 'adult' phase, when the failure rate is appreciably constant;
(*c*) the 'wear-out' phase, when the failure rate increases.

Clearly, it is desirable that the initial phase should be as short as possible, and to this end manufacturers may 'load' or 'burn-in' their products before sending them to the user, so that the consumer meets the product at the beginning of its 'adult' or 'useful' life. The constant value of the failure rate which pertains during most of the adult life of the product is the value usually implied when reference is made to 'the failure rate of the component'. When the failure rate has increased to a value twice that during the constant failure rate period the 'wear-out' phase is said to start, and the time to this start is said to measure the *longevity* of the product.

Significance of the constant failure rate. For a constant failure rate λ,

$$\lambda = \lambda_i = -\frac{1}{Q}\frac{\mathrm{d}Q}{\mathrm{d}t}$$

i.e.: $\dfrac{\mathrm{d}Q}{Q} = -\lambda \mathrm{d}t$ whence

$Q \qquad = Q_0 e^{-\lambda t}$

where Q_0 is the initial quantity functioning at the beginning of the adult life.

Reliability. The ratio Q/Q_0 is known as the *Reliability $R(t)$* of the product and for the adult phase—

$R(t) = e^{-\lambda t}$

Like all other reliability measures, reliability is time-dependent and the calculation of $R(t)$ for the 150 hypothetical components is given in column 7 of Table 5.5 and its graphical representation in Fig. 5.5.

Table 5.5

Operating period in units of time	Number operating at start of period (units)	Number failed during period (failures) (units)	Number operating at end of period (survivors) (units)	Failure rate for period (%/unit time)	Total number failed to end of period (% of original group)	Total number survived at end of period (% of original group)
0– 1	150	26	124	17·2	17·2	82·8
1– 2	124	17	107	13·7	28·5	71·5
2– 3	107	12	95	11·2	36·5	63·5
3– 4	95	8	87	8·4	42·0	58·0
4– 5	87	7	80	8·0	46·5	53·5
5– 6	80	5	75	6·3	50·0	50·0
6– 7	75	5	70	6·7	53·4	46·6
7– 8	70	4	66	5·7	56·0	44·0
8– 9	66	4	62	6·0	58·8	41·2
9–10	62	3	59	4·8	60·6	39·4
10–11	59	3	56	5·0	62·5	37·5
11–12	56	3	53	5·3	64·8	35·2
12–13	53	3	50	5·6	66·7	33·3
13–14	50	3	47	6·0	68·5	31·5
14–15	47	3	44	6·4	70·5	29·5
15–16	44	2	42	4·6	71·5	28·5
16–17	42	2	40	4·8	73·0	27·0
17–18	40	2	38	5·0	73·6	26·4
18–19	38	2	36	5·2	76·0	24·0
19–20	36	2	34	5·6	77·0	23·0
20–21	34	2	32	5·9	78·5	21·5
21–22	32	3	29	9·4	80·0	20·0
22–23	29	3	26	10·2	82·5	17·5
23–24	26	2	24	7·5	83·8	16·2
24–25	24	2	22	8·3	85·0	15·0
25–26	22	2	20	9·1	86·5	13·5
26–27	20	3	17	15·0	87·8	12·2
27–28	17	2	15	11·8	89·6	10·4
28–29	15	2	13	13·4	91·0	9·0
29–30	13	2	11	15·3	92·1	7·9

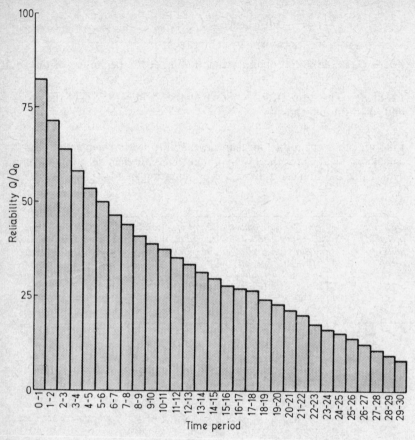

Fig. 5.5

Generalized expression for the reliability function. During the adult phase the reliability function is effectively in the exponential form above, but this does not hold during the 'infant' and 'wear-out' stages. A more generalized expression due to Weibull may be used for the whole life of the product, when—

$$R(t) = e^{-\left[\frac{(t-t_o)}{\alpha}\right]^{\beta}}$$

where t_o is the locating parameter, α is the scaling parameter, β is the shaping parameter

and by choosing appropriate values of $t_o \ \alpha \ \beta$ the whole bath-tub curve can be represented. Thus, in the simplest situation when the failure rate is constant, β is given a value of 1.0 whence—

$$R(t) = e^{-\frac{(t-t_o)}{\alpha}}, \text{ time being measured from the onset of}$$

the 'normal' period so that the reliability function reverts to the exponential form and with origin at the 't₁' point of Fig. 5.4. In the burn-in phase $\beta < 1\cdot0$, the origin being at the origin of Fig. 5.4, and in the 'aging' phase $\beta > 1\cdot0$ and the origin is at 't₂' in Fig. 5.4. Weibell paper can be used upon which a reliability plot can be made and estimates of the parameters obtained.

Mean time between failures (MTBF). The failure rate λ is usually used when discussing components, that is, devices which cannot be repaired after failure. Some products, however, can be repaired, and these are frequently referred to as *equipments*. The figure of merit which is then used is the *mean time between failures* (MTBF). Whilst this is time-dependent, during the adult life of the equipment, when the reliability function takes the exponential form, clearly

$$\text{MTBF} = \frac{1}{\lambda}$$

but this value is only appropriate during the time when the failure rate is constant. MTBF must not be confused with MTFF, the mean time to first failure.

Other expressions of reliability. There are a large number of other expressions of reliability and reference needs to be made to one of the many comprehensive texts on reliability now available.

Further Reading
This Chapter has been concerned to discuss Quality as an expression of managerial policy, whilst a later chapter (Chapter 20) displays means whereby this expression may be put into practice. This division is not a common one, and most texts treat of both subjects, so that recommendations for further reading are appropriate for either chapter. It is hoped that the more general texts appear hereunder, whilst those concentrating more on particular techniques appear on p. 234.

1. Smith, C. S., *Quality and Reliability: an integrated approach*, Pitman, London 1969.
   A most excellent introductory text which is well produced and well written. Extremely valuable for the manager.

2. Nixon, F., *Managing to Achieve Quality and Reliability*, McGraw-Hill, London 1971.
   Without using any mathematics at all, the author discusses comprehensively management's role in achieving, setting, and carrying out a sound Q. & R. policy. Comprehensively referenced and illustrated it confirms the author's position as one of the leading U.K. authorities on Q. & R.

3. Juran, J. M., *Quality Control Handbook*, McGraw-Hill, New York 1962.
   A comprehensive work, edited by the doyen of quality control engineers,

which discusses quality in both general terms and in particular industries. For the worker who needs to resolve a particular problem this book forms a most useful starting point.

4. Bazovsky, J., *Reliability: Theory and Practice*, Prentice Hall, Englewood Cliffs, N.J., 1961.
The classic book on Reliability. Whilst using mathematics freely, it will repay careful study.

5. Ireson, W., *Reliability Handbook*, McGraw-Hill, New York 1966.
A compendious work parallelling 3 above.

6. Dummer, G. W. A. and Winton, R. C., *An Elementary Guide to Reliability*, Pergamon, Oxford 1968.
Written in non-technical, non-mathematical terms, this short work covers the field of reliability in a brisk and sometimes amusing fashion. Useful as an introduction, it will have little of interest for the serious student.

7. Weinberg, S., *Profit through Quality*, Gower Press, 1969.
A broadly based book for the manager who wishes to improve profitability. Valuable for the conceptual discussion this text does not use any mathematics.

Chapter 6
Design of the Product

Nowhere in industry is there more confusion in terminology than in the field of design, development or research. In order that in this volume some degree of clarification is achieved, the following working definitions are offered and will be used throughout the present text—

1. *Research*: the discovery of novel techniques, ideas or systems.
2. *Development*: the improvement of existing techniques, ideas or systems.
3. *Design*: the translation of requirements into a form suitable for manufacture or use.

Accepting the above definitions, it will be seen that design may encompass both research and development. Both of these are creative activities and hence not easy to discuss. The difficulties are so great, and in some cases the personnel concerned so unworldly, that often no attempt is made to control them. This is a policy of despair and, whilst it must be accepted that tight control is impossible, some attempt must be made to provide guidance—particularly as the size, cost and technological complexity of many of today's new products are so great that disaster can result if control is lacking. It should be noted that in other creative activities in industry, for example, work study or tool design, close control is accepted as normal.

FIVE STAGES OF A DESIGN PROJECT

In every project the design programme will pass through the following stages—

(*a*) *Conception*, when a draft specification is laid down.

(*b*) *Acceptance*, where the specification is shown to be achievable by mathematical calculation, preliminary drawings, 'bread-board' or 'mock-up' models or laboratory-scale processes.

(*c*) *Execution*, where a number of models are prepared from the work above, or pilot-plants are made up following the laboratory-scale experiments.

(*d*) *Translation*, where the project is put into such a form that it can be manufactured within the organization where it will be produced and to the specification laid down.

(*e*) *Pre-production*, where quantities are produced sufficient to check the design, tools and specification. It is not till this stage that drawings can be 'frozen', that is, considered to be final and not liable to change without authorization.

The above five steps are always present in some form, although in small organizations they may be telescoped, whilst in very small quantity production pre-production models very often coincide with the first production, possibly with the only production. In projects where large articles —boilers, power-plants—are being designed the last three stages effectively coalesce with the actual manufacturing stage.

Conception

This first stage is most important in providing the basis for control of all subsequent design activity. A specification must be drawn up in as much detail as possible by the sales department in discussion with the design department. Where highly technical and capital goods are concerned, discussions are often on an 'engineer-to-engineer' basis, as the technical requirements and consequences may be extremely taxing.

Time spent here will not only indicate to the designers exactly what is required, it will enable the sales department to discuss the project with actual or potential customers, and it will enable some measure of the cost of changes in requirement upon the design effort to be made and charged to the appropriate source. In effect this is a translation of a sales requirement into terms acceptable to the designer.

The following minimum information should be given on a design specification—

1. The technical or performance requirements.

2. The appearance or 'styling' requirements.

3. The intended selling price or factory price. This can often only be in the form: 'Price not to exceed . . . '

4. The date when manufacture must start.

5. The probable quantity which will be sold. This quantity can substantially affect the design and, as a consequence, the first cost.

6. The maximum cost of designing which can be accepted, since the final product must bear the cost of the design.

Acceptance

This is essentially a 'back-room' function carried out in the design department by designers and draughtsmen. It is usually the first stage where costs for the design work will be assigned directly to the project, and is normally initiated by a works order embodying the draft specification laid down at conception. The draft specification is tested, being subjected to calculation, model-making or such other activity as is appropriate, and is then accepted, rejected as impracticable, or modified in conjunction with the sales department. Sometimes, particularly in simple projects, this stage will coincide with the previous one, and may consist of only a meeting between all interested parties.

Execution

A working model (or series of models) is produced, being based on the ideas thrown up at stage 2, and on general design considerations, both theoretical and practical. The models should as far as possible conform to the specification: where this is not possible, the differences should be known and their effects considered. The differences usually arise either from the magnitude of the problem (for example, an oil refinery) or from the need for special parts whose cost cannot be justified until the design is finalized. Whilst cost considerations must not be overlooked, the technical and appearance requirements are most important at this stage, and the models made should indicate clearly the feasibility of the proposed design meeting the specification at all points. The cost of the final product is a matter which needs to be accepted by the design department as a factor as important as any other, but subsequent technical development (for example by the production engineers) can often produce reductions in cost figures greater than those achieved by the design team.

Translation

At this stage the production engineering department *must* be involved in the design work. It is quite common practice for the team responsible for the original work and the model manufacturer to hand over their task to a development team which, whilst appreciating the originality of the design, can also appreciate the problems involved in manufacturing. This development team should discuss at all stages the manufacturing problems with the production engineers. Detailed estimates will begin to be formed, and it will be possible to assign maximum acceptable costs to the various components. The question 'This part must not cost more than . . . Can it be made for this? If not, how should it be re-designed?' must be asked at all times. Lack of co-operation at this time between the development engineers and the production engineers will prove very costly: the design finally placed upon the production unit will be difficult to manufacture, and emergency redesigns carried out 'on the floor' will result in a debasing of the product. Too often a sense of economy on the part of the management, or of aloofness on the part of the designer, has resulted in this stage being omitted or made vestigial: in every case, an inferior product has eventually been sold.

Work will also be proceeding on preparing the final manufacturing drawings, the drawings summarizing all the design and development effort. Control of the amount of work put into drawings is both important and difficult, and it must be remembered that the drawings are intended to convey information, and not be an end in themselves.

It is not possible to generalize on the ratio of the cost of carrying out the original work (the design work) to the cost of carrying out this consolidation work (the development work). In the author's experience the development work is always more costly, often in the ratio of 1:2, but it may well be that this is not always so. This figure is quoted only in order to underline the importance of this task, and must not be considered as a recommendation of any kind.

Pre-production

Once all the foregoing has been completed, it is desirable, particularly in large-scale productions, to carry out a pilot run *under production conditions*. This will consist of completely assembling a quantity of the production from parts made by the normal production method and using the same degree of skill in the operatives as will be found in the final manufacture.

In addition, tests to the customer specification should be carried out, again using the equipment which will be used in manufacture. The tasks should be done at some time before the start of production in order that any faults or weaknesses which are shown up can be corrected. Such a pre-production run will check—

1. Drawings;
2. Final tools;
3. Production techniques and estimates;
4. Specifications;

and only after such a run should the drawing be considered to be final.

The above outline of the processes of designing for production is an attempt to separate out the various stages of a creative act. In small organizations, one person might well carry out two or more of the above tasks, and indeed it may then be impossible to analyse the work done. Nevertheless, it is suggested that some process similar to the above must be carried out whenever design for production is necessary.

THE CONTROL OF A DESIGN PROJECT

As pointed out above, it is not possible to exert the same tight control on design effort as on manufacturing effort, yet the costs involved and the time used are often substantial. The following points are worth considering—

1. No design will ever be 'complete' in the sense that, with effort, some modification (improvement?) cannot always be made.
2. Few designs are *entirely* novel. An examination of a 'new' product will almost certainly show that it largely employs existing techniques, components or systems to which have been added a comparatively small novel element. Figures are difficult to obtain here, but the author believes that in most 'new' products the 'novel' design work rarely exceeds 10 per

cent of the total design work, the rest being modifications to existing material. The effort which must go into these modifications is likely to be reasonably predictable.

3. There appears to be a 'law of diminishing returns' on design effort. The longer the time which is spent on a design, the less the increase in the value of the design unless a technological breakthrough is achieved.

4. External and/or internal circumstances will impose limitations on design time and cost. It is as difficult to imagine a design project whose completion date is not implicitly fixed, either by a promise to a customer, the opening of a trade show or exhibition, a seasonal 'dead-line', a production schedule or some other constraint, as it is to imagine an organization whose funds are unlimited, or a product whose price has no ceiling.

THE USE OF CRITICAL PATH ANALYSIS IN DESIGN

The most effective tool for the control of design is Critical Path Analysis. This will exert a discipline and enforce a degree of pre-planning upon the design effort which is invaluable. It will ensure that the sequence in which design tasks are undertaken is determined by need rather than by interest, and it will enable the supervisor concerned to compare the progress made with the progress planned.

A common difficulty in using C.P.A. in design tasks is the belief that it is not possible to assign duration times to design activities. When dealing with this problem the following steps are useful:

1. Determine the design specification as accurately and in as much detail as possible.

2. Involve the people concerned in the drawing of the network. (It will be found that the logical basis of C.P.A. is appealing to most designers.)

3. Establish any fixed dates. If a fixed completion date is not available, agree a reasonable completion date.

4. Assign duration times on non-contentious activities.

5. Break contentious activities into smaller parts, on some of which times can be readily agreed since past experience can be of a guide.

6. Examine the remaining activities to see whether there are any historical precedents. If not, then assign to them as much time as possible without over-running the fixed completion date. It is then possible to pose the question, 'There are Y units of time in which to design X—is this possible?' which is often found to be more stimulating than the question, 'How long will it take to design X?' If at this stage the designer will not, or cannot accept the available time, then either the logic or the resources must be changed, or a re-negotiation of the completion date must take place.

Once a network has been completed and analysed it *must* be used as a control device, otherwise much of its potential value will not be realized.

This is probably done most simply by holding a regular meeting at which all those concerned report on progress. This meeting should be a progress meeting, not a design meeting to which problems are brought for solutions. Problem solving is best treated separately. It will be found that the effectiveness of this meeting will depend almost entirely upon the manner in which it is run. A tradition of the accepting of the discipline of time is an invaluable asset to the design department.

Many design offices undertake a number of projects simultaneously, and the problem of sharing limited resources amongst these projects is an important one. Here it is probably simplest to draw a network for each project, to translate each of these into bar charts and to superimpose the various bar charts upon each other. From this superimposition it will be possible to read off the total resources of any type required at any time and if this exceeds the resources available, then some float manipulation must take place. It must be remembered that the more float is absorbed by resource allocation, the more critical the project becomes, and the more serious will the effect of over-running of time. *Float represents flexibility.* A network for the design of a machine tool is shown in Fig. 6.1. (See fold-out opposite.)

PROJECT COST CONTROL

An estimated cost for design should be one of the figures submitted at the design acceptance stage. It must be recognized, however, that the calculation of this cost is not easy, and no general recommendations can be made since different situations will require entirely different systems. Thus, a design office set up to deal with one special project will need to be controlled more carefully, and in more detail, than a department which undertakes all the design tasks within a consumer product company, and both need different treatment from a design office which exists to produce designs for other organizations to use.

The purpose of the costing system must be clearly established before any system is installed. Essentially the purpose *must* be to enable the design manager to manage: to extract figures 'because they would be interesting' is expensive but valueless. As with any other situation, detail should be minimized.

In setting up an estimate and subsequently using it for control, it must be remembered that labour costs are derived from labour times, so that if times are controlled, the derived costs are also controlled. This means that using a network to control times will automatically control labour costs— and in design projects it is these labour costs which form by far the largest portion of the total costs. *Consumable* items (wire, solder, drawing paper, pencils, developing fluid . . .) are best dealt with as burden spread over all projects and included in the on-costs assigned to direct labour costs, leaving the design manager to control these as items appearing on his budgetary control returns. *Special* items, purchased solely to meet the needs of particular tasks must, of course, be assigned to those tasks.

REDUCING DESIGN COSTS

Buying Design Effort

Design effort is expensive: a qualified engineer or scientist not only has a high basic pay, he attracts to himself considerable support staff and sometimes heavy capital equipment. It is frequently possible to avoid the heavy fixed costs of permanent staff by purchasing design effort. There are a number of sources:

1. *Research Associations*: At the moment there are 52 of these in the U.K. covering most industries. Their income is partly derived from Government grants and partly from members' subscriptions. They offer information services, bulletins, and research/development facilities.

2. *Government research stations*: These can often undertake development work for companies.

3. *Educational establishments*: Within the technical colleges, polytechnics and universities there are substantial resources which can be tapped. Staff will sometimes undertake work at very low cost if it is academically interesting and capable of being published, or they will act as consultants charging a normal consultant's fee. Most academic and learned societies have extensive libraries which can be used at negligible cost.

4. *Private design companies*: There are an increasing number of commercial design companies who undertake fee-paid assignments. These include 'Industrial Designers', and though most industrial designers have specialist training and ability in aesthetics, they will frequently bring to a task a fresh and uninhibited attack on function and cost. It is foolish to introduce an industrial designer to a product when all the 'real' design is complete and expect him to carry out some painless cosmetic surgery. The industrial designer should be involved in a design project from its inception.

Frequently, the fee required by a commercial designer appears high, but it must be remembered that it does not involve the user company in the heavy fixed expense of employing his own staff.

5. *Licences to Manufacture*: It is often possible to buy the results of other companies' efforts by negotiating licences to manufacture new products. This is most commonly done with companies in other countries, and it should be remembered that conditions may be different in those countries, and that there will usually be a need to ensure that any drawings, specifications, methods are appropriate to the licensee.

Use of a Computer

The tremendous speed, and vast storage capacity, of a computer assists the designer in a number of ways—

(*a*) Frequently repeated, and long, tedious calculations can be carried out in real time. Without a computer a designer will reduce the need for calculations by using tables or graphs of 'established standards' or 'good practice'. These, to become manageable, are the abbreviated results either of a few calculations or of a series of trials, and in either case contain ample 'safety' factors which usually over-compensate for the inadequacies of the calculations. As a result, the design produced may be unnecessarily costly in some way. The computer enables these calculations to be carried out as and when needed, reducing wasted effort.

(*b*) A lengthy calculation by hand will produce an acceptable result, but the effort of examining the effect of changing one or other of the constituent parameters may be so great that no such examination is made. This may result in accepting a result which could be modified. Again, the computer's abilities could be used to check the effect of modification. Time sharing is particularly appropriate here.

(*c*) Quantities of data can be held in the computer's store and withdrawn with such ease that it becomes possible to refer readily to previous designs, experience, data.

In order that the designer can use the computer to advantage he must be able to communicate readily with it. Much work is going on in this field—'light pens' which enable drawings to be made (and modified) on the face of a display tube are becoming practicable devices. The less spectacular, but equally useful 'conversational' mode of 'talking' to a computer is now highly developed so that a designer can readily use the computer without a 'language barrier'. In addition, the computer can store the results of the design process and issue it in a useful form often obviating the need for the preparation of drawings.

Specialization by Designers

Concentration upon a limited field allows a designer to build up a body of knowledge which will permit him to answer questions within that field very much more rapidly than if his interests ranged over a wide area. This again does not produce stagnation, since the concentration brings with it a deepening knowledge and a more fundamental understanding of the problems within that field of limited study. This is generally recognized, so that there are now no individual designers responsible for, say, the complete design of an aeroplane; there are design teams, each member of which specializes upon a few aspects.

Use of a Logical Coding System

The fewer the number of piece-parts designed, the greater the productivity of the design and drawing office. It is frequently found that a part will be designed which could be identical to or is replaceable by an existing part. This wastes not only design effort but subsequent production, production control, and production engineering effort. Often minor modifications to existing parts will render it useful for a number of functions other than that for which it was first designed. At first this might appear to impose restrictions upon the designer which might inhibit his creative ability, yet in fact it will release him from the drudgery of detailed designing. No designer calls for special screws, nuts, wire diameters, sheet metal thicknesses—standardization is accepted here, yet the variety of products which can be made from these items is infinite.

It has been pointed out earlier that it is necessary to be able to identify like components readily, and it was there suggested that a simple method of achieving this is to use a logical coding system.

It would seem that the characteristics of a satisfactory coding system are—

1. any 'code-name' should indicate only one item,
2. any item should bear only one 'code-name',
3. coverage should be adequate and comprehensive,
4. it should be wholly numerical,
5. a code-name should be of constant length,
6. a code-name should not be excessively long,
7. the simpler the item, the simpler the code-name,
8. classification should be by permanent features.

One such numbering system is the *Family Name-Christian Name* method. In this, the whole range of components used *or likely to be used* is considered, and the components grouped in families, the families all having strong similarities in some important characteristics. Each family will then be given a number (the Family name) and each component in that family will be given a second number (the Christian name) differentiating it from its fellows. Then, if a new component appears to be required, an examination of the drawings of the family to which it belongs is made, and suitable components selected. This technique is very flexible, capable of considerable expansion, and when filing drawings will cause drawings of a similar size to be filed together. An initial problem arises in the original definitions of the families: this must be carefully done, and the definitions written down—that is, a dictionary formed. Once this has been done the running of the system is extremely simple, and its results felt not only in the design and drawing office but throughout the factory, where other departments will rapidly be able to recognize numbers as relating to certain components.

As an example, reference is made to a company with which the author was associated. There were some 3,000 drawings extant which had been drawn over the course of some fifteen years. The number chosen for any drawing was the next number in the series of natural numbers, so that the twenty 'pointers' used, for which tools and drawings existed, had numbers spread at random throughout the number series. Thus, if a pointer were designed it would be given a number—say 2948. The next item to be designed might be a bracket, which would have the number 2949 and so on. To identify all the pointers therefore it was necessary to search through all the drawings—a virtually impossible task. It was then decided to re-number all drawings in accordance with a Family Name-Christian Name technique. Sixty-four families were identified, and in order to allow for expansion these were numbered 000 upwards, pointers being numbered 012. A four figure number was assigned to each member of the family, since it was felt unlikely that there would be more than 10,000 drawings in any one family. All the pointers then carried numbers as follows—

012	0000
012	0001
012	0002
012	0003
——	——
——	——
——	——

These were then filed together, and when a pointer was required, reference had only to be made to the 012 file, and a search carried out amongst twenty drawings only.

The changing of all numbers to a logical system showed that some items had been drawn three, four and in some cases five times under different numbers. When the items were stored according to drawing numbers (so that the drawing number became virtually a stores location number) all similar items were grouped together physically. Other departments rapidly became familiar with the various 'family names' and it was found that, in the cost department for example, errors in pricing became more readily noticed since all 012 . . . components had similar prices and those which were substantially incorrect were very easily observed.

An elaboration of this system is suggested by Brisch ('Maximum ex Minima', *J.I.Prod.E.*, June, 1954), whereby all the integers in a part-number have a precise and unique significance. This will permit a much more minute description to be incorporated into a code number: for example, bright mild steel tube, round seamless, 0·750 in. O/D × 10 S.W.G. could be coded 1174-401, the code number being analysed as follows—

        1 . . .-. . . is a primary material.
        . 1 . .-. . . is of iron or carbon steel.
        . . 7 .-. . . is of tubular form.
        . . . 4-. . . is of mild steel.
        . . . .-4 . . is round, seamless, of specified lengths.
        . . . .-. 01 is 0·750 in O/D × 10 S.W.G.

A similar tube in brass could have a number of the form 1275-401, whilst one of aluminium might have the form 1377-401.

Whatever the classification system used, it is important that it should be clearly defined, and that the numbers should have only one meaning, that is, they should be unique. In a small company or one where the total number of items to be classified is small, it is probably unwise to attempt too great an elaboration with the code number: however, the benefits of changing from a random coding to a logical coding are so great that the apparent difficulties in changing code numbers, even with all the attendant upheaval in renumbering in stores, in the design department, in the cost office, should be accepted and a logical system installed.

Use of a Library and Technical Information Service

Considerable savings in time and money can often be effected within a project by reference to published information. This is equally true of production engineering, research or development, but it is usual to house all technical sources within one area which forms part of the design department.

In its simplest form, a library consists merely of a passive collection of books, but it can play a very positive function by being an information department from which information can be requested. A librarian trained in searching and abstracting can rapidly and cheaply produce information from which problems can be solved or new developments advanced. With the present enormous flood of technical information being published each day no scientist, technician, or technologist can hope to be up to date with his subject except in a very narrow field. The librarian, by discriminating and abstracting, can assist by limiting any field of inquiry to that of immediate interest.

Within a small company it is probably more effective to employ an information officer than to start a library. The information officer would rapidly build up the comparatively small volume of essential reference books, but would be able, by collaborating with local municipal libraries, national libraries, professional institutions, and research associations, and the excellent lending libraries, to provide quickly any reference book needed. He would also be able to abstract appropriate journals and cir-cularize bulletins of information to all who require them. This would enable the engineers and designers to assess their need for the journal and save much wasted time in examining articles of no interest to them. Of course, all journals should be available for inspection, and 'browsing' can be a very effective method of cross-fertilization. The various makers' catalogues and data sheets can also be housed in the library rather than in the buyer's office. These will be readily accessible to all, and should be kept up to date as a matter of course. The collection of such catalogues by the librarian or information officer rather than by the more directly interested persons has the practical advantage that designers—for example —are insulated from the enthusiastic representatives of firms who *will* call upon the request for a catalogue. Requests from librarians are not usually followed up so vigorously by personal calls.

Properly organized, controlled, and supported by management, an information department can be a tool as useful to a designer as a slide-rule. Regrettably it is found all too infrequently, and expensive effort has often gone to waste carrying out work which has already been published and completed. It has been estimated that up to thirty per cent of the cost of a development project can be saved by an effective information department, and the savings in time can be equally great.

THE DRAWING OFFICE

An essential part of a design department is the drawing office, since it is by means of drawings that information is conveyed to the manufacturing departments. In some industries drawings may be replaced by manufacturing specifications or by process layouts, but throughout the following section the word 'drawing' will be used to indicate any device from which manufacturing information is derived.

The authority for publishing *and amending* finalized drawings must be vested in one department only, which must also be responsible for ensuring that all drawings held by that department are up to date and represent current practice in that organization. Drawings should contain all the information necessary for the manufacture of the article concerned, either explicitly or by reference to published standards, specifications, or codes of practice.

No drawing should be issued which has not been checked by some authorized person, since a drawing error, even though apparently trivial, can have a profound effect upon production. Some organizations require not only that the drawing be checked before issue but that the drawing itself be authorized by the engineer responsible for the whole project. If this is done, care must be taken to avoid any very great reliance on the value of this 'authorizing' signature, since in a complex project the signature becomes a purely automatic device, since the authorizer has no time to check each drawing personally.

Drawings once issued may be found to be required to be modified or changed. It may appear that should any member of the organization wish to change a drawing he should have freedom to demand that the change be made. However, it will be found that this freedom will permit changes to be made either irresponsibly or without a realization of the full implication of the change. For example, a change on one small component may render the complete stock of mating components obsolete, or a change permitting easier assembly may require re-tooling, the cost of which far outweighs the saving in assembly cost.

Change System

To control changes (or modifications) to drawings, a formalized change system is usually necessary. This can take a form similar to the following—

1. *A change proposal* is raised by any interested person, but, to avoid any changes of a frivolous nature, this should be countersigned by the appropriate departmental supervisor. This proposal should state—

(*a*) Drawing concerned;
(*b*) Change required;
(*c*) Reason for the change;
(*d*) Degree of urgency—that is, whether 'retrospective', 'immediate', 'as convenient', or 'as from . . . date'.

2. *Comments* on this proposal must be made by departments concerned. Thus, the production control department might comment on the stock situation and the cost of scrapping that stock, and the work study department would discuss the changes in method, the buyer the availability of the new materials and so on.

3. *Acceptance* is given by a committee sitting to consider all the changes and the comments arising from them.

4. *A Change Note* is originated if the change proposal is accepted, and this note is published generally, being used by the drawing office as an authority to change the drawing concerned. The drawing itself will be changed, a note of the date of the change and a brief description of the change made on the drawing, and a new drawing issued, the number of the issue also being recorded. Ideally all old drawings should be withdrawn and destroyed, but it is found in fact that this is very difficult to do, and in practice new drawings are issued to departments with a request (frequently pious) that all old drawings are destroyed.

Once a change system is in being it must be clearly understood that no person has the right to change a drawing without recourse to a change proposal. At the design stage this can often be a considerable hindrance, and drawings are often assumed to be free from the change system until they are 'frozen' at the completion of the 'consolidation' stage. Before drawings are so frozen it is unwise to engage in any substantial expenditure or action derived from the drawings, and often drawings are not published until they are frozen. Should preliminary drawings be required, for example, for estimating purposes, they are best issued suitably marked across their face FOR ESTIMATE ONLY or some other appropriate wording.

Further Reading

1. Collinson, H. A., *Management for Research and Development*, Pitman, London 1964.

One of the few U.K. books to deal with the R. & D. function from a practical standpoint.

2. Burns, T. and Stalker, G. M., *The Management of Innovation*, Tavistock Publications, London 1966.

This classic work 'is a contribution to the study of problems related to the exploitation of scientific discovery in peace time conditions'. Whilst it will not help the reader to design a single control document for an R. & D. department, it will give him a substantial insight into the behaviour of the people who make up that department.

3. Stanley, A. O. and White, K. K., *Organizing the R. and D. Function*, American Management Association, 1966.

Presents charts and descriptions of the R. & D. organizations of forty-two industrial companies in the U.S.

4. Seiler, R. E., *Improving the Effectiveness of Research and Development*, McGraw-Hill, New York, 1965.

Contains useful chapters on Budgetary Control and the Selection of Projects.

5. *Computer Aided Design*, Institution of Electrical Engineers.

A collection of papers presented at an international conference, 15th–18th April 1969, which brings together a great deal of current experience.

6. Monteith, G. Stuart, *R. & D. Administration*, Iliffe Books, London 1969.

This book attempts to discuss the problems of planning and administration when applied to research and development. It gives answers based on current practices both in the U.K. and the U.S.A. It is an essentially practical work.

7. Orth, C. D., Bailey, J. C., and Wolek, F. W., *Administering Research and Development*, Tavistock Publications, London 1965.

A set of 36 cases on the management of research and development groups, and a set of research study papers. Probably of more use to the professional teacher than to the R. & D. manager.

8. Mitchell, H., *Codification in Manufacturing and Materials Management*, Gower Press, London 1972.

An excellent discussion, illustrated by examples of coding systems used in some leading U.K. companies.

Section Three   The Factory

Chapter 7
Location of the Factory

The location of the factory may well have a substantial effect upon the operation of the unit, and upon the group as a whole if the factory is within a geographically dispersed group. No set of rules can be laid down whereby the solution to the problem of location can be programmed. There are, however, a number of factors which should be considered, and these are discussed in this chapter. It is worth differentiating between the problems of *location* and of *site*: the *location* is the general area, and the *site* is the place chosen within the location. The decision on siting thus probably proceeds in two stages: in the first the general area is chosen, and then a detailed survey of that area is carried out to find possible sites. The final decision is then probably made by taking into account the more detailed factors (. . . is the view pleasant? . . . is there a good restaurant nearby? . . .).

CHOICE OF LOCATION

The following are some of the factors which will influence the choice of location—

1. *Integration with Other Group Companies*
   If the new factory is one of a number of factories owned or operated by a single group of companies, the new factory should be so situated that its work can be integrated with the work of associated factories. This will require that the group should be considered as an entity, not as a number of independent units.

2. *Availability of Labour*
   Labour may be more readily available in some cases than in others— the Department of Trade and Industry can provide information on this point. Certain areas, however, have traditional skills—for example, furniture making is well established in High Wycombe. It is very rare today that a location can be found which has appropriately skilled and unskilled labour both readily available. The choice has to be made between a location where skilled men exist but are not readily available, and one where there is a supply of unskilled labour. It must be remembered that

new skills can be taught, processes simplified and made less exacting, and key personnel moved. Most technical colleges and polytechnics are eager to co-operate in training staff, and there are a number of courses available for assisting in the training of supervisors.

3. *Availability of Housing*

Where staff has to be recruited other than locally, housing will need to be available. It is general experience that the offer of good housing can be of greater assistance in attracting staff than almost any other factor. Sometimes local councils will make houses available, whilst under other circumstances companies find it worthwhile assisting employees in the purchase of their own houses.

4. *Availability of Amenities*

A location which provides good amenities outside the factory—shops, theatres, cinemas, restaurants—is often much more attractive to staff than one which is more remote. This is particularly so where a large proportion of married women are employed who find it convenient to shop for the family during the lunch break and on the way to and from work. One important amenity in this connexion is good personnel transport—buses and trains—and some companies find this so vital that they provide special company buses.

5. *Availability of Transport*

In some cases where products or purchased parts are heavy and bulky it is important that goods transport facilities shall be readily available. Goods intended largely for export indicate a location near a seaport or a large airfield.

6. *Availability of Materials*

Whilst it is true that good transport facilities will enable goods to be obtained and delivered readily, a location near main suppliers will help to reduce cost and permit staff to go readily to see suppliers to discuss technical or delivery problems. Any buyer who has tried to improve deliveries from an inaccessible supplier will bear witness to the very considerable difficulties involved.

7. *Availability of Car Parking Space*

There is no doubt that the use of cars as a means of transport to and from work will continue to increase, whatever public transport facilities are provided. A ratio of 1 car to every 1·8 workers is already found in some U.S. plants, and a ratio of 1:3 is suggested as being a reasonable one in the U.K. upon which to base calculations, whilst an allowance of 175 cars to the acre appears satisfactory. If open space is not available for car parking, special car-park structures may be necessary.

8. *Adequacy of Circulation*

The movement of transport to and from a factory—goods, visitors, and staff—presents a problem not only of easy access but also easy control.

There is also a need for emergency access—fire-fighting equipment or ambulances—which, if impeded, could endanger life and seriously affect the company.

9. *Availability of Services*
There are five main services which need to be considered, namely—

1. Gas;
2. Electricity;
3. Water;
4. Drainage;
5. Disposal of waste.

Certain industries use considerable quantities of water—food preparation, laundries, metal plating, etc.; others use a great deal of electricity for chemical processing and so on. An assessment must be made of the requirements of the factory for as far ahead as possible. Underestimating the needs of any of the services can prove to be extremely costly and inconvenient.

10. *Suitability of Land and Climate*
Here not merely must the geology of the area be considered, that is, whether the subsoil can support the loads likely to be placed on it, but also whether the climatic conditions (humidity, temperature and atmosphere) will adversely affect manufacture. Modern building techniques are such that almost all disadvantages of terrain and climate can be overcome, but the cost of so doing may be high and a different locality could avoid an inflated first cost.

11. *Local Building and Planning Regulations*
It is important to check at an early stage that the proposed location does not infringe any local regulations. A study must be made not only of the appropriate bye-laws but also of any special regulations concerning the disposal of effluents and the presence of any ancient lights in the immediate vicinity. A discussion with the surveyor's department of the local authority is most desirable.

12. *Room for Expansion*
It is most unwise to build a factory to the limit of any site unless the long-range forecast indicates very definitely that the initial building will never be required to increase in size. This is a most unlikely circumstance and adequate room for genuine expansion should be allowed. It is dangerous to assume that at a later date the car park can be built on, or that the canteen can be used as a productive area.

13. *Safety Requirements*
Some factories may present, or may be believed to present, potential dangers to the surrounding neighbourhood—for example, nuclear power stations, and explosive factories are often considered dangerous. Location of such plants in remote areas may be desirable.

1. Integration with other group companies
2. Availability of labour
3. Availability of housing
4. Availability of staff amenities
5. Availability of transport
6. Availability of materials
7. Availability of car parking space
8. Adequacy of circulation
9. Availability of services
10. Suitability of land and climate
11. Local building and planning regulations
12. Room for expansion
13. Safety requirements
14. Site cost
15. Political situation
16. Special grants

Factors Influencing the Choice of Location

14. *Site Cost*

As a first charge, the site cost is important, although it is important not to let immediate gain jeopardize long-term plans.

15. *Political Situation*

The political situation in potential locations should be considered. Even if other considerations demand a particular site, knowledge of the political situation and local prejudices can assist in taking decisions.

16. *Special Grants*

Governments and local authorities often offer special grants, low interest loans, low rentals and other inducements in the hope of attracting industry to particular locations. As these are often areas with large reservoirs of labour, these offers can be most attractive.

Selection of a Particular Location

In most location problems there are some 'mandatory' factors—those which must be fulfilled. Thus, an oil refinery *must* have excellent main services, in particular, fresh water; also the author recalls an occasion when the site chosen had to be within twenty miles of the managing director's home. Once these key factors are identified the location problem ceases to be an open, 'Where shall the factory be located?' question, but rather a choice: 'Which out of a number of sites shall be chosen?' Here, a ranking technique, with an appropriate weight of the various factors, can be helpful. There are a number of methods of ranking and weighting, for example—

(*a*) Examine the various factors and assign to them weights representing the importance of the factor to the situation being studied. It is convenient to isolate the least important factor and give it a weighting of 1. All other factors are then expressed as multiples of this; that is, all other weights are whole numbers. It may be that in doing this a rather coarse scale is produced, but extreme accuracy is not possible and time should not be wasted striving after unnecessary precision. A panel of three persons can be helpful in setting these weights.

(*b*) Each of the locations is examined and 'ranked' for each factor, this ranking being carried out factor by factor, not location by location.

Factor	Weight	Possible Location A	B	C	D	E
Integration	0	– 0	– 0	– 0	– 0	– 0
Labour	9	1 9	5 45	4 36	2 18	3 27
Housing	6	3 18	3 18	2 12	5 30	1 6
Amenities	6	1 6	2 12	4 24	5 30	3 18
Transport	4	5 20	4 16	3 12	2 8	1 4
Materials	4	4 16	1 4	2 8	3 12	5 20
Car park	6	3 18	4 24	5 30	1 6	2 12
Circulation	6	1 6	4 24	3 18	5 30	2 12
Services	5	1 5	2 10	2 10	5 25	4 20
Land and climate	2	4 8	2 4	5 10	3 6	1 2
Planning regulations	8	5 40	2 16	4 32	3 24	1 8
Expansion	2	3 6	4 8	2 4	5 10	1 2
Safety	0	– 0	– 0	– 0	– 0	– 0
Cost	1	5 5	1 1	2 2	3 3	4 4
Political situation	0	– 0	– 0	– 0	– 0	– 0
Special grants	2	2 4	1 2	5 10	4 8	3 6
TOTALS		161	184	208	210	141

Fig. 7.1. Assessment of Possible Factory Location

(*c*) Each ranking is then multiplied by the appropriate weighting factor and the scores totalled for each possible location. These totals indicate the desirability of the possible locations compared with each other.

The results *for a hypothetical case* are shown in Fig. 7.1. The matrix form is convenient: the rank is placed in the left hand side of the cell, above the diagonal, whilst the result of multiplying the ranking by the weight is placed in the right hand side of the cell, below the diagonal. The total score is the sum of these right-hand entires.

Note: It must be emphasized that this is a hypothetical example: the weights assigned to each factor must not be taken to be recommendations of any kind.

Use of Linear Programming in Location Problems

The technique of linear programming can be used in locating a factory/ warehouse site provided that the determining factor is quantifiable and distance-dependent. The most common example of this type of problem is that where a factory 'feeds' a number of warehouses—or, inversely, where a producing unit is 'fed' from a number of sources—and the site location must be chosen to give a minimum total transportation cost. If the cost of transporting a 'load' is directly proportional both to the distance travelled and the number of units in the 'load', then a set of equations can be set up relating the total cost to the number of 'units' transported to/from each source and to the distance between the 'feeder' and the 'fed'. These equations are then solved to give the location which will minimize total transport costs, and this location is then accepted as the recommended site for the plant.

Whilst this 'transportation problem' is solved rather more easily than the 'product-mix' problem, it is still tedious to perform the manipulations manually and the computer is generally used for this purpose. Many programs are already available and there should be no need to write a special program. Although the mathematical and computational problems associated with this problem have been extensively explored its actual use is rare and confined to a few multi-location multi-market organizations.

Further Reading

Many economic texts discuss the problems of choosing a satisfactory location, but the only text directed specifically at the manager is—

Haines, V. G., *Business Relocation*, Business Books, London 1970.

Subtitled 'a guide to moving business', this is the most useful and wide treatment of all aspects of the subject. Should be read by any executive who is contemplating moving his business.

In addition to more formal works, much valuable information can be obtained by writing to County Councils, Chambers of Commerce and

Development Corporations. In the United Kingdom a set of very helpful booklets 'Room to Expand' is published by—

The Department of Trade and Industry,
(Distribution of Industry Division),
1 Victoria Street,
London SW1H 0ET

The staff of this department will also provide advice on location problems and help to pilot the prospective factory-builder through the maze of current legislation governing the choice of a site.

Chapter 8
Design of the Factory

The detailed design of a factory is clearly the responsibility of the architect, who will work within a brief set him by his client. The brief should indicate—

1. Accommodation required, both immediate and potential;
2. Latest possible completion date;
3. Quality/Life of the new building;
4. Proposed site;
5. Maximum cost.

All the above should derive explicitly from the long-term plans for the organization; if they are not so derived then it could well follow that the 'immediately useful' building could, in the long term, be a useless embarrassment to the company. As an example of the way in which long-term considerations affect the design of a new factory, it is worth considering a new plant built for a leading cigarette manufacturer. Believing that the consumption of cigarettes might fall away substantially, the directors decided that all floors of the new factory should be capable of supporting loads at least five times greater than those imposed by the relatively light-weight cigarette-making machines. In this way the company would be able, if necessary, to diversify into any enterprise requiring heavy plant, or alternatively to offer the plant more easily to a wider range of potential buyers.

It should also be noted that it is unlikely that the brief will be finalized at the first attempt: management is unlikely to be able to estimate for the cost of a new building unless very recent and comparable experience of building costs is to hand. Commonly an outline brief is given to the architect who will produce sketch plans from which some tentative estimates are produced. If these plans meet the brief, then it can be finalized, but if it does not—and usually the estimated costs are higher than the management had anticipated—then the brief must be modified and the process repeated.

During discussions between the architect and his client a number of points will arise requiring managerial decision. These should be resolved with the future use of the factory clearly borne in mind. Amongst the problems will be the following—

1. *Head Room Required*

Many modern production techniques require the use of overhead conveyors, suspended plant and above-head-height storage—in fact a plant can often be considered to be formed in two layers, one from the floor upwards, and one from the ceiling downwards. Furthermore, temporary increases in productive storage and office space can often be gained by mezzanine constructions, whilst the claustrophobic effect of a low ceiling is well known. Since inadequate head room cannot easily be remedied after the building is complete, and since the increase in cost for an increase in head room is comparatively small, it would seem to be unwise to curtail the distance between floor and ceiling too severely. A minimum clear height of 18–20 ft. is not considered excessive, or if the product is large, at least twice the height of the finished article.

2. *Loads to be Carried*

The loads developed in a work area arise not only from the immediate production equipment itself, but also from the storage of raw material, work-in-progress and finished goods around the production equipment, and from any material-handling equipment (trucks, etc.) likely to be used even occasionally in conjunction with the plant. Furthermore, the plant itself must be moved into position and the moving equipment bearing the plant must move over the gangways and floor space, which must therefore be capable of carrying the combined weight. If the floor is the ceiling of the lower storey it may also be required to carry the weight of any suspended conveyors, tools, trunking or similar fixtures.

3. *Access*

Free movement of goods in and out of the factory is as important as free movement within the plant. The architect therefore will need to know the anticipated frequency and weight of all goods moving between the factory and its environment. Here it is most important to try to forecast for as long ahead as possible: breaking new doors into a surrounding road may be very costly, if not impossible. There may be a need to consult both the Ministry of Transport and the Local Authority to ensure that current regulations are obeyed.

4. *Lighting*

There may be special requirements on lighting which must be considered; for example, colour-matching processes are most easily carried out in daylight, whilst some photographic processes require a complete absence of light. Wherever possible it seems desirable to provide natural lighting with a sight of the outside world, so that island offices and departments are best avoided. Care must be taken to control glare and distraction from outside, and the use of glass-brick walls with a viewing strip is favoured by some authorities.

Both the accident rate and productivity are affected by lighting, and all lighting should be ample for the task being carried out whilst avoiding excessive contrasts. Certain statutory requirements are laid down in the Factories Acts, and some standards are imposed in the 1941 Factory Regulations (Standards of lighting). These standards are minimal and may be varied from time to time, so that reference to H.M. Inspector of Factories is desirable if there is any doubt. The Illuminating Engineering Society has published a code of practice setting out levels of illumination suitable for various tasks.

Artificial lighting can give rise to undesirable effects other than the obvious difficulties of colour rendering. Fluorescent lamps, now very widely used because of their high efficiency, can produce an irritating flicker and, if used in conjunction with rotating machinery, a stroboscopic effect which may appear to slow down or stop a machine. This illusion is, at best, trying, and at worst highly dangerous. By using a number of lamps and designing the power supply to them correctly, the stroboscopic effect can be reduced or completely avoided.

The effectiveness of lighting can be improved by the choice of light colours in the walls and ceilings and by the use of contrasting colours on plant and fittings. Dirt will rapidly reduce the output from any lighting fitting, and all fittings should be so designed and located that they can be easily and safely cleaned.

5. *Ventilation and Heating*

Heating and ventilation are problems which, particularly in small and in narrow factories, are often treated very casually. Windows are assumed to be adequate for fresh air, and draughts—with all their consequent annoyance—are very common. The whole problem requires to be treated from the start of the design of the factory: running costs of heating plant often form a substantial part of the total running costs of the factory, and every effort should be made to conserve, and usefully distribute, heat and fresh air. Insulation, draught screens, warm air blankets, and heating ducts are best installed during construction, and not later when their installation can be costly, unsightly and disruptive.

It may be necessary, depending upon the proposed use of the factory, to incorporate air-cleaning, humidifying or drying plant within the ventilation system. This point needs careful consideration since later additions of this nature, after the factory has been built, can be unsatisfactory and uneconomical. Location of noxious processes should be determined early in order that outlet flues may be well clear of any fresh-air intake points.

6. *Services*

An essential estimate required before a factory design is started is the type and quantity of power and other supplies to be used. Gas, water, electricity and compressed air require to be freely available, and ample provision made for computer terminal points, telephones, and public address, burglar and fire alarm systems. Fire prevention and control systems—fireproof doors, sprinkler systems, hoses, fire escapes—are invariably best 'built-in' rather than applied as after-thoughts.

7. *Disposal of Waste*

Inevitably factories generate waste and—sometimes—noxious effluent. The social consequences of uncontrolled waste disposal are rapidly and sadly becoming apparent, and all waste products and effluents must be readily dispersed without damage or inconvenience to anybody. Reference must be made to local regulations, since there may be restrictions on the emission of smoke, the use of rivers as receivers of waste water, or other special regulations. Specialist advice on these matters is readily available from government sources.

8. *Special Process Requirements*

If possible, any special process requirements must be made known to the architect at the outset. Typical examples of such requirements are—

(*a*) Need for particularly close temperature control—for example, in calibration or measuring departments.

(*b*) Need for stable floors—for example in laboratories, where transferred vibrations can upset accurate readings and cause considerable waste of time and effort.

(*c*) Need for special security measures—in noisy, dangerous or secret processes.

(*d*) Need for special lighting requirements.

(*e*) Need for any special amenities.

9. *Number of Floors*

A problem requiring very early resolution is that concerning the number of floors. The choice between a single and a multiple storey building is one which, unless it is resolved by the circumstances of the site, is difficult to make. Although at first sight a single-storey building may appear desirable, many factors could indicate otherwise.

```
1. Head room required
2. Loads to be carried
3. Access
4. Lighting
5. Heating and ventilation
6. Services
7. Disposal of waste
8. Special process requirements
9. Number of floors
```

Matters Affecting the Design of a Factory which Require Managerial Consideration

Office Accommodation

Office accommodation can often be of a different standard from factory accommodation: ceilings can be lower, spans smaller, lighter floor loading ... and it is sometimes worth specifying it separately as its construction costs are lower. Against this economy must be set the loss of flexibility, resulting in a possibly more rigid factory layout later. It must be remembered that there are now statutory regulations concerning office accommodation and facilities which must be obeyed.

Advantages of a Single-storey Building

These may be summarized as follows—

1. *Quicker Building Time*
    This was more true previously than at present, since modern constructional techniques have reduced the difference in building times considerably. However, a difference does still exist; furthermore a single-storey building is more readily occupied in stages whilst construction is going on.

2. *Lower Building Costs*
    Here again modern techniques have reduced the difference between the cost of building a single- and a multi-storey building, but it is stated by some authorities that a single-storey building will cost 10–20 per cent less than the equivalent multi-storey factory.

3. *Maximum Use of Natural Light*
    In a single-storey building not only can daylight be obtained from side windows but also from roof-lights which, by correct design and location, can be completely glare-free.

4. *Easier Ventilation*
    Ventilation can be readily affected through the roof of a single-storey plant, avoiding long, unsightly and costly ventilation ducts.

5. *Easier Location*
    Should any process require isolation, whether it be noisy, dangerous, unpleasant, noxious or secret, it can be much more easily arranged in a single-storey building. This is particularly true where noisy equipment is used: in a multi-storey building the floors and ceilings will act as sounding boards, and the framework itself may well transmit machine noise throughout the whole plant. Reduction of overall noise is both difficult and expensive.

6. *Minimum Loss by Providing Circulating Facilities*
    No space is lost in a single-storey building (nor is any expense incurred) in providing lift-shafts, stairwells and escalators, whereas in a multi-storey plant this loss can be considerable, increasing with the number of storeys, since more than one lift must be provided in a tall building to

avoid serious loss of time whilst waiting for a lift. Furthermore it may be necessary to exert some form of control on the use of the lift by providing a lift attendant, thus increasing the running costs of the building, although automatic lifts are becoming more readily available.

A report in *The Times* (London, 12th June, 1962) stated that: ' . . . lifts, lavatories and passages in badly planned buildings can account for as much as 40 per cent of the space on a single floor; and the lift itself will occupy 100 square feet.'

7. *Simpler Internal Transport*
When all work is carried out on one floor the use of trucks and trolleys is simplified.

8. *Greater Flexibility*
In a single-storey building there are unlikely to be any restrictions on the disposition of heavy loads and machines.

9. *Maximum Free Floor Space*
As the ceiling is not required to support any floors above it, upright columns can be widely spaced or avoided altogether, thus considerably increasing the flexibility of use of the building. In multi-storey buildings the distance between columns is commonly 30 feet or less, in some cases only 15 feet. This can be extremely wasteful of floor space, not only because the columns themselves occupy space but because the distance between columns might be excessive for one row of machines or operators, but inadequate for two.

10. *General Supervision Easier*
The overlooking of a complete plant from a strategically placed vantage point—for example, a balcony or mezzanine floor—is possible in a single-storey plant.

1. Quicker building time
2. Lower building costs
3. Maximum use of natural light
4. Easier ventilation
5. Easier isolation
6. Minimum loss by providing circulating facilities
7. Simpler internal transport
8. Greater flexibility
9. Maximum free floor space
10. General supervision easier

Advantages of a Single-storey Building

Advantages of a Multi-Storey Building

Here again there are an appreciable number, of which the following is a summary—

1. *Lower Site Cost*
   For the same usable floor space the site area of a multi-storey building will be smaller than that of a single-storey plant. This will tend to offset the lower building cost of a single-storey building.

2. *Easier Siting of Service Sections*
   To site toilets, canteens, maintenance departments, libraries and other generally used sections in order to be readily accessible to all staff is easier in a multi-storey building than in a single-storey building.

3. *Shorter Service Runs*
   Gas, water, electricity, compressed air, telephones and other service runs are shorter in a multi-storey plant where access between departments can be seen through the floor. Moreover lift-shafts can be used to enclose unsightly pipes, ducts and trunking.

4. *Lower Heating Costs*
   Heat loss through the roof of a single-storey building is greater than that in a multi-storey plant, where heat rising from one floor will tend to warm the floor above. This can be of some importance, since heating is a considerable item in the running costs of a factory.

5. *Reduced Circulation Time*
   The distance between extreme points in a multi-storey building is less than that between the equivalent points in a single-storey plant. This, combined with the use of lifts, can reduce circulation time very substantially, particularly in large plants where internal travelling can be substantial.

6. *Use of Gravity Possible*
   In a multi-storey building, gravity conveyors and chutes can be used, and as the motive power is free, and upkeep of equipment very simple, this can be of great value in plants where there is much movement of material. For example, in some bottling plants, bottles are raised to the top of the building and then placed on roller conveyors on which they stay throughout the whole of the processing, finally being delivered at tailboard height to lorries.

7. *Better Departmental Supervision*
   With the smaller floor areas visible it is easier for local supervisors to control staff. It is also claimed that with the greater feeling of intimacy in a multi-storey plant it is possible to engender a better departmental spirit

than in a large flat building where an employee may suffer a sense of loss of identity. The use of partitioning can help to overcome this in a single-storey plant.

1. Lower site cost
2. Easier siting of service departments
3. Shorter service runs
4. Lower heating costs
5. Reduced circulation time
6. Use of gravity possible
7. Better departmental supervision

Advantages of a Multi-storey Building

Further Reading
1. *Factory Building Studies*, H.M.S.O., London 1960 onwards.
A whole range of studies covering most aspects of the design of factories.

2. Wilkinson, E., *Production Methods and Services*, Pitman, London 1964.
Discusses the services necessary for manufacturing activities to be undertaken. Material includes chapters on buildings, lighting, heating and ventilation, power, its generation, provision, commission and utilization, machinery layout and materials handling. Most useful.

Chapter 9
Layout of the Factory

The disposition of the various parts of a plant, along with all the equipment used therein, is known as the *plant layout*, which should be designed to enable the plant to function most effectively. The designing of a layout is fundamentally a work-study problem, but since factors are often involved which are outside the normal experience of a work-study engineer (for example, factors concerning the structure of the plant), work is often carried out in conjunction with the maintenance department. In very large organizations specialist engineers, whose sole task it is to design layouts, are often employed, and these layout engineers often form part of the maintenance manager's department.

PRODUCT AND PROCESS LAYOUT

The word layout is here used to indicate the layout of parts of a plant as well as of the whole plant itself. Upon consideration it will be found that all layouts fall into one of two types, product or process layouts, and it is rare to find that only one type is present in a single factory; usually they both exist side by side.

Product, Flow, Sequential or Line Layout

Here the plant is laid out according to the requirements of the product. This is typical of flow production, but it may also be found in non-manufacturing activities. For example, the provision of individual typists for separate departments is a type of product layout, as is the carrying out of a complete design task by a project engineer.

Diagrammatically this is illustrated in Fig. 9.1, where product 1 goes first to machine A, then to machine B, then to machine C, these machines being used exclusively for product 1. Products 2 and 3 have their own line of machines (K, L, M, and R, S, T, respectively) and, even though machines A, K and R are identical and interchangeable, work is not transferred from one product line to another even though some machines are severely underloaded.

Advantages

1. Easier control due to more easily seen routes. This tends to reduce paper work and material handling, and simplifies process inspection.

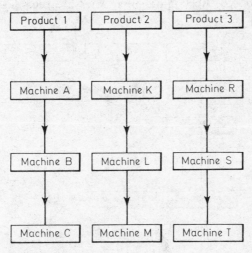

Fig. 9.1. Product Layout

2. Total 'through-time' is minimized.

3. Minimum need for buffer stocks between operations. (*Note.* Unless the production is true flow production and all operations balanced, buffer stocks will be inevitable.)

4. Maximum possible use of unskilled and semi-skilled labour.

Disadvantages

1. Unless volume is very high, machine utilization may be low, with a subsequent high capital investment.

2. One machine breakdown may immobilize a complete production line.

3. The system is inflexible, being unable to accommodate changes readily.

Process or Functional Layout

In this type of layout, plant is grouped according to its function: thus, all drills will be together, as will all mills, presses, lathes and so on. This is most commonly met with in jobbing product, but again may be found in non-manufacturing activities. Provision of typing from a typing pool is a form of process layout, whilst in design departments it is often found necessary to divide the designers into specialist teams, each team dealing with all the problems of a similar type.

This is illustrated in Fig. 9.2, where products 1, 2 and 3 all go to machine A, then after processing product 1 goes to machine B and thence to machine C, whilst products 2 and 3 go to machine L, product 2 then going to machine C, whilst product 3 goes on to machine T. To allow all machines to be fully loaded, work-in-progress stores are necessary between each machine.

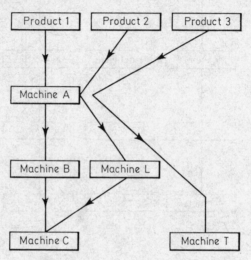

Fig. 9.2. Process Layout

Advantages
1. Extremely flexible.
2. Machine utilization higher with correspondingly low capital investment.
3. Individual operator efficiency tends to be high, since operators are required to be versatile and have some degree of skill.
4. Mechanical breakdowns do not immobilize complete production.
5. Specialist supervision possible.

Disadvantages
1. Substantial pre-production planning required if machine loading is to be high.
2. Control difficult.
3. Buffer stocks essential, hence relatively high investment in raw material and work-in-progress.

Note. The term 'group layout' is sometimes used for this type of layout, but the term is probably better reserved for the group of machines used in 'Group Technology,' which is an attempt to combine the low throughput time of Product Layout with the flexibility of Process Layout. This technique is discussed more fully later (Chapter 18).

Criteria for a Good Layout

Whilst the techniques employed in making a layout are normal work-study techniques, the process is a creative one which cannot be set down with any finality, and one in which experience plays a very great part. Furthermore it is not possible to define a good layout with any precision. However, there are certain criteria which will be satisfied by a good layout, and these are discussed below.

1. *Maximum Flexibility*

A good layout will be one which can be rapidly modified to meet changing circumstances. In this context particular attention should be paid to supply points, which should be ample and of easy access. These can usually be simply and cheaply provided at the outset of a layout, and failure to do so can often prevent very necessary modifications to unsatisfactory, outdated or inadequate layouts.

2. *Maximum Co-ordination*

Entry into, and disposal from, any department should be in such a manner that it is most convenient to the issuing or receiving departments. Layout requires to be considered as a whole and not parochially.

3. *Maximum Use of Volume*

A factory must be considered as a cubic device, as there is air-space above the floor area. Maximum use should be made of the volume available: conveyors can be run above head height and used as moving work-in-progress stores, or tools and equipment can be suspended from the ceiling. This principle is particularly true in stores, where goods can be stacked at considerable heights without inconvenience, especially if modern lift-trucks are used. In some cases material can be moved by conveyors slung outside the building.

4. *Maximum Visibility*

All men and materials should be readily observable at all times: there should be no 'hiding-places' into which goods can get mislaid. This criterion is sometimes difficult to fulfil, particularly when an existing plant is taken over. It is also a principle which is strongly resisted, and special offices, stores, cupboards and enclosures are often requested, not because of their utility but because they form a symbol of office or status. Every piece of partitioning or screening should be scrutinized most carefully as introducing undesirable segregation and reducing effective floor space.

5. *Maximum Accessibility*

All servicing and maintenance points should be readily accessible. For example, a machine should not be placed against a wall in such a manner that a grease-gun cannot easily reach the grease nipples. The maintenance under these circumstances is likely to be skimped—at best it will occupy an excessive time. Similarly, a piece of plant placed in front of a fuse box will impede the work of the electricians and may cause an unnecessary stoppage of the machine when the fuse box is opened. If it is impossible to avoid obscuring a service point, then the equipment concerned should be capable of being moved—it should not be a permanent installation.

6. *Minimum Distance*

All movements should be both necessary and direct. Handling material adds to the cost of the product but does not increase its value, consequently any unnecessary or circuitous movements should be avoided. It is a common failing for material to be moved off a work-bench to a temporary storage place whilst waiting finally to pass to the next storage point. This intermediate rest-place is often unnecessary and unplanned, being used only because an empty space appears convenient. The providing of 'extra' shelves, benches and tables should be questioned very thoroughly and avoided if possible.

7. *Minimum Handling*

The best handling is no handling, but where handling is unavoidable it should be reduced to a minimum by the use of conveyors, lifts, chutes, hoists and trucks (see Chapter 17). Material being worked on should be kept at working height, and never placed on the floor if it is to be lifted later.

8. *Minimum Discomfort*

Draughts, poor lighting, excessive sunlight, heat, noise, vibrations and smells should be minimized and if possible counteracted. Apparently trivial discomforts often generate troubles greatly out of proportion to the discomfort itself. Attention paid to the lighting and general decoration and furniture can be rewarding without being costly. Recommendations on the intensity of lighting for various tasks are published by the Illuminating Engineering Society, and most manufacturers of lighting equipment will provide useful advice on this subject.

The avoidance of over-crowding is a statutory requirement in the U.K. The Factories Act, 1937, states—

'A factory . . . shall not, while work is carried on, be so overcrowded as to cause risk of injury to the health of the person employed therein. Without prejudice to the generality of the foregoing a factory shall be deemed to be . . . overcrowded . . . if the number of persons employed at a time in any workroom is such that the amount of cubic space employed in the room is less than four hundred cubic feet . . . In calculating . . . the amount of cubic space . . . no space more than fourteen feet from the floor shall be taken into account . . . '

9. *Inherent Safety*

All layouts should be inherently safe, and no person should be exposed to danger. Care must be taken not only of the persons operating the equipment but also of the passers-by, who may be required to go behind a machine, the back of which is unguarded. This is both a statutory and a moral requirement, and great attention should be paid to it. Adequate medical facilities and services must be provided, and these must satisfy H.M. Inspector of Factories. Experience shows that the Factory Inspector is not only most competent to advise on these matters, he is always most anxious to be of assistance.

10. *Maximum Security*
Safeguards against fire, moisture, theft and general deterioration should be provided, as far as possible, in the original layout rather than in later accretions of cages, doors and barriers.

11. *Unidirectional Flow*
Work lanes and transport lanes must not cross. At every point in a factory material must flow in one direction only, and a layout which does not conform to this will result in considerable difficulties, if not downright chaos, and should be avoided.

12. *Visible Routes*
Definite lines of travel should be provided and, if possible, clearly marked. No gangways should ever be used for storage purposes, even temporarily.

The coexistence of a large number of criteria makes the definition of an 'optimum' schedule virtually impossible. Furthermore, the writing of a computer program for plant layout becomes a task of some considerable difficulty *unless some very drastic simplifications are made.*

Advantages of a Good Layout

A layout satisfying the above conditions will have the following advantages over one which does not—

1. The overall process time and cost will be minimized by reducing unnecessary handling and by generally increasing the effectiveness of all work.
2. Labour supervision and production control will be simplified by the elimination of hidden corners in which both men and material can be misplaced.
3. Changes in programme will be most readily accommodated.
4. Total output from a given plant will be as high as possible by making the maximum effective use of available space.
5. A feeling of unity amongst employees will be encouraged by avoiding unnecessary segregation.
6. Quality of the products will be sustained by safer and better methods of production.

1. Maximum flexibility
2. Maximum co-ordination
3. Maximum use of volume
4. Maximum visibility
5. Maximum accessibility
6. Minimum distance
7. Minimum handling
8. Minimum discomfort
9. Inherent safety
10. Maximum security
11. Unidirectional flow
12. Visible routes

Principles Satisfied by a Good Layout

Preparing a Layout

A suggested procedure is shown below, but this must not, of course, be regarded as definitive—

1. *Information Required*

The following information should be available before a layout can be planned—

(*a*) Type and quantity of labour, along with the company organizational structure.

(*b*) Dimensioned plan of the space to be laid out. Whilst it is not essential to have accurate scale drawings of the plant, it is usually essential to have an accurate knowledge of dimensions. Thickness of buttresses and skirting boards, and dimensions of protrusions on walls (switchboxes, fuseboards) are sometimes overlooked yet may be significant. The availability of existing supplies (gas, water, electricity, compressed air, telephones and drainage) and the locations of existing offices, toilets and permanent structures must also be indicated.

(*c*) The volume of work to be produced from the space, both immediately and in the foreseeable future.

(*d*) The operations to be undertaken, their descriptions, sequence and standard times. Note must be taken of any dangerous, noisy, dust- or smoke-producing, or otherwise special, operations.

(*e*) The equipment needed to carry out the operations.

(*f*) Any 'dead,' 'ageing,' 'stabilizing', or other process storage time.

(*g*) The volume of material, sub-stores, or buffer stocks required at each work station.

(*h*) The volume of main stores and finished part stores required. This depends not only on the output but also upon the supply and dispersal situations.

(*i*) What lines of communication and fire exits are required.

(*j*) What special requirements—burglar alarming, for example—are imposed by the local authority or by the company's insurer.

(*k*) What special inspection requirements exist.

(*l*) What special geographical requirements must be met—for example, the specific location of a dispatch department.

(*m*) If any spare plant will need to be stored in the space under consideration.

2. *Suggested Procedure*

Making a layout is not an operation to which a rigid technique can be applied. The process is largely one of trial and error, of laying out, modifying and re-laying out. It is desirable therefore that a layout should first be planned not on the space itself but upon models. These models can take one of two forms—

(*a*) Two-dimensional models which consist, in the simplest form, of a plan upon which is laid cut-out representations of the space required by the various items of equipment. It is convenient to make these cut-outs of stiff card or a colour different from that of the plan itself. Similar types of equipment in the same colour are often found helpful, and gangways can also be represented by coloured strips of card.

(*b*) Three-dimensional models, which are built up from scale models of the equipment to be used, and of the operators using them. These models can either be represented by simple blocks of wood, or they can be castings purchased from a company specializing in making such models. Three-dimensional layouts tend to be expensive, and are therefore not used in simple layouts. On the other hand, in a complex or large layout the three-dimensional layout has such substantial advantages that it is wise to consider its use. Amongst the advantages are clarity, vividness, demonstration of the use of headroom, and an ability to photograph and transmit elsewhere (e.g. to customers) the proposed new layout. It must be remembered that like any other work-study solution, the idea must be 'sold' to the user, and a three-dimensional model is useful here.

Having decided on what type of model to use, the operation sequence should be studied. It is usually found that there are one or two 'key' operations whose positions are fixed by external requirements. For example—

Packing should be near the point of dispatch, that is, a convenient outside door.

Inspection may require daylight and should therefore be near windows.

Painting may require fume extraction, and a location near an outside wall is indicated.

First operations may need to be near a stores whose position is fixed.

The planning sequence can then be as follows—

1. Locate the 'key' operations.

2. Locate main gangways: it is usually better if these are parallel to the main walls rather than running diagonally across a floor space. It is also usually more convenient if these start and finish at outside doorways.

3. Locate the remaining work areas to allow work to flow naturally between key operations. At this stage it is not necessary to locate plant in detail but to fix areas occupied by types of plant, that is, departmental or sectional areas.

4. Locate minor gangways.

5. Locate plant in detail with departments or sections.

6. Complete the layout by locating all subsidiary equipment—rubbish bins, telephones, etc.

7. Test the layout against the principles stated above. A string diagram (i.e. the representation of the route of material by a piece of string or cotton) is often helpful in establishing the distance of travel.

8. When satisfied with the layout itself, view the actual space if possible. Visualize the installed proposed layout, walk over the proposed gangways and check the installation. This should be unnecessary if the original plan was both correct and complete, but it is often found that time spent here can often be handsomely repaid by discovering features not apparent on drawings.

9. Check the final layout against the company's general policies and specifications.

---

1. Prepare model
2. Study operation sequence
3. Choose 'key' operations
4. Locate 'key' operations on plan
5. Locate main gangways
6. Locate remaining work areas
7. Locate minor gangways
8. Plan individual areas in detail
9. Locate subsidiary equipment
10. Test completed layout against principles of good layout
11. Verify layout on floor
12. Check against company policy

Suggested Sequence in Preparing a Layout

Machine Layout

All the above suggestions apply equally to assembly or machine layouts. However, there are a number of special points which must be borne in mind when making a machine layout. These are—

1. The space occupied by a machine must include any overhang caused by the travel of any moving parts or moving material.

2. Gangways must be adequate for the collection and delivery of material.

3. Floors must be strong enough to carry not only the machine but also the completed work and the goods locally stored.

4. Servicing facilities and safety devices must be accessible.

Installation of a Layout

Once a new layout has been finalized, it must be put into practice. This involves two separate and distinct steps—

(*a*) planning the way in which the new installation is to be carried out;
(*b*) supervising that this plan is carried out.

The planning technique known as Critical Path Analysis is ideally suited for both these tasks, and its use will avoid the common 'Here's the machine—where's its plinth?' type of situation. Every manager will have seen (in other people's factories!) the newly constructed wall which has had to be demolished to allow entry of a new machine. Time spent in planning is invariably time well spent.

The Use of the Computer in Preparing a Layout

At the time of writing there are four well-known computer programs available to assist in the preparation of a layout. The oldest and most widely discussed is CRAFT (Computerized Relative Allocation of Facilities Technique) which was written in 1963/64 by Armour, Buffa and Vollman. It adopts as the criterion to be minimized that of total handling cost. CORELAP (Computerized Relationship Layout Planning), ADLEP (Automated Layout Design Program) and RMA Comp 1 (Richard Mather and Associates) all adopt some form of proximity criterion, attempting to assemble the resources being planned in such a way as to ensure that those items which need to be near each other are in fact so placed. It is worth quoting from a paper by Muther & McPherson on the topic of the use of the computer in this area. ' . . . Computer-aided layout planning is still in its infancy. In our opinion none of the programs discussed here really solve the problem . . . '

The authors go on to suggest that computer programs may assist the planning function by avoiding an oversight and this is a common experience when using computers, in that the preparation of input data enforces a discipline which is often useful. It is the author's experience that layouts are currently, in fact, prepared entirely manually, and his belief that the use of the computer in this area will, for very many years, be extremely limited.

Further Reading
1. Apple, J. M., *Plant Layout and Materials Handling*, The Ronald Press Company, New York 1963.
See under 'Further Reading'—Chapter 17.

2. Moore, J. M., *Plant Layout and Design*, Macmillan, New York 1963.

Lavishly illustrated, uses mathematical techniques—queuing theory, linear programming—to deal with some problems. Assumes a knowledge of basic statistical methods.

3. Muther, R., *Practical Plant Layout*, McGraw-Hill, New York 1965.

A comprehensive text, useful to all serious students of the problems of plant layout. Very liberally illustrated with both line drawings and photographs. Mr. Muther's interest in Plant Layout has continued and developed after the publication of this book, and any articles appearing under his name will undoubtedly repay study.

4. Muther, R. and McPherson, K., Four approaches to computerized layout planning. *Industrial Engineering*, February, 1970.

Chapter 10
Equipment

The purchase of any piece of equipment—whether it be plant, tool, production aid—can be justified only on economic grounds, namely, whether the cost of the new equipment can be recovered from the selling price of the goods made or the services offered. Other criteria may be taken into consideration—for example, prestige—but in general these will be of marginal importance, and of significance principally when deciding between a number of possible pieces of equipment all of similar cost.

PLANT SURVEY

Assuming that it is decided to consider the purchase or manufacture of a piece of equipment, a plant survey is carried out, usually by the production engineering department. This survey is conveniently done in two stages, firstly a *use* or technical sifting, to reduce the range of possible equipment to manageable proportions, and secondly a *cost* or economic analysis.

Use

The following are factors which should receive careful consideration when investigating the technical specification of a piece of equipment—

1. *Capacity.* The capacity of a piece of plant needs to be ample for the purpose envisaged during the foreseeable future, and in this context reference must be made to the long-term forecast, particularly when the cost is heavy. Whilst it is foolish to purchase a machine which will soon be overloaded, it is almost certainly unnecessarily expensive to purchase one of a very much higher capacity than will ever be required unless there are other determining factors. If a total output of 10,000 parts a week is all that can be foreseen, then to purchase a machine which will produce 250,000 parts a week instead of one with a capacity of 25,000 parts a week is unjustified on the grounds of capacity: other factors may be involved, but in the case quoted the lower capacity machine should be chosen if capacity is the only criterion.

2. *Reliability.* Plant breakdown can be costly and can also jeopardize delivery dates, hence the reliability of equipment is very important.

3. *Ease of maintenance.* Maintenance costs need always to be as low as practicable, and a machine which is difficult to service will not only have a high maintenance cost—it will also be an inducement to carry out maintenance inadequately.

4. *Preparation.* Ancillary time (setting up, breaking down, cleaning) is expensive and reduces the running time of the plant, so the ease of preparation of the equipment should be considered.

5. *Compatibility.* Whenever possible, new plant should be of a type similar to or identical with existing plant. The resultant simplification in the provisioning of spare parts, in maintenance, in operator training, in setting and preparation, and in machine loading, are enormous.

6. *Safety.* Plant needs to be safe, and, though it is very rare to find unsafe plant on the market today, this aspect repays study. Accidents are costly in a lowering of output, in deterioration of morale and in bad labour relations. The onus of preventing them is firmly on the employer, both in law and in common humanity.

7. *Ease of installation.* This point can be easily overlooked, when it may then be found that access doors are too low, or permissible floor loading exceeded by the new plant on installation.

8. *Delivery.* The delivery situation needs to be investigated to see that the needs of the organization can be matched by the delivery promised. An investigation into the reliability of the supplier in this respect is worth making.

9. *State of development.* Newly designed plant is sometimes marketed before the design has been entirely finalized or stabilized. Guarantees on this are highly desirable, although it must be recognized that no guarantee can compensate for the loss of goodwill attendant upon broken delivery promises.

10. *Availability of associated equipment.* Much of the new, highly complex plant now available can only be fully utilized if a wide range of associated equipment is employed, and the availability of this equipment can often dictate the choice of plant. This is particularly true of computers and computer controlled plant which is of minimal value without its associated 'software'.

11. *Effect on existing organization.* Some new plant, when installed, will demand changes in the existing organization. Thus, a numerically controlled machine tool for example, will require that considerable managerial re-thinking takes place. Pre-planning is vital and this is often centralized in the P.C.D. and the production planning department. The 'route card' is replaced by a 'part program' which specifies the machining sequence to be performed on the work-piece. Not only are the tasks to be done specified but also the precise speeds and feeds, the flow of coolant and every other task.

The Design Office and Drawing Offices will need to realize that N.C. is being used so that for example, dimensioning is always taken from a datum. Absence of co-ordination at this stage can lengthen enormously the task of preparing programs. As with any planning technique N.C.

concentrates the planning into action *before* the work commences. If the need for this planning is not accepted, then the benefits of the N.C. tool will not be realized.

From an examination of makers' catalogues, visits to showrooms and other plant, discussion with colleagues and other interested people, a 'short list' of equipment will be drawn up using considerations similar to the above. This list must then be subjected to a cost analysis to determine between the various items listed. A useful device for carrying out this sifting is a matrix, similar to that which was described in Chapter 7, where the choice of a factory location was discussed.

> Capacity
> Reliability
> Ease of maintenance
> Ease of preparation
> Compatibility
> Safety
> Ease of installation
> Delivery
> State of development
> Availability of associated equipment
> Effect on existing organization

Use Factors Affecting Choice of Plant

Cost

There are a number of ways of carrying out an economic analysis, and it must be understood that whatever technique is used it must be consistently applied to all equipment. An economic analysis is more useful in differentiating between different items of plant than in setting an accurate figure on the absolute cost of the plant.

The requirements of an economic analysis is to appraise the *cost of producing* from a given piece of plant, not just the cost of the plant itself. This can be considered to be made up of two parts: (*a*) the standing cost, which is the cost incurred by the equipment installed and ready for use but not being operated; and (*b*) the running cost, which sets down the cost of running the equipment in order to produce the required articles.

The Standing Cost

In the calculation of standing cost, board decisions have to be made: notably, what depreciation should be considered, what is the expected return on invested capital, what allowance should be made for taxes, insurance and rates, and what rent is charged to the floor-space occupied. These, together with the purchase price, are summed to give an average annual standing cost. The above discussion implies that the plant is being *purchased outright*. There are, of course, other ways of obtaining plant, for example—

1. *Hire purchase*. Contracts can be negotiated for long periods (up to 10 years) with the interest tied to the bank rate. In some cases payments can fluctuate with a known seasonal variation in output.

2. *Leasing*. Here the user never actually *owns* the equipment leased, it being argued that the *use* of the plant is more important than its *ownership*.

3. *Hiring*. Effectively, this is leasing, but usually a maintenance contract is implied or required.

All these methods should be considered as they may well have substantial tax and cash advantages over outright purchase. In these cases, of course, the annual charges are the standing charges discussed above.

The Running Cost

To calculate the average running cost, a knowledge of the average annual total output is required. For plant producing for stock this is a comparatively simple piece of information derivable from the sales forecast. For a jobbing machine, making entirely to customer's order, the details of output cannot be forecast in such detail. The most satisfactory approximation is obtained by forecasting the anticipated output of average components and using this forecast as the basis of the calculations. From the figure of expected output, the cost of power and supplies, the factory cost of producing the articles, the cost of ancillary labour and the cost of upkeep and maintenance are calculated, and then added together to give the average annual running cost. It must be remembered that the material cost may vary with the type of equipment, since different plant may require material to be presented in different ways, and so may generate different waste.

The annual cost is the sum of the standing and running costs, and it is calculated for each piece of plant in the short list. Obviously, the final decision will depend on the results of both the use and the economic analysis.

ECONOMIC APPRAISAL OF PLANT

A 'use' or technological survey may reveal that for a project there are a number of equally acceptable pieces of plant: the choice between them must then be resolved on cost or economic grounds. There are a number of methods used to carry out this resolution, and to illustrate these the following example will be used:

Project X will involve the manufacture and selling of 100,000 units a year at a unit selling price of 5p. There are two alternative pieces of equipment, A and B with the following characteristics:

	A	B
Installed price	£6,000	£8,000
Direct labour costs/unit	0·833p	0·625p
Direct material costs/unit	2·50p	2·605p
Indirect labour/year	£400	£330
Services charges/year	£180	£150
Maintenance charges/year	£ 80	£150
Economic life	7 years	10 years

Defining 'profit' as the difference between income and necessary out-of-pocket expenses, the annual 'profit' achievable from A and B can be derived—

	A (£)	B (£)
Annual direct labour cost	833	625
Annual direct material cost	2,500	2,605
Annual indirect labour cost	400	330
Annual service charges	180	150
Annual maintenance charges	80	150
Total out-of-pocket expenses:	3,993	3,860
Annual income	5,000	5,000
∴ Annual 'profit'	1,007	1,140

The Payback Period

In this technique of capital appraisal, the time taken to recover the initial investment from the 'profit' is calculated:

$$\text{Payback Period} \quad A = \frac{6,000}{1,007} \text{ years} = 6 \text{ years} \qquad B = \frac{8,000}{1,140} \text{ years} = 7 \text{ years}$$

Return on Investment

Here, the 'profit' is considered as a return upon the investment. There are a number of different definitions possible, for example the investment can be considered as the total initial investment (£6,000 in the case of A, £8,000 in the case of B) or the average investment, assuming the value of the plant is depreciated to zero (that is £3,000 for A, £4,000 for B). Taking this latter definition we have—

	A (£)	B (£)
Annual depreciation charge (depreciating to zero by the end of economic life)	6,000 ÷7 = 857	8,000 ÷10 = 800
'Profit' as defined above	1,007	1,140
∴ Return	150	340
∴ Return on investment	$\frac{150}{3,000} \times 100\%$ = 5%	$\frac{340}{4,000} \times 100\%$ = $8\frac{1}{2}\%$

The above results thus conflict: by the 'Payback Period' techniques Equipment A is the more desirable since it is 'bought' quicker, whilst the 'Return on Investment' system suggests that equipment B should be chosen since it has a higher rate of return. Both methods, however, suffer from the same weakness, that is, that no account is taken of the *time* at which earnings are made. A more precise technique, known as Discounted Cash Flow, enables this, and other pertinent aspects of the movements of funds to be considered.

Discounted Cash Flow

The appraisal technique known as the Discounted Cash Flow (D.C.F.) method takes cognizance not only of the earnings made, but also of the *time* at which they are made. Thus, the method recognizes that £1 now, and £1 in a year's time have today quite different values, and that a profit of £1,000 obtained in a stream of £200 a year for 5 years has a different value to a stream of £100 a year for 10 years.

The Concept of Present Value

If £1 were available now, and invested to produce an income of 10 per cent a year, this income, being immediately reinvested, would grow as follows—

			£	£
Now, beginning of year 1			1	
end	of ,,	1	$1 \times \cdot 1$	$= 1 \cdot 1$
,,	,, ,,	2	$1 \cdot 1 + \cdot 11$	$= 1 \cdot 21$
,,	,, ,,	3	$1 \cdot 21 + \cdot 121$	$= 1 \cdot 331$
,,	,, ,,	4	$1 \cdot 331 + \cdot 1331$	$= 1 \cdot 464$

and so on. It is thus possible to say that £1·464 in 4 years time, at an earning rate of 10 per cent has a *present value* of £1. The figure of £1·464 in 4 years time is an inconvenient one, and it is usually reduced to £1, which thus has a present value of $£\frac{1}{1 \cdot 464} = £0 \cdot 683$, and the table above could be rewritten—

Present value of £1, at earning rate of 10 per cent

obtained one year hence	$= £\frac{1}{1 \cdot 1}$	$= £0 \cdot 909$
obtained two years hence	$= £\frac{1}{1 \cdot 21}$	$= £0 \cdot 826$
obtained three years hence	$= £\frac{1}{1 \cdot 331}$	$= £0 \cdot 751$
obtained four years hence	$= £\frac{1}{1 \cdot 464}$	$= £0 \cdot 683$

and so on. The validity of the above table can be checked, and the meaning of present value underlined by taking the present value of £1 obtained 4 years hence and calculating backwards, that is, calculating the value to which £0·683 would increase in four years if invested in an enterprise continuously producing a 10 per cent return on income—

£0·683 at the beginning of year 1 would become by year end
$$£0·683 + £0·0683 = £0·751$$
£0·751 at the beginning of year 2 would become by year end
$$£0·751 + £0·0751 = £0·826$$
£0·826 at the beginning of year 3 would become by year end
$$£0·826 + £0·0826 = £0·9086$$
£0·909 at the beginning of year 4 would become by year end
$$£0·909 + £0·0909 = £0·9999$$

which is effectively £1.

Had there been a steady stream of £1's received at the end of each year, then the following table could have been constructed:

Present value of £1 received annually at earning rate of 10 per cent:

for one year $= 0·909$
for two years $= 0·909 + 0·826 = 1·735$
for three years $= 1·735 + 0·751 = 2·486$
for four years $= 2·486 + 0·683 = 3·169$

and so on. Thus £1 a year received annually for four years is equivalent to £3·169 available now, which is *invested in a project which produces a return of 10 per cent. Note*: it is assumed that the project earns at a rate of 10 per cent and that the earnings are immediately reinvested to earn at the same rate, the original capital investment remaining unchanged. If the capital had been invested in material at the rate of £1 each year, and the material had lain idle but still useful, then this would have had an earning rate of 0 per cent and a present value of £4.

If the annual £1 had been received in amounts of $£\frac{1}{12}$ at the end of each month, or continuously throughout the year, different tables of present value would have been constructed. Such tables are readily available commercially.

Discounting

The act of taking a sum in the future and calculating its present value, assuming some particular rate of return, is called *discounting*, and it can be considered the inverse of compounding. To return to the original table, a single sum of £1 in 4 years time is said to be discounted at a rate of 10 per cent to a value of £0·683. If there is a stream of £1 in cash, or a cash flow of £1 at the end of each year, then it can be said to form a *discounted cash flow* with a present value of £3·169 if the earning rate is 10 per cent. Clearly, different earning rates will produce different present values.

Present value of £1 received annually at earning rates of:

	1%	2%	4%	6%	10%	20%	50%
for one year	0·990	0·980	0·962	0·943	0·909	0·833	0·667
for two years	1·970	1·942	1·886	1·833	1·735	1·528	1·111
for three years	2·941	2·884	2·775	2·673	2·486	2·106	1·407
for four years	3·902	3·808	3·630	3·465	3·169	2·589	1·605

If we now return to Equipment A, which involved an initial investment of £6,000 and produced an annual 'profit' of £1,000, it can be said that for the equipment to be justified, a cash flow of £1,000 a year, if discounted backwards to produce a present value of £6,000 must have an earning rate and a duration which will produce a factor of $\frac{6,000}{1,000} = 6$. There are a number of different combinations of rate and duration which will produce this result.

Present value of £1 received annually at earning rate of:

	1%	2%	4%	6%	10%
for 1 year					
2					
3					
4					
5					
6	5·795	5·601	5·242		
7	6·728	6·472	6·002	5·582	
8				6·210	
9					5·759
10					6·145

or, interpolating simply—

if the duration is $6\frac{3}{12}$ years the earning rate is 1%
$6\frac{6}{12}$,, ,, ,, ,, ,, 2%
7 ,, ,, ,, ,, ,, 4%
$7\frac{8}{12}$,, ,, ,, ,, ,, 6%
$9\frac{9}{12}$,, ,, ,, ,, ,, 10%

As the economic life is stated to be 7 years, the equipment can be said to have an earning rate of 4 per cent. Taking equipment B, this has a present value factor of $\frac{8,000}{1,140} = 7$, which can be produced as follows—

if the duration is $7\frac{6}{12}$ years the earning rate is 1%
$7\frac{7}{12}$,, ,, ,, ,, ,, 2%
$8\frac{5}{12}$,, ,, ,, ,, ,, 4%
$9\frac{4}{12}$,, ,, ,, ,, ,, 6%
$12\frac{7}{12}$,, ,, ,, ,, ,, 10%
$16\frac{1}{12}$,, ,, ,, ,, ,, 12%

and as the economic life is stated to be 10 years, the equipment can be said to have an earning rate of about 6 per cent over the economic life of the equipment. If the desirability of purchasing only B were being considered, then this earning rate would be a representation of the earning capacity of equipment B. However, since B is being compared with A, the time periods must be the same: thus, either we have to assume A has a life of 10 years, or B has a life of 7. To compare A at 7 years with B at 10 years is to ignore that the capital for A is continuously reinvested, and that when A is exhausted, the available funds are immediately reinvested, again producing a return which must be taken into account. In this case, assume that B has an effective life of 7 years: the earning rate is then less than 1 per cent, and it is this which is compared with the earning rate of 4 per cent derived from A. Under these circumstances, A is clearly the more desirable purchase.

The above discussion takes into account only the 'profit' and ignores any other sources of cash movement. In practice, however, there may be effective movements of funds due to factors such as—

> taxation,
> allowances for depreciation,
> various government grants,
> maintenance effect,
> training effort,

and so on. Further, these, and the income from sales, may not be constant over the various periods of time: taxation allowances and grants tend to be substantial in the early periods, and output may increase as sales demand increases. In addition, the 'profit' may not appear in the year in which goods are made—it is not uncommon to find that goods made in one year are paid for in the next, so that the 'profit' accrues in the year after manufacture. All these points must be taken into account in order to produce as accurate an assessment of the flow of *cash* as possible, and it is *this* cash flow which is discounted back. The D.C.F. technique is thus one which takes account not only of the effect of time upon earnings ('a £1 *now* is worth more than a £1 *later*'), but also of the other factors which affect profitability and which are not easily dealt with by other techniques.

Appraisal rather than Costing

It must be emphasized that the above techniques and their variants are methods of judging the desirability of alternative capital expenditure decisions—they permit comparison of one project with another, or one project with a standard set for use in the company. They do not readily form the basis of costing systems, and they should not be used as such.

The Loss of Value of Plant

Once a piece of plant has been installed it will—in general—immediately start to lose value. This arises from two main causes, namely: *Depreciation*, which is 'the diminution in the intrinsic value of an asset due to use and/or the lapse of time', and is a result of normal usage, bad handling, bad maintenance, accidents, or wear due to disease or chemical action; and *Obsolescence*, 'the loss in the intrinsic value of an asset due to its supercession', and is a result of a reduction in market for the product for which the plant is intended, a change in design of the type of plant or a change in legislation.

Depreciation
The purchase of a piece of equipment involves an expense which must, if the organization is to continue independently in being, be recovered

from the proceeds of running the organization. The usual way of recovering this expense is by a charge in the Profit and Loss account against the profits before arriving at the net profit, and of showing the loss of value of the equipment by reducing the value of the asset in the Balance Sheet. This reduction in value is known as the *depreciation* suffered by the equipment.

Recovery can be effected in a number of different ways. Ideally, of course, the total cost of the equipment should be recovered when its 'life' has been spent. Since it is extremely difficult to predict the life of a machine, arbitrary methods of writing down depreciation are adopted as company policy. These may vary from company to company but should remain constant within a company. The Institute of Costs and Management Accountants lists nine different methods of calculating depreciation, and many others can be found. The choice of depreciation method depends largely upon convenience, and the effects of the prevailing tax laws. Two of the most common methods are—

Straight Line or Linear Depreciation. In this method the same absolute value is deducted each year from the value; for example, if a plant is depreciated over five years, its value each year will be (as a percentage): 100; 80; 60; 40; 20; and from the sixth year onwards it will have no book value.

Algebraically this is represented by—

$$\text{Value} = P - \frac{P(n-1)}{N}$$

where P is the initial installed price, N the number of years over which is is being depreciated and n the number of years at which the value is being calculated.

Reducing Balance Method of Depreciation. In this a constant percentage of the book value is deducted each year from the book value. For example, if the depreciation each year were 50 per cent *of the remaining book value* then the value each year would be (stated as a percentage of the initial value): 100; 50; 25; 12·5; 6·25; and in fact would never become zero, although when its value became negligible (say 1 per cent of initial cost) its value would be 'written off'. Algebraically this is represented by—

$$\text{Value} = P(1 - R)^{n-1}$$

where P and n have the same significance as previously and R represents the depreciation rate.

This method is simple to calculate, and provides heavier charges at the beginning of the equipment's life—when maintenance costs can reasonably be expected to be lighter—and lighter charges at the end of the equipment's life, when maintenance costs are likely to be heavier. Against these two advantages can be set the apparent disadvantage that, unless the sum of the depreciation and maintenance charge is constant each year, the apparent cost of producing from a piece of plant will change from one accounting period to the next.

The 'Life' of Plant
It is helpful to recognize that plant may have several different 'life-spans.'

1. *The Physical.* This is the length of time over which the plant can be usefully and *economically* used. It depends upon a number of factors including the maintenance carried out and the use to which the plant is put, and it is usually determined by the maintenance and breakdown costs which become excessive at the end of physical life.
2. *The Technological Life.* This is the length of time elapsing before a new machine becomes available which makes the existing plant obsolete.
3. *The Product (or Market) Life.* This is set by the product which is made (or the service offered) by the plant no longer being required. This may be very much shorter than the physical life, and the plant may be in excellent physical condition. Whilst normal market conditions will force recognition of the product life, there is a danger of plant in large groups of companies being worked beyond the product life, since the products are perforce being sold to captive purchasers within the group. The author recalls vividly one company in a group which had to design its products around, and later use, a completely obsolete component because a sister company in the group had recently installed a new, costly plant for producing that component.
4. *The 'Book' Life.* This is the time during which the equipment is depreciated to a nominal value. This is often calculated on the basis of minimizing tax, rather than any other consideration.
5. *The Economic Life.* This is the shortest of the first three lives. If it can coincide with the Book Life, then there may be some agreement between the book-keeping and the financial considerations.

Further Reading
1. Merrett, A. J. and Sykes, A., *Capital Budgeting and Company Finance*, Longmans, London 1960.
The source-book of much current writing and thinking on capital budgeting.

2. Garbutt, D., *A Simple Introduction to Capital Expenditure Decisions*, Pitmans, London 1967.

3. Wright, G., *Discounted Cash Flow*, McGraw-Hill, London 1970.
Two basic books, both excellent, designed to be useful to the practising manager.

Chapter 11
Maintenance

Maintenance of plant and equipment in good working order is essential to the efficient working of any factory—the best machines will not work satisfactorily unless they are cared for, and the cost of a machine breakdown can be very high, not only in financial terms but also in poor staff morale and bad relations with customers.

Some idea of the magnitude of the identifiable costs can be obtained from the report of a Working Party set up by the U.K. Government in 1968 to look at the status of maintenance engineering in the U.K. This report, published in 1970, and summarized in an article 'Terotechnology—a New Approach to an Old Problem' by Major-General Sir Leonard Atkinson in the July 1971 supplement to *The Radio and Electronic Engineer* showed that—

'. . . maintenance engineering costs the U.K. manufacturing industry some £1100 million per annum . . . ' of which ' . . . it should be possible to save £200–£250 million per annum on direct costs and a further £200–£300 million on the cost of lost production due to down time . . . ' The author states that in the manufacturing industry, direct maintenance costs are made up as follows—

	£m p.a.
Direct labour	388
Direct material	286
Payments to contractors	41
Maintenance done by production staff	5
Direct overheads	366
Total	1,086

The same article defines *terotechnology* as 'the technology of installation, commissioning, maintenance and removal of plant; of feedback of operating and design experience thereon; and of related subjects and practices'. Since the author feels that it is unlikely that this name will supplant the more commonly used word *maintenance*, he will not use it further in the present text.

The Maintenance Department

The concept of the operator maintaining his own machine is now completely dead, although operators are often required to keep their machines clean, and it is now generally accepted that maintenance is a specialized service to production. In order to take advantage of the benefits of specialization, all maintenance should be carried out by one department under a maintenance supervisor, plant engineer, or works engineer, who will be responsible for duties other than the maintenance of machines.

The duties of the maintenance department include the care of plant, buildings and equipment, the installation of new equipment, and the supervision of new building. Typical sections of the maintenance department are—

1. *The Millwrights*, who install, maintain and repair all mechanical equipment.

2. *The Electricians*, who install, maintain and repair all electrical equipment including power plants and all communications equipment. Although the actual maintenance of some of these may be in the hands of the owners of the equipment—for example the G.P.O. or the local Electricity Board— all dealings with the owners should be through the maintenance department, so that individual complaints or comments should be made first to the appropriate maintenance engineer.

3. *The Building Department*, which will include any carpenters, bricklayers, plumbers or painters. Included in the responsibilities of this section will often be the provision and upkeep of all fire-fighting equipment (hoses, extinguishers, sprays, sprinklers) unless a separate department exists only for this purpose, and the care and control of the heating and ventilating plant.

4. *General Labourers*, who will carry out the moving of material and equipment. These will usually include a 'heavy gang' equipped for and capable of man-handling bulky and heavy loads.

5. *Cleaners*, who will be responsible for all cleaning and sweeping, including the care of lavatories and wash-places.

6. *Sub-contractors*, who are useful, not only to carry excess loads, but to maintain specialist equipment—for example, telephones and office machinery.

Rules Governing Maintenance Work

In order that there should be some control over the work of maintenance, two rules should be rigidly enforced—

1. All requests for maintenance work must be made (preferably in writing) at one central control point. No work should be carried out without the knowledge and approval of the maintenance supervisor at that point. Lack of strict adherence to this rule will result in a wasteful use of skilled staff and an inability to keep to any schedule of essential work.

2. No maintenance work should be undertaken by productive staff (except in an emergency) unless that work is done under the supervision

of the maintenance department—that is, unless the operator concerned is effectively seconded to the maintenance department.

3. Maintenance stores must be as carefully controlled as any other of the company's stores, as the absence of a vital part can lead to an expensive plant shut-down.

4. Records of all work carried out, including a statement of materials required, should be kept as these may assist in setting rational maintenance, replacement and depreciation policies.

Planned Maintenance

As with any other department, the work of the maintenance department requires to be planned—that is, thought out before it is actually undertaken. This is necessarily difficult in maintenance work, since a sudden breakdown may require action so immediate that any schedule is upset. To avoid this, the maintenance department should be deliberately underloaded in order to be able to carry out emergency repairs. Any unloaded time not occupied in this way can be taken up by carrying out those items of work which can neither be scheduled as routine nor considered as emergencies. Clearly, however, the bulk of the time of the maintenance department should be taken up with Planned or Routine Maintenance. Such plans should cover at least twelve months, during which time all normal items of upkeep should be covered.

A routine maintenance plan can be set up in the following way—

1. List all work which is required to be carried out by external authorities, that is, by the Department of Trade and Industry, the local government regulations, or by the company's insurers. This will include—

(*a*) The washing and/or the painting of all inside walls, partitions, ceilings and staircases.

(*b*) The thorough examination, followed if necessary by an overhaul and accompanied by a written report issued by a competent person on—

(i) every hoist and lift—usually twice a year;
(ii) all parts and working gear of lifting machines and cranes, including the rails upon which travelling cranes move—usually annually;
(iii) every steam boiler and all its fittings and attachments—usually annually;
(iv) all compressed-air reservoirs—usually annually;
(v) all fire extinguishers and fire-fighting equipment—usually annually;
(vi) all weighing machines and weighbridges—usually annually;
(vii) all postal and insurance franking machines—usually quarterly.

2. List, with the frequency required, all work deemed desirable by the factory manager. This will include the overhaul and servicing of all machines and items of plant, including office equipment and any company cars or other transport.

The frequency of maintenance should be set initially by the 'best guess' but thereafter it should be verified against records kept of performance and breakdown. For most plant, records are most conveniently kept in terms of weeks or months of elapsed time between overhauls, rather than in terms of hours worked.

3. Prepare standard instructions covering the maintenance required on each item listed. These instructions should be *in detail* and should avoid the 'overhaul as necessary' type of instruction. The purpose to which the plant is put should be considered when deciding the scale of the overhaul, as identical pieces of plant being used for different purposes may well need entirely different levels of maintenance.

In setting up these standard instructions C.P.A. can be invaluable in examining and determining the methods and, in instructing the staff in their duties. C.P.A. is extensively used here for all types of maintenance, from short duration overhauls with individual activities of only a few minutes, to very lengthy plant shut-downs.

4. Prepare a plan of work covering at least twelve months, in such a way that no maintenance section is in any way overloaded. This is very conveniently done on a Gantt chart or one of the equivalent mechanical loading charts.

5. From the plan made in (4) above, issue instructions to the appropriate staff when necessary, requiring them to carry out work, and record on the plan when the work has been done.

To ensure that all items of plant are included, it is desirable to number all plant and then to make a plant register. At the outset this is prepared from a physical inventory which is then checked against the company's asset register. This is thereafter kept up to date by advice from the buying office of each new piece of equipment purchased. This can be very conveniently kept in a visible-edge ledger, and the servicing date signalled along the edge.

The effectiveness of the maintenance department should be judged not by the vigour with which emergency repairs are carried out but on the freedom of the factory from such emergencies. This principle has been made the basis of incentive schemes for the maintenance department, although many other schemes can be set up. Owing to the difficulty in checking the thoroughness of maintenance work, however, it is probably better to rely on a sound departmental pride rather than on a financial incentive. Maintenance—particularly in flow production—is a key function and must be treated as such.

REPAIR AND REPLACEMENT

The Repair Limit

Repair—the replacement of defective, damaged or worn parts—is clearly part of maintenance. However, when the costs of repairing are substantial and unforeseen, it is necessary to consider whether it is more economical to replace the equipment rather than to repair it. One simple method whereby this problem is not overlooked—or resolved by default—is to set a *repair limit*. If the estimated cost of the repair exceeds the repair limit, the piece of plant is considered as an active candidate for replacement. Easily obtainable, low cost items are probably replaced automatically, whilst high cost or difficult to obtain items are referred to a replacement committee. The value set upon the repair limit is likely to be a complex function, depending upon age, availability of replacement, possible loss of output and resale value. Certainly repair limits must not be set 'once-for-all'—they need to be regularly reviewed.

Replacement Due to Failure

1. *Group Replacement*

When it is necessary to maintain a group of items in working order, it is sometimes more economical to replace the group as a whole *even if some of the items are still functioning satisfactorily* than to replace each item as it fails. Such a situation may arise when the cost of replacement of an item as an individual is greater than the cost of replacement of an item when it is replaced as one of a group. This is so well exemplified by the problem of replacing electric light bulbs that it is frequently referred to in the literature as *the light bulb problem*. The method of treating this problem is best demonstrated by an example.

The Light Bulb Problem

Assume that past records reveal that, out of 100 new light bulbs, on an average—

> 80 survive for at least 1 week
> 40 survive for at least 2 weeks
> 10 survive for at least 3 weeks
> 0 survive for more than 4 weeks

Furthermore, it is found that the cost of replacing a light bulb is made up of two parts—

(*a*) the cost of bringing the electrician, his mate and his equipment to the site, and this cost is £25
(*b*) the cost of replacing a light bulb once the electrician is available, and this cost is 20p.

Thus the replacement cost:

for a group of n bulbs is	£(25 + 0·2n)
for an individual bulb is	£25·2
and for n bulbs replaced individually is	£25·2 × n

The problem can now be stated as follows—

Should each bulb be replaced as an individual when it fails, or should the whole group of bulbs be replaced after some interval of time?

For the sake of arithmetical simplicity, it will be assumed that there is a total of 100 bulbs at the site, although this restriction is not necessary.

Average Bulb Life

From the available data it can be seen that, on an average, out of 100 bulbs initially good,

by end of week 1   20 lamps will have failed
„ „ „ „ 2, a further 40 „   „   „   „
„ „ „ „ 3, „   „   30 „   „   „   „
„ „ „ „ 4, „   „   10 „   „   „   „

Hence, there are, on an average,

   10 lamps with a life of 4 weeks, that is a life of 40 lamp weeks
$+30$ „   „ „ „ „ „ 3 „   „ „ „ „ „ 90 „   „
$+40$ „   „ „ „ „ „ 2 „   „ „ „ „ „ 80 „   „
$+20$ „   „ „ „ „ „ 1 „   „ „ „ „ „ 20 „   „
——   „   „
  100 lamps thus have a total life of ..   .. 230 „   „

that is, the average bulb life is 2·3 weeks.

Individual replacement. Replacing each bulb singly as it fails would entail replacing 100 bulbs in 2·3 weeks at a cost of
$$£(100 \times 25·2)$$
that is, an average weekly cost of
$$£\left(\frac{100 \times 25·2}{2·3} \text{ a week} = £1100 \text{ a week}\right.$$

Group Replacement. As it is necessary to keep the total quantity of working bulbs constant at 100, group replacement will involve (*a*) replacing defectives *as they occur*, and (*b*) replacing 100 bulbs *at fixed intervals of time*. To examine this situation it is therefore necessary to calculate the rate at which individual replacements are necessary. This can be done analytically (for example, see Ackoff & Sasieni, *Fundamentals of Operations Research*), but the underlying processes are probably most clearly shown by a *failure tree* (Makower & Williamson *Teach Yourself Operational Research*).

At the beginning of week 1, there are 100 bulbs working satisfactorily, but by the end of that week, only 80 of the original bulbs are functioning—this is shown by the horizontal branch—

$$100^{0·8}\text{———S———}80$$

where the transfixed S indicates survival, and the elevated 0·8 indicates the survival rate. In order to keep the number of bulbs constant, the 'dead' 20 bulbs must have been replaced, and this is shown by a diagonal line—

so that at the beginning of the next week the 100 bulbs are made up from 80 'originals' and 20 'replacements'. By end of the week, the 80 originals will have dropped to 40 originals (a survival rate of 0·5) and 40 replacements. Of the 20 bulbs replaced at the end of week 1, 0·8 × 20, that is 16, will have survived, and 4 will have needed to be replaced. At the end of week 3, 10 'originals' will have survived, and 30 will have been replaced; of the 40 replaced during week 2, 32 will have survived and 8 will have been replaced, and so on—see Fig. 11.1. In drawing a replacement tree of

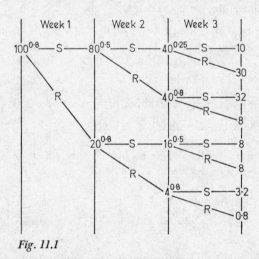

Fig. 11.1

this sort, it must be remembered that replacements initially represent 'original' bulbs, and hence survive on an average at the rate shown in the initial data, namely—

Out of 100 bulbs—

> 80 survive for at least 1 week
> 40 survive for at least 2 weeks
> 10 survive for at least 3 weeks
> 0 survive for more than 4 weeks

A complete survival tree for 5 weeks is shown in Fig. 11.2. From this it is possible to calculate the number of bulbs replaced on an average from an original group of 100 new bulbs—

> 20 replaced in week 1
> 44 replaced in week 2
> 46·8 replaced in week 3
> 42·96 replaced in week 4
> 42·512 replaced in week 5

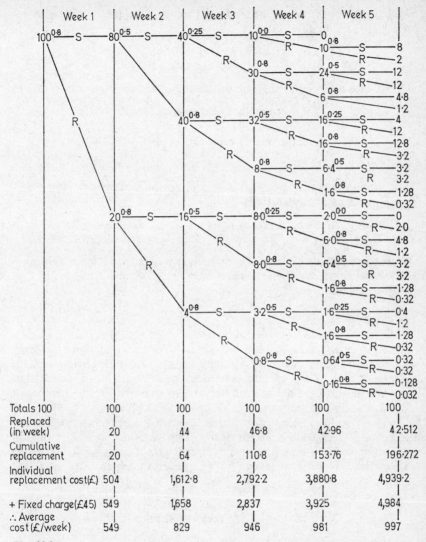

Fig. 11.2

It is now possible to deduce the total cost of replacing the group each week, every two, three, four . . . weeks—

Group Replacement at end of week 1. There will be 20 bulbs replaced as individuals at a cost of

$$£(20 \times 25·2) = £504$$

+ 100 bulbs replaced as a group at the end of the week at a cost of

$$£(25 + 0·2 \times 100) = £45$$

$$\therefore \text{ total replacement cost} = £549$$

125

Group Replacement at end of week 2. There will be (20 + 44) bulbs replaced as individuals at a cost of

$$£(64 \times 25 \cdot 2) = £1612 \cdot 8$$
$$\text{— say £1613}$$

+ 100 bulbs replaced as a group at the end of the period at a cost of £45

$$\therefore \text{ total replacement cost } = £1658$$

$$\therefore \text{ Average weekly replacement cost } = £\frac{1658}{2}$$
$$= £829$$

Similarly the average weekly costs of group replacement at the ends of 3, 4, 5 weeks can be calculated—

Group replacement at end of week	1	2	3	4	5
Average weekly cost (£ a week)	549	829	946	981	999

and comparing this with the average weekly cost of individual replacement—£1100 a week—it will be seen that the most economic policy will be to group-replace at the end of each week.

2. *Failure which can be tolerated*

The above situation implies that failure brings with it penalties so large that replacement must be carried out *upon* or *before* failure. In some situations the costs incurred by failure are such that inactivity, both of equipment and of the maintenance department, can be tolerated until some convenient time has elapsed, for example, until a specific number of items are not working, or until a shift has ended.

In this case, it is necessary to balance the costs due to inaction against the costs of replacement. Here again, it is necessary that information concerning failure frequency rates and replacement costs are available, as well as the costs due to inactivity. The necessary criterion then is that

the cost attributable to inactivity during time T
must be less than
the cost of replacement at time T.

Knowing the various failure parameters, the above conditions enable the optimum replacement time to be calculated.

Replacement Due to Deterioration

Inevitably all equipment deteriorates with time, although in some cases the time span may be extremely long. To decide whether equipment should be replaced is a problem identical with that which was considered under the heading 'The selection of plant—economic appraisal' (page 110). Here one of the pieces of plant being considered is the *existing* plant, and it is this which is compared with the alternative plant available. Clearly the

various factors ('installed price', 'indirect charges', 'maintenance charge'
...) refer to the values applicable at the time when the appraisal is being
made, not the initial values which were usable when the plant was first
installed.

Further Reading
1. Corder, G. G., *Maintenance—Techniques and Outlook*, British Productivity Council, London 1965.
Its title describes the text admirably. A useful, practical work.

2. Morrow, L. C. (Ed.), *Maintenance Engineering Handbook*, McGraw-
Hill, New York 1966.
An encyclopaedia setting down detailed maintenance methods.

3. Clements, R. *Manual of Maintenance*, Business Publications, London
Vol. 1, 1965, Vol. 2, 1966.
An amalgamation of a number of handbooks on maintenance written
by authors with intimate knowledge of specialized aspects of the subject.
Contains much useful, detailed information and guidance.

Chapter 12
Budgets and Budgetary Control

THE BUDGET

As pointed out earlier, a budget is essentially a quantitative statement of a policy, and is an effective summary of the decisions taken concerning the factory. In general, the word 'budget' is used to imply a *financial* statement, and it will be so used here, but it is worth realizing that other budget statements can be made—for example, a time-budget or schedule can be drawn up which is equally a statement of policy. Clearly these different budgets should all be drawn together into one comprehensive statement, but there are still some technical problems which prevent this being done in all cases.

Given a sales forecast, the factory manager can use it as a basis from which to prepare his factory budgets. These are usually expressed in financial terms, since all activities in a factory are capable of being so expressed, and hence a budget covering many different activities will be homogeneous. The method of preparing a factory budget may be as follows—

1. From the sales forecast an estimate is made of—
   (*a*) the material content,
   (*b*) the direct labour content in operator-hours, of the required production.
2. From the direct labour estimates, estimates are made of—
   (*a*) the direct labour: estimates are made for each of the departments—that is, the direct labour force required in each department;
   (*b*) the supervisory labour necessary to control the direct labour in each department;
   (*c*) the ancillary labour required to support the work of each department.
3. From the above estimates and the sales forecast the service and control staffs (the maintenance, inspection, wages, costing, accounting, production control, production engineering, design and development, and managerial staffs) required to achieve the sales forecast are estimated.
4. From the long-range forecasts and the general objectives and policies of the company an estimate is made of any other indirect staff—

for example, research and training—which may be required to be employed during the current financial year, but whose efforts will not produce revenue during that time.

5. Calculations of overhead expenses—rent, rates, insurance, tax, heating, lighting and so on—are made.

6. All the above are then consolidated into an estimate of what the total expenditure will be during the financial period under consideration.

7. The difference between the total estimated expenditure and the total revenue is the profit which should be achieved.

8. This profit, added to the estimated expenditure, gives the factory budget for the financial year. (See Appendix I, p. 397).

The budget is clearly a very complex statement, embodying both policy decisions (for example, those concerning the methods of depreciation to be used) and organizational assumptions (for example, those concerning the acceptable levels of support staffs). None of these can be justified except on pragmatic grounds, and it is therefore impossible to produce a budget which is clearly 'correct': what is required is an *acceptable* budget, that is one which does not conflict with *any* of the corporate objectives. It is unlikely that such a document will be produced at a first attempt, and it is usually necessary to make a series of drafts, starting with one in fairly broad terms, and amending and refining it successively until acceptable results are obtained.

It must be stressed that the budget should be an *agreed* document representing a consensus of the views of all whom it directly concerns. The executive who co-ordinates the drawing up of the budget must actively involve the appropriate supervisors in the preparations, discussions and analyses required in preparing the budget. The budget is not an *order-giving* but a *situation-displaying* document, and the manager needs ' . . . to unite all concerned in a study of the situation, to discover the law of the situation, and obey that'. (M. P. Follett, *The Giving of Orders*).

The importance of the preparation of a budget cannot be stressed too greatly, since it results in management knowing *in advance* the activities to be undertaken in the budget period and their probable results. Beside this very obvious benefit, the act of preparation itself produces other gains—notably it requires that the organizational structure and the staff required should be carefully considered. Without a budget a decision concerning the employment of—for example—extra staff can only be made on the grounds of immediate expediency. On the other hand the budget will show immediately what effect the extra expenditure will have on the year's trading, and whether the benefits to be gained justify that expenditure. The structure discussed and agreed when preparing the budget will also result in a clarification of the duties of each individual so that each person can know what is expected of him.

During the initial stages of a company's existence, the preparation of a budget is difficult, and the results inaccurate. But, as information is accumulated, a budget becomes both easier to prepare and much more accurate. Thus early difficulties must not be allowed to prevent the preparation of the budget—it is one of the most important weapons in the armoury of the factory manager. Furthermore, once the budget is prepared it can be used as a very simple yet accurate, means of controlling activity by continually comparing budgeted with actual performance. Finally, should circumstances change during the year, the budget can be used to show what steps need to be taken to compensate for the altered circumstances.

The Capital Expense Budget

From the preparation of the factory budget, and knowing the long-term requirements of the company, the factory manager will build up a list of new plant and equipment required. This will be cast into the form of a capital expense budget, which, when ratified by the board, will permit the purchase of the new equipment. Subsequent purchasing will depend upon the cash resources of the company, and the actual placing of an order for such items must be authorized by the financial accountant, who will verify that the placing of the order at that time will not prove embarrassing.

The Break-even Chart

The derivation of a break-even chart from a budget enables rapid assessments of the effect of variations in the budget factors to be made, and thus

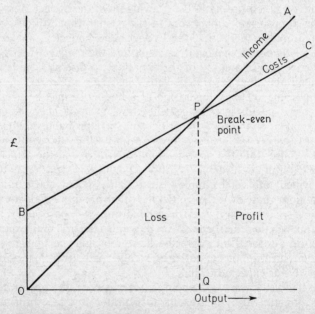

Fig. 12.1. Break-even Chart

increases the overall value of the budget. In its simplest form it consists of the graphical representation of costs at varying levels of activity shown on the same chart as the variation of income with the same variation in activity. The point at which neither profit nor loss is made is known as the 'break-even' point, and is represented on the chart by the intersection of the two lines. On Fig. 12.1 the line OA represents the variation of income with output, and BC the variation of costs with output. At low output costs are greater than income, whilst at high outputs costs are less than income. At the point of intersection P, costs are exactly equal to income, and hence neither profit nor loss is made. If the budget figure for output is below the break-even point (i.e. less than OQ) then the organization is said to be budgeted for a loss. A more usual situation is for the budget figure to exceed the break-even figure (i.e. to exceed OQ), when the organization will be budgeted for a profit.

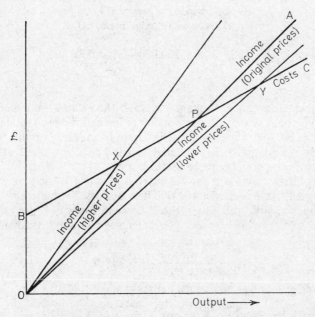

Fig. 12.2. Break-even Chart showing Effect of Variation in Selling Price

Variations in either income (i.e. sales prices) or costs will result in the slopes of the respective lines varying, causing the break-even point to slide up and down. Fig. 12.2 shows the same organization as in Fig. 12.1, the costs being assumed to remain constant. With the income as in Fig. 12.1, the income line OA intersects the cost line at P. Assuming that the sales prices are increased (i.e. the income increases) the income line intersects the cost line at X, which is lower than the original break-even figure, whilst if the sales prices are decreased (i.e. the income decreases) the break-even point slides up to Y. A similar set of graphs will show the effect of a variation in costs, and by combining the two effects a rapid assessment of the effect of any course of action can be made.

The Margin of Safety

In practice, it is clearly desirable for budgeted income to exceed break-even income by as large an amount as possible—working at or near the B/E point is very difficult as the ability to accept changes is small. A measure of this ability is given by the *margin of safety*, which is the ratio of the amount by which budgeted income exceeds B/E income to the budgeted income itself; that is—

$$\text{Margin of Safety} = \frac{\text{Budgeted income} - \text{B/E income}}{\text{Budgeted income}} \times 100$$

For example, if—

$$\text{Budgeted income} = £200,000$$
$$\text{Break-even income} = £160,000$$

then—

$$\text{Margin of Safety} = \frac{200,000 - 160,000}{200,000} \times 100$$
$$= 20\%$$

Clearly, the smaller this percentage becomes, the more the company is at risk. (*Note*: some workers refer to the difference between budget and break-even—£40,000 above—as the margin of safety. As this is only significantly meaningful if it is related to the budget or the break-even, the above ratio is probably more useful.)

An alternative expression for the margin of safety is the *percentage of capacity* figure. Here it is assumed that the budgeted volume employs all the capacity available, and that at the B/E point, capacity is used in direct proportion to the volume made. The percentage of capacity therefore is given by—

$$\frac{\text{B/E income}}{\text{Budgeted income}} \times 100\%$$

which would give, using the above figures—

$$\text{Percentage of Capacity} = \frac{160,000}{200,000} \times 100\%$$
$$= 80\%$$

Drawing a Break-even Chart

Trading expenditure can be considered to be made up of two parts, the *fixed* costs and the *variable* costs. The fixed costs are those which do not change with variations in output, and include such items as rent and rates. Variable costs on the other hand are the costs which do change with variations in output, and these include labour and material costs, insurance, supervision and similar items. Together they form the total cost. This is shown diagrammatically in Fig. 12.3, where the fixed cost is OB, and is

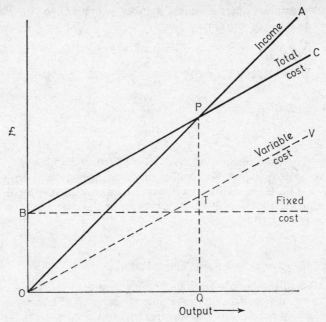

Fig. 12.3. Make-up of a Break-even Chart

shown by a line parallel to the abscissa, and the variable cost by the line OV which passes through the origin. The total cost is the result of adding these two and will be shown by the line BC. This can be considered to be drawn either by *first* setting off the fixed cost (OB) and then drawing the variable cost through B at the correct slope, or by drawing the variable cost through the origin and then drawing a line parallel to it, spaced by a value equal to the fixed cost.

If the latter technique is used, then the distance between the income and variable cost lines is known as the contribution, and at the break-even point the contribution PT is equal to the fixed cost OB; that is to say—

at Break-even, Contribution = Fixed cost.

This gives a simple method of calculating the break-even point. For example: in a company whose income is £100,000, the profit is 10 per cent and the fixed cost is £15,000. What is the break-even point?

Income	= Variable cost+fixed cost+profit
i.e. £100,000	= Variable cost+£15,000+£10,000
∴ Variable cost	= £75,000
	= 75 per cent of income

At break-even—

Contribution	= £15,000
Income	= Variable cost+contribution
Income	= 75 per cent income+£15,000
25 per cent Income	= £15,000
Income	= £60,000

The same result is obtainable in a number of other ways: the choice of method is dictated by the circumstances.

$$\text{Margin of Safety (£)} = £100{,}000 - £60{,}000 = £40{,}000$$

$$\text{Percentage of Capacity} = \frac{60{,}000}{100{,}000} \times 100\% = 60\%$$

$$\text{Profit/Volume ratio} = \frac{10{,}000 + 15{,}000}{100{,}000} \times 100\%$$
$$= 25\%$$

Note: it is not always obvious which costs are fixed, and which are variable. Indeed, some may be semi-variable, changing 'step-wise' with volume. The decisions on these matters may be arrived at historically by observing how the expense varied with varying volume in the past, or an arbitrary decision may have to be made.

The Profit Graph and the Profit/Volume Ratio

In place of the B/E chart, a *profit graph* may be drawn. This relates profit earned to output (see Fig. 12.4). At outputs below B/E losses are made, so that the profit graph is on the negative side of the output axis, whilst at B/E neither profit nor loss is created, and the graph crosses the output axis. Above B/E profit appears and the graph rises above the axis. The increase in profit for a unit increase in output is said to be the Profit/Volume ratio (P/V ratio), and is the slope of the profit graph; that is, it is the ratio—

$$\frac{KM}{FM}$$

The length FM is the budgeted output, and KM is the sum of KL (the profit generated at the budgeted output level) and LM, which is equal to OF, the loss at zero output, that is, the fixed cost. Hence—

$$\text{P/V ratio} = \frac{KL + LM}{FM}$$
$$= \frac{\text{profit} + \text{fixed costs}}{\text{output}} \times 100$$

Alternatively—

$$\text{P/V ratio} = \frac{KL}{PL} = \frac{\text{Profit}}{\text{Margin of Safety}}$$
(expressed in £)

Using the same figures as previously—

$$\text{Margin of Safety (as a \%)} = \frac{100{,}000 - 60{,}000}{100{,}000} \times 100$$
$$= 40\%$$

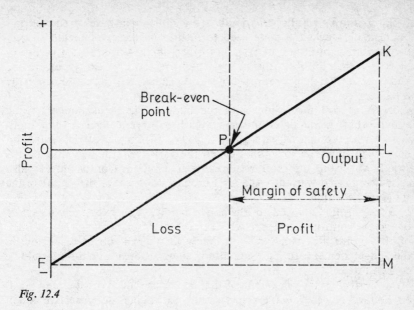

Fig. 12.4

BUDGETARY CONTROL

Once a budget has been drawn up it can be used as an instrument of control by continually comparing actual with budgeted performance. Since all activities in a factory are ultimately capable of being expressed in financial terms, the breadth of control possible is very great. This comparison is known as Budgetary Control, and the essential features of this, like any other control system are—

1. *Planning*, that is, the preparation of the budget. This is discussed briefly in Chapter 1, and an example is given in Appendix I. In general there is a Master Budget which summarizes a number of detailed or departmental budgets. The departmental budgets are produced first, then amalgamated into the master budget which will need to be compared with the directives issued by the board. Drawing up a budget in the absence of past information is difficult, but the act of preparation *forces* consideration of organization and potential.

2. *Publishing*, that is, informing each executive of that which is expected of him. This is often done implicitly in the very act of planning a budget, but once the whole budget is complete an explicit statement should be made. This 'selling' of the budget is most important, since no system is able to work unless the people concerned with it understand it and are prepared to make it work. At the initial inception of a budgetary control system there is always great reluctance on the part of a departmental manager to co-operate, and a fear that 'they' are going to show him how to do his job.

3. *Measuring* results; this is always a difficult task since engineers—for example—who are quite used to measuring pieces of metal, suspect the measurement of output, wages or other similar features. It is necessary of course that the items being measured are those which appear in the budget, and that they are measured in the same units as those originally used.

4. *Comparing* the results with the budget. The measurements taken above, whilst being significant in themselves, have a much greater significance when compared with a budget. The difference between actual and budgeted expense is sometimes called the variance, although this term is strictly applicable only to deviations from standard. Confusion may also arise here in that 'variance' is a term used in statistics for the square of the standard deviation.

5. *Reporting* the results of the above activity. This is done by means of budgetary control statements, which enable the factory manager and such of his subordinates as necessary to know whether the objectives set out in the budget are being fulfilled, and if not, in which areas attention should be concentrated.

6. *Correcting* the behaviour of the system or modifying the plan itself. As pointed out earlier, the responsibility for taking the corrective action often lies outside the 'control' department, being the responsibility of the departmental manager or supervisor.

Preparation of Budgetary Control Statements

The preparation of a budgetary control statement requires care, and the following points should be observed—

1. *Information should be accurate*, or at least of a *known* inaccuracy. If it is known that inaccuracies are present then consistency of measurement and presentation is vital. The basing of action upon incorrect data may lead to incorrect action being taken, which will bring the whole scheme of budgetary control into disrepute. An unwarranted air of accuracy is sometimes given by quoting figures to too many significant places. For example, if the number of hours worked is 123, and the wages earned are £74·25, and it is known that both the hours and wages figure are in error, there is no point in calculating that the average rate (that is, wages ÷ time, or £74·25 ÷ 123) is 60·36485p an hour. The derivation of the ·36485 portion is not only meaningless, it is also expensive to achieve. Even if the initial figures were correct and the ·36485 correct, it is difficult to conceive of any circumstances when it could be used.

2. *Information should be pertinent*, and no information should be presented to an executive concerning matters over which he has no control. The simpler the control statement can be, the more use will be made of it. Two sources of useless information are: (*a*) the recording of expenditures which are fixed, such as rent and insurance; and (*b*) the presentation of information to one departmental executive of expenditure incurred in another department.

3. *Information should be adequate*. Nothing is more frustrating than an inability to make a decision because some information is missing. This can lead to the collecting of excessive data, and a balance must be struck between 'too little' and 'too much'. Probably the only useful test which can be applied here is that of *usefulness*. Will the operating manager *use* the information? Clearly, the detail required varies with hierarchical level: information needed in one position will probably be excessive in a superior position and inadequate—but too broad—at a subordinate one.

4. *Information should be up-to-date*, so that action, if required, can be taken. The presentation of data concerning matters over which, by virtue of the time which has elapsed, nobody has any control, is of little more than historical interest, and as such can only be useful as a guide to future action. The frequency with which statements should be issued depends very much on local circumstances: usually monthly is adequate in stable organizations although weekly may be necessary in times of rapid change. A useful criterion concerning the frequency of reporting is given by Antony, who suggests that a useful measure of the time interval is 'the shortest period of time in which management can usefully intervene and in which significant changes in performance are likely'.

> Accurate
> Pertinent
> Adequate
> Up-to-date

Information Requirements for a Budgetary Control System

Example of a Budgetary Control Statement

A complete budget for an imaginary company (the 'F.M.' Factory) is presented in Appendix 1. Of the thirty or so items presented in the master budget a number are fixed, or so slow-moving as not to warrant issuing in the weekly budgetary control statement. The others are presented to the factory manager in a form as shown in Table 12.1. This shows immediately that the actual output of £122,000 is below budget by some £12,500, yet the direct wage bill is effectively as planned, and the direct material usage is high. The only figure which may be of significance is that of indirect labour in the production department. The factory manager would probably call first for a statement of the work-in-progress and the scrap generated. Should these figures indicate that there was no apparent pilfering, but that the productivity was low, giving an excessive direct labour cost for the output, and that excessive scrap had been produced, he would then call for an analysis of the production department's indirect labour costs. These would already have been prepared and submitted to the production manager in a form similar to Table 12.1, and would reveal a shortage of

Table 12.1. Budgetary Control Statement for Week 26

Item	Amount this week	Total to date 26 weeks	Budget 26 weeks	Budget Comparison Above	Budget Comparison Below
	£	£	£	£	£
Output—	4,700	122,000	134,500		12,500
Small tools and tool maintenance	91	220	200	20	—
Telephones	120	320	330	—	10
Travelling and entertaining	9	200	210	—	10
Canteen	4	100	100	—	—
Staff advertising	110	300	250	50	—
Welfare	3	70	75	—	5
Bank charges	4	90	85	5	—
Cleaning materials	5	135	135	—	—
Insurances	4	111	111	—	—
Printing and stationery	20	500	370	130	—
General expenses	5	125	130	—	5
Indirect wages—					
Accountancy/Costing	95	2,200	2,400	—	200
Personnel	104	2,200	2,000	200	—
Engineering	54	1,400	1,450	—	50
Inspection	182	4,700	4,750	—	50
Production	1,000	24,000	29,100	—	5,100
Holiday pay	58	1,500	1,650	—	150
N.H.I.	126	3,300	3,425	—	125
Pension Fund	27	700	800	—	100
Direct labour	1,560	41,000	41,155	—	155
Direct material	1,000	26,000	25,321	679	—

fitters, an understaffed production control department and a severe shortage of supervision on the production floor itself.

In the absence of a budget, the lack of production might well be noticed, but the probable causes—that is, the lowered productivity due to shortage of service, control and supervisory staff—could not be *known*, and great reluctance might have been felt in employing more chargehands in the situation as outlined. In practice, of course, the statement shown would have been one of a series which would have shown the trends developing, and remedial action would have been taken before. The production manager would have been in a position earlier to discuss his problems authoritatively with his superior by virtue of the accumulation of information.

Two points must be borne in mind when operating a budgetary control system—

(*a*) Budgets, and the derived control documents, are *tools* of management, not punitive weapons. They should exist to help the manager, not to punish him.

(*b*) No budget should ever be considered to be fixed and immutable: differences between performance and budget (the cost accountant's 'variances') may arise from changes in external circumstances, and if these are significant, then the budget must be revised.

Further Reading
   1. Jones, E., *Finance for the Non-Financial Manager*, Pitman, London 1972.
   This work covers much more than the material of this chapter. Its content and style make it a useful text for the production manager.
   See also the recommendations to Chapter 21 (p. 246).

Section Four   Manufacture

Chapter 13
Types of Production

It is usually accepted that there are three main types of production, namely: job, batch and flow production. It is important to realize at the outset that these types of production are not necessarily associated with any particular *volume* of production, and that depending upon the circumstances the same task can be undertaken by any of the above methods.

These three different types of production all exhibit distinct characteristics and require different conditions for their effective inception and working. The circumstances in any factory at any time must be carefully considered before a decision is taken as to the method of production to be used. Frequently the type of production employed depends on the development of the company concerned. Many factories start on a job production basis; proceed, as volume increases, to batch production methods in part at least; and finally manage to flow-produce all or some of the products concerned.

It might be said that it is rare to find in any factory that only one type of production is carried on, so that, in a radio factory for example, the final assembly of the receiver might well be carried out under flow production conditions, whilst the manufacture of the raw chassis was carried out under batch production conditions, the manufacture of the jigs, tools and fixtures proceeding under job production conditions.

JOB PRODUCTION

Job or 'make complete' production is the manufacture of a single complete unit by an operator or group of operators, and a number of identical units can proceed in parallel under job production conditions. Bridge building, dam construction and shipbuilding are common examples of job production industries, although even in these fields batch production techniques are being used. Job production is characterized by the fact that the whole project is considered as one operation and work is completed on each product before passing on to the next. Labour tends to be versatile and highly skilled, capital investment is high, while control is relatively simple, being largely exerted by the operator or group. In the case of the production of single specialized equipments, it is inevitable that job production should be used, but in the case of quantity manufacture it is conceivable though unlikely that job production could also be used.

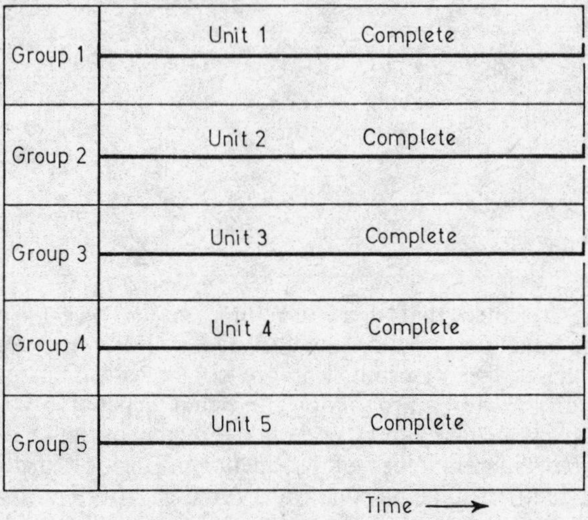

Group 1	Unit 1	Complete
Group 2	Unit 2	Complete
Group 3	Unit 3	Complete
Group 4	Unit 4	Complete
Group 5	Unit 5	Complete

Time ⟶

Fig. 13.1. Job Production of Five Units

BATCH PRODUCTION

As quantities increase beyond the few made during the earliest history of many companies, work may be carried out under batch production methods. Such methods require that the work on any product is divided into parts or operations, and that each operation is completed throughout the whole batch before the next operation is undertaken. This technique is probably the most common type of production in the United Kingdom, typical examples being the production of electronic instruments, transformers and so on. By its use some degree of specialization of labour is possible, and capital investment is kept low, although the organization and planning required to ensure freedom from idle and waste time is considerable. It is in batch production that the production control department can produce most benefits, and these can often be spectacular, but it is also in batch production that it will be found most difficult to organize the effective working of a production control department.

In order to clarify the difference between job and batch production, consider a small quantity of units, say five, being made by a number of operators (see Fig. 13.1). Under job production conditions the operators would be divided into five groups, and each group would be responsible for the complete manufacture of one unit. Under batch production conditions, however, the work content of each unit would be broken into a number of operations not necessarily of equal work content, and the

144

operators would again divide into groups. The first group would then complete the first operation on all five units, passing the batch as a whole on to the next group and so on until the manufacture was complete. In general the batch is not passed on from one operator or group to the next until all work is completed on that operation: transferring part batches can often lead to considerable organizational difficulties.

It should be noted that, during the batch manufacture of the five units mentioned above, four units are always at rest, no work being carried out on them. Referring to Fig. 13.2, if material is issued at time 0, work will be

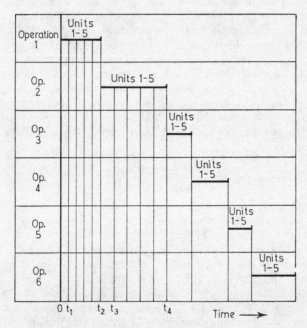

Fig. 13.2. Batch Production of Five Units

carried out on one unit during time t_1. This unit will remain stationary till time t_2 whilst work is being carried out on the other four units. Work will then restart on this unit during time t_2-t_3 when it will again rest till t_4, and so on. In fact, the rest periods of any one unit from a batch of a total $\frac{n-1}{n} \times 100$ per cent, of the total batch production time. This is characteristic of batch production, where the work-content of the material increases irregularly and results in a substantial work-in-progress.

In addition to the rest period indicated above, the organizational difficulties of batch production may well generate other rest times. Where numbers of batches are passing through the same production stages, and competing for resources, it is usual to move a batch from an operator or machine into a 'buffer' or 'work-in-progress' store, to wait there for the

145

next operator or machine to become available. The sequencing of batches from different jobs to reduce this source of 'rest' is one of the most difficult problems encountered in the management of a production unit, and however successfully it is solved, there will inevitably be some element of rest time brought about by this competition for resources. Thus, in batch production, there is a rest period for each unit in the batch, whilst work is proceeding on other members of the batch, and another rest period whilst the whole batch is in buffer store. This often results in the time between the origination of work on a batch and its eventual completion being much greater than the simple manufacturing time for the batch.

The effect of the considerable time lag between an initial investment in material and its subsequent translation into cash upon the sale of the finished product can be very serious in terms of the investment in capital which is tied up in the work-in-progress. On the other hand, the presence of the buffer stores permits the production unit to absorb shocks and changes, thus building in some element of flexibility, and it assists in making more effective use of the various limited manufacturing resources. This balancing of investment in material against investment in resources is a continually recurring task, and one to which there is rarely a simple, unique answer.

FLOW PRODUCTION

Batch production is characterized by the irregularity in the increase of work added to the basic material. Batch production turns into flow production when the rest period mentioned above vanishes. In other words, flow production can be defined as production during which the work content of the product continually increases, or as Woolard put it 'the processing of material is continuous and progressive'.

Flow production, then, means that as the work on each operation is complete the unit is passed to the next work stage without waiting for the work to be complete on the total batch. In order that this can flow smoothly the times for each operation must be of equal length, and there must be no movement off the production line. For example, inspection must be physically located within the flow production line and the inspection function must not occupy more than the unit operation time. Furthermore since the whole system is balanced any fault affects not only the stage at which the fault occurs, but also all the stages in the production line.Thus a fault, occurring at one stage of a flow production line which cannot be cleared within the time cycle of the line, will result in that stage being held up. This in turn causes all the stages previous to it to be held up and all the stages subsequently to run out of work. The line as a whole, therefore, must be considered as a single entity and not allowed to break down at any point at all.

It is sometimes believed that flow production is a comparatively recent technique, but this is far from the truth. In 1784, Oliver Evans in Pennsylvania had designed and operated a completely mechanized grain mill, whilst in 1804 the British Naval Arsenal at Deptford had created a flow line of skilled workers, along with a kneading machine, which turned out 70 ship's biscuits a minute. The most comprehensive example of flow production did, however, come very much later in 1914–1916, when the Ford Company, in its Highland Park factory, set up an extensive flow production plant to make the Model T car.

In order that flow production can function satisfactorily, the following requirements must be met—

1. *There must be Continuity of Demand.* Should demand be spasmodic there will be a build-up of finished work which can give rise to storage difficulties. Alternatively, if production is caused to fluctuate along with demand, then the setting-up and balancing of the flow line will need to be carried out frequently, giving an excessively high total cost. In industries with widely varying demands, a levelling-out is achieved by making for stock during the 'flat' periods, the stock supplementing the current production during 'peak' periods. The price paid for this organizational simplification is, of course, the cost of holding the completed products.

2. *The Product must be Standardized.* A flow line is inherently inflexible and cannot accommodate variations in the product. A quasi-variety is achieved by varying finishes, decorations and other externals.

3. *Material must be to Specification and Delivered to Time.* Due to the inflexibility mentioned above the flow line cannot accept the variations in material which can be incorporated in a batch or job production process. Furthermore, if material is not available when it is required the effect is very serious, since the whole line will be frozen.

4. *All Stages must be Balanced.* If the requirement that the material does not 'rest' is to be fulfilled, then the time taken at each stage must be the same. This can lead to an inefficiency due to an inability to balance stages. For example, assume a product with a work content of 10 hours has to be made at a rate of 400 a week, and the normal working week is 40 hours, then—

$$\text{The total weekly work content} = 400 \times 10 \text{ hours}$$

$$\text{Hence the number of operators required} = \frac{400 \times 10}{40}$$

$$= 100$$

$$\text{And the time for each operation} = \frac{10}{100} \text{ hours}$$

$$= 6 \text{ minutes}$$

To meet the required production then, a flow line with 100 stages needs to be set up, the work content of each stage being 6 minutes. It may be found, however, that one stage has a work content of only 3 minutes and that it cannot be compounded with any other stage. Under these circumstances this stage (and another congruent stage) must have an idle time content of 3 minutes. This is known as a 'synchronizing loss' and the only way of avoiding this would be to increase the rate of production so that, in fact, all stage times could be reduced to 3 minutes. In the situation when an element cannot be reduced to the required stage time—for example, a machine controlled operation is 10 minutes—then resources must be increased so that the effective operation time becomes less than the stage time. This can lead to an under-utilization of resources.

5. *All Operations must be Defined.* In order that the line will maintain its balance, all operations must remain constant. This can only be done if the operations are recorded in detail.

6. *Work must Conform to Quality Standards.* In job or batch production variations in quality at one stage can be compensated for by extra work elsewhere: in flow production this cannot happen, since each stage has a defined operation.

7. *The Correct Plant and Equipment must be Provided.* Lack of correct apparatus will unbalance a line, causing weaknesses throughout the whole sequence.

8. *Maintenance must be by Anticipation not Default.* If equipment breaks down at any one stage, the whole line is halted. To avoid this a programme of preventive maintenance must be in force.

9. *Inspection must be 'In Line' with Production.* Unless the inspection stage is balanced with the rest of the production, a dislocation to the flow will inevitably take place.

The achievement of the above requires considerable pre-production planning, particularly in assuring that the correct material is delivered on time, and that the operations are of equal length of time. Common examples of flow production are the manufacture of motor-cars, watches, domestic radio receivers, etc.

It must be noted that flow production is not necessarily large-scale production. For example, one firm found it profitable to flow-produce three equipments a day, a task which they had previously undertaken by batch production methods. The following advantages can be derived from the effective institution of flow production techniques—

(*a*) The direct labour content will be reduced, since the comprehensive pre-production planning which is necessary will often produce economies in time.

(*b*) Assuming the product is initially designed correctly, the reproducibility, and hence the accuracy, is high.

(*c*) Since inspection is 'in line' deviations from standard are rapidly picked up.

(*d*) Since there is no rest period between operations, work-in-progress is at a minimum.

(*e*) Again, since there is no waiting period, the provision of work-in-progress stores is unnecessary, and the total storage space required is minimized.

(*f*) Handling is reduced.

(*g*) Control (including production, budgetary, quality and supervisory control) is simplified, the flow line being virtually self-controlling.

(*h*) Any weakness in materials or methods is immediately high-lighted.

(*i*) Material requirements can be planned more accurately.

(*j*) Investment in material can be more rapidly translated into income from sales.

> Continuity of demand
> Standardized product
> Material to specification and to time
> Stages must be balanced
> Operations must be defined
> Work must be to quality standards
> Correct plant and equipment must be provided
> Maintenance by anticipation not default
> Inspection 'in line' with production

Requirements for Flow Production

Line Balancing in Flow Production

In practice, the setting up of a flow production line involves two associated problems—

(*a*) the minimizing of synchronizing loss;

(*b*) the maximizing of resource utilization.

Where a product is complex, there are certainly a large number of possible sequences in which the operations can be carried out, and the choice of sequence will affect both the above. The choosing of a sequence gives rise to the class of problems known as *Line Balancing*, and a wholly logical solution to these has yet to be found.

Continuous Production

This term usually refers to production which continues for 24 hours a day, 7 days a week, throughout the year. Clearly this must be a flow production process, and it usually implies a very high volume, very capital-intensive situation—for example, oil refining, sheet glass making.

JOBBING PRODUCTION

The term *jobbing production* is usually used to imply production carried out only against customers' orders, and not for stock. It does not indicate any particular type or method of manufacture.

MASS PRODUCTION

There is in common use the term *mass production*, which is often loosely used to imply a particular type of production. In fact, mass production is nothing more than production on a large scale, and as such can be manufactured under either job, batch or flow production methods. The greater volume of mass production will usually result in a reduced unit direct labour cost, since a greater total expenditure on production aids and service functions will produce increases in productivity without an increase in unit indirect costs. Thus, if a number of small factories all producing identical articles coalesce into one large unit producing the same total quantity of the same articles, it is possible to increase considerably the effort on *work study, tooling, plant, inspection* and *production control* beyond that in any of the individual factories. The total cost could then be lower than the sum of the costs in all the individual factories—although flexibility may be lost, inertia may be increased and morale may suffer.

It is sometimes assumed also that during mass production quality will of necessity suffer. This is not so: it is not correct to equate mass production with *low* quality but generally with *uniform* quality, and this quality level depends on managerial policy and not on the scale of production.

Another equally invalid assumption is that increased production *necessarily* leads to increased profits. This is not always so: increased production may lead to reduced *manufacturing* costs, but the total net return to the enterprise may be diminished by the need to reduce selling prices or increase promotional expenses in order to sustain the volume of production.

Further Reading

1. Demyanyuk, F. S., *The Technological Principles of Flow Line and Automated Production*, Pergamon Press, Oxford 1963.

An excellent study in depth of the requirements of Flow Line production. The translation from the Russian is good, and the realization that managers in the U.S.S.R. have the same problems as elsewhere is heartening.

2. Nevins, A., *Ford, the times, the man, the company*, Scribner's Sons, New York 1954.

A fascinating biography which discusses some of the early attempts at flow production.

3. Woolard, F. G., *The Principles of Mass and Flow Production*, Iliffe, London 1956.

An excellent text, predating the Russian work by several years. It is readable, and extremely practical.

Chapter 14
Work Study I

Work Study is 'a *management service* based on those techniques, particularly method study and work measurement, which are used in the examination of human work in all its contexts, and which lead to the systematic investigation of all the resources and factors which affect the efficiency and economy of the situation being reviewed, in order to effect improvement'.

This definition indicates clearly where present-day work study differs from earlier job improvement schemes: a systematic discipline has been set up, providing a framework in which to work. Regrettably, work study has been endowed with a glamour which leads newcomers to believe that it is a panacea for all manufacturing ills. This, of course, is not so: it is one of a number of equally important management tools and cannot replace good management, although it may indicate areas requiring investigation.

In a Joint Industrial Training Boards report on *Training for Work Study Practice*, the following excellent statement occurs: 'Work study attains its benefits through, firstly, investigation of the current situation, examining especially any apparent weaknesses (for example, poor performance by an operating team or machine or the high cost of a job): this diagnosis is followed by the determination and introduction of appropriate improvements in operating methods. The investigation and review will cover operating methods, selection of type of equipment, usage of equipment, layout, supply and usage of materials, availability of ancillary services, e.g. materials handling, organization of work, effectiveness of planning procedures and progress control, and the potential effect of the investigation on overall cost and profitability.' By virtue of its far-reaching nature, the inception of work study must be undertaken most carefully. For example, in developing a new manufacturing technique, investigations may show that a substantial cause of inefficiency is the lack of adequate supplies of the correct material: this will appear to be a criticism of the buying department which, in turn, may be revealed to be conditioned by the general financial policy of the company. Thus what may start as a simple improvement of method programme may call into question the action of a number of senior executives. Such a situation could well cause considerable resentment and in some cases active opposition. An equally difficult situation is the employment of a work study engineer in a factory or department without adequate managerial support, so that any suggestions or improvements are not implemented. This results in bitterness on the part of the work study engineer and work study itself being brought into disrepute.

At the outset, therefore, of any work study programme, it is vital that all concerned should understand the principles, techniques and limitations of work study. As with any facet of management, success depends upon the co-operation of the people concerned, and positive steps must be taken to obtain the goodwill of those whose work is to be studied. *Secrecy, or the appearance of secrecy, must be avoided at all costs.* The ideal situation is one where work study is not considered as a separate entity but as an integral part of all activities. For this reason it is highly desirable for 'appreciation' courses to be run for all management down to shop floor supervisor level so that all concerned may learn something of work study. Many technical schools and polytechnics will run such courses, and a number of employers' organizations and trades unions mount special courses for their members.

Present day work study includes two closely allied techniques. *Method Study*, which is the critical study of ways of doing work, and *Work Measurement*, which is the assessment of the time which a job should take. Both are carried out systematically and follow very similar patterns.

Work Study

Method Study	*Work Measurement*
1. Select task to be studied	1. Select task to be studied
2. Record the facts	2. Record the facts
3. Analyse the facts	3. Analyse the facts
4. Develop the new method	4. Measure the task
5. Install the new method	5. Define method and its related time
6. Maintain	6. Maintain

By carrying out an investigation along the above lines, the ordinary engineer will be most likely to achieve useful results. This is not to say that brilliant ideas never occur: of course they will, but their occurrence will be irregular and not to order. A systematic technique will certainly result in an improved method at all times.

METHOD STUDY

Select

The selection of the task to be studied is a *managerial* responsibility: the attitude 'go and have a look around the production floor and find something to deal with' is irresponsible and not likely to produce long-term benefits. As with any other factory activity, a method study—and its subsequent implementation—will cost money, and an estimate of the likely costs should be made before starting. Should these costs exceed probable savings, then the study should only be carried out *if there are other valid, identifiable reasons*. Look particularly carefully at the task which is intrinsically interesting, or about which the managing director has 'a good idea'. Some indications of the possible need for a method study are—

Bottlenecks generating high work-in-progress, long delivery times, or unbalanced work-flow.

Idle plant or people giving rise to an under-utilization of resources.

Poor morale, evidenced by petty or trivial complaints, poor quality and/or high absenteeism. These may all arise from tedious or unnecessarily tiring work.

Inconsistent earnings where the earnings are tied to output.

A Critical Path Analysis of a project will show where effort must be applied to reduce total project time.

It is unwise to carry out a study on a job where there is any form of industrial unrest—*the motives for the study will be suspect*. Once a task has been chosen, all involved—however remotely—should be informed, and the reasons for the choice and the desired outcome should be explained. Even quite innocent studies can take on a sinister appearance if the reasons for them are not known and understood.

Record

Once the task is agreed, the study will start by the engineer concerned *recording the facts* by direct visual observation. 'What the soldier said' is not accepted as evidence either in a court of law or in a method study. This recording requires to be carried out extremely carefully, since important factors may be overlooked or ignored. *All* facts require recording, preferably at the time and place of occurrence. A number of different recording methods are available, and that which is used must be appropriate to the circumstances.

Process charts

These are 'charts in which a sequence of events is portrayed diagrammatically by means of a set of *process chart symbols* . . .'. Their purpose is to provide an unambiguous, succinct record of a process so that it may be examined, analysed and—desirably—improved, usually away from the workplace.

Five symbols have been generally agreed and are in current use. These are illustrated in Fig. 14.1.

It is useful to differentiate between two types of operation—

'*Do*' *operations* where work is actually performed on the material or plant, resulting in an increase in added value.

'*Ancillary*' *operations* where material or plant is prepared, cleaned down, or put away.

○   Operation: '. . . usually the part, material or product . . . is modified or changed.'

⇨   Transport: '. . . movement of workers, materials or equipment from place to place' without otherwise furthering the process.

▽   Permanent Storage: '. . . a controlled storage . . .'

D   Delay or Temporary Storage: '. . . a delay . . . for example, work waiting between consecutive operations or . . . temporarily laid aside.'

☐   Inspection: 'Inspection . . . for quality and/or . . . quantity.'

Fig. 14.1. Work Study Symbols

Cross-hatching may be used to emphasize the 'do' operations, as in Fig. 14.2.

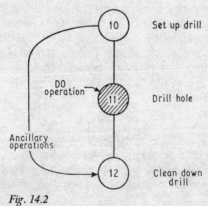

Fig. 14.2

Distances are recorded to the left of the transport symbol, and brief descriptions are written on the right of each symbol.

These symbols, combined in a process chart, give a rapid picture of a process, showing clearly where a process is worked on, where it is transported and so on. The care with which this recording is done will largely determine the final success of the study.

There are basically two types of process chart, differing in the level of detail recorded—

(*a*) *Outline Process Chart.* In this, the overall picture of the sequence of events and of the introduction of materials in a process is given by recording operations and inspections, using only two symbols (the circle and the square) of the five available.

(*b*) *Flow Process Chart.* This provides considerably more detail than the Outline Process chart, and all five symbols are used. Flow Process charts refer either to the *Man* (or Machine), that is, to the activities performed by the man, or to the *Material* (the activities carried out upon the material) and not to both simultaneously. Two-handed charts can be drawn, and pre-printed forms (see Fig. 14.3) are often found to be most economical.

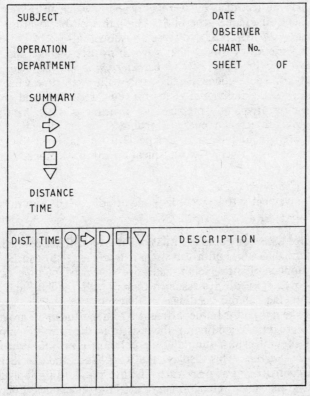

Fig. 14.3. Pre-printed Form for Flow Process Chart

Time-Scaled Charts

These are charts where two or more activities which are proceeding concurrently or simultaneously are shown on a common time scale. Again there are broadly two sets of time-scaled charts, differing in the level of detail.

(c) *The Multiple Activity Chart.* A multiple activity chart, which may be considered to be a vertical Gantt chart, is used to show the time relationships between two or more men, machines or materials. Essentially, a vertical column is erected for each of the protagonists, and the work performed is recorded as shading within the column. Time is recorded on the left and a brief description of the activities on the right. From the chart the ratio of working to non-working time can be determined, and an attempt at balancing can be made.

(d) *The Simultaneous Movement Chart* (SIMO *chart*). In this the movements of two or more parts of a worker's body are recorded. The movements are generally of very short duration—of the order of milliseconds—and the preparation of a SIMO chart usually requires a frame-by-frame analysis of a cine film of the work being studied. The elements of work may be recorded by *therblig symbols*, which were first used by Gilbreth, hence the name—therblig is Gilbreth spelt backwards (almost!). There are now 17 therbligs, and these are shown in Fig. 14.4. There are a number of varieties of SIMO charts which do not use therblig symbols, but employ one or other of the *Predetermined Motion Time Systems* (PMTS) codes. These codes usually carry with them time values for the performance of the individual elements being recorded, and the PMTS charts are most frequently prepared as a means of work measurement. Whilst SIMO charts can enable imbalances to be detected, they are difficult to prepare, and likely to be expensive both in time and equipment. They are used only if very great justification can be demonstrated.

Movement Charts

When movement is to be recorded, one or other of the movement charts is employed—

(e) *Travel Chart.* In complex situations it is sometimes confusing to try to use a flow diagram, and a travel chart (see Fig. 14.5) can be used. In this, the number of movements made over a period of time can be recorded. Movement is always assumed to start with the left hand row title and move to the column headings, so that movements from department 7 to department 4 and from department 2 to department 16 are as shown by the two crosses. By adding up the crosses in the rows the 'movements out' can be found, whilst summing the columns gives 'movements in'.

(f) *Flow Diagram.* This displays the work-place and the locations of the various activities, drawn to scale. The five standard symbols are used, and the diagrams again refer to man, material or machines. Effectively, it can be considered to be a Flow Process Chart drawn upon a scale-drawing of the work-place.

(g) *String Diagram.* Here again a scale drawing is used which is mounted upon a wooden panel. A preliminary survey identifies the locations of terminal points, and a fine string is wound between these pins to represent movement, supplementary pins being inserted where directions of movement change. The advantage of string over pencil marks on a piece

Symbol	Name	Colour
(Search)	Search	Black
(Find)	Find	Grey
(Select)	Select	Light Grey
(Grasp)	Grasp	Red
(Hold)	Hold	Gold ochre
(Transport Load)	Transport Load	Green
(Position)	Position	Blue
(Assemble)	Assemble	Violet
(Use)	Use	Purple
(Disassemble)	Disassemble	Light violet
(Inspect)	Inspect	Burnt ochre
(Pre-position)	Pre-position	Pale blue
(Release load)	Release load	Carmine red
(Transport Empty)	Transport Empty	Olive green
(Rest)	Rest for overcoming fatigue	Orange
(Unavoidable delay)	Unavoidable delay	Yellow
(Avoidable delay)	Avoidable delay	Lemon yellow
(Plan)	Plan	Brown

Fig. 14.4. Therbligs

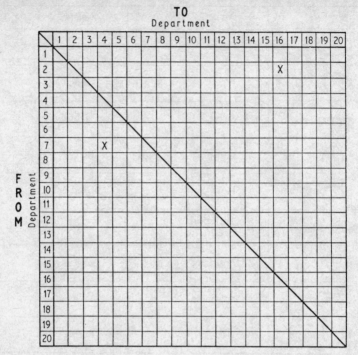

Fig. 14.5. Travel Chart

of paper is that repeated journeys over common paths can be shown without risk of obliteration or confusion. Unwinding and measuring the strings will enable the distances moved to be discovered. The string diagram will display vividly faults in a layout which cause bottlenecks, back- or cross-tracking or other movement difficulties.

Analyse and Develop

The analysis of the facts and the development of a new method can, and in general should, be carried out away from the place where the task is being performed. It is not easy to separate the development from the analysis, and for this reason these two are considered together.

In order to ensure that a new method is developed, there are two essentials—

    (*a*) an open mind
    (*b*) a systematic approach

and within particular organizations, a 'laundry list' of possible alternative methods and materials may be found useful. The open mind is largely a matter of experience and climate within the company: recriminations about past decisions, and investigations into past reasons and behaviour serve little purpose and invariably generate ill-feeling. The systematic approach can be assisted by the questioning technique.

The Questioning Technique

The activities in a process are subjected to an interrogation which follows a fixed pattern. It may be thought that 'delays' and 'transportations' should be attacked first, but this is not so: an 'operation' which is eliminated may well cause a 'delay' or a 'transportation' to disappear. Similarly, a modification to a 'do' operation may remove the need for an 'ancillary' operation. Hence *attack 'do' operations first.*

Activities are tested by asking five sets of questions:

1.	*Purpose*	What is being done? Why is it being done? What else could be done? What should be done?
2.	*Place*	Where is it being done? Why there? Where else could it be done? Where should it be done?
3.	*Sequence*	When is it done? Why then? When else could it be done? When should it be done?
4.	*Person*	Who does it? Why that person? Who else might do it? Who should do it?
5.	*Means*	How is it done? Why that way? How else can it be done? How should it be done?

These questions are asked in *the above order:* if the purpose is dislodged, all other questions are meaningless. If the place is changed, then the sequence, person and means may be altered. If on the other hand the means is questioned *first,* then a great deal of effort may be expended in analysing and improving a method which is later found to serve no useful purpose.

From the above recording and analysing, a picture of a new method will begin to emerge. This is a difficult step to systematize, and the speed with which a new method is proposed will depend on the experience, background and ingenuity of the engineer concerned. Nevertheless, the more closely is the job analysed, the easier it will be to *develop the new method.*

It may be that the new method will require the design of a jig, tool, or other production aid beyond the ability of the work study engineer. In this case he will need to recruit the assistance of an expert—for example a jig and tool designer—and he must be able to specify in some detail the performance of the device required. It must be remembered that the best solution is always the most simple, and, if a block of wood with a nail in it will do the job required, a more elaborate device would be undesirable. The new method should be recorded in the same way as the existing method, the two compared, and a summary of the advantages made, along with the cost of the new installation. Any new method must, of course, be inherently safe.

Install

The new method, once approved by the work study man, and the expenditure (if any) authorized by the appropriate person, requires to be *installed*. A process layout must be written and the technique 'sold', first to the foreman and the management, and then to the operators concerned. Without goodwill the new method may well fail—no system or method is any better than the persons operating it. Many a good idea has fallen down because the operator concerned has not accepted the idea. In 'selling' the idea, the work study engineer must first 'sell' himself: this does not mean that he must be offensively 'hearty' or friendly, but he must be respected and trusted by the operators. During the course of a study the engineer will have much information thrust upon him and he must not abuse the confidence placed in him by disclosing information intended for his ears alone. Once the idea is accepted, the operator must be trained in the new ideas by precept and example, and a habit of good working developed. Training is not considered complete until the productivity expected is achieved.

Maintain

Inevitably habits of work different from those desired by the work study engineer will develop unless the new technique is *maintained*. This may require continual visits from the engineer concerned, but it is better if this is done by the operator's immediate supervisor. To be able to do this the method must be written down clearly and concisely and thoroughly understood by the supervisor. If variations in the method then arise he can either correct them, or, if they appear desirable, submit them to the work study department for incorporation into the process layout.

Further Reading

1. *Introduction to Work Study*, International Labour Office, London 1970.

2. Currie, R. M., *Work Study*, Pitman, London 1972; for the British Institute of Management.

The above two books are both equally valuable introductions to Work Study.

3. *Glossary of Terms in Work Study* (BS 3138), British Standards Institution 1969.

One of the few glossaries of terms in the management field published in the U.K. The subjects covered include 'associated subjects'.

Very useful.

4. Barnes, R., *Motion and Time Study*, Wiley, New York 1969.

A thorough discussion of Work Study by one of the most respected workers in this subject. The comprehensive text includes detailed material on PMTS. Liberally illustrated.

5. Randall, P. E., *Introduction to Work Study and Organization and Methods*, Butterworths, London 1969.

A highly compressed, inexpensive outline of Work Study and O. & M. It is designed to appeal to the layman and as such must be accounted a success.

6. Fields, A., *Method Study*, Cassells, London 1969.

Comprehensive and well illustrated, it also discusses briefly associated topics such as ergonomics, network analysis and value analysis.

Chapter 15
Work Study II

Work measurement techniques are intended to reveal the work content of a task. In order that different tasks may be compared, the work content is always measured in the same units, those of *time*, and the time taken to complete any job is considered to be the time which a qualified worker— that is, one who has the necessary physical and mental attributes and has acquired the necessary skill—would take if working without over-exertion throughout a normal working period whilst applying himself to the job. Such a worker would be said to be working at *Standard Performance* and in one hour would produce *1 Standard Hour* or *60 Standard Minutes* of work.

Confusion often arises between the various times which are used in work measurement, and in order to clarify the terminology, an example is given. It should be noted that in practice the element being measured would generally be of very much shorter duration than the figure quoted, but use of the more practical figure would generate very small numbers which, in isolation, would seem to be trivial.

An operator is observed to carry out a given task in 60 minutes. This is known as the *observed time* and takes no account either of any allowances or of the ability of the operator—it is just the time which the operator being observed took whilst actually working, from the moment of starting to the moment of finishing. In order that operator's ability and effort can be compensated for, the operator is *rated*, that is, he is mentally compared by the observer with a qualified operator working at standard performance. An observer is thus required to have a very clear concept of the rate at which a worker who possesses the necessary physical and mental attributes, and the required skill, would satisfactorily carry out the task under observation safely, accurately, at the correct speed and without undue strain. Having this concept, the observer then must assess the worker being studied against this criterion. It is clearly an extremely difficult task, since it involves the comparison of a number of different yet dependent features of the subject's work with those of the 'qualified worker'. For example, the subject may be working at the right speed, yet at a lower level of quality or in a less safe manner. Alternatively, the quality produced may be much higher than necessary, yet the quantity produced may be too low. All the factors concerning the work being carried out must be assessed and integrated into a single rating figure, and this done whilst the task is actually being carried out. Assuming that the operator observed in our example has been working one-third as hard again as a qualified operator he would be said to have a rating of 133. In practice, rating is never assessed in increments smaller than 5 units, so that the figure of 133 would normally be rendered as 135, and the time which a *qualified* operator would have taken—known as the *basic time*—is

$$60 \times \frac{135}{100} \text{ minutes}$$

that is 81 minutes.

This rating is essentially a matter of proper training and considerable experience on the part of the observing engineer, and obtaining consistency in rating both between different engineers at the same time, and the same engineer at different times, is extremely difficult, and is a matter to which much attention has been paid. A common technique for obtaining consistency is by means of *rating films*. In these the same operations are performed at various ratings. The work study engineer views these, rates the operations, and then compares his rating with the rating given by the film. He then views the same operation performed as before but in a different sequence, and again rates the operations. This is repeated until consistency is obtained. The whole process is repeated after a convenient interval of time—say one month. By means such as this some considerable degree of consistency is obtained and it is claimed that ratings can be consistent to ± 5 per cent—a very necessary requirement if an accurate measurement of work content is required.

There are a number of different *Rating Scales*, just as there are different temperature scales. These differ by the value put on and the derivation of the fixed point—the *Standard Rating* point. This rating corresponds to the average rate at which qualified workers will naturally work, providing that they are properly educated, equipped and motivated. Probably the earliest rating scale is that which assumes that the unmotivated worker (the so-called 'day-worker'—one who is paid at 'day-rate' and does not earn any financial incentive) works at a 60 rating, and that the motivated worker will work one-third as hard again, that is at an 80 rating. The standard rating on this '60/80' scale is thus 80. Other scales which are 'pegged' to the 'un-motivated' worker are the 75/100 and 100/133 scales.

The British Standard rating, for reasons which are cogently argued in B.S. 3138, 'pegs' the rating scale to the performance of the motivated worker, and gives a value of 100 to the standard rating point, making no assumption about the rating of the 'un-motivated' worker. This recommendation has been rapidly accepted by U.K. practitioners, and it is now becoming rare to find rating scales other than the B.S. scale in British companies.

During a day the operator will need to relax in order to overcome fatigue—whether mental or physical, real or imaginary—and to attend to various personal needs such as drinking a cup of tea or going to the lavatory. These factors are taken into account by adding to the basic time a *Relaxation Allowance* which has been previously agreed within the organization for each type of work and each circumstance. Within the organization being discussed let us assume that the relaxation allowance for the task in question is $12\frac{1}{2}$ per cent. The relaxation allowance would thus be—

$$81 \times \frac{12\cdot5}{100} \text{ minutes;}$$
that is $10\cdot125$ minutes;
or effectively 10 minutes.

Under some circumstances there may be small irregularities in work— for example, due to small quantities of defective material—for which some allowance should be made. This is done by adding an allowance—a *contingency allowance* for extra work—which in our example might be $2\frac{1}{2}$ per cent, that is—

$$81 \times \frac{2\cdot5}{100} \text{ minutes;}$$
which is effectively 2 minutes.

The *work content* of the task is then defined as—

> Basic time
> + relaxation allowance
> + contingency allowance for extra work.

that is—

$$81 + 10 + 2 \text{ minutes}$$
or 93 minutes.

This represents the working time for the operation being studied throughout the 'attended time'. There are, however, allowances which have to be made for non-working time before it is possible to calculate the daily output. These allowances arise out of the process itself: for example there may be a dead period whilst a machine is slowing down, or there may be idle time due to an overlapping in two machines required for the same task. These are known as 'process allowances for unoccupied time' and 'interference time'. Once these are added to the work content the average operation time is obtained. This is the *standard time* and is—

> Work content
> + contingency allowance for delay
> + unoccupied time allowance
> + interference allowance.

Assuming the last three factors are 1 per cent, 1 per cent and $1\frac{1}{4}$ per cent respectively, in our example—

$$\text{Standard time} = 93 + 0\cdot93 + 0\cdot93 + 1 \text{ minutes}$$
$$= 95\cdot86 \text{ minutes—say 96 minutes.}$$

so that 100 operations carried out consecutively would occupy 100 × 96 minutes, *not* 100 × observed time. The operation in question is said to contain 96 standard minutes of work and if, in fact, the actual time taken for 100 operations was 100 × 90 minutes (= 150 hours), it would be said that 9,600 standard minutes were produced in 9,000 minutes. If the operator concerned had taken 4 × 40 hour weeks to produce this work, and had been occupied at Trades Union negotiations for perhaps 10 hours, then the *attendance time* would be 160 hours, and the *diverted time* 10 hours.

Two performance figures could then be defined:

$$\text{Operator performance} = \frac{\text{standard time}}{\text{time taken}} \times 100 = \frac{9,600}{9,000} \times 100$$
$$= 107\%$$
$$\text{Overall performance} = \frac{\text{attendance time}}{\text{standard time}} \times 100 = \frac{9,600}{9,600} \times 100$$
$$= 100\%$$

More precise definitions of these and other ratios used for managerial control purposes are given in the British Standard already quoted.

Most financial incentive schemes require yet another time, the *allowed time*. This is the time which, if fully used, will earn for the operator, no bonus or premium. Any time less than the allowed time generates a *Time Saved,* and it is very common to gear bonus earnings to this time saved (see Chapter 31). The *allowed time* is derived from the *standard time* by the addition of a *policy allowance*, the magnitude of which depends upon a managerial policy concerning the acceptable level of earnings of the grade of operator concerned. The relations of these various times to each other is shown in Fig. 15.1.

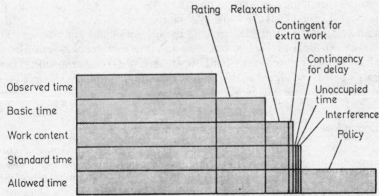

Fig. 15.1

Methods of Work Measurement

There are a number of different work measurement techniques of which the best known is—

Time Study

Time study is a direct observational technique in which an experienced engineer watches a worker, times what is being done, and 'rates' the work. Unfortunately it is viewed with great suspicion by many operators who remember the days of rate-cutting, where the usual reason for using a stopwatch was either to set a rate (that is, a bonus price) or to cut it. On the other hand it is a completely intelligible technique which can be understood with the minimum of explanation, unlike some other techniques which are so esoteric that they smack of black magic. Much suspicion will be removed if a clear explanation is given to the person being timed of the reason for the timing, if the timing is carried out in a perfectly open manner and if the operator has been given ample time to settle into an orderly rhythm of work carried out in accordance with a method laid down by a proper method study. No attempt should be made to carry out a time study if the work is not capable of being done correctly—for example, if the correct tools or the required material are not to hand.

Synthesis and Analytical Estimating

Within any organization the same elements of work will recur, even if the total jobs differ. Work measurement can be achieved by adding together the times for these elements. If originally these times had been obtained by time study, then the process is known as *synthesis*, whilst if they had been obtained by estimating, using the best available knowledge and experience, then the process is called *analytical estimating*.

Many organizations will build up books of tables of these times, entering new elements as they are discovered. In some cases it is possible to reduce the figures to simple charts or (less frequently) algebraic expressions. A good classification system for the retrieval of the data is essential, and the master file, carrying the original data, must be carefully preserved. The loss of a set of synthetic data can be extremely serious.

Since working conditions, traditions and work patterns differ from place to place, *it is most unwise to try to transfer synthetic, or analytical estimating data from one company to another.*

Predetermined Motion Time System (PMTS)

When extremely small work elements are used, then the system of work measurement is known as a PMTS. One of the earliest of these—MTM or Methods Time Measurement—uses hand and arm movements, recognizing a number of basic motions (reach, move, turn and apply pressure, grasp . . . and so on), and tables of times for these elementary movements under varying conditions are published. Other systems identify different elements, or use figure movements as a basis for calculation. The duration of these basic movements is small (of the order of $\frac{1}{30}$ second), and they are usually determined by studying cine film records. In all cases the times given are 'levelled', and the need for rating vanishes.

PMTS requires training in use since the definitions of the basic elements are not always immediately obvious. It is most unwise for an untrained person to try to derive a work content from a PMTS table. Much work has gone into the simplification of these systems, and second and third generation systems have been evolved. Unlike synthesis or analytical estimating, the basic data for PMTS can be transferred, not only from company to company, but from one part of the world to another.

The advantages of the three synthesizing techniques are—

1. Short-run tasks can be work measured.
2. Rating, the most difficult part of a time study, is not necessary.
3. The results obtained are consistent. This is particularly important in small batch production where there are too few repetitions carried out for an accurate time study.

Activity Sampling

In order to determine the stoppages taking place in a factory or department a large number of time studies can be made, forming a production study. This can be extremely costly in manpower, particularly if the behaviour of a large department is under investigation. A sampling technique known as *activity-sampling* has been developed following some work by a statistician (L. H. C. Tippett) on spot observation of machines and operatives. Essentially this technique consists in taking a large number of 'snap' observations on the activity or otherwise of the department under observation. For example, in a machine shop with a number of machines, frequent observations at random times throughout a week of the number of machines actually at work would give an indication of the average percentage of active machines. The larger the number of observations the more accurate does the indication become. The number of observations required for any particular circumstances can be simply calculated (see below), but in practice it is often adequate to continue to take readings until the results obtained have stabilized.

Surprisingly little used, this is quite a simple technique, extremely economical in manpower and capable of giving information which could not reasonably be obtained any other way. It can be applied to tasks where a stop watch could not be used—for example, to measure the idle time in a typing pool, or to analyse the time used in a drawing office into that spent on drawing, seeking information, checking, calculations and so on.

Activity Sampling—Number of Observations Required

N random observations of the proportionate occurrence of a statistic form a sample, size N, of mean proportionate occurrence π drawn from a population with a true proportionate occurrence P and a standard error—

$$\text{S.E.} = \sqrt{\frac{P(1-P)}{N}}$$

In repeated sampling—

67% of the values of π lie between $P \pm 1$ S.E.
95% of the values of π lie between $P \pm 2$ S.E.
99·7% of the values of π lie between $P \pm 3$ S.E.

The inaccuracy resulting from taking π as an estimate of P may be expressed as LP and for the 95% (confidence) limits—

$$LP \leqslant 2 \text{ S.E.}$$

that is—

$$LP \leqslant 2 \sqrt{\frac{P(1-P)}{N}}$$

Thus, the number of observations N necessary to achieve an accuracy LP at the 95% confidence level is—

$$N \leqslant \frac{4(1-P)}{L^2 P} \text{ (see Table 15.1 and Note (iii) below)}$$

P is the proportionate occurrence, and L is a fraction of P so that if—

$$P = 0\cdot20$$

and $\quad L = \tfrac{1}{5}$

(that is, the value of P lies between $0\cdot20 \pm \tfrac{1}{5} 0\cdot20$, i.e. $0\cdot16$ and $0\cdot24$) then—

$$N \leqslant \frac{4(1 - 0\cdot20)}{(\tfrac{1}{5})^2\, 0\cdot20} = 400$$

It may be more convenient to express the inaccuracy in absolute terms, that is, as a fraction of the total population rather than as a fraction of the occurrence, so that the previous example would be quoted as—

$$P = 0\cdot20 \pm 0\cdot04$$

In this case, if the inaccuracy is l—

$$l = LP$$

and

$$N \leqslant \frac{4P(1-P)}{l^2} \text{ (see Table 15.2 and Note (iii) below)}$$

and using the previous figures—

$$l = \tfrac{1}{5} \times 0\cdot20 = 0\cdot04$$

and

$$N \leqslant \frac{4 \times 0\cdot20\,(1 - 0\cdot20)}{(0\cdot04)^2} = 400$$

Notes: (i) *P* is initially estimated from a preliminary survey of—say—50 observations, and its value later confirmed as more observations are taken;

(ii) *N* is the number of *observations*, not the number of 'tours'. Thus if there are 50 work-stations being observed in a 'tour', then when *N* = 400, 8 tours are required *not* 400;

(iii) for 67% and 99·7% confidence limits, the 4(= 2²) above becomes 1(= 1²) and 9(= 3²) respectively.

Table 15.1.

L = Acceptable Accuracy in *P* as a proportion of *P*

		0·01 1%	0·05 5%	0·10 10%	0·20 20%
	1	3,960,000	158,400	39,600	9,900
	2	1,960,000	78,400	19,600	4,900
	5	760,000	30,400	7,600	1,900
Percentage	10	360,000	14,400	3,600	900
Occurrence	20	160,000	6,400	1,600	400
P	30	93,300	3,730	930	230
	40	60,000	2,400	600	150
	50	40,000	1,600	400	100

Maximum number of observations required, calculated from

$$N \leqslant \frac{4(1-P)}{L^2 P}$$

Table 15.2.

l = Acceptable Accuracy in P as a proportion of the whole population

		0·05 1%	0·05 5%	0·10 10%	0·20 20%
	1	396	16	4	1
	2	784	31	8	2
	5	1,900	76	19	5
Percentage	10	3,600	144	36	9
Occurrence	20	6,400	256	64	16
P	30	8,400	336	84	21
	40	9,600	384	96	24
	50	10,000	400	100	25

Maximum number of observations required, calculated from

$$N \leqslant \frac{4P(1-P)}{l^2}$$

THE CONTROL OF INDIRECT LABOUR

Traditionally, work study is associated with 'shop-floor' or direct labour; however, the costs associated with so-called 'indirect' labour are often as high or *very much higher* than the direct labour costs (page 14 gives some idea of the ratio of total labour to 'administrative and clerical labour'). To control these costs, work study has been applied to indirect labour, and in order to try to avoid any antagonisms, special names have been invented for the various techniques.

Organization and Methods

Organization and Methods (always abbreviated to 'O. & M.') is substantially method study in the office. Some practitioners would claim that they have a particular right to lay down the organizational structure of the department or company, but this claim is difficult to sustain, and the 'M' part of 'O. & M.' invariably predominates. The techniques of the 'O. & M.' man are exactly those of the Work Study Engineer, but applied to all clerical and administrative procedures. It is quite common to find that an 'O. & M.' department will also be responsible for job evaluation and merit rating systems.

Recording Methods

Whilst many O. & M. officers use the standard work study symbols of pages 154 and 157, some workers have added special symbols of their own devising, a procedure to be deplored. The increasing use of data processing equipment over the last decade, and the consequent need to analyse data flow systems has brought about a genuine need to produce a set of flow chart symbols for data processing. These symbols were internationally agreed at a meeting in Tokyo in 1965 where representatives of 11 countries were present. The British Standard Specification B.S. 4058, Part 1, 1966, *Data Processing Problem Definition and Analysis, Part 1: Flow Chart Symbols* embodies these symbols—some 30 in all—and gives some recommendations upon the conventions to be used in drawing data flow charts. It must be recognized that these charts record the flow of *data* rather than the activities of men or machines, and they thus serve purposes quite different from work study charts.

Work Measurement

Work measurement in offices presents—*or is often said to present*—problems of such magnitude and complexity that its use is severely limited. These problems when examined seem to be—

(*a*) *the creative nature of the task*. It is argued that many office workers are involved in creative tasks, and ' . . . it's impossible to time thinking'. Upon examination, however, it will be found that the creative content is frequently such a small proportion of the whole that it can be absorbed within an associated physical activity.

(*b*) *the irregularity of the work*. It is true that the work of—say—a secretary may be highly irregular. Thus in the middle of typing a letter she may be required to stop and take dictation, make coffee, welcome a visitor, answer the telephone . . . Frequently it will be found that much of the irregularity is entirely unnecessary, arising principally from the lack of organization and discipline of the supervisor.

(*c*) *prejudice*. The belief that the office worker is necessarily superior to other employees dies hard and this belief often carries with it the concept that they must not be subjected to such 'indignities' of the shop floor as the measuring of work. Fortunately more sensible attitudes are replacing these prejudices, but it is obviously vital that the warning against secret work measurement must be heeded. Knowledge is the greatest enemy of prejudice, and any attempt at clerical work measurement must be preceded by full and comprehensive discussion on the purpose of the measurement.

Clearly it is not usually possible *or useful* to measure indirect work as accurately as highly repetitive, large volume machining work. However, it will often be found that high accuracy is not necessary.

Methods of Clerical Work Measurement

All the techniques of work measurement are available, but it is found in practice that Time Study—the use of the stopwatch—is rarely satisfactory, partly because of the difficulties of rating and partly because of prejudice. Activity-sampling is widely used for departmental studies, whilst there are a wide range of proprietary PMTS available. These include—

Master Clerical Data (M.C.D.)
Clerical Standard Data (C.S.D.)
Universal Office Controls (U.O.C.)
Clerical Milli-Minute Data (Clerical M.M.D.)
Office Staffing Standards (O.S.S.)
Basic Work Data

All these appear to have been developed from MTM

Mulligan Clerical Standards—This is said to be directly derived from micro-motion studies of clerical work.

Usually and desirably associated with the measurement of indirect labour is some form of control system. These systems, like the PMTS above, often have proprietary names, and are often sold as complete packages by consultants. At one time the 'package' implied a particular type of work measurement technique, but most practitioners now use whichever technique is most appropriate. Amongst the best-known names in this field are *Variable Factor Programming* (VFP) and *Group Capacity Assessment* (GCA). Considering GCA as representing this general class of measurement and control system, it proceeds by identifying the various factors in a task, measuring the unit time for a factor and determining the frequency of occurrence. The product of the frequency and the factor time will give the time for the task—

Task: Post 100 stock-control cards

Factor Description	Time (mins.)	Frequency	Product (mins.)
1. Post stock movement to card and calculate balance	0·5	100	50·0
2. Open purchase requisition	0·64	5	3·2
3. Create extra/new card when required	1·4	3	4·2
		Total	57·4

This calculation will be repeated for each task identified.

Allowance must be then made for time not spent on the various tasks but which is necessary to the running of the office—

Time Not Spent on Measured Tasks During Week

			Hours
Miss A	—	filing	2
Miss B	—	restocking stationery	1
Miss C	—	general administration	2
All	—	telephoning	2
		Total	7 = 420 minutes

A count is made of the various tasks undertaken and a calculation can then be made of the output of the office—

Task	Standard time (mins.)	Count	Product
1. Record cards	57·4	80	4,592
2. Audit reports	150·0	6	900
3. Allocations	91·2	4·5	410
		Total	5,802
Plus: Personal allowance 20%			1,160
Time spent on non-factor but necessary work			420
∴ Total output in *Standard Minutes*			7,382

This can then be compared with attendance time and a group efficiency figure calculated—

Hours worked:

Miss A	36
Miss B	36
Miss C	18
Miss D	36

Total   126 hours = 7,560 minutes

$$\therefore Performance\ index = \frac{7,382}{7,560} \times 97\cdot2\%$$

As with any other form of work study, it is essential that the purpose and the methods to be used are fully and clearly explained. *Never carry out a secret work study.*

Further Reading
All the texts recommended for Chapter 14 also provide additional reading for this chapter. The following books deal principally with office procedures.

1. *The Practice of O. & M.*, H.M.S.O., London 1965.
Although compiled by the Management Services Division of the Treasury and therefore reflecting Civil Service practice and attitudes, this is a useful introductory work by some of the pioneers.

2. Milward, G. E. (Ed.) *Organization and Methods—a service to Management*, Macmillan, London 1967.
An excellent British text.

3. O'Shaughnessy, J., *Analysing and Controlling Business Procedures*, Cassell & Co., London 1969.
This book provides a basis upon which to build that experience of office procedures which allows the user to discriminate between the trivial and the essential. Whilst at first glance it may appear to be a conventional text on Work Study, it is soon apparent that all examples and applications are to office procedures.

4. Cemach, H. P., *Work Study in the Office*, Maclaren, London 1969.
A thorough, well-illustrated book for the serious worker.

5. Whitmore, D. A., *Measurement and Control of Indirect Work*, Heinemann, London 1971.
Intended for practitioners of work measurement, office managers and manufacturing and functional heads who wish to extend their activities into the wider realms of non-repetitive work control. Most useful.

Chapter 16
The Work Place

The effectiveness with which work is carried out is conditioned not only by *method* but also by *environment*. Indeed, it is artificial to separate these factors since they are clearly interdependent, and the only justification which can be offered here is that of practical convenience. A further simplification will also be introduced, namely that of considering only the *physical* environment and ignoring the more subtle and probably more important psychological aspects of work.

The study of man in his working situation is known in the U.K. as *ergonomics*, from the Greek word for work, or, in the U.S.A. as *human engineering*. Whilst the intuitive use of ergonomic concepts is not new, the codification and classification of knowledge received a very considerable impetus from the demands of the armed forces during World War II. Regrettably, however, much of the material currently available is either not used or ignored by the designers of machines and equipment, so that it is still not uncommon to find controls so placed that they cannot be conveniently operated, or adjustments which can only be carried out by three-armed midgets.

Man and his dimensions

It is a matter of common observation that man, like all other products of man, is variable. As a consequence, equipment for general use should either be capable of simple and rapid adjustment (for example, the typist's chair) or it should be so designed that it will cater for the majority of persons likely to use it (for example, the access door to a workroom). To be able to ensure that one or other of these conditions be met, it is necessary to know something of the significant dimensions of the human body and how they vary across the population being examined.

There are numbers of anthropometric tables available, some of which can be found in the texts listed in 'Further Reading' and whilst useful they must be treated with care as the information set out in them may depend upon many factors including sex, geographical origin, age, occupation. Thus, the figures obtained from a study of—say—recruits to the City of London Police Force are not likely to be of immediate application when designing equipment for—say—the use of drivers of the Paris Metro.

If a table of dimensions is available from a population which differs from that which is required, then all dimensions can be multiplied by the ratio of the mean height of the initial population to that of the required population. Possibly more useful than the sample tables of human dimensions are the recommendations for equipment dimensions published by the British Standards Institution.

Man at the Workplace

Without suggesting that the psychological circumstances of work are not of very great importance, man can also be regarded as a machine with well known physical requirements. These requirements are frequently ignored, and the ability of man to function in unsuitable situations is quite remarkable. However, to ignore them will inevitably result in stress and discomfort, and therefore any such action should be *as a result of a positive decision* and not as a result of apathy or drift.

Man's physical requirements at the work place have been, and are still, the subject of considerable research. The results of this research and much experience are here summarized:

1. *Sit rather than stand.* Unless there is some overwhelming reason work should be carried out seated. Even when work demands that the operator stands then a comfortable seat should be provided for use whenever the work-cycle permits.

2. *Permit a change in position.* The workplace should not be so designed that the working posture cannot be changed. A fixed position is invariably tiring, and should be avoided.

3. *Aim for a natural working position.* Any working position which involves an unnatural posture—a twisted trunk, or an extended arm position for example—will create undue fatigue.

4. *Keep movements symmetrical.* Balanced movements are not only less tiring they are also more easily controlled.

5. *Ensure adequate working space.* A confined space is not only psychologically distressing, it may increase physical fatigue by causing muscles to be tensed in an effort to avoid the constrictions.

6. *Ensure working area is at a comfortable height.* The correct height of a working area will depend on the nature of the work, fine work—for example, watch assembly—needing to be nearer to the eye than coarse work—for example, ironing in a laundry. Since the possible occupants of a working area differ in size, adjustable heights and distances are desirable.

7. *Use mechanical devices to hold work.* The use of the hands to hold work is generally unnecessary and always tiring. Jigs and/or fixtures can usually be designed to remove the need for the hands to act as clamps.

8. *Support arms.* Support can often be usefully provided for elbows, forearms and hands. These should be upholstered, adjustable, generous in size and robust.

9. *Support feet*. Feet should, if possible, be placed firmly and comfortably upon the floor. If this is not possible, a robust footrest should be provided. A single bar, or an up-turned transit box is generally not satisfactory.

1. Sit rather than stand
2. Permit a change in posture
3. Aim for a natural working position
4. Keep movements symmetrical
5. Ensure adequate working space
6. Ensure comfortable working height
7. Use mechanical devices to hold work
8. Support arms
9. Support feet

Man as a Machine

Man and the Machine

Man is essentially a tool-using animal, and the earliest tools, often extensions of their users, were built for an individual's personal use and modified to have the correct 'heft' and 'feel'. Today, tools tend to be much more complex, and the working power provided from sources outside the user. This results in a loss of direct contact between the operator and the work-piece, so that he will need to receive information concerning the work, and transform this into action by operating some form of control. Care must be thus taken to ensure that the operation of the machine does not become so complex that it is an end in itself and either the work or the operator suffers.

Information

All information provided should be *pertinent, adequate, timely* and *accurate*. (See Chapter 12 for a discussion of the presentation of information in Budgetary Control Statements.) Broadly there are three ways of presenting information—by sound, by vision and by touch.

Sound

Sound signals are extremely useful for alarm and warning purposes, and are most effective if used intermittently. Continuous sound signals—for example, those sometimes used in tuning radio equipment—can become tiring and ineffective, and are best replaced if at all possible by visual displays. One advantage of the audible signal is that it can force itself upon the operator's attention, so that a worker engaged upon a task can readily have his attention drawn to a breakdown or malfunction.

Sight

Measurements, except in very special circumstances, are usually displayed visually. Such displays may be *continuous*, where a pointer moves over a scale, or *digital*, where a set of digits is displayed. Where rates of change need to be observed, the continuous display is most useful, particularly where a moveable pointer traverses a fixed scale: for absolute readings digital displays are to be preferred. In addition, warnings may be given by flashing lights or 'blinking' shutters, although these require that the operator's attention be directed to the warning device as they do not 'command' in the same way as sound signals.

Controls

Controls operate by touch, and serve both to communicate information and to operate the machine. The suitability of various controls for different purposes is shown in Fig. 16.1, taken with permission from the D.S.I.R. publication *Men, Machines and Controls*, by K. A. Provins.

Layout of Displays and Controls

If poorly used, a display or control can lose much of its effectiveness. Whilst man is extremely adaptable and capable of considerable accommodation, it is wasteful to require him to stretch, bend or otherwise contort himself if this can be avoided by sensible layout of the control and display devices. The 'Cranfield Man' was 'created' to use the controls of a lathe in current use—he was required to be $4\frac{1}{2}$ feet tall, 2 feet across the shoulders and have an 8 feet arm span! Regrettably, he is still not yet 'dead'.

Controls should be located so that they are easily handled by the operator. When it is necessary to mount a large number of controls, then locate the 'fine' controls as near to the operator as possible and the 'coarse' controls farther away. Try to 'fit' the control devices to the scale of the work—a delicate knob for light work, a more robust one for heavier work.

Displays should, if possible, be located near, or in relation to, its control device. Where a number of displays are required try to:

(*a*) group them according to purpose,
(*b*) differentiate them by colour and/or position.

Wherever possible, try to standardize upon the direction of travel of pointers or scales, and try to align the 'key' points of the display so that they are all in the same direction. Thus if a battery of dials is used in the control of a process, reading is simplified if the 'normal' position of all dials is at 12.00 o'clock.

In the final analysis a good design is one which 'feels' right, where the hands of the operator fall naturally upon the controls and his eyes fall easily upon the displays. Such an integration is neither easily described, nor easily achieved, and however much care is taken in the design stage, testing *by operators of skills comparable to those for whom the machine is designed* is most desirable.

TYPE OF CONTROL	Suitability for tasks involving:				
	Speed	Accuracy	Force	Range	Loads
Cranks Small	Good	Poor	Unsuitable	Good	Up to 40 in/lb
Large	Poor	Unsuitable	Good	Good	Over 40 in/lb
Handwheels	Poor	Good	Fair/poor	Fair	Up to 150 in/lb
Knobs	Unsuitable	Fair	Unsuitable	Fair	Up to 15 in/lb
Levers Horizontal	Good	Poor	Poor	Poor	Up to 25 lb*
Vertical (to–from body)	Good	Fair	*Short*: Poor / *Long*: Good	Poor	Up to 30 lb*
Vertical (across body)	Fair	Fair	Fair	Unsuitable	{ one hand up to 20 lb* / two hands up to 30 lb* }

 Joysticks	Good	Fair	Poor	Poor	5–20 lb
 Pedals	Good	Poor	Good	Unsuitable	(30–200 lb depends on leg flexion and body support) (ankle only up to 20 lb)
 Push buttons	Good	Unsuitable	Unsuitable	Unsuitable	2 lb
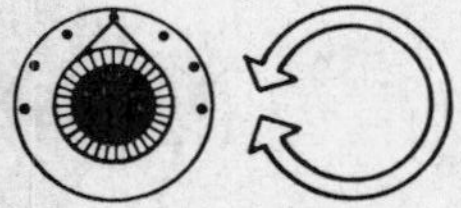 Rotary selector switch	Good	Good	Unsuitable	Unsuitable	Up to 10 in/lb
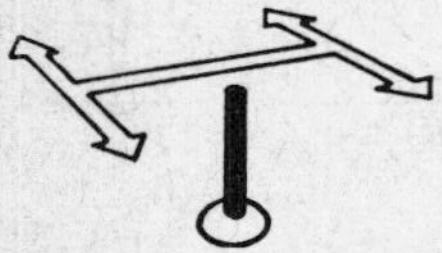 Joystick selector switch	Good	Good	Poor	Unsuitable	Up to 30 lb

* When operated by a standing operator depends on body weight.
(Based on Table 4 in British Productivity Council Seminar on *Ergonomics Fitting the Job to the Worker* by K. F. H. Murrell 1960.)

Fig. 16.1 *Suitability of various controls for different purposes*

Man and the working environment

1. *Lighting*

Good lighting is important: it assists in the efficient performance of work, it allows people to move easily *and safely*, and it creates and displays the character of the item being illuminated. Present illumination technology permits virtually any type of light to be provided, no matter how intense or how constituted. Broadly the visual efficiency with which a task can be carried out increases with the illumination provided in the way shown in Fig. 16.2. whilst the likely cost to provide that illumination

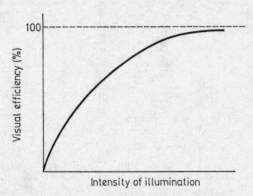

Fig. 16.2

varies with intensity as in Fig. 16.3. (Note: compare these diagrams with those shown on pp. 52–3 relating the cost of achieving precision to process capability.) Clearly the aim must be to choose an illumination level which will produce an acceptable visual efficiency and the definition of ' . . . acceptable efficiency' will vary from place to place, ' . . . reflecting differences in prosperity, standards of living and the whole national climate'

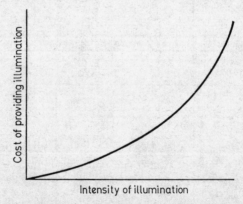

Fig. 16.3

(*Interior Lighting Design Handbook*, published by the I.E.S.). The current British I.E.S. code (see Table 16.1) is based on the belief that ' . . . a visual efficiency of at least 90 per cent in poor conditions of contrast' is 'always justified economically'. The corresponding American code is based upon a much higher requirement for visual efficiency (99 per cent) and Larson (see Further Reading) discusses the validity of these choices and gives tables comparing recommended intensities in a number of countries.

Table 16.1. Recommended minimum service values of illumination for different classes of visual task.

Class of visual task	Examples	Minimum service value of illumination (lux)*
Casual seeing	Locker rooms	100
Rough tasks with large detail	Heavy machinery assembly; stores	200
Ordinary tasks with medium size detail	Wood machining; general offices; general assembly	400
Fairly severe tasks with small detail	Food can inspection; clothing, cutting and sewing; business machines; drawing offices	600
Severe prolonged tasks with small detail	Fine assembly and machining; hand tailoring; weaving silk or synthetic fibres	900
Very severe prolonged tasks with very small detail	Hosiery mending; gauging very small parts; gem cutting	1,300–2,000
Exceptionally severe tasks with minute detail	Watchmaking; inspection of very small instruments	2,000–3,000

(I.E.S. Code, 1968)

*Note: the lux is a measure of the intensity of light. 10 lux are approximately equal to 1 foot-candle, or more precisely 1 lux = 1 lumen/sq. metre. The output from a 100 watt filament lamp is (again approximately) 1,200 lumens, so that if 25 per cent of the light from a 100 watt filament lamp falls upon a bench measuring 2 metres × 1 metre, the average illumination on the bench is $\frac{0.25 \times 1,200}{2 \times 1}$ lux = 150 lux. In practice the light intensity can be directly measured by means of an appropriately calibrated photometer which is readily obtainable commercially.

Glare and Contrast

The overall effectiveness of a lighting system will depend not only on its intensity, but also upon the *glare* and *contrast* generated. Glare is said to occur when the intensity of light is such that it does not contribute to useful seeing, and may arise either *directly*, when it is caused by the

181

primary light source or *indirectly* when it is generated by reflections from surfaces of some sort. Thus, an observer looking directly into the sun suffers from *direct glare* whilst if he is troubled by reflections from a surface he suffers from *indirect glare*. It is desirable always to reduce glare, although this is frequently not possible particularly if the primary designer does not recognize the dangers of indirect glare, and it is not at all uncommon to find multiple reflecting paths giving rise to glare.

Contrast exists when *differences* in brightness exist, and frequently the existence of adequate contrast can enormously improve the modelling of the task being illuminated. Furthermore, a contrast between the task and the general areas can be psychologically very satisfying: the apparently 'simple' solution to the lighting problem of illuminating all areas to a uniformly high level tends to produce a deadly uniformity and mindlessness which is depressing and unnecessarily costly.

Climate

The 'climate' of work, as used here, is affected by—

(i)   air temperature;
(ii) air movement;
(iii) air pollution;
(iv) relative humidity of air.

General recommendations for levels of the above factors are clearly impossible since the type of work being carried out will affect the requirements. Thus, a skilled instrument maker, whose work involves little physical effort, considerable precision and much concentration will demand a higher air temperature than the operator of a heavy press. He will tolerate very little air movement, whilst a very active operator will need some movement to help him cool himself. He will be very sensitive to air pollution—smells—and he will wish to avoid too high a humidity.

The measurement of 'comfort' levels for climatic factors is difficult and different authorities recommend different values. In a paper 'An Approach to Environmental Engineering' (*I.E.E. Journal*, May 1972, pp. 167–170) Platts suggests that:

'For comfort, the air temperature should be about $21°C \pm 1°C$. The mean radiant temperature should not be more than $5°C$ below the room-air temperature . . . The range (of moisture content) for comfort is quite variable around a relative humidity of about 35–55 per cent . . .'

It must be remembered that the climatic factors are invariably better and more cheaply dealt with at the initial design stage of the building, therefore any special requirements concerning climate should be made known to the designing architect. As the use of any building is likely to change throughout its life provision should be made for the modification and control of environment factors.

Fortunately, the human body has a high adaptation to climatic conditions, and frequently all that is required is to provide adequate means of heating. If more comprehensive control is needed it is possible to provide it by means of complete air conditioning plants.

Noise

Noise, which is best described as any unwanted sound, will not merely cause annoyance, it may also affect efficiency by inducing stress and may mask communications. The Department of Employment in the U.K. has been considerably concerned with the problems generated by noise and has recently published a very thorough *Code of Practice for Reducing the Exposure of Employed Persons to Noise*. This document is so thorough that it would be presumptuous to try to improve upon the recommendations set out therein and all managers should make reference to it since it contains much sensible advice.

Broadly, it suggests that noise should first of all be reduced wherever possible and recommendations for doing this are given; and thereafter, where it is not possible to reduce noise then ear protectors should be worn.

It is worth noting that too little noise can be almost as great a problem as excessive noise. The author recalls that when engaged upon the design of acoustic devices, he found that working in an acoustically 'dead' room produced feelings of fear which were extraordinarily distressing, and which must have affected his work adversely.

Further Reading

1. Kellerman, F., van Wely, P., Willens, P., *Vademecum—Ergonomics in Industry*, Philips Technical Library, published in the U.K. by the Cleaver-Hume Press, London 1963.
A terse, well-written, 'cook-book' of good ergonomic practice. Presents recommendations rather than discussions.

2. Lighting Industry Federation Ltd, *Interior Lighting Design Handbook*, 1973.
An extremely valuable discussion of the principles and practice of good interior lighting.

3. Larson, L., *Lighting and its Design*, Whitney Library of Design, New York 1964.
This beautifully produced book questions some of the presuppositions of the U.S. illuminating engineers, and examines the aesthetic and design problems and looks at the points of view of the opthalmologist, the psychologist and the psychiatrist. It is very copiously illustrated with many marvellous photographs.

4. BS 3044, 1958, *Anatomical, physiological and anthropometric principles in the design of office chairs and tables*, British Standards Institution.

5. BS 3079, 1959, *Anthropometric recommendations for dimensions of non-adjustable office chairs, desks and tables*, British Standards Institution.

6. BS 3404, 1961, *Anthropometric recommendations for dimensions of office machine operator's chairs and desks*, British Standards Institution.

7. BS 3893, 1965 *Specification for office desks, tables and seating*, British Standards Institution.

The above codes and specifications crystallize the best U.K. thinking on some aspects of man in his working environment.

8. Whitfield, D., 'British Standards and Ergonomics', *Applied Ergonomics*, 1971, Vol. 2 No. 4.

9. Illuminating Engineering Society of Great Britain, *Code of Recommendations for Lighting Building Interiors*, I.E.S. Code, 1968.

Chapter 17
Materials Handling

The movement of material from one place to another is found within every organization, and its study—Materials Handling—is sometimes considered to be a separate discipline. It is, in fact, one aspect of work study, and any materials handling problem must be solved by normal work study techniques. The purpose of this chapter is to introduce some of the specialist equipment available for materials handling.

The costs of materials handling are often difficult to identify: however, it seems likely that in many factories, *at least* one-quarter of the final cost is attributable to the handling of the material. It is suggested that every factory manager should cause an investigation to be carried out on the handling costs within his factory. The results would certainly be illuminating and probably alarming. It is frequently found that improvements in materials handling provide the quickest and cheapest ways of improving productivity.

Unlike many other operations studied in a factory, the movement of materials adds to the cost of the product whilst leaving its value unchanged. It is therefore important first to *reduce the need* for the handling, and second to *reduce the cost* for that handling which is inevitable. Any materials-handling problem must thus start with the layout of the factory or department (the criterion of minimum distance 'all movements will be both necessary and direct' must be applied), and with the design of the product which should be such that, during the various stages of manufacture, no unnecessary material is transported. This latter aspect coincides with the view that the most economical design is that which requires least material to be removed. It is often said that the best materials handling is no materials handling.

Accepting that there is an inescapable need for some handling, attention should be given to—

(*a*) *Correct identification of material.* The cost and frustration of trying to identify anonymous material is high.

(*b*) *Correct packing of material.* Easily damaged material requires careful handling and this in itself is costly.

(*c*) *Capacity of equipment.* To try to economize by purchasing light or near-capacity equipment is frequently a false economy since it may result in multiple loads being required, rather than single loads.

(*d*) *Size of load.* Always move the largest possible loads, again to avoid multiple handling.

(*e*) *Weight of container.* The heavier the load, the more difficult it is to move. Effort should be expended in moving the material, rather than the container—hence, use the lightest possible container.

---

1. Identification of material
2. Method of packing
3. Capacity of equipment
4. Size of load
5. Weight of container

Check-list when Handling Material

The reduction of cost of residual movement can be considered under the following five headings.

Use of Manpower

The use of manpower for moving material is so flexible that it tends to be used extravagantly. The following rules apply—

1. Do not use productive workers for moving material: use labourers.

2. Do not move in small quantities: the use of a full wheel-barrow or sack-truck is easier and cheaper than the movement of single items.

3. Do not require loads to be manually raised above shoulder height or set upon the floor. Keep the loads at working height.

Use of Gravity Conveyors

Gravity is always present, and can provide a cheap and reliable source of motive power. Slides, chutes, roller conveyors and ball tables all will assist in the easy movement of material, and roller conveyors can be assembled in very many ways, incorporating junctions, branches, gates and traps of all sorts. A large bottling plant will usually provide an ex-hilarating view of the adaptability of the roller conveyors. By mounting lengths of roller conveyor on wheeled frameworks, portable unloading conveyors can be made, and these are much used in industries such as the building industry, where loads have to be deposited at widely different points which vary from day to day.

When considering the use of gravity conveyors, the following points should be noted—

1. The gradient required is often less than imagined. For a roller-type conveyor a drop of $\frac{1}{2}''$ in a foot is usually adequate, whilst a polished metal

chute may need 4" drop in the same distance, although this will very much depend on the state of the two surfaces in contact.

2. If physical circumstances prevent an adequate drop being obtained, it is sometimes possible to insert a short length—a hump—of powered conveyor to give the load an initial 'push'. Alternatively, the load can be raised mechanically to a level from which the required drop can be obtained.

3. The load bearing capacity must be adequate. Roller conveyors are obtainable in a range of loadings, and the pitch of the rollers should be such that there are always at least three rollers in contact with the load. It is often desirable to strengthen loading and unloading areas and curves.

4. When using roller conveyors, the base of the load should be firm and —preferably—flat. This may necessitate the provision of subsidiary trays or tote boxes, and the expense of these must be considered in the costing of the conveyor system.

5. Where cylindrical loads are to be moved concave shaped rollers can be useful.

Use of Power Conveyors

Gravity conveyors are limited in that they will work only on a downward incline and they are not suitable for moving certain types of goods—for example, powders and liquids—without subsidiary containers. For any movements on the level or uphill, therefore, powered conveyors are necessary. The addition of power often permits operations to be carried out by the conveyor system itself, and many multi-stage plants are machines linked by conveyors or conveyors with machines added to them. The power is not only available to carry out the work; it can also control the flow and precise timing of movements is possible. An ingenious use of a powered conveyor for this purpose is found in some clock manufacturing, where an endless conveyor is driven at a constant speed around a factory, the total transit time being 24 hours. Clocks are loaded on to the conveyor at one point, being wound and set to a master clock at that point, so that when they return to that point the accuracy of the clock can be very simply checked. Again, short lengths of power conveyor can be made self-contained and portable, enabling rapid and/or temporary changes of location to be made.

In some cases, it is possible to use the conveyor itself to carry out part of the production process. For example, the author once needed to varnish some waxed components. The component was such that it could not be force-dried—a gentle current of air was all that could be used. The varnishing took place at the loading point of a conveyor which then rose, in an inverted V, into the roof of the workshop and descended to a discharge point, only about 4 feet from the loading point. The journey was sufficient to dry the component, and little floor space was used in the drying process.

There are a number of types of powered conveyor, namely—

1. *Powered—or Live—Roller Conveyors*—these consist of a set of rollers to which some driving mechanism has been added giving conveyer speeds

of up to 60 feet a minute. One way of doing this is by a drive belt below the carrier rollers, a set of pressure rollers beneath this belt ensuring contact between drive and driven. In one ingenious design these pressure rollers are cam-shaped, having a 'flat' along part of their cylindrical surface. 'Sensing' rollers spaced along the conveyor indicate when loads are near each other and the appropriate pressure rollers are turned, flat side upwards, thus removing drive from a section of the conveyor. This prevents collisions between delicate loads, and also allows work to 'bunch' or 'accumulate' in the dead section of the conveyor. The absence of motive force in this section ensures that the accumulated work is not crushed together.

2. *Belt Conveyors*—these can be of wire mesh, chain-and-slat, or belting. Wire mesh conveyors are used widely in industries where washing or spraying is carried out, and there is a need to heat and cool products, since the conveyor itself can be heat resisting. Examples will be found in food preparation, annealing (glass and steel) and paint stoving. A chain-and-slat conveyor is useful for the movement of heavy loads, particularly since the traction provided by the chain(s) and driving wheels is positive and free from slip, although this can be a disadvantage if materials jam, when crushing and damage can take place. Flat belt conveyors are simple, relatively cheap and easy to maintain, and suitable for the movement of small parts. For the movement of granular or powdered materials a 'dished' or 'troughed' belt can be used, which will give a substantial increase in carrying capacity compared with a flat belt. All types are used during assembly work, where operators sit on one or both sides of the conveyor and carry out work on items placed thereon. Control of operation speeds is thus possible, and the use of the conveyor in this way will require careful balancing of operations.

In general, belt conveyors are used for transport in the horizontal plant: slight inclines can be achieved depending upon the friction between the belt and the load. It is impossible to make any sort of recommendations as to the degree of lift achievable with a belt conveyor, since considerable effort is continually being carried out to increase the angle of lift and at least one company has produced a conveyor running over a magnetized bed, allowing ferrous components to be raised up inclines of up to 72 degrees above the horizontal. When loads have to be raised beyond the normal angle of lift, trays, pans or flight bars can be fitted to the belt, and the conveyor then effectively becomes an elevator. The trays or pans can also be used as a means of delivering measured quantities of material, either horizontally or inclined.

3. *Suspension Conveyors*—these run above normal head height and carry arms, pans or containers for the movement of goods, and are mono-rail devices. They are particularly useful in that they make use of 'free' space, and can be used as travelling stores. A very wide field of application is in the finishing industry, where a suspension conveyor, with suitable rises and falls, can carry goods from one finishing tank to another, resting in each for a predetermined time. Care must be taken, in designing suspension conveyor systems, to ensure that there is clearance between the top of the load

in the pan and the bottom of the conveyor system *particularly when the conveyor rises or falls.*

A first cousin to the above type of conveyor is the drag-chain conveyor which is sometimes used in warehouses for moving floor trucks, the truck being 'hitched' to a suspended chain.

4. *Spiral Conveyors*—these are probably the earliest of all powered conveyors, being often known as Archimedean spirals. Basically they consist of a ribbon-bladed screw rotating either in a cylinder (for vertical movement) or in a trough (for horizontal movement). Since they can be completely enclosed, they are widely used in the food industry, where they can be kept very clean. One factory actually uses an air-tight spiral conveyor for the pre-cooking of food, heat being applied by steam passing through the screw itself. Substantial volumes of finely divided material can be moved by means of a screw, and in one installation grain is lifted at the rate of 35 tons an hour.

A type of spiral conveyor known as the 'Spiraveyor' dispenses with the outside cylinder or trough, replacing it by a second screw being parallel to, but apart from the first screw, the two screws acting in opposition. Bagged or sacked material can be conveyed at speed (up 90 feet a minute) with this useful device.

5. *Tubes.* These are often used for conveying articles placed in containers which fit snugly into the tube. Message-carrying tubes are well known for this purpose and are often used in factories and shops to pass information to and from central locations, although tubes using containers with code-rings are now available, permitting the free dispersal of containers between a number of different points all located in a pneumatic 'ring'. A different method of use of pneumatic tubes is in the bulk conveyance of granular substances—grains, fine powders and similar articles. Effectively a current of air is caused to flow along the tube of such a velocity that the articles to be transported 'float' along. Air velocities up to 2,500 feet a minute are sometimes used and movements of up to 20 tons an hour are not unusual.

The choice of air velocity is quite critical: too high, and the transported material scours the tube, causing wear particularly at bends; too low and the material falls and may build up, blocking the tube. Material which is lumpy, or likely to coagulate is not transported very satisfactorily by air.

An associated method of movement is the hydraulic conveyor, where liquid replaces the air in the pneumatic tube. This is often very useful in the movement of materials which are too large or too heavy for pneumatic conveyance, for example coal, grit and sand. The movements of liquids along tubes is, of course, as old as plumbing. It is interesting to note, however, that deliveries of *different* liquids (for example, different fractions of oil) can be made down one tube by using a plastic 'separator' between the end of one liquid and the beginning of the next. The movement in tubes of liquid metals (for example, sodium) has been highly developed in the nuclear engineering field. An alternative method of tube conveying is by means of alternately compressing and releasing a flexible tube, generating a movement much in the way that peristaltic action moves food in the human digestive tract. Tube transmission has the advantage of security— it is difficult for goods in transit to be lost from a tube.

6. *Lifts.* These may be of many types, from large, closed door goods-lifts to continuous moving 'Paternoster' lifts. All are of fixed location and their positions are determined at the layout of the plant. Essentially they are vertical conveyors, usually working between various floor levels.

Use of Package Loads

Conveyors in general can be used for the continuous movement of goods, and the conveyor itself can be allowed to run whether it is carrying material or not. An alternative method of moving material is by means of devices which convey discrete loads. These have been widely developed and are particularly useful in the storage of material rather than in the processing of material. They include—

1. *Hoists and Cranes.* These are flexible in use, cranes in particular being capable of being moved. Most hoists can run along a fixed line, and the electrically powered block and tackle which can be operated by a hand-held switch is extremely useful in stores, and receiving and dispatch departments, where it can be used to load and unload lorries, large versions being capable of moving up to 20 tons weight. There are often statutory requirements concerning the maintenance, overhaul and inspection 'by an approved person' of hoists and cranes.

2. *Trucks.* These may be either physically or mechanically propelled, and consist of a platform upon which loads of any shape and size may be placed for onward transmission. Since the platform is fixed, loading and unloading must be performed by hand—when weight becomes significant— or by crane or hoist—where availability of loading equipment is important. This can result in a poor utilization of truck and driver.

3. *Lifting Trucks.* These are rapidly replacing ordinary fixed-bed trucks. They are either hand or power propelled, the most common being driven by battery operation, and their use has revolutionized storage and handling of material.

Most lift trucks are of the so-called 'fork-lift' type: lifting is performed by a pair of projecting arms (the forks) which can rise up a pair of parallel uprights. The method of operation revolves around the use of 'pallets,' which are portable platforms upon which work is loaded. The forks are inserted below the platform of the pallet, then raised to clear the ground, and the truck moved to the new destination of the material. The essential difference between a pallet and a stillage is that pallets are intended to be stacked upon each other, and herein lies the greatest virtue of the fork-lift truck and pallet. The fork-lift can raise pallets, in some cases up to 20 feet, although heights of 8-10 feet are more common at the moment. By storing loaded pallets on top of each other, maximum use can be made of head room, and so the floor area of stores can be reduced to a minimum. Gangways must be adequately large to allow a truck to operate.

Pallets are of two main kinds, the flat pallet without sides, and the box pallet with sides. Each of these can be of many designs, as at the moment there is no standardization of pallet design or size in the U.K., although the B.S.I. has published a booklet—*Pallets for Materials Handling*—making recommendations on dimensions. By co-operation between supplier and receiver, goods can be loaded on to pallets at the supplier's factory, transported to the customer and there off-loaded into the factory or stores, still on the pallets. This can prove very economical in handling time, but the volume occupied by the pallets in transit and the cost of returning the empty pallets may be of importance. In some metal-using industries this is overcome by casting the raw material into pallet rather than ingot form so that the pallet itself is used in final manufacture, whilst in other cases the pallet can be caused to collapse for return.

As well as moving palletized loads, fork-lift trucks can be used for moving articles such as barrels and drums, coils of wire and strip metal. By moving the forks horizontally they can be made to grasp loads, and some forms have hooks whereby suspended loads can be shifted. The lift truck is a very versatile device which can considerably increase the utilization of space and reduce the physical effort involved in moving material. A very wide range of accessories is available.

Use of Motor Transport

Delivery vehicles are used extensively, both within large complexes and for collection and delivery of goods. The cost of such transport is often high, but its magnitude may either be unrecognized or assumed to be too difficult to assess. Many companies arrange contracts with specialist delivery organizations, and this has the twin advantages of relieving management of a task for which they have little or no liking or ability, and of producing a known cost figure.

If a company decides to employ its own motor transport, attention should be given to—

1. *Utilization.* Work study applied to vehicle operation will enable methods to be improved and standard times developed for loading, transit and unloading. From these standards, routes should be developed in advance by the transport manager with a view to reducing total cost. Success here depends on the ability to—
   (a) improve 'turn-round' methods by materials handling studies,
   (b) choose minimum distance/time routes,
   (c) amalgamate loads.

2. *Drivers.* Direct physical supervision of drivers is virtually impossible, and indeed it is this aspect of the job which makes it appealing to many drivers. This is not to suggest that drivers are inferior in behaviour to other employees: however, loss factors which would be seen by internal supervision may escape notice. These include excessive times spent at depots, waiting for work to be loaded/unloaded and queueing times, when

the vehicle with its driver waits to enter the delivery point. Reducing such losses without impairing morale or curtailing initiative requires carefully designed and intelligible control systems based on the standards discussed above.

3. *Vehicle maintenance.* A sound preventive maintenance system is essential and, if the volume justifies, an internal maintenance garage can be set up. Management of an internal vehicle repair workshop presents considerable problems if the supervisor is to avoid diversion of time in the garage on to the overhauling of private cars. To reduce the need for a wide variety of spares, fleet vehicles should all be of the same make. The extent of both standardization and specialization within the automobile industry, together with the wide spread of well equipped service stations suggest that sub-contracted maintenance is likely to be much easier and cheaper than 'domestic' maintenance arrangements.

4. *Design of loading/unloading bays.* Value is received from a van only when it is actually moving material, and not when it is stationary. The layout of the loading/unloading bay and the provision of appropriate cranes, hoists and conveyors can often reduce turn-round time and reduce queueing.

5. *Statutory constraints.* The operation of goods vehicles is subject to many constraints arising from legislation. A change in the maximum permitted weight carried, the maximum permitted length, maximum permitted driving hours or minimum insurance requirements can have substantial effects on total cost.

---

1. Utilization of vehicles
2. Utilization of drivers
3. Vehicle maintenance
4. Loading/unloading facilities
5. Statutory constraints

Check-list for Motor Transport Operation

Further Reading

1. Apple, J. M., *Plant Layout and Materials Handling*, The Ronald Press Company, New York 1963.

Deals with the problems from an engineering standpoint, but avoids too great a study of the technical problems. Contains valuable appendices on the operating details of conveyors, trucks and pallets, and on suggested methods of preparing layouts.

2. Woodley, D. R., *Encyclopaedia of Materials Handling*, Pergamon, Oxford 1964.

Without doubt the most exhaustive work on the subject ever written. Contains everything known on the subject—a series of addenda keeps the matter up-to-date.

Chapter 18
Group Technology

When small batches are produced, three sources of value-less cost are important—
- (a) costs due to difficulties in scheduling,
- (b) set-up costs where preparation for production takes place,
- (c) handling costs, where work is transferred to or from work stations.

It is clear that the unit cost of each of the above increases as the batch size decreases. However, it is often not appreciated how frequently small quantities are, in fact, produced. Representative figures are difficult to obtain but Seizo Nishizaka and Jumio Endo remark that '. . . at present in machining production in U.S.A., lot sizes smaller than 50 pieces occupy 75 per cent of all production', and they go on to say '. . . in the factory we are concerned with . . . the batch size is a maximum of 30 pieces . . .' with '. . . an average batch size of 3–10'. In the U.K., work by G. Baguley, while a final-year student at Loughborough University, within his sponsoring company showed that on one type of machine 80 per cent of the set-ups were for batches of less than 30 parts.

The effects of these large numbers of small batches may be seen by any observer who cares to carry out an activity sampling exercise within a machine shop. Such an exercise was carried out by the Machine Tool Industry Research Association in 'four selected shops', with the following result—

Activity	Percentage of Machine Time Available		
	Centre Lathes	Turret Lathes	Capstan Lathes
Loading and unloading	7·4	7·3	7·7
Idle, loaded, operator absent	17·9	16·0	16·7
Idle, loaded, operator under instruction	2·1	1·2	1·3
Miscellaneous	0·3	1·1	1·2
Setting and handling	25·4	27·8	32·0
Gauging	6·0	4·2	3·6
Cutting	40·9	42·4	37·5
Totals	100·0	100·0	100·0
Proportion of time employed	76·8	82·9	79·8

(*Machinery and Production Engineering*, February 9, 1966)

Note: the difference between the totals of 100 per cent and the 'proportion of time employed represents . . . the time that the machines were out of use due to breakdowns, lack of operators and similar causes'.

Thus, of the total time the machines were nominally available, metal was actually being cut for only about 40 per cent of the time, whilst for over 25 per cent of the time 'setting and handling' was carried out.

The student survey previously referred to obtained similar results in a rather different way. The process layouts for six months for all jobs of 15 components or less for three types of component were surveyed and the standard times both for 'set-up' and for machining were calculated with the following results—

Family	Total Machining Time (Hours)	Total Set-up Time (Hours)
A	402	479
B	460	473
C	541	398
Totals	1,403	1,350

The effect of these observations is to illustrate that, at least in jobbing machine-shops, the time spent on setting up is comparable with the time spent on cutting metal. In general the technology of metal cutting is well known and high: substantial increases in productivity are therefore likely to derive from other causes—for example, better scheduling and lower set-up times, and it is with these areas that Group Technology is concerned.

AN HISTORICAL NOTE

Possibly the earliest discussion of a form of G.T. was at a National Engineers Conference in the U.S.S.R. in 1938 when Sokolovsky presented a paper on 'Standardization of Technological Processes'. Korling, of Scania Vabis, Sweden, was discussing group machining in the late 1940s, and at a Stockholm conference in 1947 C. B. Nathhorst described the basic principles of Group Production.

The major publication on this subject was in 1956 by S. P. Mitrofanov who produced *Scientific Principles of Group Technology*, which included the first discussion of the composite component. In 1962, P. A. Sidders in *Machinery* described work done at Forges et Ateliers de Construction Electriques de Jeumont. This work was largely carried out by the Brisch organization and its French Associates C.O.P.I.C., and it released in the U.K. a flood of articles by members of the Brisch company.

Complementary work on the utilization of plant, and upon work-piece statistics was carried on at Aachen and in 1962 Opitz published his 'Principles of Coding and Definitions for a system of Classification to Describe Work-pieces', and subsequently a number of conferences on G.T. were held in both East and West Germany.

Undoubtedly, the leaders in the use of G.T. are to be found in the

U.S.S.R.—at a recent conference, one Russian speaker mentioned that there were 800 G.T. applications in the U.S.S.R. It is difficult to discover how many users there are today in the U.K., but it is probably less than 50. Hardly any reference to its use in the U.S.A. has been found in the literature. At the First International Seminar on Group Technology, Professor V. B. Solaja of Belgrade is reported by Drurie as saying—

'Group Technology is the realization that many problems are similar and that by grouping similar problems, a single solution can be found to a set of problems, thus saving time and effort.'

In essence, Group Technology seeks first for similarities, not differences. Similar parts are then collected into 'families', and these families manufactured on groups of associated machines. A typical family is shown in Fig. 18.1.

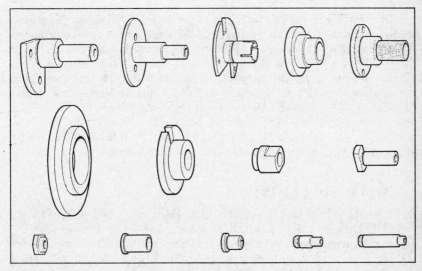

Fig. 18.1

Once a family has been identified, a *composite component* may be envisaged, such a component being one which contains all the features of all members of the family—see Fig. 18.2. Although this component may have neither physical form nor physical expression, the concept itself is

Fig. 18.2. The Composite Component Derived from the Family.

found to be an extremely useful one in later work. The available machines are then surveyed to find which group of machines can best be put together to produce the composite component, and this group of machines then physically moved together to form a 'cell' or 'group'. The group is set up to make the composite component, and the actual parts then produced by leaving out those operations not appropriate to the particular part being made. The effect of this grouping is to reduce total set-up time, and Drurie records[1] that at Ferranti Ltd. in Edinburgh, after having completed a first run on a family of components ' . . . a detailed analysis on 55 of the jobs picked at random' gave the following results—

	Setting time taken:
Conventional	219 hr. 52 min.
G.T.	73 hr. 16 min.
Saving:	146 hr. 36 min.

. . . Our previous ratio of machining to setting was 60:40, so this gained us 36·6 per cent in machining time, i.e., the three first operation machines were producing the output of four conventional machines . . . ' The Central Machine Tool Institute, Bangalore, reported (*Machinery and Production Engineering*, September 6, 1967) ' . . . overall setting times have been reduced from 225 to 50 min. with respect to four different work pieces'. Hopkinsons Ltd claimed (*Metalworking Production*, March 1, 1967) ' . . . set-up times slashed by 50–70 per cent'; Metal Box at Perivale stated (*Metalworking Production*, June 25, 1969): ' . . . the system is found to cut setting times over a period by up to 50 per cent . . . '; and so on.

FAMILIES OF PARTS

From what has been said it is clear that the key to using Group Technology successfully is the ability to identify readily items within the same family. In an extremely small organization it is possible that this may be done 'by eye', but this is both haphazard and difficult, and it is desirable that a more systematic technique should be used. A 'coding' or 'classification' system for this task is indicated, the purpose of such a system being to group items together according to their common features (' . . . to seek for similarities'). The characteristics of a satisfactory coding system have been discussed in Chapter 6. Many systems have been—and will continue to be—invented, fulfilling some or all of the desirable characteristics. A study of current G.T. literature reveals that four systems have been extensively used—

(*a*) the Brisch system (U.K.)
(*b*) the Mitrofanov system (U.S.S.R.)
(*c*) the Opitz system (W. Germany)
(*d*) the Vuoso system (Czechoslovakia).

[1] Drurie, F.R.E., *The Production Engineer*, February 1970.

The Brisch system

When applied to G.T. this requires an eight-digit primary code or mono-code which effectively sets down the design characteristics of the part, followed by a secondary code, or polycode, identifying the manufacturing characteristics. Usually the first digit of the primary code is derived from the series—

0 — Organization and operations
1 — Primary materials
2 — Bought-out commodities
3 — Components
4 — Sub-assemblies and products
5 — Tools and portable equipment
6 — Plant and machinery
7 — Buildings, services, utilities
8 — Scrap waste
9 — Reserved

All other digits are 'tailor-made' to the client organization. The polycode requires reference to a 'code-book', which again will be 'tailor-made' to the user's need.

The Mitrofanov system

This was created by S. P. Mitrofanov, one of the earliest known workers in G.T., who first conceived the idea of the composite component. It is essentially a production-orientated code of seven digits—

First digit (0–9)	Section:	
Second digit (0–9)	Class:	parts characterized by common function and structural shape.
Third digit (0–9)	Sub-class:	parts characterized by common shapes and similar processing methods.
Fourth digit (0–9)	Group:	characterized by similar shapes and number of manufacturing operations.
Fifth digit (0–9)	Type:	operation type
Sixth, seventh (0–99)	Size	

No reference has been found to the use of this code outside the U.S.S.R. (*Note*: Mitrofanov concentrated his work upon single-machine groups—for example, capstan lathes).

The Opitz system

H. Opitz, working at Aachen University, investigated the requirements of machine tools needed to produce the parts used by industry in W. Germany.

197

In doing so he found a need to devise a coding system to identify components, and it is the development of this system which is the Opitz system. It is applicable only to machine parts, and uses 5 digits to define shape, followed by four 'optional extra' digits specifying size, material, original shape of raw materials and accuracy. The complete code is contained on eight quarto sheets, and it is stated that it can be used with reasonable confidence after several hours' tuition. The code is so comprehensive that it is unlikely that any single organization will ever use more than a small part of the available identifiers, and this may result in an apparent loss of cohesiveness. It is discussed more fully by Haworth, E. A., in *The Production Engineer*, January 1968.

The Vuoso system

This was developed in the Vuoso Research Institute for Machine Tools & Metal Cutting in Czechoslovakia in 1959. It is a simple, four digit code, all details of which are contained on a single sheet of paper. Inevitably it lacks the detail of the Brisch or Opitz systems, but its simplicity is such that it should be carefully considered. Before a component is placed into a family, it is necessary to refer to the appropriate drawing—an unnecessary act with Brisch.

CHOICE OF FAMILY

The composition of the family of parts which are 'housed' in a group is largely determined by the equipment available within the organization—too large a family will require a large number of machines in the machining group: too small a family may result in duplication of plant. Four aspects of the group likely to result from a family should be examined—

1. What load will the family generate?
2. What capacities and capabilities would be needed?
3. Is it possible to set up the group for the family?
4. Are the necessary machines available or obtainable?

It should be noted that—

(*a*) a group may in fact comprise only one machine (for example, a capstan lathe). This was generally the case with the Mitrofanov groupings.

(*b*) it is unlikely that all the machines in a group are equally loaded—some degree of under-utilization is probably inevitable.

Ideally the family should be so chosen that it is economical to set up the group once and then leave it thus set up indefinitely. This is not always practicable, and a group may accommodate two or more related families whose set-ups differ from each other. In these cases it may be considered desirable to code the set-ups themselves, so that the production order not only directs the material to a group, but also indicates which set-up should be used. Note that the group should carry out the *complete* machining of a family in order to achieve the benefits of reduced handling and reduced synchronization loss.

RESULTS OF GROUP TECHNOLOGY

The most exhaustive discussion of a G.T. application in the U.K. is embodied in a N.E.D.O. publication *Production Planning and Control*. This describes work at Serck-Audco, and the benefits claimed are—

Sales	Up 32%
Stocks	Down 44%
Stock/Sales ratio	Down from 52% to 25%
Manufacturing time	Down from 12 to 4 weeks
Overdue orders	Down from 6 weeks to under 1 week
Dispatches/Employee	Up about 50%
Capital investment	Cost recovered 4 times by stock reduction alone.

Since the G.T. (called at Audco 'Cellular Group') programme was carried forward by the personal efforts of the directors of the company it may be felt that these benefits owe something to the personality and leadership exerted by these senior executives; this may, of course, be so. However, there are many very similar claims—for example, a French company stated in *Metalworking Production*, February 12, 1964—

Machine costs declined an average of	15%
Set-up and adjustment time diminished	70%
Machine utilization increased on average by	32%
Scrap fell from 4% to	2%
Through-put time reduced from 5–6 weeks to	2 days
Investment in semi-finished parts down	90%
Transport equipment diminished by	35%

The English Electric Co. at Bradford reported in *Machinery and Production Engineering*, June 1, 1966—

'... Output has increased by at least 75% ... Down time has been reduced to a maximum of 15 min. ... there is a substantial reduction in paperwork. ...'

Nishizako & Endo at the 10th International M.T.D.R. Conference at the University of Manchester, 1969, claimed—

'... Production output increased by 30% ... rejects reduced by 50%.' June 11, 1960.

Similar claims are made in the U.S.S.R. See, for example, Ivanov.

Even were all these claims to be vastly inflated, there is no doubt that remarkable results can be obtained from G.T., *provided* that the initial investment in planning and coding is not foregone. The cost of this work, and the time taken for its execution can be very substantial; but the benefits will be found throughout the company, not only in the manufacturing departments, but also in the service departments.

Summary of Benefits usually claimed for Group Technology

1. Reduced unit set-up time.
2. Improved learning, resulting in lower machining times.
3. Improved labour efficiency resulting from standardization and simplification.
4. Improvement in the effective use of machines.
5. Lower handling times due to reduction in transport distances.
6. Simplification in planning procedures.
7. Need for buffer (inter-stage) storage reduced with consequent reductions in—
    (*a*) stocks
    (*b*) W.-i.-P.
    (*c*) storage space.
8. Through-put times reduced.

Application of G.T. to Non-machining Activities

All the above discussion has been around machining activities. Clearly, G.T. can be used elsewhere: plastic moulds with removable inserts are a form of G.T. The literature describes a number of non-machining applications—see, for example, Ivanov, or an article in *Metalworking Production*, June 11, 1969.

Further Reading
1. Ivanov, E. K., *Group Production Organization and Technology*, Business Publications Ltd., 1968.
An invaluable basic text setting our experience in the U.S.S.R.

2. Edwards, G. A. B., *Readings in Group Technology*, Machinery Publishing Co. Ltd., 1971.
Essential reading for all serious workers in the G.T. field.

3. Gallagher, C. C. and Knight, W. A., *Group Technology*, Butterworths, 1973.
A comprehensive and well referenced text.

4. *GROUP Technology*, British Productivity Council, 1970.
This is one of the last of the excellent sets of seminar papers produced by the now sadly defunct B.P.C.

Chapter 19
Estimating and Planning

Estimating and planning in industrial plants are related activities in that they both deal with the manufacturing methods and costs of a product. However, the purposes to which these activities are directed are quite different and the method of carrying them out may be substantially different, although this is not necessarily so. Basically an *estimate* is produced before there is an authority to manufacture, and a *plan* is produced after.

ESTIMATING

An estimate may be required for any or all of a number of quite separate reasons, namely—

1. *To Assist in the Setting of a Selling Price.* A product having been designed, it is necessary to sell it; or alternatively, a potential customer requires to know what a company would charge to manufacture a product to his specification. In either case an estimate of the probable cost of manufacture and/or design is required in order to form a basis for a selling price. Whilst the actual selling price is a matter of policy, that policy cannot be determined with any realism unless an estimate has been first made.

2. *To Assist in Making Policy Decisions.* Many policy decisions—for example, what new plant should be purchased, or whether the manufacture of a new product can be entertained—require estimates to be made.

3. *To Assist in the Setting of a Target Purchase Price.* It is not necessarily true that the lowest purchase price is that which is least costly to a company. If the vendor underestimates his own costs and so quotes a price which it is uneconomical for him to meet, then his deliveries and service are likely to suffer, and at worst he will go out of business, causing trouble and expense for the purchaser. To avoid accepting such a price the buyer will find it useful to have a *target purchase price* against which he can match incoming tenders. The provision of such a target purchase price may be usefully carried out by the estimating department, although some companies have special 'purchase price analysis' departments.

4. *To Provide a Basis for Control Activities.* Whenever a new product is incorporated in a production programme, an estimate will be required (*a*) to assist in forward loading a shop or department (that is, by production control), and (*b*) as a criterion against which actual costs can be measured (that is, by cost control). This estimate may well be rapidly superseded by a definite production plan once design and volume are crystallized, but in the early stages this may not be practicable.

Types of Estimate

Estimates will cover three main areas: (*a*) design and development; (*b*) manufacture and construction; (*c*) installation and maintenance, although this is not a factory activity and will not be discussed. All require experience within the organization concerned, since in any but the simplest tasks it is extremely difficult to translate performance in one organization into performance in another.

Estimating for Design

It is often held, particularly by designers, that since designing is a creative activity it cannot be shackled by the chains of an estimate, and that 'nobody knows how long it takes to think of an idea'. Nevertheless, before embarking on a new design project it is vital to know what expenditure will be incurred and over what period. This is inherently a difficult and inaccurate task, particularly since no design can ever be considered 'complete', all designs being capable of improvement. This in itself constitutes one further reason for estimating at the design stage, since it allows some measure of control to be exerted on the designer.

In general a design project will encompass five stages (see Chapter 6), namely—

1. *Conception*, when the initial specification is laid down.
2. *Acceptance*, where the specification is shown to be achievable.
3. *Execution*, where working models based upon the activity in stage 2 are made up. These models should substantially meet the specification initially laid down.
4. *Translation*, where the design is rendered into such a form that it can be manufactured by the unit for which it is intended.
5. *Pre-production*, where final working models are made under production conditions.

Of the five stages the first, 'conception,' is the most difficult to estimate, since it may involve long discussion with the customer and/or the sales department. At the same time, however, it is the most important to the estimator since the greater the detail in which the project can be specified the more accurate will be the succeeding estimate. Time spent here will be amply repaid in accuracy and in subsequent ease of control of the work of the design department.

The other four stages are derived from the first, and require an intimate knowledge of the persons concerned, their abilities, personalities and past experience. Usually the estimator will discuss the project with the chief designer and/or draughtsman who, by virtue of experience and technical knowledge, will be able to compare the proposed project with past projects upon which costing information is available. The estimate, when complete, will include the designers' time, split into appropriate grades, draughtsmen's time, also split into grades, the material required for experimental work, and what special equipment will be needed. Critical Path Analysis can be of considerable assistance here.

Estimating for Manufacture

When estimating for manufacture it is desirable to break down the product into elements of such a nature that existing information on similar elements can be used. Since the estimate is not intended to be used as an instruction to manufacture, the elements into which it is broken need not necessarily be those into which actual production will fall. The estimate, once complete, should contain the following—

(*a*) *Indirect Labour Times, Rates and Overheads.* These will include—

(i)   Production engineering;
(ii) Inspection;
(iii) Model-making;
(iv) Tool-making;
(v)   Special machine designing and manufacture.

(*b*) *Direct Labour Times, Rates and Overheads.* These should be departmentalized; for example, into—

(i)   Machine shop;
(ii) Press shop;
(iii) Assembly shop;
(iv) Finishing;
(v)   Packing.

Standard times should be used throughout, and all ancillary times noted separately.

(*c*) *Direct Material Costs.* This will include raw material costs and bought-in component or sub-assembly prices. Scrap allowances where appropriate *must* be included.

(*d*) *Equipment Costs.* This will specify any new machinery, plant, tools and buildings which may be required.

The above items are not necessarily added together to give an estimated factory cost, since the inclusion or otherwise of various items will depend upon the cost policy of the company concerned. It is necessary to consider each factor, however, in order to forward load each department and to

Prepared by.................... Date.................... Summary for Estimate No....................

Indirect Labour

Department	Hours	Rate	L/Cost	O/H Rate	O/H Cost
Design Dept.					
Drawing Office					
Production Eng.					
Model Shop					
Tool Design					
Tool Making					
Inspection					
Totals					

Direct Labour

Department	Hours	Rate	L/Cost	O/H Rate	O/H Cost
Machine Shop A					
Machine Shop B					
Sub/Assy. Shop A					
Sub/Assy. Shop B					
Sub/Assy. Shop C					
Finishing Dept.					
Assembly Shop K					
Assembly Shop L					
Calibration Dept.					
Packing Dept.					
Totals					

Indirect Material

Direct Material

	£	p
Special Tool		
Special Test Equipment		
Total		

Total Cost

Fig. 19.1. Estimate Summary Sheet (All columns to be filled in)

assess capital expenditure. In order to ensure that no factor is overlooked it is useful to prepare a master form to be filled in for each estimate (see Fig. 19.1).

Accuracy of Estimates

Estimating in itself is inevitably costly, involving both the expenditure of money and the use of valuable skilled personnel who could make useful contributions to the company in other, more direct, departments. The accuracy of an estimate will, in general, be directly proportional to the time spent on the estimate, that is, to its cost. Clearly, the cost of making an estimate must be related to its value to the organization, and care must be taken to avoid too much time and money being spent on trivialities. The accuracy of the estimate must be enough to enable sensible decisions to be taken, yet the estimate must contain safeguards, probably in the shape of contingency allowances to ensure that the subsequent work is not required to be carried out at an impossibly low price. In 'single-shot' or 'one-off' organizations the accuracy of estimates is inevitably lower than in highly repetitive work where considerable historical data is available. In all cases it must be clearly understood that the accuracy of the estimate need be no greater than necessary to allow rational decisions to be taken, otherwise considerable time and money will be spent in trying to achieve an unnecessary precision.

It is desirable to maintain, in as much detail as available, records of *actual* performances, so that they may be compared with the previously prepared estimates. In this way it is possible to—

(*a*) detect and correct any bias in individual estimators;

(*b*) discover whether estimating information is in accord with current practice;

(*c*) build up information for use in any synthetic estimating techniques.

Organization and Location of an Estimating Department

As in any field, specialization of functions leads to greatest efficiency, and wherever possible estimators should specialize on those fields where they have greatest experience. In this there may well be a difference between the estimator and the planning engineer, for in planning, novelty of approach and lack of the prejudice conditioned by previous experience is a possible advantage. In a general engineering works it may be possible to have estimators specializing in—

1. Press-work;
2. Automatic and capstan work;
3. Machining;
4. Assembly.

Experience in the organization concerned is imperative, and a new estimator recruited from outside the organization will find it necessary to adjust his ideas on performance and efficiency to the organization in which he is working. For this reason reference to cost records, previous estimates and planning sheets must be as simple as possible both to verify calculations and assumptions, and to use existing calculations as short cuts to new estimates. In order that this reference to past records be useful, it is important that estimates be consistent: for example, if it is decided that on some small parts used in assembly a loss factor should be allowed, the *same* factor should be used throughout all estimates. Any assumptions used should be stated on the estimate form.

In preparing any estimate there is a great deal of repetitive calculating of the following type—

Labour cost = rate × time + overheads.
Material cost = area of material used × cost per unit area.
Time taken = number of joints × time per joint.

These calculations can conveniently and economically be carried out by special calculating clerks, rather than by highly skilled and expensive estimators, or by using pre-calculated tables, graphs or nomographs. Estimate sheets should be put in such a form that the repetitive calculations are clearly seen.

Where a computer is used for other purposes—for example, stock control or costing—it will be likely to have on file current information concerning prices and rates of pay, so that estimates can be produced which reflect recent conditions.

The responsibility for running an estimating department varies considerably from company to company, and no general rule can be made. Wherever the organizational responsibility lies, it must be clearly understood that the estimator *must* have ready access to all other departments in order that he can check records, verify techniques and examine equipment. *The marketing department* is sometimes responsible for the estimating section: this is most satisfactory when the product being manufactured is highly standardized, varying only in detail between one customer and the next. In this case the basic information upon which the estimating department bases its calculations is agreed with the production department, which produces a formula or series of formulas covering all the most likely cases. An example of such a situation arises in a transformer factory, where the products vary in known manner between each other, and a schedule of all possible variations with estimates attached can be made.

In a small factory, particularly one working on general engineering, it is convenient to make the estimating department part of the *production department*, since estimating does not occupy the whole attention of an integral number of people. In this case estimating and production engineering can be combined, thus simplifying records and filing. Estimates made under these circumstances tend to be comfortably achieved and hence less competitive, since the department making the estimate will eventually be required to accomplish it.

For highly repetitive work, where constant reference is required to be made to past cost records, it is possible to combine the estimating depart-ment with the *cost department*. This will tend to be unsatisfactory, since the general atmosphere of the department is not one of manufacturing, as the head of the department is an accountant rather than a production manager. Furthermore, the estimates, being based entirely on past records, will tend to be very conservative.

Probably the most satisfactory organization is for the estimating de-partment to have full departmental status and report directly to the *factory* or *general manager*. This is more possible in large organizations, and will result in the estimating department 'pace-making' the organization by providing very competitive estimates which act as stimuli to the pro-duction department.

PLANNING

Planning as a description may be used to cover many activities within the factory, and its use is a constant source of confusion. However, it is well established to mean *the preparation of manufacturing instructions*, and it is in this sense that it will be used in the present discussion. This work may be carried out by specialist engineers known variously as method, process, planning or work study engineers in conjunction with jig, tool or fixture designers, or, more generally by production engineers whose knowledge and skills embrace all the previously mentioned specialities. The present chapter will be concerned with the instructions themselves and with the provision of production aids whilst Chapters 14 and 15 deal with work study. This breaking-up of planning is done on the grounds of convenience rather than on those of validity, since the functions cannot be carried out independently.

The Initiation of Production—the Works Order

Manufacture can be required to start either *externally*, that is, by the receipt of an order from a customer; or *internally*, that is, by a requirement to manufacture for stock either for subsequent direct sale or for use in later assemblies. In either case it is probably simplest to deal with both requests in the same way and consider the sales department as the customer and the factory as the supplier, and to start all production activities only upon receipt of an order from the sales department. This order may be known as a sales order, works order, manufacturing order or job order. It will—

(*a*) Translate a customer's request into terms understandable to the recipient. A copy of the works order is often sent to the customer as an acknowledgement of his order, so that the customer may be assured that what is being manufactured is, in fact, what is required;

(*b*) Ensure that all necessary information is provided to all recipients. Many customers' orders contain phrases like '(certain stated items) as previously supplied', 'as agreed with your Mr. Brown', 'as discussed in the meeting of July 11', or simply 'as previously supplied'. This information must be expanded and made quite unambiguous.

(c) Provide a convenient method for referring to any task. All works orders will bear a number, and it is easier to refer to 'Works Order No........' than to describe the task each time. This is a convenient way of identifying a task, and simplifies all internal administration.

The W/O number can also be a code number, identifying the type of work and/or its location in the factory, or referring to the delivery required. This last device is very useful in a company dealing with a large number of small orders where delivery is most important.

The works order will usually be received by at least the production, inspection and costing departments, although it may also be convenient to distribute copies more widely. There is a tendency to broadcast copies of works orders far and wide, and it is not unknown for many copies to be distributed 'in case they might be useful': in the author's experience, one company distributed 17 copies of all works orders, at least 9 of which were never used.

Upon receipt of the works order, the production manager will need to decide how exactly work shall proceed, and to do this he will instruct the planning department to produce an *operation* or *job sheet* or *layout*. This is a statement of the manner in which a task should be carried out in order that production proceeds most economically within the plant concerned. If the total production is carried out in a number of operations then there will be a series of operation sheets which can in turn be consolidated into a *route*, which is a complete description of all the stages through which a job will pass.

The Operation Layout

The detail shown on an operation layout will depend on the quantity being produced, the type of labour available and the quality of the product required. A mass-produced article of high quality made with semi-skilled and unskilled labour will require considerable detail, and the preparation of the operation layouts will take considerable time and effort. On the other hand a simple unique article produced completely by an experienced craftsman would require a very brief layout. However, all operation sheets should carry the following information—

1. *Works Order Number.*
2. *Date Layout Originated.*
3. *Originator's Name.* This will enable reference to be made to the originator and hence to the information upon which he decided the method.
4. *Quantity to be Produced.* Whilst this is defined by the works order it is useful to repeat it explicitly, since the operation layout may change if the quantity produced is changed. For example, if an operation can be

carried out on Machine A with an ancillary time of 2 hours and a standard time of 2 minutes, and on machine B with an ancillary time of 8 hours and a standard time of 1 minute, then, all other considerations apart, small quantities are produced more quickly on machine A and large quantities on machine B (see Fig. 19.2).

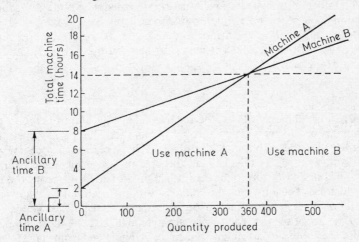

Fig. 19.2. Effect of Ancillary Time on Total Machine Time

5. *Method of Manufacture.* This should be a clear unambiguous statement in as brief a form as possible. Standard or obvious abbreviations should be used wherever possible.

6. *Equipment to be Used.*

7. *Production Aids Needed.* These include any jigs, tools, fixtures, gauges, small tools and any other devices required to carry out the manufacturing method laid down.

8. *Standard Time.* This is 'the total time in which a job should be completed at standard performance: work content, contingency allowance for delay, unoccupied time and interference time where applicable' (B.S. 3138, item 35009), and may be set by use of any of the techniques of work study. These time standards may be used—

(*a*) For shop loading;
(*b*) For estimating;
(*c*) As a basis for efficiency measurements;
(*d*) As a basis for budgetary and cost control;
(*e*) To set up a direct incentive scheme;
(*f*) To assist in line balancing;
(*g*) To assist in determining improved methods.

9. *Ancillary Time.* This is the time when a machine or process 'is temporarily out of productive use due to change-overs, setting, cleaning, etc.' It is important that this be shown, since it would substantially affect the scheduling of a process or plant.

10. *Material Used*. This may well be specified on the drawing to which the manufacture is being made: however, the operation layout will need to specify it *in the form in which it is required*: for example, metal might be in sheet or strip form. The drawing may only define the metal itself, and then the operation layout would need to define whether it were in strip or sheet.

The information listed above must be regarded as a minimum: further data might appear, for example information relating to bonus schemes. From the information given much of the work of the production control department will stem, whilst it may also be used by the costing and estimating departments.

The Route

The operation layout will list the separate elements of an operation most articles are made by passing through a number of separate operations. In order that the whole manufacture may be recorded, a *route* or *route card* is drawn up, consolidating all the operations into a single reference. By careful design of the route card it can also be used to record the complete history of a job from the initial issuing of material to the eventual passing of the completed and inspected goods into a finished goods store. Many means of using a route card are available, but the most usual is to require the route card to stay with the job, being passed from stage to stage, and annotated by the inspection department when appropriate.

The Provision of Production Aids

In the preparation of operation layouts the need for devices to assist in manufacture may become apparent. These production aids ('prodaids') are usually designed by the production engineering department, and include devices such as—

Jigs: which hold the work and guide the tool;
Fixtures: which hold the tool;
Tools: which remove material;
Special machines: which replace standard equipment but carry out a special task.

Clearly the line of demarcation between plant and production aids is tenuous but in general *plant* is characterized by having a relatively long economic life, by being used repeatedly to furnish a series of services, and by not being purchased with a primary intention to resell. *Prodaids*, on the other hand, are usually designed for a particular job or process, and their costs recovered against that job or process.

The calculation of the cost of a piece of plant is lengthy, and the calculation of the economic cost of, say, a fixture can be very much simpler. If the savings produced by use of a production aid are S per piece, then the cost C of the tool will be justified if the number of parts produced is N where—

$$C = NS$$

The cost can be calculated as the cost of plant, using exactly the same criteria. However, as a first-order approximation, accurate enough for many purposes, the cost can be considered to be the initial cost.

For example, how much can be spent on a device which reduces factory cost by 2p a piece if 20,000 pieces are being made?

$$\text{Cost permissible} = 2 \times 20,000\text{p}$$
$$= \pounds 400$$

Alternatively, if a production aid will cost £100, what savings must it produce if 10,000 parts are being made?

$$\pounds 100 \quad = \text{savings} \times 10,000$$
$$\text{i.e. savings} = \frac{100 \times 100}{10,000} \text{ p}$$
$$= 1 \cdot 0\text{p}$$

D. F. Galloway defines some terms useful when discussing the provisioning of production aids—

1. *The Response Ratio* which is the ratio of the net economic gain arising from a prodaid to the cost of the prodaid, that is

$$\text{Response Ratio} = \frac{\text{net economic gain arising from prodaid}}{\text{cost of prodaid}}$$

and clearly as the net economic gain can be calculated either over a year or over the total life of the device, then Response Ratio is specified either as Response Ratio Annual or Response Ratio Total.

2. *The Response Duration* which is the total time over which the effect of the production aid persists.

3. *The Response Delay* which is the interval between the incurring of costs on the production aid and the deriving of benefit from that aid.

Drawing upon the experience of the Production Engineering Research Association, Dr. Galloway suggests that ' . . . an efficient advisory service can attain an average Response Ratio of 10:1, and that in practice, average Response Duration is about three years . . . ' Whilst it might be argued that P.E.R.A.'s experience is atypical, these figures do not seem to be in conflict with the author's experience, and these values can usefully be taken as criteria against which proposals, and subsequent performance, can be judged.

Further Reading
There is a paucity of general material on the subjects of estimating and planning, probably due to the considerable variations between the needs of these two functions in different situations.

Clugston, R., *Estimating Manufacturing Costs*, Gower Press, 1971.
Derived largely from the author's personal experiences in light engineering this book needs to be read with care.

Chapter 20
Control of Quality

CONFORMANCE QUALITY

In a previous chapter (Chapter 5), the corporate implications of a positive quality policy were indicated, whilst in the present chapter, the methods whereby that policy is achieved are discussed. In general, these are achieved by some form of *inspection*, although it should already have been made clear that inspection alone will not achieve quality—'quality is everybody's business'.

Inspection

At one time, the task of an inspector was usually taken to be the passive one of sifting out any faulty workmanship—or sorting out the good from the bad. Whilst this function is still present, inspection is now thought of as an active device to *prevent* rejects. This has resulted in the inspection department being concerned, not only with finished products, but also with raw materials, tools, piece-parts and all manufacturing processes. This does not relieve the production supervisor of any of his responsibility for quality; rather it tries to assist him in this aspect of his duties through the prevention of defective work rather than generating excess cost by the rejection of defective work.

Just as the other control departments (budgetary and production control) are concerned to see 'that all that takes place is in accordance with the rules established and the instructions issued', so may the inspection department be said to be concerned with the comparison of performance with established criteria. The 'performance' may be the manufacturing process itself, when the inspector will require to be assured that the way manufacture is being carried out is as specified in the manufacturing instructions; or it may be some characteristic of the finished product or part.

Inspection Criteria

Criteria may arise in either of two ways—

    1. By use (that is, functionally). For example, dimensions may require

to be determined by the use to which the object is being put. These criteria are so chosen that the finished product has the required *performance*, *life* and *interchangeability*.

2. By user (that is, by appearance). For example, a finish may require to be acceptable to the user even though it may not affect in any way the functioning of the product.

Once a criterion has been chosen it should be committed to paper and published as a standard. Wherever possible, criteria should be expressed numerically so that objective measurements can be made: if this cannot be done, then reference should be made to existing test pieces. Expressions like 'as good as possible', 'to normal commercial standards', 'best possible', should be avoided, as they will inevitably lead, at some time, to disputes. Many criteria are set down in national or international standards, and the use of such standards promotes interchangeability and simplifies purchasing. Since many standards (particularly those published by the British Standards Institution) are generally accepted by industry in the U.K., the variety of products sold is greatly reduced, whilst the volume of standardized products is considerably increased. This leads immediately to a reduction in operating costs.

The Responsibilities of the Inspection Department

The inspection department will usually carry out the following activities—

1. *Goods inwards inspection.* When any goods are received they should be checked against the order which they fulfil. This may necessitate considerable inspection, since incorrect material can hamper manufacture: on the other hand indiscriminate inspection is costly and often unnecessary.

2. *Tool-room and 'first-off' inspection.* Where production aids such as tools are used they will need to be checked to avoid producing defective work. This may relieve later inspection stages of a great deal of work: for example, if a piece part is jig-drilled, verification of the drill jig itself may well avoid the necessity for exhaustive inspection of the piece-parts produced.

3. *Piece-part (component or sub-assembly) inspection.* Where parts are required to mate together, the components may require inspection, although this may be simplified if the method of manufacture is closely controlled.

4. *Finished goods inspection.* This may also require that the inspection department issues a test certificate, calibration chart or other form of warranty to the customer, guaranteeing that the equipment dispatched is to the customer's specification.

In some organizations the inspection department is required to prepare all specifications, whereas in others the task is undertaken by the design authority. Probably the best arrangement is for specifications to be prepared jointly by a Specifications Committee. Certainly it is unwise to publish a specification without discussions with the inspecting, designing and manufacturing sections.

The location of the quality Control Department

The quality control department may be responsible to any of the following—

1. The *General Manager* (or Senior Executive), who is presumed to be sufficiently aloof from day-to-day problems to be able to make final balanced judgements on quality matters, particularly where these requirements apparently clash with the requirements of the manufacturing departments. However carefully specifications are written, there will be some problems which arise from the interpretation of requirements, and heavy pressure may be brought to bear upon the inspector to pass material which may be suspect. In such matters the ability to appeal to an arbiter is most useful.

2. The *Chief Engineer* (or Chief Chemist, Chief Designer), who can appreciate the technical problems which arise in complex modern equipment and can thus bring expert knowledge to bear upon problems. This location is probably most appropriate to organizations producing high-technology equipment.

3. The *Sales Manager*, who is effectively the representative of the customer and can therefore ensure that decisions taken are in the best interests of the customer. This may result in an insistence upon a quality greater than contracted for in the initial price. For consumer goods, this arrangement is probably most satisfactory.

The physical location of the inspection department will depend on the geography of the plant, the type of product made, and the inspection which has to be imposed. Broadly, inspection may either be *centralized,* when all material is brought in to one central point, inspected, and then redistributed or *decentralized* (*localized*), where inspection is carried out at the point of manufacture. These correspond exactly to process and product layouts as discussed in Chapter 9, with the same advantages and disadvantages.

It should be noticed, however, that there is often friction between inspection and production, due to apparently conflicting interests. A centralized inspection may build up a feeling of remoteness on the part of the inspection department, with a consequent lack of understanding for, and resultant bad feeling with, the production departments.

Wherever possible jigs, fixtures, or production aids should be so designed that not only will they prevent incorrect work being carried out, but also check the work of preceding stages. Any checking equipment used must itself be checked on a routine basis, and the maintenance of inspection devices should be carried out just as the maintenance of any other piece of equipment. No amount of inspection will produce articles of good quality; this can only be built in, not 'inspected in'.

STATISTICAL QUALITY CONTROL

As stated above, *quality control* is a term usually used in the U.K. to cover those techniques of inspection based upon sampling methods: in the U.S. the term Statistical Quality Control (S.Q.C.) is more generally used. Sampling techniques have been used for as long as produce has been manufactured. The cheese maker, for example, tests a cheese by taking a small sample, and the housewife cuts a slice of cake to verify the whole of it. In a good number of cases sampling is the only possible way of inspection—where the tests are destructive, expensive, or lengthy, or where the quantities produced are large.

Quality control acts by taking samples and interpreting the results by means of mathematical analyses. The study of variations is so comprehensive that modern quality control techniques will give valid results of known accuracy, whereas the haphazard earlier sampling gave results of doubtful value and (most important) unknown validity. The ability to sample test derives from the fact that a stable system, subject only to random variations, obeys known mathematical laws.

It must be realized at the outset that variations in manufacture arise from one of two sources: firstly, to the assignable causes which can be removed or controlled—for example, tool wear, variations in materials, poor machine maintenance, errors in setting; and secondly, to chance or random variations—for example, movement of the machine due to passing traffic, draughts causing sudden temperature changes, sudden discontinuities in material, and random external distractions affecting the concentration of the operator.

Assignable Causes

In improving quality by attacking the assignable causes, a thorough recording system will be found invaluable. If the symptoms of defective work are identified and recorded, it will be possible to determine what percentage of rejects can be attributed to any symptom, and the probable result will be that the bulk of the rejections derive from very few symptoms (see Fig. 20.1). To improve conformance quality, therefore, the major symptoms (8. 9. 10 in Fig. 20.1) should be attacked first. Without an analysis of this sort, it is much too easy to devote resources to removing symptom 1, perhaps, because its cause is immediately apparent. Of course, any one symptom—for example, a 'dry' soldered joint—may be the result of a number of possible causes: incorrect bit temperature, poor fluxing, dirty metal, wrong solder, and a series of experiments may have to be designed and carried out to check the effects of the possible causes.

Statistical quality control can be used where the assignable causes of bad work are known and if possible removed, that is, where the system is under control. By viewing the products and checking their behaviour it will be possible to see where an assignable cause has returned to a process, and hence investigating to find what that cause is and consequently eliminating it. The presence of the random variations, of course, sets the limits to the accuracy of the process. Thus, should random variations in a system account for deviations from nominal of ± 1 per cent, an accuracy of product of $\pm$ 0·5 per cent is not achievable in that system unless a sorting procedure is imposed to select only the items within the limits of $\pm$ 0·5 per cent. This procedure is useful in those cases where the 'outside-limit' components can be used, but is otherwise wasteful.

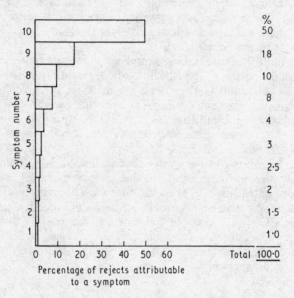

Fig. 20.1. Symptoms of Assignable Causes of Bad Work

Random Variations

A process under control is subject only to chance or random sources of variation, and such situations have been under constant study since the 1650s, when Pascal and Fermat discussed together the outcomes of games of dice. Broadly, the statistical quality controller is concerned with two main classes of problem—

(*a*) where the product has a property which *varies*. For example, if a pin is cut from a rod by a process under control, the length of the rod may have any length between the extremes set by the process. Control is here exerted by examining the variables—*control by variables*—and these usually follow the so-called 'normal' laws.

(*b*) where the produce has an *attribute* which is either 'good' or 'bad', 'right' or 'wrong', 'acceptable', or 'not acceptable', 'defective' or 'non-defective': for example, a ball may pass or fail to pass through a hole. This is *control by attributes* and is largely governed by the 'binomial' laws.

In many situations it is impossible to measure all the products and samples from the total output are therefore taken and inspected. The results of this inspection are compared with the results expected from a stable situation: if the actual results agree with the predicted ones, then no action is demanded. If they do not so agree, then it can be assumed that the process has changed and an investigation is put in hand to discover and remove the cause of the change. Frequently, these comparisons are carried out graphically on *control charts* upon which *warning* and *action* levels are marked.

These charts are often very easy to understand and interpret, and they can become, with experience, sensitive diagnostic tools which can be used by operators and first-line supervision to prevent defective work being produced. It is usual to place the control chart on a board adjacent to the process being controlled, so that the producer him/herself can see the sampling results being recorded. Time and effort spent in explaining the working of the chart to all concerned is never wasted, and Nixon suggests that the chart itself 'shall be called a "howmadoin" chart' to help to remove any feelings of oppression brought about by its presence.

The range of use of control charts is now very wide and within the present text it is not possible to indicate more than the basic principles underlying such charts. Reference is made in 'Further Reading' to some comprehensive texts, but the literature of this subject is extremely rich and the reader will readily find many other works for further reading.

Control by Variables

Assume that in manufacturing a product P it is subject to a process which should produce a property x. On measuring a sample of 1,000 Ps it may well be found that they have values of x, which when rounded off to the nearest 5 are distributed as follows—

Value of x	Number of P's
70	1
75	6
80	12
85	18
90	85
95	214
100	339
105	201
110	75
115	33
120	10
125	4
130	2
	1,000

These values are shown graphically in Fig. 20.2, and the shape and general symmetry of this histogram indicate that a Normal or Gaussian distribution conveniently describes the variation of property x. This distribution, which is symmetrical, is described mathematically by only two parameters—the

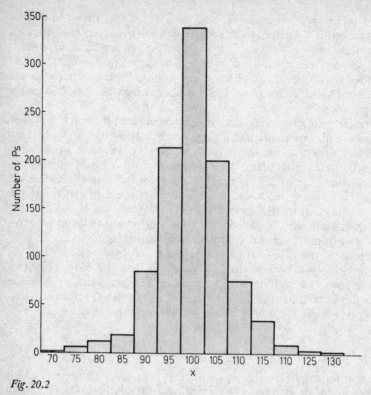

Fig. 20.2

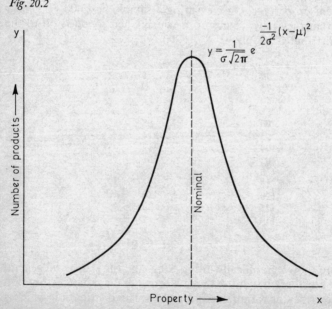

$$y = \frac{1}{\sigma \sqrt{2\pi}} e^{\frac{-1}{2\sigma^2}(x-\mu)^2}$$

Fig. 20.3. Normal or Gaussian Curve

average or *mean*, often written μ, and the standard deviation σ (see Fig. 20.3). The standard deviation is a measure of the 'width' or 'spread' of the distribution; it is calculated by adding together all the squares of the differences between the measured values and the mean value, dividing the resultant sum by the total number (n) of observations, and then taking the square root of the result, that is—

$$\sigma = \sqrt{\frac{\Sigma(x - \mu)^2}{n}}$$

The calculation of the mean μ and the standard deviation σ for the data given, is set out in full below—

x	Frequency of x	Frequency of $x \times x$	$x - \mu$	$(x-\mu)^2$	Frequency $x(x-\mu)^2$
70	1	70	-30	900	900
75	6	450	-25	625	3,750
80	12	960	-20	400	4,800
85	18	1,530	-15	225	4,050
90	85	7,650	-10	100	8,500
95	214	20,330	-5	25	5,350
100	339	33,900	0	0	0
105	201	21,105	$+5$	25	5,025
110	75	8,250	$+10$	100	7,500
115	33	3,795	$+15$	225	7,425
120	10	1,200	$+20$	400	4,000
125	4	500	$+25$	625	2,600
130	2	260	$+30$	900	1,800
	1,000	100,000			$\Sigma(x-\bar{x})^2 = 55,700$

$$\therefore \text{Mean} = \mu = \frac{100,000}{1,000}$$
$$= 100$$

$\therefore$ Standard deviation

$$= \sigma = \Sigma \frac{(x-\mu)^2}{n}$$

$$= \sqrt{\frac{55,700}{1,000}}$$

$$= 7 \cdot 46$$

It should be noted that in practice there are 'short-cut' methods of calculation available, and that all computers, including small 'desk-top' and time-sharing computers, have existing programs which will very readily and speedily handle these calculations.

The formal mathematical statement of the normal distribution is—

$$y = \frac{1}{\sigma\sqrt{2\pi}} e^{-1/2\sigma^2 (x - \mu)^2}$$

and for the population as a whole the area under this curve between any two values of x measures the probability of an observation falling between these two values. For the data already examined where—

$$\mu = 100$$
$$\sigma = 7\cdot46$$
$$y = \frac{1}{7\cdot46\ \sqrt{2\pi}}\ e^{-1/111\cdot3\,(x-100)^2}$$

so that, for example, the probability of finding a value of $x = 85$ is given by the area under the curve between the values $x = 82\cdot5$ and $x = 87\cdot5$. Fortunately, it is rarely necessary to carry out this calculation as tables are available from which all the necessary information can be deduced.

One of the valuable properties of a normal distribution is that the proportion of items within a 'slice' bounded by the $\mu \pm t\sigma$ values depends only upon the value of t and not upon the values of μ and σ. Thus, the percentage of items falling between the mean -1σ and the mean $+1\sigma$ is always 68·3 per cent—or put another way, the percentage of observations lying *outside* these values is $(100 - 68\cdot3)$ per cent $= 31\cdot7$ per cent. Values for these percentages are readily available in many reference books—an abbreviated and simplified table is given below—

Width of 'slice'	Percentage of population lying outside 'slice'
Mean ±0·5	61·7
Mean ±1·0	31·7
Mean ±1·5	13·4
Mean ±1·96	5·0
Mean ±2·0	4·55
Mean ±2·5	1·24
Mean ±2·58	1·00
Mean ±3·0	0·27
Mean ±3·09	0·20

The significance of these figures is two-fold—

(*a*) they indicate the economic consequences of any particular tolerancing. For example, if limits of $\pm1\sigma$ are adopted, then 31·7 per cent of the production will be rejected. A very common 'acceptability' level is taken as 'not more than 2 in every 1,000 shall be rejected', and this would indicate limits of $\pm3\cdot09\sigma$. This is commonly rounded off to $\pm3\sigma$, and the 3σ limits are often assumed to be the 'natural' limits.

(*b*) if a sample of, say, 1,000 items is taken at random from production, and *more than* 3 of them lie outside the 3σ limits calculated from previous measurements, then it is extremely likely that there are causes other than random causes at work, that is, there are *assignable* causes operating which may be traced and eliminated.

Sampling for Variables

A process under control will very often generate a normal distribution of the feature being measured. It is frequently difficult to measure the total production, and so random samples, of size n may be taken. If the mean values of each of these samples (the *sample means*) are calculated, they will be effectively normally distributed, even if the original population itself is not truly normal. The standard deviation of the sample means—often called the *standard error* to avoid confusion with the standard deviation of the parent population—is smaller than the parent standard deviation—

$$\text{standard error of the sample means} = \frac{\sigma}{\sqrt{n}}$$

where σ is the standard deviation of the parent population. For example, if samples each of 4 units are taken from the above population (page 217), then the means of these samples will form a normal distribution which has a mean of 100 and a standard error of $7 \cdot 46/\sqrt{4} = 3 \cdot 73$. This is not to say that *each* sample will have a mean of 100 and a standard deviation of $3 \cdot 73$, but that the population formed by the sample means has these values. Thus the values of the means of the samples could well be—

Mean value of x from a sample	Number of times the mean value is found
90	1
92	1
94	3
96	12
98	18
100	20
102	19
104	15
106	8
108	2
110	1
	100

Mean	$= 100$
Standard error	$= 3 \cdot 7$

Fig. 20.4 shows the comparison between the parent and the derived sample populations.

In practice, a useful value for the standard deviation of the parent population is derived from the average *range*, that is the average over a number of samples, of the differences between the extreme values of the samples. If this average range is $\bar{w}$, then an approximate value for σ is: $\bar{w}/d$, where d is obtained from the following table—

Sample size n	2	3	4	5	6	7	8	9	10
d	1·13	1·69	2·06	2·33	2·53	2·70	2·85	2·97	3·08

For those interested, this is discussed more fully in Pearson, E. S. and Hartley, H. O., *Biometrika Tables for Statisticians*, Vol. 1, Second Ed., pp. 43–49, Cambridge University Press.

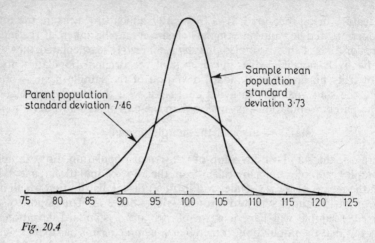

Fig. 20.4

Control Charts for Variables

Control charts for variables make use of the above properties of samples, and in practice a continuing series of samples is taken, their means calculated and each mean plotted on a simple chart.

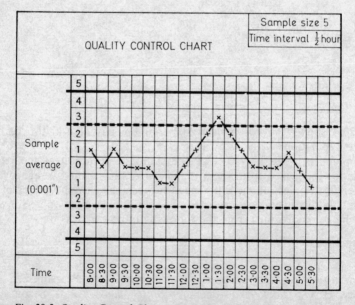

Fig. 20.5. Quality Control Chart—Dimensions Recorded

The probability that a sample mean will fall above the mean $+2$S.E. values is—very nearly—0.025, or $\frac{1}{40}$, and that it will fall above the mean $+3$S.E. values is—again very nearly—0.001 or $\frac{1}{1000}$. Any value which is in fact outside the mean $+2$S.E. value thus acts as a warning that the process is, or may be, changing from its desired performance, whilst two values in a succession of samples above this value have a probability of chance occurrence of $0.025 \times 0.025 = 0.000625$—which is so small that it must be ignored; the two values can be taken together as signals that the process has drifted out of control and must be investigated. Similarly, a value of the mean of a sample which lies above the mean $+3$S.E. value can occur so infrequently that action must be taken to investigate the process. Two sets of lines are commonly imposed upon the control chart—the warning, or $\frac{1}{40}$ lines, and the action, or $\frac{1}{1000}$ lines. These are set at ± 2S.E. and ± 3S.E. away from the mean value—

$+3$S.E.	ACTION
$+2$S.E.	Warning
Mean	
-2S.E.	
-3S.E.	Warning
	ACTION

Clearly, the mean and standard error referred to here are those applying *to the samples*, and they are derived from taking a number of successive samples—20 is a common number—and hence deriving values for the mean and standard error. In the case of the data given on page 217, assume that the samples are represented by the table on page 221. The value of the mean and S.E. have been found to be—

$$mean = 100$$
$$standard\ error = 3.73$$

hence the warning and action lines would be set at—

Lower warning line = $100 - 3 \times 3.73 = 88.91$, say 89.0
Lower action line = $100 - 2 \times 3.73 = 92.54$, say 92.5
Upper warning line = $100 + 2 \times 3.73$ say 107.5
Upper action line = $100 + 3 \times 3.73$ say 111.0

and the control chart would appear—

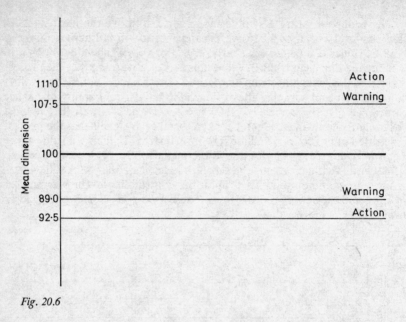

Fig. 20.6

Again, sets of tables are readily available from which action and warning line values may be obtained.

Control by Attributes

When it is not possible to measure a product except in terms of 'good' or 'bad', the quality control process is effectively that of determining which one, out of two possible decisions, is appropriate. This 'one out of two' situation is a *binomial* situation, and the sampling process is governed by the laws of the *binomial distribution*.

If the proportion of the production which is not acceptable (the 'fraction defective') is p, and the 'fraction non-defective' is q, clearly $p + q = 1$, and when a large number of samples, each of size n is taken, then the mean number of defectives which will be found is np. If only one sample is taken, then the probability of finding 0, 1, 2, 3 ... defectives in any sample is given by the successive terms in the expansion of $(q + p)^n$, that is—

the probability of 0 defectives $= q^n p^o = q^n$

the probability of 1 defective $= nq^{n-1}p^1$

the probability of 2 defectives $= \dfrac{n(n-1)}{1 \times 2} q^{n-2}p^2$

$$\text{the probability of } x \text{ defectives} = \dfrac{n!}{x!(n-x)!} q^{n-x}p^x$$
$$= {}_nC_x\, q^{n-x}p^x$$

The average number of defectives obtained in a large number of samples is called the *expected number defective* and is given by—

$$\text{expected number defective} = np$$

The standard deviation for the number of defectives in samples of size n, fraction defective p fraction non-defective q, is—

$$\text{standard deviation} = \sqrt{npq}$$
$$= \sqrt{np(1-p)}$$

Thus, if the fraction defective is 0·1 (that is, 10 in 100) and the sample size is 20 then the Expected Number Defective will be—

$$20 \times 0{\cdot}1 = 2$$

and the standard deviation will be—

$$\sqrt{20 \times 0{\cdot}1 \times 0{\cdot}9} = 1{\cdot}34$$

and the probability of a single sample containing—

0 defectives will be $(0{\cdot}9)^{20}$		$= 0{\cdot}122$
1 defective	$20 \times (0{\cdot}9)^{19}(0{\cdot}1)$	$= 0{\cdot}270$
2 defectives	$\dfrac{20 \times 19}{1 \times 2}(0{\cdot}9)^{18}(0{\cdot}1)^{2}$	$= 0{\cdot}285$
3 defectives	$\dfrac{20 \times 19 \times 18}{1 \times 2 \times 3}(0{\cdot}9)^{17}(0{\cdot}1)^{3}$	$= 0{\cdot}190$
4 defectives		$= 0{\cdot}090$
5 defectives		$= 0{\cdot}032$
6 defectives		$= 0{\cdot}009$
7 defectives		$= 0{\cdot}002$
8 defectives		$= 0{\cdot}000$

These probabilities may be represented graphically, as in Fig. 20.7.

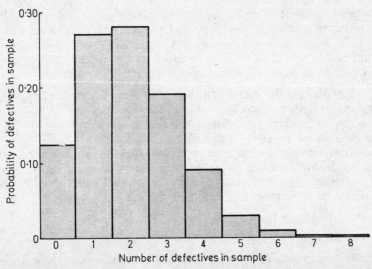

Fig. 20.7

225

If now from a population which previously had the above characteristics a sample of 20 items is taken and, say, 7 of these are found to be defective, then it can be said that the likelihood of this happening is so very small (2 in 1,000) that it is extremely likely that the process producing the population has changed.

The control chart for attributes operates in a similar way to that for variables, except that it is usually 'one-sided' in that there is only one set of warning and action lines. These lines are again set by reference to the standard deviation of the number of defectives in the samples, although in the case of the binomial distribution the $+2\sigma$ and $+3\sigma$ values do not present constant risk levels as in the 'control by variables' case. Tables are again available from which the warning and action levels may be deduced for any risk levels from knowledge of the expected number defective and the standard deviation of the number of defectives.

Proportion defective charts

The above discussion deals with charts requiring samples of a constant size and from which the number of defectives in each sample is plotted. These are known as *number defective* or *np* charts: in some situations it is not convenient to take samples of constant size and so the *proportion* of defectives in a sample is used as the quality indicator. In these *proportion defective* or *p* charts the warning and limit values are not constant, having to be calculated—or in practice read from the tables—for each sample.

Acceptance Sampling Plans

Any consumer must accept that amongst a batch of goods delivered to him there will be some which are *defective*. The proportion of defectives which can be tolerated in a batch (or, to use the U.S. term, in a lot) must be agreed between the supplier (or producer) and the consumer. Thereafter, the consumer must take such action as he feels appropriate to ensure that the goods delivered do not contain more defectives than can be tolerated. Assuming that it is decided that some form of 'goods-inwards' inspection must take place, then one of two courses of action is possible—

(*a*) 100 per cent inspection can be carried out. This involves inspecting every item received, a costly, tedious and possibly unreliable process which in some situations—for example, where destructive testing is essential—cannot possibly be carried out.

(*b*) Samples may be inspected and the batch or lot accepted on the results obtained from these samples. This sort of sampling is often called *acceptance* sampling and since it is concerned only with 'good' or 'bad' items, it is an attribute-sampling situation.

The Operating Characteristics of a Sampling Scheme

The simplest type of acceptance sampling scheme is one where a single sample (size *n*) is taken from the batch (size *N*) and the whole batch is accepted if the number of defectives found in the sample is equal to, or less than, an agreed figure (*d*). Ideally, this scheme should be such that *all* batches which have an actual proportion of defectives equal to or less than a tolerated proportion are accepted on the basis of the single sample, and *all* batches which have an actual proportion of defectives greater than the tolerated figure are rejected by the sample. The way in which this scheme would operate is shown in Fig. 20.8, the Operating Characteristic (O.C.) curve of the scheme.

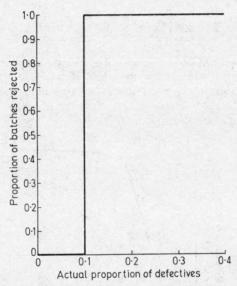

Fig. 20.8

In practice, such an O.C. is only attainable if the sample size is equal to the batch size, that is, if there is 100 per cent inspection; when the sample size is less than the batch size there must always be a risk that an unsatisfactory batch is accepted (the 'Consumer's Risk') or that a satisfactory batch is rejected (the 'Producer's Risk'). To illustrate how an actual O.C. is generated, consider again the situation set out previously (page 225) where the initial population—the batch—had an *actual* proportion of defectives of 0·1, and a sample of 20 was taken. Assume that the rejection level was 2, so that if 2 or more defectives were found in the sample then the whole batch would be rejected, whilst if 0 or 1 defectives were found, the whole batch would be accepted.

From the calculations on page 225 it is known that for this proportion of defectives—

the probability of 0 defectives being found in a sample of 20 is 0·122
the probability of 1 defective being found in a sample of 20 is 0·270
∴ the probability of 0 or 1 defective being found in a
sample of 20 is 0·392

Thus, in this sampling scheme, when the actual defective proportion is 0·1, the proportion of batches accepted will be 0·392, and the proportion rejected will be 1 − 0·392 = 0·608. Similar calculations can be carried out for other actual defective proportions—

Actual proportion of defectives	Proportion of batches rejected
0·01	0·017
0·05	0·264
0·10	0·608
0·20	0·931
0·30	0·992
0·40	0·999

and these give the O.C. of Fig. 20.9. (*Note*: in practice it is not necessary to calculate the above values, as again, tables of values are readily available.)

Taking the operating characteristics of single sampling schemes where the sample size is 20, for various values of *d*, the numbers of defectives rejecting the sample are shown in Fig. 20.10.

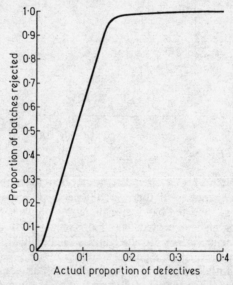

Fig. 20.9

From the above discussion it must be clear that in any sampling scheme there are risks that incorrect decisions will be taken. These are described as—

1. *The Producer's Risk*, which is the risk that a batch of goods of acceptable quality will be rejected as a result of a sample inspection.
2. *The Consumer's Risk*, which is the risk that an unsatisfactory batch will be accepted as a result of a sample inspection.

3. *The Acceptable Quality Level* (*A.Q.L.*) which defines the highest percentage of rejects in a batch which the receiver will regularly accept, whilst at the same time the risk that good batches will be rejected is specified. For example—

A.Q.L. = 5 per cent with a producer's risk of 0·01

means that in any batch 5 per cent defectives will be tolerated, any rise above this being rejected. The risk of 'false' rejections, that is, that a batch is rejected whilst containing less than 5 per cent defective, is 0·01, i.e., 1 per cent.

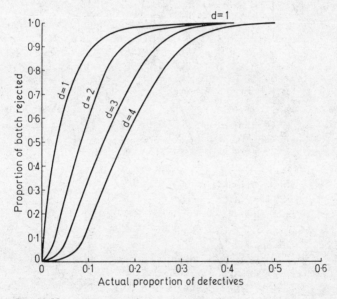

Fig. 20.10

4. *The Lot Tolerance*, which is the percentage of defective which is unacceptable to the recipient. Batches of this quality or worse should be rejected. The risk of accepting worse qualities than this is the consumer's risk.

These can be shown graphically by the *operating characteristic* of the particular scheme (see Fig. 20.11).

A further description of the effectiveness of a sampling scheme is given by the A.O.Q., that is, the Average Quality of the Outgoing batches—

$$\text{A.O.Q.} = \frac{\text{Actual number of defectives in accepted batches}}{\text{Total number of items in accepted batches}}$$

When the initial quality of the goods inspected is high, the outgoing quality will be high since there were few defectives present in the first place: similarly, when the initial quality is poor, the outgoing quality will again be high, since the sampling scheme will have rejected easily the low quality batches. A high outgoing quality is represented by a low value for A.O.Q., and a curve representing the variation of A.O.Q. with the actual proportion of defectives in the batches presented for inspection is shown in Fig. 20.12. The peak represents the poorest quality of the accepted batches which will be regularly accepted, and this is known as the *accepted outgoing quality level*, A.O.Q.L., of the sampling scheme.

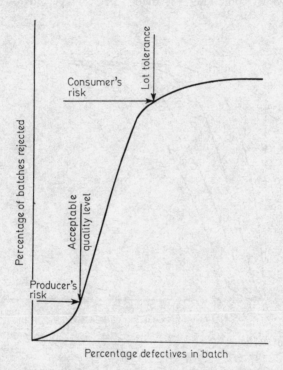

Fig. 20.11. Operating Characteristic showing Producer's Risk, Acceptable Quality Level, Consumer's Risk and Lot Tolerance

In addition to the single sampling scheme discussed above, there are in common use, double, multiple and sequential schemes. As an example of these, consider the usual type of double sampling scheme. This type of scheme is more economical to operate than a single sampling scheme if the quality of the incoming goods is high. The procedure is as follows—

1. Collect sample at random from batch. (*Note*: in general the sample taken is smaller than that which would be taken in a single scheme.)
2. If the number of defectives found is below acceptance number, accept whole batch.

3. If the number of defectives found is above the rejection number, select second sample.

4. If total rejects found in both samples is less than acceptance figure, accept entire batch.

5. If the total number of defectives found exceeds acceptance figure, *either* 100 per cent inspect and segregate defectives *or* reject entire batch.

Example—

> Take sample of 100 from batch and inspect.
> If 2 or less defectives, accept batch.
> If 5 or more defectives, reject batch.
> If 3 or 4 defectives, take a second sample of 100.
> If total defectives less than 5, accept batch.
> If total defectives above 5, reject batch.

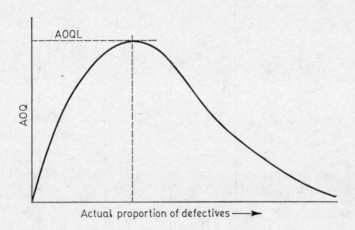

Fig. 20.12

Inspection Records

The results obtained from such sampling schemes are useful as a means of accepting or rejecting batches of work, and if they are recorded they will give a picture of the stability of a particular supplier. This can be done by means of a simple record such as Fig. 20.13, and this will provide useful information upon which to base future buying policy. Clearly where a vendor rating system (page 330) is in use, the information derived from the inspection records can be invaluable.

Sampling Plan	AB/784/K			Part No.	38.243

Supplier.........J. Smith...........................

Date	Order No.	G.R.N. No.	Batch Size	No. of Defectives in Sample	Accept or Reject
6.1.71	32749	0842	5,000	4	A
17.1.71	32749	0896	4,000	3	A
27.1.71	33864	1260	5,000	3	A
12.2.71	33865	1570	2,000	1	A
22.2.71	34126	1635	10,000	10	R
6.3.71	34239	1765	4,000	2	A

Fig. 20.13. Inspection Record

Statistical Quality Control—Conditions for Use, and Advantages

Statistical sampling techniques can be used if—

1. The process is under control, *and*

2. The quantity being produced is sufficiently large to enable realistic samples to be taken.

If these conditions are satisfied, then quality control can provide the following advantages over a 100 per cent inspection—

1. Reduction in defective work, resulting in a reduction of production cost.

2. A smoother production flow.

3. A more economical use of inspection personnel and a substantial reduction in inspection costs.

4. Warning being given of a process drift.

5. Rejection of a complete batch is more compelling than rejecting only the defectives.

6. The inspection process is less tedious, and will therefore tend to be carried out more responsibly.

Installation of Statistical Quality Control

As with any other new management tool, statistical quality control needs to be installed with care. For an organization used to 100 per cent inspection the idea of making judgements—indeed of halting production altogether—upon the results of tests or measurements on small samples will be both revolutionary and suspect. Should an ill-devised quality control system fail—that is, give results which are demonstrably at variance with a 100 per cent inspection—then subsequent efforts to extend quality control will be very difficult.

At the outset, management must be made aware of the logical basis upon which statistical quality control is built. The ideas of probability may appear strange, although the idea of 'odds' on a horse-race is well accepted. Senior staff should attend a series of appreciation lectures where they can learn of the methods of quality control, though there is no need for them to learn the detailed processes. At the same time the senior engineers responsible most directly for inspection should learn as much as possible of the mathematical theory underlying this new technique. Regrettably, too few engineers have any knowledge of statistical methods, a shortcoming which is increasingly appreciated by many universities who now include some study in their degree courses.

When management is well grounded in quality control ideas, a similar grounding should be given to the production supervision. This should be as practical an approach as possible and should avoid any superfluous 'jargon'. The ideas need to be put over, rather than teaching a new terminology, and films and visits to other companies can be very usefully employed here. Once a thorough understanding is obtained throughout the factory, a practical demonstration within the factory itself should be set in train. This should be on a simple part made in quantity and of known quality. The results given by quality control will rapidly be seen to be in line with those of the existing 100 per cent inspection, whilst being obtained more cheaply and quickly. The installation of quality control should continue once the results of the initial experiment are accepted. This installation is probably better if carried out throughout one workshop at a time. Part of the installation should be the explaining to the individual operators of the meaning of the quality control charts and how they are used, and it will be found that operators respond rapidly to the information given on the charts and can take great pride in them.

Further Reading
1. Moroney, M. J., *Facts from Figures*, Penguin Books, Harmondsworth 1969.
This is a 'must' for anybody seriously wishing to study the use of statistical techniques.

2. Smith, C. S., *An Introduction to Quality Control*, 1964.

3. Anson, C. J., *Quality Control as a Tool for Production*, 1962.

4. Desmond, D. J., *Quality Control—Short runs and Small Batch Production*, 1965.
The above are three of the seminar papers produced and published by the British Productivity Council. All are valuable, and can be profitably studied. The mathematical complexity increases from 2 to 4.

5. Juran, J. M., *Quality Control Handbook*, McGraw-Hill, New York 1962.
A comprehensive work edited by the doyen of quality control engineers.

6. King, G. K. and Butler, C. T., *The Principles of Engineering Inspection*, Cleaver-Hume Press, London 1965.
This discusses some of the basic principles underlying inspection itself.

7. Hume, K. J., *Engineering Metrology*, MacDonald, London 1970.
The authoritative work on measurement.

8. Rissik, H., *Quality Control in Production*, Pitman, London 1947.
A useful basic book.

9. Huitson, A. and Keen, J., *Essentials of Quality Control*, Heinemann, London 1970.
A short, basic text covering the concepts and practice of Statistical Quality Control. Valuable for newcomers to the subject.

Chapter 21
Costing

Whilst budgets and budgetary control apply to the whole organization—that is, expenditure concerning the factory as a unit is analysed—costing is the ascertaining of the amount of expenditure incurred on a single item or group of items. There are two principal different types of costing: *historical* costing, where the costs are collected and analysed after the expenditure has taken place, and *standard* costing, where costs are compared as they occur with an estimated cost, prepared in advance of production, and known as the Standard Cost. Both have their place in industry. Standard costing is particularly useful in repetitive manufacture and is a type of control (cost control) exhibiting exactly the same features as other managerial control, namely—

1. *Plan*
2. *Publish*
3. *Measure*
4. *Compare*
5. *Report*
6. *Correct*

In certain types of manufacture the extraction of costs of individual projects may be a process more costly than justified by the results obtained —for example, in jobbing shops where very few processes are repeated and the time cycle for a complete task is extremely low. As with any other data-collecting project, consideration must always be given to the use to which the information obtained will be put. Unless there is an immediate need for data it is probably unwise to collect it: too many filing cabinets are filled with information which is awaiting analysis. 'The figures will come in useful one day' is heard all too frequently.

THE SOURCES OF COSTING INFORMATION

No costing system can be any more accurate than the information which is fed into it, although once considerable data is accumulated it is often possible for the cost department to observe probable errors which can then be referred back to the originators. All information used by the cost department originates elsewhere, and it is important to realize this, as often criticisms of the cost department for costs being 'wrong' should in fact be aimed elsewhere. The cost accountant will require to know, when costing a job—

1. The *time spent* and by whom;
2. The *material used* and its cost;
3. The *overhead expenses* incurred.

Labour

Time recording is done either by means of time sheets (Fig. 21.1), which are filled in daily or weekly by hand, and which summarize the total hours spent, or by job cards (Fig. 21.2), each job having a separate card, the time spent on the job being recorded on the card by hand or by a clock (a job clock). In this case, the cost department will receive from each operator one card for each job undertaken, and in a jobbing shop with short time-cycles this will result in a large number of cards. However, the assignment of the time to the individual job is much simpler than in the case of the summarized job sheet. In the case of large-scale flow production, where an operator is engaged wholly upon one job for extended periods, the need for individual time recording vanishes. Where time recording is

Name......J. Brown............ Dept....D1......... W/E...1-1-71.................

Job No.	Mon.		Tue.		Wed.		Thur.		Fri.		Sat.		Totals
	N	o/T	N	o/T	N	o/T	N	o/T	N	o/T	N	o/T	
4261	2						2		1				5
4773	3		3		3				1				10
3648	1		2		2		3		1				9
4355	1				1				1				3
4343			1				2		1				4
5160	1		2		2	1	1		3				10
Totals	8		8		8	1	8		8				

Fig. 21.1. Weekly Time Sheet

needed it must be realized that the accuracy of recording will be low unless there is some incentive towards accurate time booking. This inaccuracy will arise from—

Description of Job				Job No.	
Assembly of				1001	
F.M.I.				Op. Name	
				J. Brown	
ON		OFF		TIME	
				N	*O/T*
1.1.61	*11.30*	*1.1.61*	*12.30*	*1*	
2.1.61	*9.00*	*2.1.61*	*12.30*	*3½*	
4.1.61	*10.00*	*4.1.61*	*12.00*	*2*	
5.1.61	*9.00*	*5.1.61*	*4.00*	*6*	
Total Time				*12½*	

Fig. 21.2. Job Time Card
(*Note:* 'Time on' and 'Time off' are recorded by means of a job clock)

1. Reluctance on the part of an operator to carry out a tedious and often apparently useless task.

2. Reluctance to book 'waiting', 'idle', or 'lost' time, out of loyalty to his supervisor and his colleagues.

3. Reluctance to book 'extra' time arising from operations carried out above those anticipated (for example, in rectifying bad material), again out

of loyalty to supervisors and fellow workers. Some attempt to prevent incorrect booking can be made by requiring the supervisor to countersign the time records, but this places a considerable strain on the supervisor and can result in a substantial part of the supervisor's time being used signing clock cards.

An incentive bonus scheme, as pointed out in Chapter 31, will usually result in much more realistic time-recording, and this may, in fact, be one of the most substantial advantages of such a scheme.

Material

Material recording is usually carried out by means of requisitions (Fig. 21.3) and the simple rule to be observed is that no material should be issued from stores without a properly authorized material requisition being presented, this requisition bearing the cost allocation. Care must be taken to avoid cost recording of stock for items of insignificant value, otherwise the cost of costing itself will be abnormally high. This can be avoided by 'bulk issuing' small items and charging the cost of these 'bulk issues' to an overhead or 'spread-over' account.

MATERIAL REQUISITION			
Originator's Signature	Dept.	Date	Job No.
Material Required			Qty. Required
Material Issued			Qty. Issued
Issuer's Signature	Date	Receiver's Signature	

Fig. 21.3. Material Requisition

Material Pricing

The quantity of material being known, it is necessary to assign to it a price. If the price actually paid (the 'specific price') for the material is known, then no particular problem presents itself—

Price charged = Number of units used × unit price

However, it may happen that quantities of the same material are purchased at different prices, and that 'issues' take place between the various receipts of material. For example—

100 units at 10p a unit are received on January 1, and there are thus 100 units available in store. 50 and 30 of these are issued on February 1 and March 1 respectively, and clearly the unit price for each of these 'issues' is 10p. On April 1, a further 100 units are received to give a total of 120 available in store, but unfortunately the unit price for this delivery has risen to 15p. On May 1, 50 units are issued, and it is impossible to identify the source of this 50—that is, whether it comprises 20 of the original 100, 50 of the second 100, or some combination of the two. What unit price should be set for this issue?

| | *Received* | | *Issued* | *In Store* |
	Unit Price (p)	Quantity (units)	Quantity (units)	Quantity
January 1	10	100		100
February 1			50	50
March 1			30	20
April 1	15	100		120
May 1			50	70

There are a number of methods available to deal with this problem, amongst which are—

1. *Weighted average pricing.* Here an average is struck by adding together the values of stock already in store and stock added, and dividing by the total quantity of stock. Thus, on April 1, the value of stock already in store is $20 \times 10p = 200p$. To this is added 100 units of stock at 15p a unit = value 1500p. The total value of stock is thus $(200 + 1500)p$ and the *weighted average unit price* is—

$$\frac{1700}{120} p = 14 \cdot 17p.$$

The stock issued on May 1 is thus issued at a price of $(50 \times 14 \cdot 17)p = 708 \cdot 5p$. If now further stock were received—say 100 units at 20p a unit—the weighted average price would be $\left(\frac{70 \times 14 \cdot 17 + 100 \times 20}{170}\right)p$ a unit.

(*Note*: this averaging should be contrasted with the *simple averaging* method where the price is derived by adding together the unit prices $(10p + 15p = 25p)$ and dividing by the number of orders—in this case 2—to give the average price—$(25 \div 2)p$ a unit. This method has nothing to commend it but its simplicity.)

2. *LIFO pricing.* Here the price charged is the last price paid (—hence Last-In-First-Out). Thus, the May 1 stock is charged out at the last price paid, that is at 15p a unit, so that the total price out would be $(50 \times 15)p = 750p$. If another order for—say—60 units had to be fulfilled, then 50 would

be priced at the last price (15p). This 50 units would have exhausted the April delivery, so that the remaining 10 units would be priced at the next latest price, that is at 10p a unit. Hence, the price out for 60 units on June 1, assuming no new deliveries, would be—

$$50 \text{ units at } 15p = 750p$$
$$10 \text{ units at } 10p = 100p$$
$$\therefore \text{ total price } = 850p$$

3. *FIFO pricing.* Here the price charged is the first price from which the issued material could have been drawn. Thus, on May 1 the issued material would be charged out at 10p a unit for 20 units. The '10p a unit' stock having then been exhausted, the remaining 30 units would have been charged out at 15p a unit, so that the total price out would be $(20 \times 10)p + (30 \times 15)p = 650p$.

These three systems would give the following prices out for the May 1 issue—

Weighted Average	LIFO	FIFO
700p	750p	650p

4. *Standard pricing.* Here a fictitious price is assumed for the material, and all material issued at this *standard* price. Where the actual price varies from standard, a *variance* is declared, a positive variance indicating that the purchase price is greater than standard, a negative variance indicating that it is less. Standard pricing is only used as part of a complete standard costing system.

5. *Replacement pricing.* Here again a fictitious price is set, this being the price which it is anticipated will be paid when the material is replaced.

The various methods of pricing above each have their own advantages. Probably the weighted average method is most common in the U.K. except where a complete standard costing system is in use. Whichever method is used, it must be applied consistently and continuously.

Overhead Records

Overhead records are derived partly from the normal financial records of the factory, and partly from returns from the manufacturing departments. A policy decision is required to decide which items shall be recorded as direct expenses, and which as indirect expenses. Those operations which constitute an inherent part of the job are usually considered as direct expenses, so that the calibration or setting of apparatus is usually a direct expense even if carried out under the supervision of the chief inspector whose own cost is spread over. No general rules can be laid down, however, each case being entirely dependent upon local circumstances.

Other indirect expenses are those which arise from lost time and lost materials. These have been mentioned above very briefly, and require very careful consideration. Analysis of both, particularly if reasons can be assigned to the expenses, can be extremely helpful in pin-pointing weaknesses. One method of preparing such analyses is to set up a code of indirect expenses, each common source of such expense bearing a number. For example, idle time may be coded as follows—

W1 Waiting for material
W2   ,,   ,, drawings
W3   ,,   ,, fitter
W4   ,,   ,, maintenance
W5   ,,   ,, supervisor

and so on. Any idle time is then 'booked against' the appropriate number, and a summary of costs readily prepared against each code. These summaries will then indicate weaknesses, and also show the financial importance of any weakness. This can be of great importance when subsequent decisions on the strength of departments have to be taken. For example, if W3 ('waiting for fitter') has cost the factory £2,500 in one year, there is a strong case for the employment of at least one more fitter.

THE LOCATION OF COSTS

Data on costs are collected only in order to help the manager control his work. To do this, the figures need to be organized in some useful way, that is, they need to be grouped around *cost centres*. A cost centre is a division, part or function of the whole enterprise wherein *responsibility* can be meaningfully located, for it is only when responsibility can be sensibly identified that control can be properly exerted. There are no simple rules for identifying a cost centre beyond that of requiring an unambiguous definition of responsibility. Clearly the size and complexity of a cost centre will vary from company to company, although it is desirable to make it small enough to enable *rapid* action to be taken if the figures generated indicate a need for this.

The cost centre itself may well include the provision of a number of different activities or the production of a number of different products, and it may also be useful to discover the cost of each activity and/or product, that is, of each of the various *cost units*. As with a cost centre, the definition of a cost unit is a matter of judgement, and again, the overriding requirement is that the results obtained should be *useful*. It should be noted that a cost unit need not necessarily be a unit in the sense of an individual item—it might be a batch of identical items (a dozen, a hundred . . .), or a group of similar products, or a single item. Each organization needs to define its own cost centres and units, although within any industry common practices will probably have grown up and these are often usefully followed.

THE RECOVERY OF OVERHEADS

Consideration of the budget will show that trading expenditure falls into three main categories—

    1. Direct wage costs, which can be allocated to specific jobs.

2. Direct material costs, which again can be allocated to specific jobs.
3. Those other costs which cannot be allocated to specific jobs; that is, the aggregate of the indirect material cost, indirect labour cost and indirect expenses. This aggregate is known as the overhead.

So that this overhead charge can be recovered, some method must be available for sharing it amongst the production. The apportionment of overheads to particular jobs or products is a technical problem of some complexity, and reference needs to be made to a good text-book on costing for a full discussion of the alternatives available. For the purposes of the present text, however, the two most common types of overhead recovery procedure will be briefly described, using the following example—

A company makes and sells during a year 200 units of A (unit selling price £18) and 100 units of B (unit selling price £19). The direct costs in £s are—

	Unit		Total	
	A	B	A B	
wages	4·0	5·0	800+500 =	1,300
material	2·5	3·0	500+300 =	800
totals	6·5	8·0	1,300+800 =	2,100

The total trading expenditure of the organization is £5,350.
The total income is £ $(200\times18+100\times19)$ = £5,500
∴ the profit is £ $(5,500-5,350)$ = £ 150

and the overhead is £ $(5,350-2,100)$ = £3,250

Absorption Costing

Here, all overhead items are aggregated and the resulting total divided amongst all products or jobs by means of an agreed rate, the *overhead recovery rate*.

In the example given, the aggregated overhead is £3,250, and one common absorption costing method spreads this over all jobs by adding on a fixed percentage to the wage cost:

Total overhead = £3,250
Total wage cost = £1,300
∴ Overhead recovery rate = $\frac{3,250}{1,300}\times100 = 250\%$
(as a % of direct labour)

The assigned costs in £s would then appear—

	Unit		Total	
	A	B	A	B
Wages	4·0	5·0	800	500
Material	2·5	3·0	500	300
Overhead	10·0	12·5	2,000	1,250
Total	16·5	20·5	3,300	2,050
Selling price	18·0	19·0	3,600	1,900
∴ profit	1·5		300	
loss		1·5		150

and final profit = £(300−150) = £150

Marginal Costing

Here, overheads are divided into *fixed overheads*, being those which do not
change with output, and *variable overheads*, being those which do depend
on output. Only the variable overheads are assigned to products or jobs,
the fixed overheads then being recovered from the contributions to expenses left when the direct costs and variable overheads are subtracted
from the selling price. This is sometimes known in the U.S. as *direct
costing* or *differential costing*, and the cost figure so produced is sometimes
referred to as the *out-of-pocket manufacturing cost* to express the fact that
it is a cost which would have been avoided if the product or job had not
been undertaken.

In the example used so far, the overhead cost was given as £3,250.
This must be scrutinized to decide how much is fixed (for example, rent,
rates . . .) and how much is variable (for example, power to run machines,
oil to lubricate tools, cotton waste . . .). Assume the investigation shows—

	£
Variable overheads	650
Fixed overheads	2,600
Total	3,250

$$\text{Overhead recovery rate expressed as a percentage of wages} = \frac{650}{1,300} \times 100$$
$$= 50\%$$

The assigned costs in £s would then be expressed:

	unit A	unit B	total A	total B	
Wages	4·0	5·0	800+	500 = 1,300	
Material	2·5	3·0	500+	300 = 800	
Overhead	2·0	2·5	400+	250 = 650	
Total	8·5	10·5	1,700+	1,050 = 2,750	
Selling price	18·0	19·0	3,600+	1,900 = 5,500	
Contribution	9·5	8·5	1,900	850 = 2,750	

∴ Final Profit = contribution − fixed overheads = £2,750 − 2,600
= £150

In both cases, the final profit figure is the same, £150, and in static
conditions, where no changes are contemplated, possible or enforced, there
is little to choose between the two methods. However, in the more usual
situation of fluidity, marginal costing is more likely to give meaningful
answers. For example, if output of B can be increased by 20 units without
additional capital charges (that is, from the same plant and equipment),
what costs are involved?

Absorption costing would show—at first sight—

$$\text{additional costs} = £20 \times 20·5 = £410$$

However, this has assumed a constant overhead rate, derived from an output of 200 As and 100 Bs. Since the output of B is being increased to 120, then the overhead rate must be revised. To sweep through a range of alternative levels of A and B becomes a tedious procedure, often more honoured in the breach than in the observance. On the other hand, marginal costing would give immediately—

$$\text{additional costs} = £20 \times 10 \cdot 5 = £210$$
$$\text{additional income} = £20 \times £19 = £380$$
$$\therefore \text{ additional contribution} = £170$$

Again, if examining the product mix, absorption costing would indicate that, by manufacturing 100 Bs, a loss of £150 was being incurred. The deduction that total profit would increase if the number of Bs made and sold were decreased is appealing—indeed, it would seem that total profit could be increased by £150 if B was discontinued altogether. In fact, of course, this would not be so, since the fixed overheads would remain.

These problems, and others of a similar nature, are most readily dealt with by marginal costing, and techniques concerned with changing situations usually need marginal data. The extraction and manipulation of the fixed and variable elements of the overhead often appears difficult, and for this reason marginal costing is not so widely used as the simpler, blunter weapon of absorption costing.

It must be noted that since the overhead cost contains elements which are the results of managerial decisions (a good example of this would be the rate of depreciation) then the factory cost too will be the result of a managerial decision, that is, cost is a matter of policy.

It is a common failing to assume that high overheads are a sign of inefficiency: this of course is not so, and the relation between cost, direct labour and overheads, must be clearly understood. Any increase in direct labour cost must always be accompanied by a reduction in overheads if the factory cost is to remain the same. There is little point in reducing overheads whilst at the same time causing the direct labour charge to increase.

Standard Costing

Standard costing is analogous to budgetary control, but deals with cost units rather than the whole organization. Values for all the elements of cost are estimated prior to their commitment, and the actual cost is then shown as the standard cost plus or minus a difference, always known as the *variance*. For example, the standard cost for product C might be made up as follows—

	p
Standard Wage Cost	20
Standard Material Cost	30
Standard Overhead Cost	50
	100

In practice it might be found that the *actual* costs were—

	p
Wages	25
Materials	25
Overheads	60
	110

and this could be shown in a standard costing system as—

	Standard (p)	Variance (p)
Labour cost	20	+5
Material cost	30	−5
Overhead cost	50	+10
	100	+10

Since the standard values had previously been fixed and recorded, there is no need to repeat them in the report, and so they could be presented as—

	Variance (p)
Labour	+5
Material	−5
Overheads	+10

This method has the advantages of (*a*) giving price estimates of achievable costs, and (*b*) enabling management's attention to be directed to those places where effort is needed, that is, to those places where performance differs significantly from plan.

Variance Analysis

The three principal variances (Labour, Material, Overheads) may arise from a number of causes, and the reduction of variances to their constituent parts, and the subsequent discovery of reasons for these variances is known as *variance analysis*. A complete discussion of this topic is beyond the scope of this text, and recourse to one of the works shown at the end of this chapter is recommended. As an illustration of the method, however, consider the wage variance. This may arise from one or both of two causes—

(*a*) a difference in the time taken for the job (the 'Labour Efficiency Variance'),

(*b*) a difference in the wage rate (the 'Wage Rate Variance').

Thus, the standard wage cost of 20p may have been calculated from a standard time of 20 minutes and a standard wage rate of 1p a minute, hence—

$$\text{standard wage cost} = 20 \times 1p$$

In practice, however, it might have been found that the actual time taken was 12½ minutes and that the wage rate was 2p a minute, thus giving the actual wage cost of 25p. The Labour Efficiency Variance would then be −7½ minutes, and the Wage Rate Variance would be +1p a minute.

Note: it should not be assumed that a negative variance is necessarily desirable, since although it represents an expenditure less than anticipated —and hence it is a saving—it may also indicate an error in setting the standard. If, as is usual, the standard cost is examined when a selling price is fixed, a high standard cost may result in a high selling price and a consequent loss in the volume of sales.

Further Reading

1. *Terminology of Cost Accounting*, Institute of Cost and Management Accountants, London 1966.
A valuable reference book.

2. Batty, J., *Management Accountancy*, Macdonald and Evans, London 1969.
Useful for the serious student, covers a diversity of topics.

3. Dickey, R. I., *The Accountant's Cost Handbook*, The Ronald Press, New York 1960.
Like its companion, *The Production Handbook*, this encyclopaedic text is most useful in conjunction with more detailed studies. Reflects American usage.

4. Sidebotham, R., *Accounting for Industrial Management*, Pergamon, Oxford, 1964.
A valuable, simple book, useful to managers who, having little or no knowledge of accountancy, wish to understand something of it.

5. Buyers, C. I. and Holmes, G. A., *Principles of Cost Accountancy*, Cassell, London 1967.
A most useful text, which, whilst written with the needs of examination candidates in mind, will be found to be equally useful to the practising manager. Cannot be recommended too highly.

Section Five The Timetable

Chapter 22
Production Control I

GENERAL

Every organization produces—or should produce—a 'hierarchy' of plans to enable it to fulfil its corporate purpose. These plans differ from each other in the level of detail at which they operate, and detail is in itself a reflection of the time-span covered by the plan. The largest time-span is exhibited by the overall company policy as determined by the Board of Directors. Conforming with this, but spanning a shorter period of time is the Sales Forecast which quantifies and identifies the products which will be made over the foreseeable future. From this forecast the Production Control Department prepares a *Production Schedule* which in turn generates a *Production Load* which is finally translated into action by the *Production Supervision* (see Fig. 22.1).

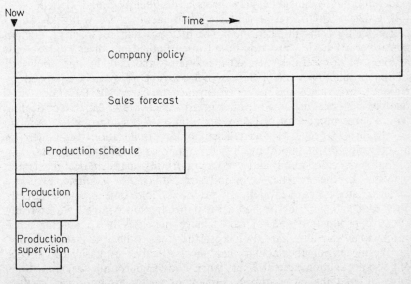

Fig. 22.1

The P.C.D. thus is one of the planning departments within an organization and indeed some authorities refer to it as the Production Planning and Control Department. In the present text, however, Production Planning will be reserved for that function which concerns itself with the determination of the manufacturing *method*, and 'Production Control' will be understood to comprise *all* the control functions first discussed in Chapter 1, namely—

Plan
Publish
Measure
Compare
Report
Correct

In essence, the P.C.D. should be able *at all times* to answer two basic and apparently simple questions—

1. Can a particular task be undertaken, and if so, when?
2. How far have the tasks in hand proceeded?

and in trying to provide these answers, P.C.D. must attempt to organize the most effective use of manpower, materials and plant.

Inevitably the Production Control Department will generate written instructions and as a result it is often considered to be the paper-work-producing department. As such it is much maligned and its duties misunderstood. This misunderstanding is as frequently found at high as at low levels, with the result that staff and facilities are withheld, duties consequently being ill-performed. The qualities required of a production controller are no less exacting than those required of, for example, a cost accountant or chief designer, yet it is often found that the staff employed in the production control department are not adequately equipped by training, experience or innate intelligence to carry out the duties adequately. The production controller needs a clear brain, capable of dealing with a large number of problems simultaneously, a thorough knowledge of production processes and efficient office organization techniques, an appreciation of the importance of controlling costs, and an understanding of mathematical methods and—more important—mathematical reasoning.

Many of the weaknesses of industrial units—for example, excessive material stocks, broken delivery promises, idle time—can be directly attributable to inferior or non-existent production control, whilst really effective production control can achieve increases in output far more spectacular and at a far lower cost than any other management tool. Furthermore, no other activity can show effective results in the absence of good production control. Every work study engineer must, at some time, have suffered the bitter disappointment of seeing his improved method made ineffectual by the absence of material due to poor production control. In any plan for improving efficiency or reducing losses throughout a factory, the organization of a really efficient production control department must come very high in priority: certainly no incentive scheme will work without an effective P.C.D.

Marketing Policy and Production Control

Broadly, there are two possible ways by which a manufacturing company can derive its income—

(*a*) by *receiving* orders from customers, and thence generating work to fulfil these orders;

(*b*) by *obtaining* orders from customers, these orders being filled from work generated *before* the receipt of orders.

Much of the task of production control is concerned with *future* action, and therefore the more accurately the future can be predicted, the better chance the production controller has of making effective plans. An order-receiving policy will inevitably produce greater uncertainty than an order-obtaining policy which will carry with it greater risk. The Marketing Department will need to forecast future sales, and bear responsibility for unsold stocks if the forecasts are incorrect.

The decision to change from 'order-receiving' to 'order-obtaining' is an extremely important one, whose effects, whilst felt throughout the organization, are of paramount concern to the production department and to P.C.D. The value of good market research and sales promotion must not be underestimated, and failure to align marketing with manufacturing will result, at best, in chaos, and at worst, in failure.

Outline of the Functions of Production Control

Scheduling and Loading

At the time of issuing a sales programme (in the case of making for stock), or at the time of acknowledging the receipt of an order (in the case of making to customers' order), the sales department will issue a works order (see Chapter 19) which will authorize the manufacture of a product or group of products. This order is the starting point for all P.C.D. activities concerned with actual manufacture, although P.C.D. will already have assisted the sales department in fixing the delivery date shown on the works order.

From the works order a *master schedule* (or programme) is prepared, which involves assessing labour and material requirements and availability, and thence laying down the dates by which major functions must be complete. This master schedule will be issued to the labour control section, wherein labour availability (both men and machines) is verified, detailed programmes prepared and the various departments *loaded* in as much detail as is useful. At the same time, a copy of the master schedule will be passed to the *material control* section, which will check material availability, putting in train whatever action is necessary.

Material Control

Material Control is the reverse of the coin of which labour control is the obverse. Since the number of items of information is so very much greater in the case of material than in that of labour, the same techniques are not necessarily appropriate. In general the task of the material controller can be said to be that of assessing the need for material, and then taking appropriate action to see that this need is met. This subject is discussed later in Chapter 27.

Dispatch and Progress

At the appropriate time, manufacture is actually initiated by the *dispatch* section, which collects together all relevant documents, verifies the detailed availability of labour, materials, tools, equipment and production aids, and issues authorizing documents. Throughout the whole of this time, and during the subsequent manufacture, the *progress* section will observe performance, verifying that the requirements of the master schedule are being fulfilled. Any deviations from this schedule are brought to the notice of the appropriate supervision, and any necessary modification to schedule made in order to overcome the results of these deviations. Should the final delivery date appear to be endangered, it is unquestionably the responsibility of the production control department to inform the sales department in order that, if deemed desirable, the customer can be advised. Avoidance of this simple courtesy will inevitably lead to a severe deterioration in customer relations, which in turn will eventually be reflected in the intake of orders. A delivery date should be considered sacrosanct, and every endeavour made to maintain it, but if it proves quite impossible so to do, the customer should be informed, and this information can only originate from the production control department. The dispatch and progress tasks are discussed further in Chapter 26.

Sequence of Operations

The sequence of operations is represented in Fig. 22.2 and the five main functions of P.C.D.—Scheduling, Loading, Dispatching, Progress and Material Control—will be discussed in detail later. It must be realized that these functions, although separate, are not necessarily carried out by different persons, the detailed organization depending upon the local conditions, such as size of plant, volume and type of work, and the geographical disposition of the plant.

Production Control and the Computer

The computer is able to store enormous quantities of information and carry out calculations very rapidly, in so-called 'real time', that is, within

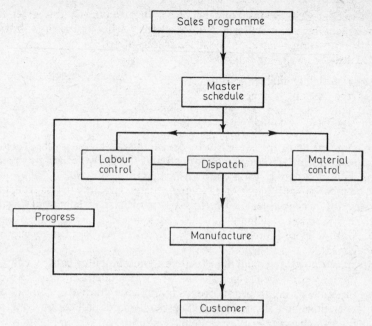

Fig. 22.2. Outline of the Function of the Production Control Department

such a time that information is available early enough to permit useful action to be taken. Furthermore, the computer will tirelessly repeat calculations for as long as it is required to do so: it will not, if properly instructed, generate mistakes either through fatigue or personal inaccuracy. These characteristics are clearly most valuable to the Production Controller.

The scheduling of production presents an enormous challenge to the computer programmer. In special cases where some logical basis for the schedule can be set down—linear programming, critical path analysis, line of balance—the computer can be of great assistance. Similarly, if a schedule has been established, loading—the assigning of work to individual work stations—is a comparatively easy task, particularly if the load nowhere exceeds the capacity. The greatest difficulty arises where products have to go through a number of work stations, and the products compete for limited resources. This sequential scheduling problem is characteristic of batch production, and a general solution in logical terms has not yet been produced although a great deal of effort is being expended on this.

Particular solutions, however, can be produced, providing that any restrictions, and the rules governing the scheduling method (see page 261) are capable of explicit statement. The derivation of a load from the schedule is again possible, given that the schedule within which loading must operate is known, although again, a set of decision rules is necessary.

Material Control is, as has been pointed out, a task analogous to, and

often overlapping the task of scheduling. It is frequently a simpler task than scheduling since material is derived from without the organization, and the constraints can often be more readily stated.
These are—

(*a*) the cash available;
(*b*) the costs of storage;
(*c*) the acceptable risk level;
(*d*) the costs of being out of stock.

A material control system can be operated with a computer, providing the above information can be quantified and the likely variations in stock usage and in supply lead time are known.

The most difficult parameters to express numerically are the acceptable risk level (ninety-five per cent certainty—or the risk of being out of stock once in every twenty demand times is not unusual) and the costs of being out of stock. Here again the necessity of making decisions is thrust upon management.

In addition to its calculating facilities, the computer can be provided with ancillary equipment—peripherals—by which documents can be typed. Thus, again with appropriate programming, the computer can act as a 'big typewriter' actually producing the bonus cards, job tickets, material requisitions . . . needed in manufacture. Similarly, if reports of actual performance are fed back into the computer, progress reports can be prepared virtually in any form which the user requires: in some cases— material control for example—these reports can be accompanied by the appropriate documentation.

Without doubt, the speed of the computer opens new possibilities to the Production Controller. The writing of a new Production Control program is a task of very considerable difficulty and not one to be undertaken except in the most exceptional circumstances. All computer companies, and many bureaux and consultancies, already have available programs which have been tested in action. Choice should be made from one of these, although any potential user should seek advice on the programs not only from its author but also from some person who has actually used the program in the field. Inevitably, the adoption of a program will require that some, possibly many, of the users' practices should be modified, and a wrong choice of program can wreak havoc with an established system. A two-year interval between initially deciding to use a computer for Production Control and eventually getting the first genuine 'run' on the computer is inevitable.

Further Reading

1. Burbidge, J. L., *The Principles of Production Control*, Macdonald and Evans, London 1971.
    An invaluable book written by a manager-turned-teacher. Prof. Burbidge keeps his feet well on the ground, and uses diagrams and descriptions rather than hiding behind mathematical analyses.

2. Magee, J. F. and Bodman, D. M., *Production Planning and Inventory Control*, McGraw-Hill, New York 1967.
A first class text, excellently written and presented.

3. Muth, J. F. and Thompson, G. L. (Ed.), *Industrial Scheduling*, Prentice-Hall, Englewood Cliffs, N.J. 1963.
A collection of articles on the problems of scheduling and how they are tackled in some cases. Can be very usefully read.

4. Lockyer, K. G., *Production Control in Practice*, Pitman, London 1974.

5. Corke, D. K., *Production Control IS Management*, Edward Arnold, London 1969.
A very useful practical book written by a management consultant.

6. *Factfinder 13: Production Control Packages*, National Computing Centre Ltd. 1973.
Provides factual information on the major application packages currently available for use in the area of Production Control.

7. *Computer Guide 9: Production Control*, National Computing Centre Ltd. 1973.
Discusses the potential and actual uses of the computer in Production Control. Both this and the previous text are essential reading for any manager considering the use of the computer in Production Control.

Chapter 23
Production Control II

SCHEDULING AND LOADING

A schedule is a representation of the time taken to carry out a task. It is not a simple list of the functions necessary, since it takes into account the time relationships between the various functions. For example, a product may pass through a number of functions, some of which can be carried out concurrently, and others may need to be completed before the next function is started. A route or list of work to be done would not show this overlapping, whereas a schedule would take this into account. (See Fig. 23.1.)

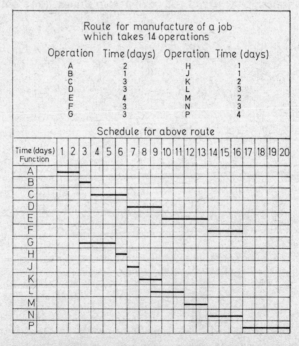

Fig. 23.1. Route and Schedule for a 14-operation Job

A *job schedule* will plan the manufacture of a particular job; once made it will not need to be changed unless there is a change either in the job (for example, in the quantity to be produced, or in the product being produced) or in the method of manufacture. A company which makes a range of products will thus derive a number of schedules which are filed and used as a basis for production control. Such schedules are not dated but specify the time taken: once a delivery date is fixed it will then be possible to date the schedule in order that positive dates for the starting and finishing of each function can be derived. When drawing up a schedule it is important to record upon it—

1. The product.
2. The quantity scheduled.
3. The labour force used.

Most manufacturing organizations produce a number of jobs simultaneously. It is necessary therefore, to amalgamate a number of schedules. This can be done only when the delivery dates for each job are known, and the whole amalgamation will then specify the work to be carried out in each department throughout the period under review. This operation is known as *scheduling*, and the result known simply as the *schedule, production schedule* or *factory schedule* for the plant as a whole.

Optimum job conditions obtain when the various job schedules can be transferred into the schedule without modification. This situation rarely arises, since a number of functions (or operations) in different jobs may require to be carried out simultaneously in identical departments. This would result in the departments concerned being at one time required to carry out more work than possible whilst at other times they would be partly idle. The preparation of a factory schedule will thus require attention to be paid to—

(*a*) The various job schedules.
(*b*) The capacities of the various sections or departments.
(*c*) The efficiencies of the various sections or departments.
(*d*) The maintenance schedule.
(*e*) Holidays.
(*f*) Anticipated sickness/absenteeism.
(*g*) Existing commitments.
(*h*) Availability of materials.

It should be noted that a schedule which completely occupies all work stations at all times gives a high utilization of resources accompanied by considerable inflexibility. When the future is known with some security— for example, in an aggressive marketing situation, where goods are mass-produced and suppliers well controlled—such scheduling may be possible and desirable. In the more usual batch production conditions, some flexibility is extremely desirable, and this can be built in by deliberately underloading resources, and by using sub-contractors. Clearly, such devices generate extra costs and these costs may be considered as the price which must be paid to be able to deal with the unexpected.

Loading

Loading differs from scheduling only in terms of detail and time-span: a schedule will timetable a department for a period of a month, a load will timetable a machine or operator for a day or a week. Not infrequently the final loading—the hour-to-hour assignment of work to individual operators—is carried out by the first-line supervisor.

The *load* is the work assigned to a machine or an operator, and *capacity* is the volume of output capable of being produced in any convenient period of time. When the load is equal to the capacity, then the department, machine or operator is said to be *fully loaded*. If the load is greater than the capacity, then the plant is *overloaded*, whilst if the load is less than capacity the plant is *underloaded*. (See Fig. 23.2).

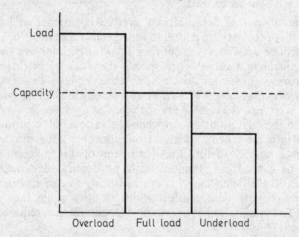

Fig. 23.2

Loading. The preparation of loading schedules for a machine or operator is capable of providing substantial improvements in productivity. Ideally, every machine or operator should know the tasks which have to be undertaken for as far ahead as possible, certainly for at least one working week. By so doing it will be possible—

1. To make maximum possible use of plant and personnel.
2. To establish and meet target dates.
3. To determine necessity for new plant.
4. To improve operator morale.

Basically it is only possible to express a load in hours of work, but it is frequently convenient to express it in other physical terms—

Money ('a machine has an output of £x an hour').
Weight ('a machine has an output of x tons an hour').
Length ('a machine has an output of x feet an hour').
Quantity ('a machine has an output of x parts an hour').

All, however, are expressions of standard hours of work at a known rate of working.

The load on a machine/operator will thus lay down the output and time for the period under consideration, and might well take the form—

Machine 'X'

Monday	8.00 a.m.– 5.15 p.m.	Operation 1	Job 001
Tuesday	8.00 a.m.–12.30 p.m.	Operation 2	Job 002
	12.30 p.m.– 5.15 p.m.	Operation 2	Job 003
Wednesday	8.00 a.m.–10.30 a.m.	Operation 1	Job 003
	10.30 a.m.–12.30 p.m.	Operation 2	Job 005

....

....

Friday	8.00 a.m.–11.00 a.m.	Operation 2	Job 019
	11.00 a.m.– 5.15 p.m.	Operation 1	Job 020

This load can be derived only from the schedule, and the schedule in turn can only be drawn up considering the load. Since delivery dates determine the schedule, the need for considering the load when setting a delivery date is clear, the relationship being as shown in Fig. 23.3.

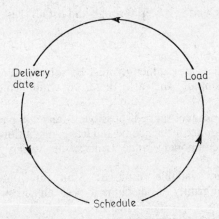

Fig. 23.3

It is a folly to set a delivery date without due regard for the load, yet this is done so frequently that it can be said to be general practice. This will inevitably lead to a costly usage of labour and to broken delivery dates, and must be discouraged at all costs: once capacity has been filled it is possible to insert other work only at the cost of existing commitments.

The Problem of Scheduling

The key to efficiency in a production unit is the ability to schedule effectively—and yet *scheduling* is an exercise which is not resolvable in unique logical terms. Two barriers to efficient scheduling exist—

1. An inability to identify the prime purpose for which scheduling is being undertaken. Many criteria exist against which the soundness of a schedule can be judged, for example—

minimum production costs
minimum storage costs

are two possible criteria. Yet they may *both* be required, and both be in conflict with each other. There are many more criteria which can be stated, and an attempt to satisfy them all can lead to a result which satisfies none. Here the most useful procedure is to try to assign costs to each of the criteria and to choose that which gives a maximum return on investment as the prime purpose.

2. The astronomical numbers involved. If there are N jobs to be processed in sequence through M machines, there are $(N!)^M$ possible schedules. This number can be reduced by requiring that the order of jobs on the first machine should be retained on all other machines. This produces a so-called 'ordered' schedule, and for N jobs there are a mere N! possible schedules. Thus, for 16 jobs there are 16!, that is—

$$20,722,989,888,000$$

possible schedules, and to sweep through and list all these is not a practical proposition.

Reducing the Scheduling Problem

The problem, however difficult, must be solved, albeit in a most imperfect way. To simplify the task, there are a number of fairly obvious commonsense steps which can be undertaken:

1. Reduce the product range if possible. Many companies manufacture products which produce little income and less contribution.

2. Reduce the component range. Unnecessary variety in components is extremely costly.

3. Examine the available resources. Many machines are needlessly complex, and uniformity in machine types can substantially ease the scheduling problem.

4. Carry out a job enlargement programme. To train staff to carry out a number of jobs rather than only one job will improve flexibility and morale.

5. Investigate the use of sub-contractors. The off-loading of peaks of work can sometimes be very rewarding in terms of the organizational simplification which results.

6. Separate out 'big' jobs, which consume a great deal of labour and 'small' jobs, which consume but little labour. To try to mix 'big' and 'small' work in the same work-places is usually very difficult, and a 'small order' shop, organized more informally than a 'large order' shop will usually be quite effective.

7. Ensure close liaison between marketing and production. Stresses can often be relieved by discussion with customers.

1. Reduce product range
2. Reduce component range
3. Examine available resources
4. Enlarge all jobs whenever possible
5. Use sub-contractors
6. Separate 'big' and 'small' jobs
7. Close liaison with marketing

Simplifying the Scheduling Problem

Use of Interstage Stores

The virtual impossibility in batch production of balancing the load on all stages results in gaps in the work available to a work station or department. To avoid this cost, it is common to find that sub-stores (interstage, work-in-progress or buffer stores) are created between departments. These form 'pools' or 'reservoirs' from which succeeding stages can draw work and thus keep all stages at work. Whilst this avoids the 'idle-time' cost of an unbalanced load, it substitutes for it the cost of holding the work-in-progress: since this cost is often difficult to identify and value, it is often ignored; yet it may well be that the idle-time costs, and the organization costs to remove them, may in fact be less than the very heavy costs of holding stock. This area of cost creation will often repay investigation.

Scheduling Rules

Whilst the above suggestions may simplify the scheduling task, they will not solve it, and the residual problem is still gigantic. There is not yet, except in various very special cases, a technique available which can be guaranteed to produce a 'correct' answer, and to enable schedules to be constructed in practical circumstances, it is useful to devise rules to follow. Possible rules are—

1. schedule first those jobs with the shortest first operation, or
2. schedule first those jobs with the shortest last operation, or
3. schedule jobs according to their total work content, or
4. schedule jobs according to their date of receipt, or
5. assign priorities to jobs according to the customer.

None of these (or any of the others which can be set down) can be shown to be 'optimizing' rules—they are entirely arbitrary. Nevertheless, the adoption of some arbitrary rule is more likely to produce a consistent schedule than an entirely random scheduling system.

Some Special Cases

1. One-off jobs can be dealt with by C.P.A. (see Appendix 2). A

multitude of such jobs will, however, produce a resource allocation problem just as intractable as a batch scheduling problem.

2. Where there are only two machines, they can be scheduled for minimum total through-put time by a system known by the name of its author—Johnson's two-machine algorithm. This is more easily used than described, and an example may help in understanding the method. Consider a series of six jobs (A, B . . . F) which all have to pass through two machines in the same order, that is, through machine I first, and then through machine II. Processing times (in whatever units are used) are given—

Job	A	B	C	D	E	F
Machine I	0	4	6	3	5	2
Machine II	3	6	8	8	0	5

A sequence table is constructed—

Sequence	1	2	3	4	5	6
Job						

The job array is then scanned and the smallest processing time(s) identified. In this case, the smallest times are O (on A, I) and O (on E, II). If the smallest time appears on machine I it is done first (so that job A is scheduled first) and if it appears on machine II it is done last (thus, E is scheduled last). The jobs thus scheduled are eliminated and the process repeated, until all jobs are scheduled. The sequence table will then become—

Sequence	1	2	3	4	5	6
Job	A	F	D	B	C	E

This schedule will have a minimum total throughput time, although it may be that there are other schedules which have an equal throughput time, or a shorter total time for particular jobs. The use of this technique is necessarily limited, but it can be useful in special circumstances—for example, where two consecutive machines are very costly, or combine to form a 'bottle-neck'.

3. Cambell, Dudek and Smith, (*Management Science*, Vol. 16, 11, & 10, pp. B630–B637, June 1970) have suggested that the Johnson algorithm may be applied to a multi-machine case, to discover a sequence of jobs which, if not minimal in total through-time, is likely to be near-minimal. This algorithm is not capable of rigorous mathematical justification: however, on the occasions when Cambell, Dudek and Smith were able to

test it against a complete display of ordered schedules, it was found that the results were very near minimal. This author has also tested it in similar fashion and has obtained equally satisfactory results—for example, for the job-machine array—

Machines	Jobs (time in hours)				
	A	B	C	D	E
1	34	67	35	48	76
2	24	80	52	40	37
3	23	20	90	25	60
4	38	31	13	11	65
5	64	3	23	66	53
6	36	69	73	61	70
7	35	30	34	26	14
8	68	66	57	48	18
9	90	55	35	75	48

Where Job A takes 34 hours on machine 1, then passes to machine 2 where it takes 24 hours, machine 3 where it takes 23 hours . . . and so on, then the through-times in hours for the 5! (= 120) feasible ordered schedules are—

636(1)	649(1)	651(1)	663(1)	681(1)
687(2)	689(1)	691(2)	693(1)	694(1)
698(1)	699(2)	704(1)	709(4)	710(1)
711(3)	713(5)	718(1)	719(2)	721(1)
722(1)	724(1)	725(1)	726(1)	727(1)
728(1)	729(1)	732(3)	734(1)	735(2)
736(1)	738(1)	740(3)	743(2)	744(3)
749(3)	750(1)	751(3)	753(1)	754(1)
755(4)	762(1)	763(1)	765(1)	767(3)
770(2)	771(4)	773(1)	775(1)	780(2)
781(2)	784(2)	786(1)	791(1)	793(1)
794(2)	795(1)	799(1)	800(1)	801(1)
802(1)	805(1)	806(1)	807(1)	809(2)
810(1)	813(4)	814(1)	815(1)	818(2)
819(1)	823(1)	827(1)	829(1)	832(1)
831(1)	841(1)			

so that the minimum possible through-time is 636 hours. Using the C–D–S– algorithm a sequence A C D B E was indicated which had a total through-time of 649 hours.

This algorithm requires the generation of a number of fictitious two-machine schedules, which are then sequenced using the Johnson two-machine method. These sequences are applied to the initial array and the through-time for the resulting sequence calculated. That sequence which then generates the least through-time appears to be likely to be a near minimal sequence.

The fictitious schedules are derived as follows—

From the initial N job/M machine array, the 'processing time' for a series of pairs of fictitious machines M_1 and M_2 is calculated as follows—

For the first pair—
 Processing time on M_1 = Processing time on first machine
 Processing time on M_2 = Processing time on second machine
For the second pair—
 Processing time on M_1 = Processing time on first two machines
 Processing time on M_2 = Processing time on last two machines
or generally, for the kth pair—
 Processing time on M_1 = Processing time on first k machine
 Processing time on M_2 = Processing time on last k machine
and the number of such pairs is clearly $M - 1$

Thus, for the array above—

First fictitious schedule

Machines	Jobs (times in hours)				
	A	B	C	D	E
M_1	34	67	35	48	76
M_2	90	55	35	75	48

giving a Johnson sequence A D B E C, which applied to the initial array has a total through-time of 713 hours.

Second fictitious schedule

Machines	Jobs (times in hours)				
	A	B	C	D	E
M_1	58	147	87	88	113
M_2	158	121	92	123	66

giving a Johnson sequence A C D B E, which applied to the initial array has a total through-time of 649 hours.

Third fictitious schedule

Machines	Jobs (times in hours)				
	A	B	C	D	E
M_1	81	167	177	113	173
M_2	193	151	126	149	80

giving a Johnson sequence A D B C E, which applied to the initial array has a total through-time of 663 hours.

Fourth fictitious schedule

Machines	Jobs (times in hours)				
	A	B	C	D	E
M_1	119	198	190	124	238
M_2	229	220	199	210	150

giving a Johnson sequence A D C B E, which applied to the initial array has a total through-time of 650 hours.

Fifth fictitious schedule

Machines	Jobs (times in hours)				
	A	B	C	D	E
M_1	183	201	213	190	291
M_2	293	223	222	276	203

giving a Johnson sequence A D B C E, which applied to the initial array has a total through-time of 663 hours.

Sixth fictitious schedule

Machines	Jobs (times in hours)				
	A	B	C	D	E
M_1	219	270	286	251	361
M_2	331	254	235	287	268

giving a Johnson sequence A D E B C, which applied to the initial array
has a total through-time of 711 hours.

The six possible sequences thus are—

	Sequence	Through-time (hours)
1	A D B E C	713
2	A C D B E	649
3	A D B C E	663
4	A D C B E	650
5	A D B C E	663
6	A D E B C	711

and of these the second (ACDBE) has the least through-time and is thus
adopted as the sequence most likely to be near optimal.

4. Line-of-balance, a special case of C.P.A., can be used in 'single
batch' situations and is particularly useful when delivery rates are not
linear with respect to time. Essentially L-o-B consists of drawing a network
for the production of a single unit, and calculating the 'latest finish' for
all activities. If the delivery activity is taken as the last activity and a
previous activity has to be finished 4 weeks previously—at week N say—
the total quantity passed through the previous activity should be equal to
the total quantity which should pass through delivery at week N + 4.

Clearly, these rules are of limited use, and a 'trial and error' system
may need to be followed. An illustration of such a system is given in the
next chapter.

Critical Path Analysis and the Batch Scheduling Problem

Every job with a definable start and finish is capable of being represented
by a network—for example, the job set out in Gantt chart form on page 256
becomes the network of Fig. 23.4. The batch production situation is one
which essentially consists of a number of discrete jobs, each with their own
'starts' and 'finishes', and it may therefore be thought that C.P.A. can be
used to schedule batches of work. Two problems however arise—

(*a*) each job will, *within itself*, generate a resource problem, and as
already discussed, this problem is not capable of any general solution;

(*b*) if, as is generally the case, each job is independent of each other
job, then the sequencing *of the jobs themselves* becomes a problem of
considerable magnitude.

Taken together, these two problems present difficulties which are, *in the
general case*, far beyond the logical and computational resources currently
available.

Recognizing these limitations, however, much work has been carried
out providing 'special' solutions to the batch production problem using

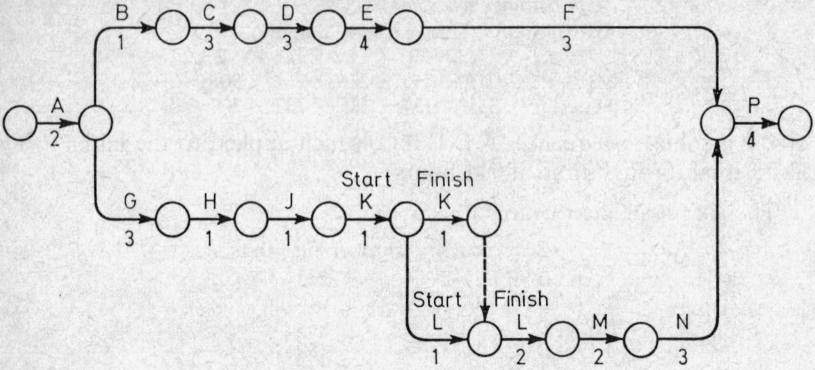

Fig. 23.4

the well-recognized methods of employing intuitively derived decision rules to constrain the number of possible solutions which might be generated. One program which has been used successfully in a number of cases is WASP (Workshop Analysis and Scheduling Program) which was first written and used at A.E.R.E., Harwell, to solve a domestic problem, and which has subsequently become available generally.

Essentially, WASP takes all the jobs submitted to it and loads them on to a machine in a sequence determined by the Work Content and the Target Date, or by a Managerial Priority Rule. Scheduling takes place only over a discrete time interval (the 'scheduling period'), this interval being related to the length of the working period (or shift) so that variations in capacity can be readily accommodated. Where the operation time at a particular machine is less than the scheduling period, the job is scheduled forward up to the end of the scheduling period. Up-dating at the end of the scheduling period then allows further job scheduling to take place, as well as accommodating any over-runs or deviations. Some idea of the number of jobs and machines which can be handled is given by the following table,

Program parameter limits	Available Core Store (Bytes)			
	54K	64K	108K	128K
Machines	200	200	300	400
Machine groups	100	100	125	200
Machine group places	500	1000	1000	1000
Components	3900	5000	7500	9800
Components assembly	150	150	300	300
Operations component	50	50	50	50
Operations assembly	2000	2000	3200	3500
First components	—	—	—	7500
Computer—4 tapes or tape equivalents required				

(*Source—Production Control by Computer*, D. N. Gower, A.E.R.E., R6259, revised 1970)

WASP is a management tool.

WASP is a job shop simulator.

WASP will *not* solve loading problems—it will advise shop management what and where they are.

WASP starts from now and loads machines in the shop up to full capacity—*not* beyond.

WASP shows the end date for each job that would be achieved if conditions do not alter and the schedule is followed.

WASP does *not* take into account possible failure, scrappings, remakes, sub-contracting—unless this is planned initially. Consequently, end dates produced will be optimistic.

WASP does *not* take into account possible future alterations to priorities and end dates therefore can be both pessimistic and optimistic. If priorities are going to be reviewed in the future, end dates produced *now* will be wrong.

WASP will always produce a good feasible schedule and end dates based on that schedule. If work is not completed to schedule the end date of that job *and* a lot of others will suffer.

The Good Manager modifies the end dates produced in the light of known shop performance and job complexity.

The Good Manager accepts that the end dates on his computer output will not remain static.

The Good Manager uses the end dates as a monitor of job progress. If they drift out too far he will examine each case *and* take the remedial action required.

WASP will always reflect the state of the shop and any action taken will be indicated in the next output.

WASP produces scheduled information in sufficient detail to enable the Good Manager to take action based on *facts*.

If the shop is overloaded and every job is top priority, WASP will show that *this cannot be done without taking some action*. The *facts* are there and action must be taken by

either	*off loading*
	extending delivery dates
or	*re-assessing priorities*
	getting a larger shop
	working overtime

WASP will analyse management action and show the resultant feasible schedule with acceptable end dates.

(*Source—Production Control by Computer*,
D. N. Gower, A.E.R.E., R6259, revised 1970)

and the salient features of WASP are shown on page 267. It must be remembered that WASP is only one of a number of computer scheduling problems and that the WASP decision rules are not necessarily the most useful in all circumstances. Before using any such program it is essential to discover what rules are built into the program, and also whether the program has actually been used in a real working situation.

Further Reading

1. Elmaghraby, S. E., *The Design of Production Systems*, Reinhold, New York 1966.

2. Conway, R. W., Maxwell, W. L., and Miller, L. W., *Theory of Scheduling*, Addison-Wesley, 1967.

Neither of the above texts is for the faint-hearted, or the non-mathematical. Probably together they set out the state of the mathematical development of this vexed and intractable subject.

3. Eilon, S. and King, J. R., *Industrial Scheduling Abstracts (1950–1966)*, Oliver and Boyd, 1967.

Chapter 24
Production Control III

AN EXAMPLE OF SCHEDULE PREPARATION IN A BATCH PRODUCTION UNIT

The previous chapter discussed the basic problems of scheduling and indicated that it was not possible, except in some special limited cases, to produce an 'ideal' schedule. In practice, of course, it is essential to produce some feasible schedule, whether it be ideal or not. The problem is at its most acute in a batch production unit, and the present chapter illustrates one way in which this is attempted. It must be stated quite unambiguously that the solution which is evolved is but one of many. It has the advantage of being workable—that is, it does not produce an overload before any work starts, but there may well be many other equally or more useful solutions. As pointed out earlier, a computer can be of assistance here, since, once programmed, it can rapidly display alternative solutions. For illustration, however, the present chapter shows a manual approach: the computer approach would be very similar except that alternatives could be produced very rapidly.

There are two main situations which occur in any factory—

1. Products are manufactured for *stock*, in which case it is possible to prepare the schedule and load at the beginning of the planning period: the 'marketing' situation.

2. Products are manufactured only against *customers' orders*, in which case it is necessary to schedule and load during the planning period: the 'selling' situation.

Manufacturing for Stock

The sales programme will be effectively in the form—

Delivery by end of Week	Product	A	B	C	D
1	... ...	20			20
2	... ...		10		
3	... ...			10	15
4	... ...	15	10		
5	... ...			20	10
6	... ...	10	10		
7	... ...			20	15
8	... ...	20			

From this, works orders, authorizing production, will be issued as follows—

```
Job Number          1001
Product             A
Quantity            20
Delivery Required   Week 1
```

```
Job Number          1002
Product             B
Quantity            10
Delivery Required   Week 2
```

and so on, covering all fourteen jobs shown in the programme.

The production control department will then obtain from the planning department a route and schedule of manufacture for each product. Assuming that the manufacture is simple, and that there is neither overlapping nor dead time in the master schedule, the route and the schedule will be identical and would take the form—

Job Number		1001	
Product		A	
Quantity		20	
Operation	Department	Time	Number of Operators
1	D.1	5 days	1
2	D.2	6 ,,	1
3	D.3	4 ,,	1
4	D.4	5 ,,	1
5	D.5	2 ,,	1

and, in all, fourteen routes would be required which, when prepared, could be summarized as follows—

Product Type	Qty.	Job Number	Work Content in Operator-days in departments					Job completed by end of week
			D.1	D.2	D.3	D.4	D.5	
A	20	1001	5	6	4	5	2	1
B	10	1002	10	10	10	10	10	2
C	10	1003	3	8	5	5	8	3
D	20	1004	12	24	32	20	12	1
A	15	1005	4	4	3	4	2	4
B	10	1006	10	10	10	10	10	4
D	15	1007	9	18	24	15	9	3
A	10	1008	3	3	2	3	1	6
B	10	1009	10	10	10	10	10	6
C	20	1010	5	15	10	10	15	5
D	10	1011	6	12	16	10	6	5
A	20	1012	5	6	4	5	2	8
C	20	1013	5	15	10	10	15	7
D	15	1014	9	18	24	15	9	7
A	20	1012	5	6	4	5	2	8
C	20	1013	5	15	10	10	15	7
D	15	1014	9	18	24	15	9	7

Note: all fractions of an operator-day are rounded up to the next whole number.

From the production manager the production control department would obtain a statement of the capacity of each department—

Department	Weekly Capacity
D.1	12 operator days
D.2	25 ,, ,,
D.3	30 ,, ,,
D.4	20 ,, ,,
D.5	20 ,, ,,

From its own records P.C.D. would obtain statements of the existing loads, holiday periods, maintenance requirements—

Existing Load

Department	Loaded until end of week
D.1	46
D.2	47
D.3	48
D.4	49
D.5	49

Holidays
All departments closed for weeks 50, 51.

Maintenance
Department
D.1
D.2
D.3 } all maintenance carried out in weeks 50, 51.
D.4
D.5

271

The existing commitments of the various departments are then as shown in Fig. 24.1 (between pages 272–3).

Since delivery dates are specified it is sensible *in this case* to schedule from completion date backwards to the starting date: in other cases it may be more useful to start each job as early as possible and schedule forward. At this stage P.C.D. should correct the standard times given on the various route cards for any known or foreseeable departmental inefficiencies or absenteeism: for the purpose of this text, it is assumed that all work is carried out 'at standard'. Under these circumstances a preliminary programme represented by Fig. 24.2 (between pages 272–3) is produced, and it will be seen that this programme generates severe overloading on a number of occasions.

Overloading is quite unacceptable since it represents a task which is incapable of being fulfilled. There are a number of ways whereby an overload can be reduced, including—

(*a*) increase available resources, either, on a short-term basis by working overtime, or, on a long-term basis by buying more plant or hiring more men.

(*b*) sub-contracting the work producing the overload. This often results in shifting effort from the direct producing departments to the support departments—for example, to the purchasing department.

(*c*) improving the manufacturing method to reduce work content.

(*d*) changing the product design again to reduce work content or to permit of the purchase of complete parts.

(*e*) negotiating a change in delivery date.

In an attempt to produce a schedule which does not involve the first four of these possibilities, a revised programme is constructed (Fig. 24.3, between pages 272–3).

The revised programme satisfies the feasibility criterion—no department is overloaded—but at the expense of delivery dates—

Job Number	Delivery Date—End of Week	
	Required	Planned
1001	1	2
1002	2	2
1003	3	4
1004	1	1
1005	4	4
1006	4	5
1007	3	3
1008	6	6
1009	6	7
1010	5	6
1011	5	7
1012	8	8
1013	7	8
1014	7	9

Clearly, these changes in delivery dates must be agreed with the customer, who, in this case, is the Marketing Department. Furthermore, two jobs (1010 and 1011) have delivery times longer than those in the preliminary programme, and there is very substantial underloading on many occasions. All these follow from the reduction of overloads in the way chosen in drawing up this particular 'Final Programme'. A number of other ways might have been chosen, and as a result different distortions might have arisen: the acceptability of any particular method can only be judged in the light of local circumstances.

The load on each department can be read straight off the programme as shown. In turn, the load on individual machines/operators can be readily deduced.

Derived load

Consider department D.1. This has a total capacity of 12 operator/days each week, and this is made up of the work of two operators (Smith and Jones) for six days each week. Their programme of work—that is, their individual loads for weeks 47–4—will be represented by Fig. 24.4.

Note: *it must be emphasized again that the solution of Figs. 24.3 and 24.4 is but one of many possible sets of solutions, and no claim is made that it is in any way 'the best'.*

It is sometimes considered not necessary to break the load down to individual operators, and the actual allocation of work left to the first-line supervisors. This is satisfactory in small departments where the machines and/or operators are completely interchangeable. If this is not the case, it will be found that much time is lost by operators waiting for a supervisor to find an appropriate job. This loss of time can sometimes assume alarming proportions, besides putting an unreasonable strain on the first-line supervisor, and causing a great deal of ill-feeling amongst the direct operators, particularly if bonus payments are involved.

Manufacturing against Customers' Orders

In the problem of manufacturing for stock, the tasks are known before the planning period is started, and time is available to adjust the programme with some precision. In the case of bespoke manufacture this will be so only if the time-cycle of manufacture is long, and the orders received well before production must start. Should the manufacturing cycle be short, and deliveries rapid, alternative techniques may be necessary, particularly if the volume of orders is great. Scheduling and loading will not be so accurate, and it is wise under these circumstances to attempt to underload each department by about 10 per cent in order that any inaccuracies or poor performances will not have too great an effect on the overall performance.

The sales programme will have been prepared in the form of the number of hours' work which it is anticipated will be received by the factory in the form of customers' orders. If the product being manufactured

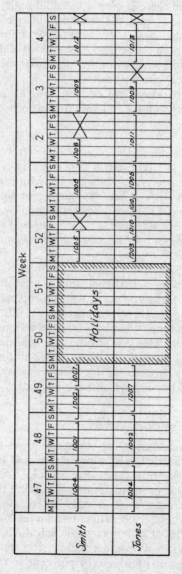

Fig. 24.4

is a stable one, i.e. one that has a stable cost pattern, it may well be that the factory load can be represented in money. For example, if it has been found over some years that the selling price is split as follows—

	Per cent
Direct Labour	20
Direct Material	30
Overheads	40
Profit	10
Selling price	100

then an overall load can be represented in terms of the selling price. Alternatively, it may be found that the labour content is directly proportional to weight, area or some other simple parameter. Under these circumstances it is convenient to build up a load in diary form, the load increasing as orders arrive. It is clearly not possible to issue a manufacturing programme in detail at the outset of the planning period. The frequency with which a programme is issued will depend on the manufacturing time, the delivery time and the volume of orders, but a factory with a one-week manufacturing cycle and a short delivery should aim to issue a four-week programme each week. Thus, in week 1, a programme covering weeks 1, 2, 3, and 4 is issued. In week 2, the programme will cover weeks 2, 3, 4, and 5, and so on. The setting of delivery dates in this circumstance *must* be a matter for close consultation between the sales department and the production control department, and unilateral decisions by one or other department can only lead to eventual disaster.

Loading against Customers' Orders

Assuming the circumstances given above, a load can be built up against a convenient physical property of the product. If there is no consistent pattern, then the loading operation becomes more difficult, since it is necessary to plan the job in detail, preparing a route for each order as it is received. Such a procedure is not, in itself, inherently difficult, becoming so only when the volume of work becomes great. The route having been prepared, there are a number of methods whereby a load is built up. The simplest is a diary, where a series of sheets (see Fig. 24.5) is drawn up, one for each week, and as orders are prepared and planned, work is loaded into the appropriate week. As with all schedules, planning must take place from the delivery date forward: if the final department is D.5, and a delivery is quoted as week 50, a route will be prepared showing the job progressing—

$$D.1 \longrightarrow D.2 \longrightarrow D.3 \longrightarrow D.4 \longrightarrow D.5$$

Department D.5 is then loaded *first* to give the required delivery, then D.4, D.3, and so on.

An alternative method is to represent the load graphically on a bar chart of a type exactly similar to Figs. 24.2 and 24.3. This will produce a

	Week No. 28
	June 30th–July 6th

D.1 Total hours available 96			D.2 Total hours available 200			D.3 Total hours available 240			D.4 Total hours available 160			D.5 Total hours available 160		
Job No.	Hours	Total Hours	Job No.	Hours	Total Hours	Job No.	Hours	Total Hours	Job No.	Hours	Total Hours	Job No.	Hours	Total Hours
2001	20	35	1984	44	94	1970	20	38	1940	24	54	1920	10	22
2002	15	59	1986	50	114	1972	18	62	1942	30	69	1921	12	32
2008	24	77	1987	20	144	1973	24	92	1943	15	85	1924	10	40
2009	18	91	1990	30	176	1974	30	142	1946	16	110	1927	8	54
2014	14		1992	32	206	1977	50	187	1950	25	130	1928	14	64
			1993	30		1978	45	222	1953	20	162	1934	10	72
						1981	35		1956	32		1936	8	84
												1937	12	

Fig. 24.5. Diary Form of Loading

much more striking effect than the diary: if there are a large number of orders, however, the chart becomes unmanageable, and the detail too fine for easy reference. The chart does have the advantage that it can be used, not only as a loading chart but also as a progress chart, and when used in this fashion it is known as a Gantt chart. Progress is shown on a Gantt chart by superimposing a line on the loading line, the length of which is proportional to the work done.

One disadvantage of a bar or Gantt chart drawn on paper is that it is inflexible; that is, that any modifications require alterations to, or complete redrawing of, the chart itself, which in a complex chart can be both costly and difficult, besides being a substantial source of error. To try to avoid this a number of mechanical devices have been designed whereon the work is represented by a card, peg, tape, or other device which is held on to a board. Changes are then made by moving the representational devices as required. The ingenuity of these planning boards and their very considerable flexibility command attention, and any executive wishing to install a loading system would be well advised to see all the boards now marketed. It must be remembered, however, that no system is any better than the people working it: no method, however good, can make up for inefficient operation on the part of staff. For this reason, if for no other, simplicity should be a primary requirement in any loading/progress system.

Chapter 25
Production Control IV

LINE OF BALANCE

Historically, Line of Balance (L-o-B) was developed before C.P.A., and the two systems are often considered to be separate but related techniques. However, if the original time-scaled stage-time diagram is abandoned, then L-o-B can be seen to be a quite conventional C.P.A. system applied to a 'single-batch' situation.

Where L-o-B Can be Used

Just as C.P.A. is used to schedule and control a single project, L-o-B can be used to schedule and control a single batch. The following requirements need to be satisfied—

  (a) there must be identifiable stages in production at which managerial control can be exerted;
  (b) the manufacturing times between these stages must be known;
  (c) a delivery schedule must be available;
  (d) resources can be varied as required.

Whilst it is possible to use L-o-B to control a number of separate batches, just as it is possible to use C.P.A. to control a number of separate projects, the computational difficulties become great. It is therefore usual to employ L-o-B in 'single batch' situations where the batch concerned is of some considerable importance to the organization. An estate of houses, a batch of guided weapons, a batch of computers, are likely to be the type of work appropriate to L-o-B control.

L-o-B in Use

The L-o-B technique will be illustrated by reference to the following hypothetical example—

Product Z is assembled from five components, A, B, C, D and E. A is purchased outright and B is made, tested and then joined with A to make Sub-Assembly 1 (S/A1). C is also made and tested, and then assembled with S/A1 to give sub-assembly 2 (S/A2). The material for D has to be purchased, and it can then be made up and tested, and then joined with S/A2 to give sub-assembly 3 (S/A3). *E* is a purchased item which is assembled to S/A3 at the final assembly stage to give the complete Product Z. This final assembly stage can be considered to include the act of delivering the product to the customer. The delivery schedule is as follows—

First delivery in week ending 1st January.

Week Number	Quantity
1	2
2	4
3	8
4	12
5	10
6	10
7	16
8	18
9	20
10	22
11	24
12	26
13	28
14	24
15	10
16	6
17	4
18	2
19	2
20	2
Total	250

Step 1. Construct a C.P.A. diagram to show the logic and timing of the production. It will usually be found most convenient to start to draw this from the end (in this case 'Final Assembly'), and work towards the various opening activities. The network need not be closed at the start—multiple starts are quite permissible and useful here—and nodes need not necessarily be identified, although for the purposes of the present text the nodes are identified here by letters. Duration times indicate the time required for unit production: these times are maintained constant during production by variation of resources. The final chart is now very similar to the 'GOZINTO' diagram discussed by—for example—Vaszonyi.

Step 2. Carry out a reverse forward pass from time 0 at the final event, that is, assign to the final node a time 0, and then successively add duration times for each activity in order. This will give the set of figures inscribed against each node, 2 at *N*, 3 at *M*, 8 at *J* and so on.

The result of this reverse forward pass can also be represented on a time-scaled diagram, which is the form in which L-o-B results are often presented.

Node Times

Whilst the node times represent the latest possible finishing times for the various activities, it is probably more useful to consider these times in

279

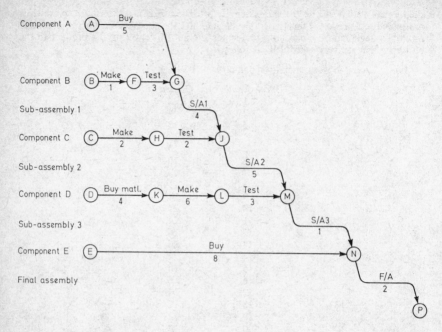

Component A — (A) — Buy 5

Component B — (B) — Make 1 — (F) — Test 3 — (G)

Sub-assembly 1 — S/A1 4

Component C — (C) — Make 2 — (H) — Test 2 — (J)

Sub-assembly 2 — S/A2 5

Component D — (D) — Buy matl. 4 — (K) — Make 6 — (L) — Test 3 — (M)

Sub-assembly 3 — S/A3 1

Component E — (E) — Buy 8 — (N)

Final assembly — F/A 2 — (P)

Fig. 25.1

relation to the quantities which would pass through the head nodes at any given time. Consider, for example, the activity 'Make component B'. Any single component B, having been made, will subsequently require three weeks for testing, four weeks to be assembled into S/A1, five weeks to be assembled into S/A2, one week to be assembled into S/A3 and a final two weeks to be incorporated into the final assembly. Therefore, the interval of time in weeks which must elapse between a unit being made and its final assembly into Product Z is—

$$\underset{\text{(test } B)}{3} + \underset{\text{(S/A1)}}{4} + \underset{\text{(S/A2)}}{5} + \underset{\text{(S/A3)}}{1} + \underset{\text{(F/A)}}{2} = 15$$

If the conclusion of Final Assembly is the delivery of the complete Product Z to the customer, then the cumulative quantity of Bs which should 'pass through' node F by time t is the cumulative quantity which should 'pass through' node P (i.e. be delivered) by a time $t + 15$. For example, two weeks *after the start of delivery of complete 'Product Z' to the customer*, the total quantity of B which should have been completed is equal to the cumulative quantity which should be delivered by week $15 + 2 =$ week 17, that is, 244. This node time obtained by the reverse

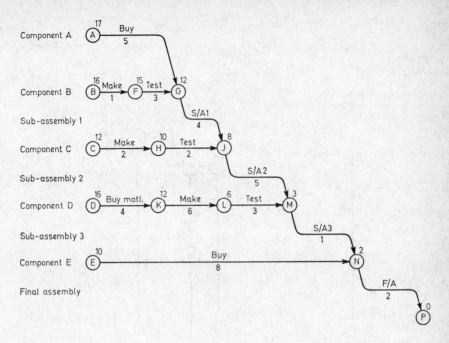

Fig. 25.2

forward pass is called elsewhere the 'equivalent week number' for all activities entering the node being considered.

Step 3. Rank the activities in descending order of 'equivalent week number'. This ranking gives the activity number—sometimes, in L-o-B, called the stage—and is carried out to produce later a tidy 'cascade' chart—

Activity	Equivalent Week Number	Activity Number
Make Component *B*	15	1
Test Component *B*	12	2
Buy Component *A*	12	3
Buy Material Component *D*	12	4
Make Component *C*	10	5
Test Component *C*	8	6
Make Sub-assembly 1	8	7
Make Component *D*	6	8
Test Component *D*	3	9
Make Sub-assembly 2	3	10
Make Sub-assembly 3	2	11
Buy Component *E*	2	12
Carry Out Final Assembly	0	13

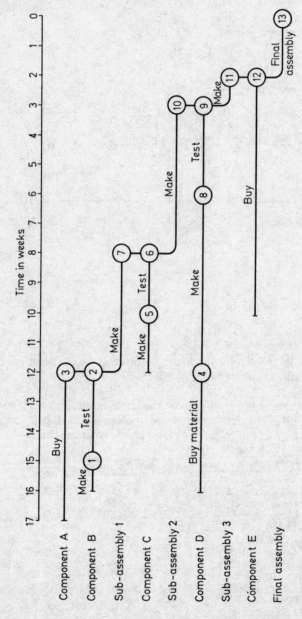

Fig. 25.3

Step 4. Prepare a calendar and accumulated delivery quantity table—

Date	Week Number	Quantity	Cumulative Quantity
4th September	−17		
11th September	−16		
18th September	−15		
25th September	−14		
2nd October	−13		
9th October	−12		
16th October	−11		
23rd October	−10		
30th October	−9		
6th November	−8		
13th November	−7		
20th November	−6		
27th November	−5		
4th December	−4		
11th December	−3		
18th December	−2		
25th December	−1		
1st January	1	2	2
8th January	2	4	6
15th January	3	8	14
22nd January	4	12	26
29th January	5	10	36
5th February	6	10	46
12th February	7	16	62
19th February	8	18	80
26th February	9	20	100
5th March	10	22	122
12th March	11	24	146
19th March	12	26	172
26th March	13	28	200
2nd April	14	24	224
9th April	15	10	234
16th April	16	6	240
23rd April	17	4	244
30th April	18	2	246
7th May	19	2	248
14th May	20	2	250

Step 5. From the above two tables deduce the quantity of each activity which should be completed by any particular date. For example—

It is now 22nd January. How many of each component should be completed?
Consider 'Make Component D'.
The time is now week 4.

The quantity through 'Make Component D' is equal to the quantity which can pass through the final stage in six weeks' time that is, in week $4 + 6 = 10$. From the table above this is a total of 122 units.
Similarly, for all the activities—

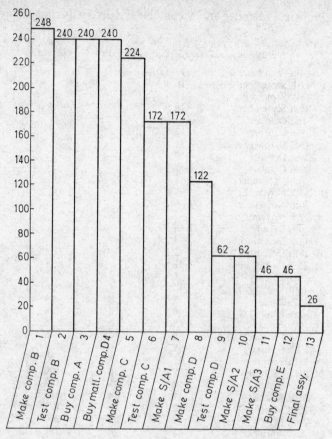

Fig. 25.4. L-o-B Chart

	Volume of Work Completed is Equivalent to Volume Delivered at Week	Total Units
Make Component *B*	4+15 = 19	248
Test Component *B*	4+12 = 16	240
Buy Component *A*	4+12 = 16	240
Buy Material Component *D*	4+12 = 16	240
Make Component *C*	4+10 = 14	224
Test Component *C*	4+ 8 = 12	172
Make Sub-assembly 1	4+ 8 = 12	172
Make Component *D*	4+ 6 = 10	122
Test Component *D*	4+ 3 = 7	62
Make Sub-assembly 2	4+ 3 = 7	62
Make Sub-assembly 3	4+ 2 = 6	46
Buy Component *E*	4+ 2 = 6	46
Carry out Final Assembly	4+ 0 = 4	26

This can be represented on a chart—the traditional L-o-B chart.

Week Number	Week Starting	1 MAKE COMP. B	2 TEST COMP. B	3 BUY COMP. A	4 BUY MATL. D	5 MAKE COMP. C	6 TEST COMP. C	7 MAKE S/A 1	8 MAKE COMP. D	9 TEST COMP. D	10 MAKE S/A 2	11 MAKE S/A 3	12 BUY COMP. E	13 FINAL ASSY.
−17	SEPT. 4			S										
−16	SEPT. 11	S		C	S									
−15	SEPT. 18	2	S	C	C									
−14	SEPT. 25	6	C	C	C									
−13	OCT. 2	14	C	C	C									
−12	OCT. 9	26	2	2	2	S		S	S					
−11	OCT. 16	36	6	6	6	C		C	C					
−10	OCT. 23	46	14	14	14	2	S	C	C				S	
−9	OCT. 30	62	26	26	26	6	C	C	C				C	
−8	NOV. 6	80	36	36	36	14	2	2	C		S		C	
−7	NOV. 13	100	46	46	46	26	6	6	C		C		C	
−6	NOV. 20	122	62	62	62	36	14	14	2	S	C		C	
−5	NOV. 27	146	80	80	80	46	26	26	6	C	C		C	
−4	DEC. 4	172	100	100	100	62	36	36	14	C	C		C	
−3	DEC. 11	200	122	122	122	80	46	46	26	2	2	S	C	
−2	DEC. 18	224	146	146	146	100	62	62	36	6	6	2	2	S
−1	DEC. 25	234	172	172	172	122	80	80	46	14	14	6	6	C
1	JAN. 1	240	200	200	200	146	100	100	62	26	26	14	14	2
2	JAN. 8	244	224	224	224	172	122	122	80	36	36	26	26	6
3	JAN. 15	246	234	234	234	200	146	146	100	46	46	36	36	14
4	JAN. 22	248	240	240	240	224	172	172	122	62	62	46	46	26
5	JAN. 29	250	244	244	244	234	200	200	146	80	80	62	62	36
6	FEB. 5		246	246	246	240	224	224	172	100	100	80	80	46
7	FEB. 12		248	248	248	244	234	234	200	122	122	100	100	62
8	FEB. 19		250	250	250	246	240	240	224	146	146	122	122	80
9	FEB. 26					248	244	244	234	172	172	146	146	100
10	MAR. 5					250	246	246	240	200	200	172	172	122
11	MAR. 12						248	248	244	224	224	200	200	146
12	MAR. 19						250	250	246	234	234	224	224	172
13	MAR. 26								248	240	240	234	234	200
14	APRIL 2								250	244	244	240	240	224
15	APRIL 9									246	246	244	244	234
16	APRIL 16									248	248	246	246	240
17	APRIL 23									250	250	248	248	244
18	APRIL 30											250	250	246
19	MAY 7													248
20	MAY 14													250

Fig. 25.5

A complete table for the whole 'Life' of the batch can be drawn up if desired—and this is shown in Fig. 25.5. The *S*s in the table indicate the latest dates by which the various chains of activities should START, this date being derived from the equivalent week numbers from the opening activities. The *C*s in the table show that work must be CONTINUED.

Step 6. Record the actual progress upon either the L-o-B chart or the 'Life' table. For example, if at 22nd January the achieved and planned results are—

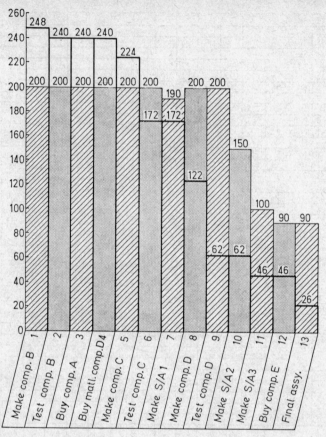

Fig. 25.6

		Achieved	Planned
1	Make Component *B*	200	248
2	Test Component *B*	200	240
3	Buy Component *A*	200	240
4	Buy Material Component *D*	200	240
5	Make Component *C*	200	224
6	Test Component *C*	200	172
7	Make Sub-assembly 1	190	172
8	Make Component *D*	200	122
9	Test Component *D*	200	62
10	Make Sub-assembly 2	150	62
11	Make Sub-assembly 3	100	46
12	Buy Component *E*	90	46
13	Final Assembly	90	26

the L-o-B chart will be as follows whilst the life table will be as in Fig. 25.7.

Despite the over-fulfilment of the delivery schedule (90 delivered and only 26 required), it can be seen that a 'choking-off' of production will

Week No.	Week Starting	1 MAKE COMP. B	2 TEST COMP. B	3 BUY COMP. A	4 BUY MATL. D	5 MAKE COMP. C	6 TEST COMP. C	7 MAKE S/A 1	8 MAKE COMP. D	9 TEST COMP. D	10 MAKE S/A 2	11 MAKE S/A 3	12 BUY COMP. E	13 FINAL. ASSY.
−17	SEPT. 4	S												
−16	SEPT. 11	C												
−15	SEPT. 18	2												
−14	SEPT. 25	6	S	S	S									
−13	OCT. 2	14	C	C	C									
−12	OCT. 9	26	2	2	2	S								
−11	OCT. 16	36	6	6	6	C								
−10	OCT. 23	46	14	14	14	2	S	S						
−9	OCT. 30	62	26	26	26	6	C	C						
−8	NOV. 6	80	36	36	36	14	2	2	S					
−7	NOV. 13	100	46	46	46	26	6	6	C					
−6	NOV. 20	122	62	62	62	36	14	14	2					
−5	NOV. 27	146	80	80	80	46	26	26	6	S	S			
−4	DEC. 4	172	100	100	100	62	36	36	14	C	C	S	S	
−3	DEC. 11	200	122	122	122	80	46	46	26	2	2	C	C	
−2	DEC. 18	224	146	146	146	100	62	62	36	6	6	2	2	S
−1	DEC. 25	234	172	172	172	122	80	80	46	14	14	6	6	C
1	JAN. 1	240	200	200	200	146	100	100	62	26	26	14	14	2
2	JAN. 8	244	224	224	224	172	122	122	80	36	36	26	26	6
3	JAN. 15	246	234	234	234	200	146	146	100	46	46	36	36	14
4	JAN. 22	248	240	240	240	224	172	172	122	62	62	46	46	26
5	JAN. 29	250	244	244	244	234	200	200	146	80	80	62	62	36
6	FEB. 5		246	246	246	240	224	224	172	100	100	80	80	46
7	FEB. 12		248	248	248	244	234	234	200	122	122	100	100	62
8	FEB. 19		250	250	250	246	240	240	224	146	146	122	122	80
9	FEB. 26					248	244	244	234	172	172	146	146	100
10	MAR. 5					250	246	246	240	200	200	172	172	122
11	MAR. 12						248	248	244	224	224	200	200	146
12	MAR. 19						250	250	246	234	234	224	224	172
13	MAR. 26								248	240	240	234	234	200
14	APRIL 2								250	244	244	240	240	224
15	APRIL 9									246	246	244	244	234
16	APRIL 16									248	248	246	246	240
17	APRIL 23									250	250	248	248	244
18	APRIL 30											250	250	246
19	MAY 7													248
20	MAY 14													250

Fig. 25.7

occur in weeks to come due to underfulfilment on some activities, and, equally important, that there is an over-investment in work-in-progress on other activities. It may therefore be possible to transfer resources from the 'rich' activities to the 'poor' ones whilst preserving the delivery schedule: decisions here can only be taken in the light of local knowledge, and will require reference to both the C.P.A. diagram and the progress results.

Design/Make Projects—Joint C.P.A./L-o-B

It is not uncommon to find projects which involve a setting-up stage (design, plan, make jigs and tools) followed by the production of a batch of equipment. Here it is possible to use conventional C.P.A. for all the work up to, and including the making of the first complete equipment, and then to employ L-o-B to control the subsequent batch production.

Further Reading
   1. Lockyer, K. G., *An Introduction to Critical Path Analysis*, Pitman, London 1969.
   Contains a comprehensive discussion of L-o-B.

   2. Lumsden, P., *The Line-of-Balance Method*, Pergamon, Oxford 1969.
   This treats L-o-B as a logical part of C.P.A. It deals in particular with the case of quantities delivered at a constant rate and on this basis carries out calculation of resource requirements. It contains summaries of a number of actual uses of L-o-B.

Chapter 26
Production Control V

DISPATCH AND PROGRESS

In any production sequence a great deal of activity takes place prior to actual manufacture. This will include—

1. Preparing manufacturing drawings;
2. Preparing material lists;
3. Designing and making special production aids;
4. Purchasing and/or allocating material;
5. Preparing job layouts/routes;
6. Setting bonus rates and preparing bonus cards;
7. Preparing material requisition.

Dispatch

All this activity must be co-ordinated, and this is done most conveniently by the production control department. Once all these preparations are complete, manufacture itself can be put in train, and the formal act of so doing is known as *dispatching*. The dispatch section will thus be seen to be the bridge between manufacturing and pre-manufacturing. When all functions are being carried out correctly and to time, the dispatching function will be of least importance, and in large-scale flow production will become vestigial, being a routine clerical task. It is then often found convenient to merge the dispatch function with the progress function, when they are both carried out by a single section.

Responsibilities of the Dispatch Section
This section will normally be responsible for the following—

1. Checking the availability of material and then taking appropriate action to have it transferred from the main stores to the point at which it is first needed.
2. Ensuring that all production aids are ready when required and then having them issued to the manufacturing departments.
3. Obtaining appropriate drawings/specifications and material lists from

the drawing office or library. These must be checked to see that they are of the correct issue required by the works order.

4. Withdrawing job tickets, bonus cards, operation layouts, route cards, material requisitions or any other paper work from the files. These are collected, together with the drawings, and are issued to the supervisors responsible.

5. Obtaining any inspection schedules or information from the design department, sales department or drawing office. This information is issued to the inspection department, along with advice that production is imminent.

6. Informing the progress section that production is starting.

7. Informing the production supervisors when manufacture is to be started.

8. At the conclusion of manufacture, ensuring that all drawings, etc., layouts, and tools are withdrawn and returned to their correct location.

Progress

Once production has been set in motion, it is necessary to check that it is proceeding according to plan. It might be considered *either* that this is unnecessary (since work is going as anticipated) *or* that it is a tacit admission of inefficiency (since work is *not* going as anticipated). On these grounds it could be argued that if a car is being driven along a straight road it is not necessary to watch the progress of the car. Just as the car will encounter irregularities in the road, which although slight, may cause it to deviate from its intended route, so it will be found that there are many factors over which the factory has no control, which will seriously deflect the production departments. For example—

1. Materials may be delivered late;
2. Associated departments may be behind in their own production;
3. There may be excessive absenteeism—an influenza epidemic can reduce the staff available to unworkable levels;
4. The customer may insist on changing his specification or delivery rate;
5. Strikes and 'Acts of God' can hold up manufacture completely;
6. Machine and tool breakdowns may be greater than anticipated;
7. There may be errors in drawings.

Furthermore, all plans are liable to be in error due to normal human failings: errors due to deliberate malignity are rare, and are usually readily observed.

The Progress Chaser

The comparison of performance with plan is the responsibility of the progress department. This is staffed by clerical workers (progress clerks) who record, sift, and compare information, and by perambulatory staff known as *progress chasers* (in the U.S. 'expediters'). The chaser is responsible for seeing that any details which have been overlooked, or which have not proceeded according to plan, are put right. These details are often of such a nature that they can be resolved only by very detailed investigations, involving much walking and talking. In small organizations these duties are carried out by the shop supervisors, but in geographically large units there may be such time taken in going from one section to another that the supervisor is away from his own department an undesirably long time.

Process and Product Responsibilities

Chasers may either be responsible for processes (that is, for the drills, or the lathes), or for products (that is, for the progress of a single job from inception to packing). The process responsibility has two advantages: firstly, that the chaser becomes very familiar with each individual in his sphere of activity, knowing the strengths and weaknesses of each; and secondly, that he knows intimately the geographical disposition of his department, knowing immediately the places where items are most likely to be mislaid. On the other hand, with highly complex products, the effects of variations in manufacture and design can be appreciated only by persons with design engineering experience; as a result, product chasing is often necessary, the chaser being dignified by the name of *Project Engineer*. The project engineer has an overall view of a project, and can foresee and counteract the effects of weaknesses in any department upon the project as a whole. There is a tendency today to employ process and product chasers simultaneously, but whatever system is used, the qualifications for a good chaser remain the same, namely—

1. Tenacity;
2. Robust health;
3. A phlegmatic disposition;
4. An ability to mix well at all levels;
5. An excellent memory.

It must be clearly understood, of course, that the chaser supplies an advisory service—he has no authority over direct production personnel. Informal arrangements may often arise whereby the chaser acts in the supervisor's place, but it must never happen that the responsibility for output, which is unquestionably the supervisor's, should devolve upon the chaser. The chaser should always discuss problems with the appropriate supervisor, never with the operator. Should the results of these discussions be unsatisfactory, he should then move up the organizational structure to the person to whom he is next responsible.

The Fundamental Problems of Progress

Ideally the progress section should always be able to provide detailed information on the location and state of work of all the materials in progress. This should be capable of being done from written records supplemented by detailed knowledge obtained by the chaser 'on the floor'. This ideal is very difficult to attain even in quite small organizations, due to the complexity of the situation which arises from two fundamental problems—

1. *The Problem of Feedback.* The returning of information from a production department to P.C.D. is usually regarded by the production operators and supervisors as an unnecessary and irritating ritual, and is carried out with great reluctance and little accuracy. Furthermore, this information must be in usable form: surprisingly enough, chasers themselves tend to record information in the most unsatisfactory way, often relying on memory or scraps of paper rather than on written records. The difficulties arising from this have to be experienced to be appreciated.

2. *The Problem of Volume.* The information once obtained will be of very great volume, yet much will excite little interest, since it will relate to work which is, in fact, proceeding satisfactorily. Hence it is necessary to sift and present the information obtained.

Feedback

Information can be obtained from a production department in a number of ways—

1. *Mechanically.* If a process is tied to a machine or conveyor, mechanical (or electrical or electronic) counting and/or recording devices may be used. These can also be employed if it is possible to guarantee that all products pass a given point. There is a great variety of such devices, many of them incorporating control mechanisms which regulate the production.

2. *Operator's Work Record.* The operator can be required to maintain a log, showing which operations, and how many of each he or she has carried out. This can be done in a very abbreviated form, involving little writing, and is probably most satisfactory in repetitive work (see Fig. 26.1). It will usually require verifying by the supervisor.

3. *Job Card.* This is a variation of the work record, in that the operator is presented with a card specifying the work to be done. It is usually prepared in P.C.D. from the route laid down by the production engineering department, and can form an authority for the operator to carry out the task specified. The operator will fill in the quantity of the operation carried out, the serial numbers if required, his own name and any other information. The cards are collected daily and returned to the progress section for analysis. This technique is particularly useful in small batch production, since the card itself can be used to instruct the operator in the task he has to carry out and will thus relieve the supervisor of this duty.

4. *Detachable Tickets.* If production is repetitive, a ticket can be prepared which accompanies each item. Each ticket will bear the job number of the product, the serial number of the individual item (if applicable) and a list of the operations through which the product will pass. This ticket will be tied to the product as part of the first operation, and as each operation is completed the operator will sign the appropriate portion of

Name	Clock No
Robinson	*43624*

Date	Dept
21/11/60	*A 36*

Op. number	Quantity	Total
1001/1	~~HHT~~ ~~HHT~~ ~~HHT~~ //	17
1001/2	~~HHT~~ ~~HHT~~ ~~HHT~~ ~~HHT~~ ~~HHT~~ /	26
1001/3		
1001/4		
1002/1		
1002/2	//	2
1002/3		
1002/4		
1003/1	~~HHT~~ ~~HHT~~	10
1003/2		
1003/3		
1003/4		
1004/1		
1004/2		
1004/3		
1004/4	~~HHT~~	5

Checked .... Date.........

Fig. 26.1. Operator's Work Record

the ticket and detach it, placing it in a box designated for that purpose. This box is emptied at least daily by a progress clerk, and the results shown by the tickets analysed. For fast-moving work this can be very useful, since the operator is involved in very little work. A disadvantage may be that the tear-off portion of the card can be easily lost (see Fig. 26.2).

5. *Walk-and-count.* This is the most primitive method of all, and relies on the progress chaser's walking round his own sphere of activity and counting the work he sees. Despite the ingenuousness of this technique it is very often resorted to, in cases of doubt, to supplement or verify information obtained in some other way, and this probably is the most valuable way to use it. It would be most unwise to depend solely on this method of collecting information, since it can be very tedious and inaccurate if carried out continuously.

The information obtained above is necessary for the production control department to carry out its duties. It must be noticed, however, that the information is very similar to that required by the costing department and the wages department if an incentive bonus scheme is in being. If possible, a bonus card should be used to provide progress information, since bonus cards will tend to be filled in promptly and accurately. Organizationally, the turn-round of information must be very rapid, since both the progress and the bonus departments require the information at the same time. Often

Job Nº	OPERATION	Serial Nº
001	FINAL INSPECTION	234
001	FINAL TEST	234
001	OPERATION 9	234
001	OPERATION 8	234
001	OPERATION 7	234
001	INSPECTION B	234
001	OPERATION 6	234
001	OPERATION 5	234
001	OPERATION 4	234
001	INSPECTION A	234
001	OPERATION 3	234
001	OPERATION 2	234
001	OPERATION 1	234

Fig. 26.2. Detachable Ticket

these cards will go first to the progress department, which after abstracting the required information will pass them on to the bonus department. This may result in bonus calculations being a week later than the work itself, and will give rise to wages being 'a week in hand,' that is, paid one week late. This is a well-known situation, and presents little difficulty once explained, except when an employee leaves, when a bonus has to be estimated.

Volume

The volume of information obtained is particularly great when items are being batch produced. Job production clearly presents little difficulty in this respect, whilst flow production can be considered to be single operation productions, where again volume is not so difficult. Furthermore, flow production has the advantage that any difficulties are immediately brought to notice, since they affect the whole production.

Batch production not only presents the most difficulty but also has the greatest need for feedback of information. There appear to be two methods of reducing the volume of information—

1. *Key Points.* In any production sequence there will be found to be a number of key, nodal or 'gate' points, arising either from the production method itself or from the geographical layout of the production depart-

ment. Such key points are often found to be inspection or finishing points, though this is not invariably so. If information is obtained only at these points, then it will be possible to localize trouble without pinpointing it. For example, Fig. 26.3 represents production with three inspection points. If returns are obtained from these points only, then it will be possible to

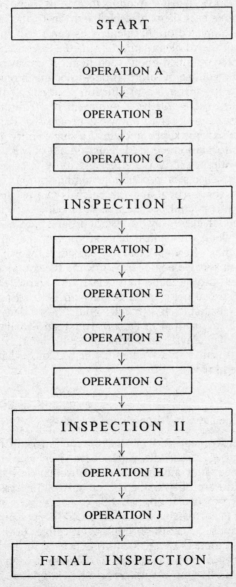

Fig. 26.3. 'Key' Points

narrow down investigation—for example, if it is found that Job 234 has passed the first inspection but not the second, then it must obviously be either in operations D, E, F, and G or Inspection II. This will enable any investigations to be made in these operations only. This type of short cut will reduce the volume of information considerably, though at the same time sacrificing some detail.

2. *Complete Batch.* During manufacture it is found that there is a temptation to move each item of each batch on to the next location as soon as work is completed on that item. This can result in a batch being spread throughout the whole organization, and as a consequence information will need to be obtained about each item. If, however, each batch is kept complete, the volume of information will be much reduced. Consider a batch of 50 passing through a production sequence. If the batch is not kept together, then there will be a minimum of 50 returns to give the information required in order to know the progress of the batch. On the other hand, if the batch is kept complete as a single entity, then one return will give all the information required. This will not only reduce the volume of information without sacrificing either clarity or precision; it will also simplify all other aspects of production administration. For example, if material is issued for a batch, and the batch is allowed to break up, the physical control of material becomes very difficult, since it is difficult to locate components. In every way the task of progressing and administration becomes more difficult with split batches, for a very doubtful reduction in overall 'through-time'. In some cases it is considered worth-while to locate the whole batch in a single box or tray, moving the container only when it is complete. If the tray is made particularly noticeable, for example, by being painted a special colour, the colour can be used as a progressing device itself. For example, if a batch should move daily through each department a red tray started in Department 1 on Monday should be in Department 2 on Tuesday, 3 on Wednesday and so on. If a chaser sees a red tray in Department 1 on a Wednesday he will know that an immediate investigation is required.

The Use of the Computer in Dispatch and Progress

As pointed out earlier (pages 251 and 266) the computer can, if appropriately programmed, produce a schedule which obeys given decision rules and lies within the framework of any imposed constraints. In verifying that the capacity constraints are obeyed, the computer would necessarily have had to carry out a load calculation, and this can readily be printed out for consideration by the dispatchers. In addition all the job cards, route cards, material requisitions . . . can be produced in legible form for use by the manufacturing personnel. These documents can be in the form of mark-sense cards and hence can be used to feed back information on the progress of any task, thus allowing status reports to be printed for use by the manager.

Presentation of Progress Information

The information collected by the progress department will provoke action only when it shows that some task is *not* proceeding according to plan. It is necessary therefore to present the information in such a manner that deviations from plan are made immediately and urgently observable. This is most easily done with the aid of charts or graphs, though the accountant's device of changing the colour of the figures presented can be used.

The type of graph chosen will depend upon the use to which the information is to be put. Broadly, however, charts may be considered as being of two types: (*a*) individual charts, showing some single aspect of production; and (*b*) overall charts, showing the progress of interrelated functions.

Individual Charts

If the output of a single operator, machine or department is required to be scrutinized and compared with plan, it can be shown up very readily by means of a cumulative graph. For example, suppose that the planned and actual outputs from allocation are as shown in the following table.

| Day | Output | | | |
| | Planned | | Achieved | |
	Daily	Cum.	Daily	Cum.
1	4		4	
2	5	9	4	8
3	6	15	7	15
4	7	22	8	23
5	8	30	9	32
6	8	38	8	40
7	8	46	7	47
8	8	54	8	55
9	8	62	7	62
10	8	70	7	69
11	9	79	8	77
12	10	89	8	85
13	11	100	8	93
14	12	112	9	102
15	13	125		
16	14	139		
17	13	152		
18	12	164		
19	11	175		
20	10	185		
I	II	III	IV	V

Examination of daily outputs (columns II and IV) will not readily reveal the failure to meet the plan: the cumulative figures (columns III and V) do in fact show the failure, but if these figures are represented graphically (Fig. 26.4) then the failure becomes more striking. This can be readily understood at all levels, and is very simple to construct and interpret. Care is needed in the choice of scales, but no difficulty will be found after a little practice. This type of graph is ideal for representing output, and with experience can be very versatile.

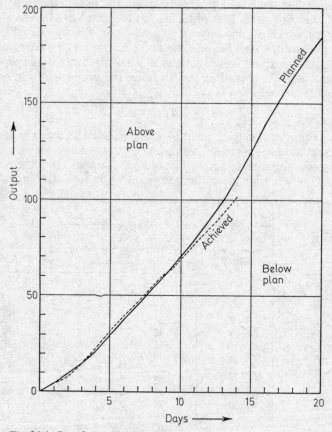

Fig. 26.4. Cumulative Output

Overall Charts

When a number of interrelated functions have to be represented simultaneously, the single line graph is inadequate. Two or three graphs can be drawn on the same axes—beyond this number the graph becomes cluttered and difficult to interpret. Furthermore, the relationship between various features is difficult to represent. For this reason it is necessary to use some other visual representation, and the most common is the Gntta chart.

When scheduling, it was seen that the simplest method of planning a complex series of functions was to use a chart relating time with required performance. Thus, if operation A is required to start on the fifth day and finish on the fourteenth day of a sequence, whilst operation B starts on the ninth day and finishes on the twentieth of the same sequence, the chart should be as follows—

DAY	1	2	3	4	5	6	7	8	9	10	11	12	13	14	15	16	17	18	19	20
OPERATION A																				
OPERATION B																				

This shows clearly the interrelation between operations A and B as far as requirements go. The length of the bar represents time: if now it is also assumed to represent performance, the chart will be able to be used to show the relation between actual and planned. Assume that at the end of Day 9 only 20 per cent of Operation A were complete: this would be represented as follows—

DAY	1	2	3	4	5	6	7	8	9	10	11	12	13	14	15	16	17	18	19	20
OPERATION A																				
OPERATION B																				

The length of the heavy bar represents performance, and it is only 20 per cent of the total length of line A. This shows clearly that Operation A is lagging behind target, since after 5 days 50 per cent of the operation should have been completed. On the other hand, assume that at the end of Day 11, Operation A was 50 per cent complete while Operation B was also 30 per cent complete, this would be represented as follows—

DAY	1	2	3	4	5	6	7	8	9	10	11	12	13	14	15	16	17	18	19	20
OPERATION A																				
OPERATION B																				

The length of the Operation B bar represents 30 per cent of the total length, and since only 25 per cent should have been completed by Day 11, it extends beyond the cursor marks.

This simple device, of permitting length to represent both time and performance is known as a Gantt chart, and is widely used in very many applications. By a series of simple annotations reasons for delays can also be represented, so that the chart can show a comprehensive picture of the state of a department. Most proprietary planning and progress boards are Gantt charts, performance being shown by coloured markers, pegs, tapes, or strings; few give information greater than the simple hand-drawn Gantt, although the use of colour may make the representation more vivid, but they often have the advantage of being able to be simply re-arranged. Once a hand-drawn Gantt chart requires to be altered it is necessary to re-draw it—a tedious operation.

Further Reading

1. Clark, W., *The Gantt Chart*, Pitman, London 1963.

A stimulating book written by an enthusiast, showing some of the ways in which the Gantt chart can be used. It is impossible not to derive some profit from reading this work.

2. Trussler, J. O. C., *Production Control by Computer*, Machinery Publications, 1968.

3. *Computer Aided Production Control*, National Computing Centre, 1973. See also references 6 and 7, page 255.

Chapter 27
Production Control VI

MATERIAL CONTROL

In most industries the cost of material forms a substantial part of the final selling price of the product. Where the interval between receiving the purchased material and its transformation into profit by selling the completed product is short, then the cost of holding the material is likely to be insignificant. However, material must be frequently stored either raw or partly finished and the cost of this storage can be high. There are a number of ways in which this cost can be computed: to the author it would seem reasonable to consider stock as an investment from which a return is expected. Should no return be forthcoming due to the investment laying fallow—that is, the material being held in stock—then the 'cost' of storage can be taken to be *at least* the 'loss' represented by failure to earn the expected return. Thus, if company policy requires that any investment should yield a return of 26 per cent of its value each year, then holding stock can be said to cost at least 26 per cent a year of the the purchase price of the stock. The holding of stocks worth £100,000 for one year will thus cost £26,000 when computed on the above basis.

However great the holding cost *as a fraction of the purchase price*, it would again be unimportant if the value of stocks held were small; if a company with an annual profit of £1m only stored, on an average, £100 worth of stock a year, then the cost of holding this stock—£26 a year—is not of any great concern. In practice, it is often found that the value of stock held is a very large part of the working capital, and Table 27.1 gives figures for a number of manufacturing companies selected at random. It should be emphasized that the value of stock held as shown in the balance sheet is correct only when the balance sheet is derived, and it may fluctuate substantially as deliveries are made or received.

The Task of the Material Control Department

The material control department is here assumed to be required to maintain an adequate supply of correct material at the lowest total cost. The department's task can be achieved in four stages, namely—

Factory and Production Management

Table 27.1. 20 Manufacturing Companies Chosen at Random

Company	Sales	Current Assets				Working Capital	Net Profit before taxation
		Stock	Debtors	Cash and short-term investments	Total		
A	210,786	77,445	60,413	17,911	155,769	95,745	24,834
B	537,800	123,900	76,300	5,900	206,100	17,300	38,100
C	203,340	53,593	40,618	4,401	98,612	47,620	32,683
D	68,371	9,226	17,933	129	27,288	8,085	5,816
E	97,133	5,447	22,975	4,087	32,509	5,324	3,762
F	29,770	3,873	8,079	1,480	13,432	4,559	2,628
G	28,800	9,591	5,309	865	15,765	5,289	942
H	485,250	121,060	119,420	13,290	253,770	121,970	43,150
J	13,023	4,207	4,264	799	9,270	4,256	1,054
K	22,875	5,156	4,403	201	9,760	3,362	1,052
L	52,520	18,079	16,091	213	34,383	23,275	5,033
M	3,845	570	1,022	78	1,670	826	321
N	40,000	12,362	14,085	1,797	28,244	12,318	4,451
P	79,118	7,230	13,653	3,042	23,925	6,825	546
Q	349,510	85,324	73,528	19,043	177,895	97,367	32,185
R	16,428	3,791	1,510	647	5,948	4,698	2,280
S	46,827	10,428	12,074	850	23,352	15,065	2,561
T	86,463	12,695	17,906	8,726	39,327	15,069	17,642
U	40,248	673	4,258	609	5,540	1,313	686
V	5,607	1,376	1,643	889	3,908	2,645	924

1. *Assessing* material requirements in agreement with the sales programme, and *requisitioning* that which is required from the buying department.

2. *Receiving and storing* material safely and in good condition.

3. *Issuing* material upon receipt of appropriate authority.

4. *Identifying surplus* stock and taking action to reduce it.

Buying itself is a function which is not *necessarily* part of the task of material control, and although in the view of the author the buyer should be part (possibly the head) of material control this is largely a matter of local organization, and will depend upon, amongst other things, the value of material compared with the value of the sales price. For convenience, buying will be excluded from this chapter and dealt with later.

Assessing and Requisitioning

Material (or stock) can be considered to be of two kinds—

1. *Direct material*, that is, material which can be allocated to a cost centre or cost unit.

2. *Indirect material*, that is, material whose cost cannot be allocated but must be apportioned and absorbed by cost centres or cost units; and indirect material may be divided again into—

(*a*) Production material—that is, material used in the product itself.

(*b*) Service material—that is, material used in service and maintenance operations, for example, rag, cotton waste, lubricating oil and grease, soap, brooms, brushes, small tools.

Where final products are few and of known design, and where all (or nearly all) material is direct, little difficulty is experienced in assessing material requirements. A works order is received from the sales office: a material list to fulfil this order is obtained from the design department. The material specified in the material list is requested (requisitioned) from the buying department, the requisition specifying a delivery date which would enable the production plans to be satisfied. This situation is typical both of the 'one off' shop and the mass production shop.

In the case of the batch production shop which makes only against customer's orders, a different situation may well arise. Consider a factory making products, all of which are variations of a basic pattern. These products will all use a number of common parts, the final product varying in the manner in which these parts are put together and any extra special parts added. To purchase only when a customer's order is received would involve the repeated cost of ordering small quantities, and an extended delivery time whilst those small quantities were being obtained. If material were ordered for stock, then, provided the stock levels were controlled, economies could result. A simple illustration is a company making a range of products, all of which use some 4 B.A. full-nuts. Works orders might well be received which require the use of these full-nuts as follows—

```
Order 1001 requires  50 4 B.A. full nuts.
     1002    „      100    „    „    „
     1003    „       50    „    „    „
     1004    „       75    „    „    „
     1005    „      250    „    „    „
```

and so on. Ordering in these small quantities (50, 100, 50, 75, 250 . . .) would obviously be both expensive and tedious. Clearly in this case one stock order, from which all the smaller quantities can be drawn, would be an advantage. It is the assessment and control of these stock orders which presents the greatest difficulty in material control, although the power and capacity of a computer can be of great assistance here.

It must be noted that the *cost* of an item it not necessarily related to its *value*: the cost of a 4 B.A. nut is trivial, but its absence can prevent the delivery of an item worth a considerable amount of money, and in this sense the value of the full-nut can be said to be equal to the value of the completed equipment in which it will be lodged.

Stocked Material

Material, whether direct or indirect, which is stocked for general use requires careful control, and here the meaning of *minimum*, *safety* or *insurance* stock must be clearly understood. It is that level below which stocks should not fall: it is an emergency device only, and is intended to prevent unusual and unforeseen circumstances (e.g. excessive scrap, or late deliveries) from stopping or hindering production.

Generation of Stock Orders

Orders for stock can be initiated either by means of signals generated by the receipt of a sales order (order point generation) or by signals arising at the stock point itself. Order point generation is an ideal to be sought in that stock will be precisely matched to needs. The difficulties arising from the sheer volume of data which has to be handled are, however, very great, and stock point generation is most frequently used. To avoid expending effort on items of low usage, an A-B-C analysis (see pages 426–33) of the annual usage of all items should be carried out. The computer, promises to offer facilities which will enable order point generation of stock orders to take place.

Forecasting Usage

In stock point generation it is necessary to forecast usage in the near future: thus, if the usage of stock over the last 7 months is as shown in the first table below, the stock controller must predict the likely usage of stock *next month*. The simplest way to forecast is to assume that usage *next* month will equal usage *this* month. Although crude, this forecast is often adequate for very low value items, but for high value, high usage items some other forecasting device is necessary. Frequently, an average of past usage is employed as a predicter of future usage, and this average may either be *simple*, where all data has the same importance, or *weighted*, where some data, usually the more recent, has greater importance than other data.

TABLE I	June	436
	July	398
	August	434
Year 1	September	417
	October	401
	November	404
	December	430
		2,920

	January	426
TABLE II	February	392
	March	434
	April	440
	May	403
Year 2	June	389
	July	405
	August	429
	September	392
	October	427
	November	441
	December	428

A very common type of weighted average is the *exponentially weighted average*, so called because the weight assigned to information decreases exponentially as time recedes. At the beginning of each new forecasting period, a new average is struck so that the average moves forward, and it is thus known as an *Exponentially Weighted Moving Average* (E.W.M.A.). As the variations in the average are less than those in the information, the process is called *exponential smoothing*.

In mathematical terms, if the actual usage at time N is P_N, and the E.W.M.A. at the same time is M_N, then—

$$M_N = a_1 P_N + a_2 P_{N-1} + a_3 P_{N-3} \ldots$$

where

$$a_1 + a_2 + a_3 + \ldots = 1$$

and

$$\frac{a_2}{a_1} = \frac{a_3}{a_2} = \frac{a_4}{a_3} = \ldots = a$$

a being a positive constant less than 1

$$\therefore a_1 + a\,a_1 + a^2\,a_1 + \ldots = 1$$

$$\therefore \frac{a_1}{1-a} = 1$$

Now—

$$M_N = a_1 P_N + a\,a_1 P_{N-1} + a^2\,a_1 P_{N-2} + \ldots$$
$$= a_1 P_N + a\,(a_1 P_{N-1} + a\,a_1 P_{N-1} + \ldots)$$
$$= a_1 P_N + a\,M_{N-1}$$

and if M_N is taken as the forecast F for the next period, that is, if—

$$F_{N+1} = M_N$$

then

$$F_{N+1} = a_1 P_N + a\,F_N$$
$$= (1 - a) P_N + a\,F_N$$
$$= P_N + a(F_N - P_N)$$

$F_N - P_N$ is the error in the forecast for the last period, so that—

$$F_{N+1} = P_N + a \text{ (error in last forecast)}$$

or expressed in words—

the forecast for any period = actual value for last period + a fraction of the error in the forecast for last period.

To see how simply this forecasting system operates, return to the first table on page 304 (*note*: the second table shows the actual usage in the months to come). If no previous forecasting has been carried out, then a simple average of the previous data is taken for the forecast for January of year 2, that is—

Forecast for January, Year 2 $= \frac{1}{7} (2920) = 417$

By the end of January, Year 2, it is known that the actual usage is 426, and accordingly the error is (417 − 426) = −9. The fraction of this error is conveniently taken to be 0·2, so that—

$$\text{Forecast for February} = \text{Actual for January} + 0.2 \times \text{error}$$
$$= 426 + (0.2 \times -9)$$
$$= 426 - 2$$
$$= 424$$

(fractions of units are rounded up or down to the nearest whole number), or, set out in tabular form—

Month	Forecast for this month	Actual for this month	Error in forecast	0·2 (Error in forecast)	Forecast for next month
January	417	426	− 9	−2	424
February	424	392	+32	+6	398
March	398	434	−36	−7	427
April	427	440	−13	−3	437
May	437	403	+34	+7	410
June	410	389	+21	+4	392
July	392	405	−13	−3	402
August	402	429	−27	−5	424
September	424	392	+32	+6	398
October	398	427	−29	−6	421
November	421	441	−20	−4	437
December	437	428	+ 9	+2	430

This result is shown graphically in Fig. 27.1.

The choice of the fraction to be fed back is initially one of judgment. In essence, the larger the fraction, the more closely the forecast follows ('tracks') recent events, and the smaller the fraction, the more importance is given to distant events. It is therefore possible to change the weight given to various time periods: in times of change and instability, a large fraction (0·4 or 0·5) is used, whilst in a stable situation a small value (0·2) is employed.

The error in a forecast system is often measured by the *mean absolute deviation* (M.A.D.) which is the mean of all errors, all being considered as positive, so that the M.A.D. for year 2 above would be calculated as follows—

$$
\begin{array}{r}
+ 9 \\
+32 \\
+36 \\
+13 \\
+34 \\
+21 \\
+13 \\
+27 \\
+32 \\
+29 \\
+20 \\
+ 9 \\
\hline
\end{array}
$$

∴M.A.D.   275 ÷ 12 = 23.

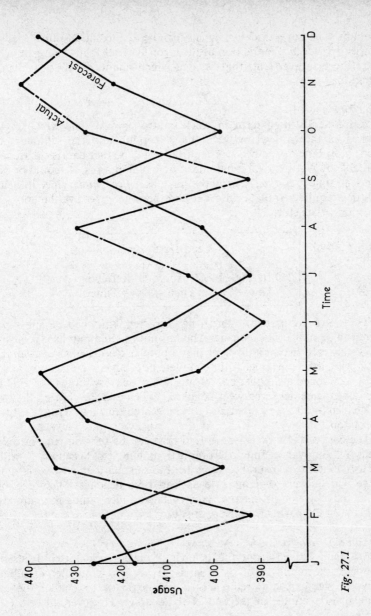

Fig. 27.1

From this measure 'tracking signals' can be derived and in turn these can be used to modify the fraction of the error fed back, thus giving an 'adaptive' forecasting system, that is, one which adapts itself to a changing situation.

Lead Time

A frequently used term in stock control is *lead time* which may be defined as the interval between the perception and the fulfilment of a need. If on January 1 a need for a part is seen, and that part is subsequently available by April 1, then it has a lead time of 3 months. It should be noted that lead time is not *necessarily* the same as *delivery time*, since it includes the time required to place an order and the time to receive the goods into the appropriate store.

Lead Time		
Ordering Time	Delivery Time	Receiving Time

These two components, 'ordering' and 'receiving' can be substantial: there can be no factory manager who has not raised a purchase requisition and discovered two months later that a purchase order has not been made out for the item concerned. Nor can there be a buyer who has not, at some time, telephoned a supplier concerning a 'late delivery' only to be told that 'the goods were delivered weeks ago' . . . and found that indeed they were so delivered but they 'had not been cleared through Goods Inwards Inspection'.

The cost of these increases in lead time can be substantial, not only in terms of annoyance and lost production, but also because, as will be discussed later, the insurance stock held to safeguard against variations in usage and delivery will increase as lead time increases. The 'economy' which reduces 'non-productive' (*sic*) costs by understaffing the purchasing and supplies departments is very costly.

Stock Point Generation

A signal derived from the behaviour of the stock itself is used to authorize the purchase of more stock. There are a number of different schemes available, and reference should be made to one of the more detailed texts quoted at the end of the chapter. However, there are two common systems—

1. *The two-bin or fixed re-order quantity system.* In this, orders are placed when the level of stock has dropped to a previously determined level (the Re-order level or R.O.L.) which is such that when material is ordered at that level, it will be obtained from its source by the time that the stock has fallen to the minimum level. The quantity of stock ordered (the Re-order Quantity or R.O.Q.) is usually constant.

2. *The fixed re-order interval system.* In this, re-ordering takes place cyclically, that is, an attempt is made to assess the usage and then re-order at fixed intervals of time, the quantity ordered being such that either a maximum stock level is replenished at each ordering, or a constant order quantity is placed at each ordering. This *cyclical ordering* has the advantage that suppliers know well in advance when orders are going to be received: alternatively, if the parts are made in the company's own workshops, the production control department can plan labour and machine loads at the beginning of the planning period and possibly adjust the dates of re-quisitioning the parts to provide maximum use of plant. It also allows the purchasing department to plan its own work to the best advantage.

Whatever method of generating orders is used, changes in demand may well force changes in the frequency of ordering. It will be found very useful to include in the material control records a note of the weekly or monthly usage of each item. This can be automatically generated as each transaction takes place, and variations in usage can act as signals to examine the ordering policy for the item concerned. The effort involved in carrying out this calculation on low value ('C') items may well be excessive, but it will certainly be justified for class 'A' stocks. The ABC classification, discussed later in this chapter, should affect and determine continuing control procedures.

Economic Batch Size

The quantity to be ordered, whether from inside sources or from outside suppliers, is dependent upon a number of opposing factors. In any purchase or manufacture there is an element of ancillary cost, either when plant is set up, cleaned or changed over, or when a purchase order is placed. This ancillary cost is spread over the quantity of goods in the batch concerned, and from this point of view the larger the batch the lower the unit ancillary cost. On the other hand the unit cost of storage increases with the batch size. The calculation of the most economical size of batch to manufacture is extremely difficult, involving, amongst other things, a knowledge of the costs attributable to unused capacity. The purchasing situation, however, is more tractable and the calculation can be usefully carried out.

Whilst all the variations of the basic economic batch size calculations cannot be displayed here, the most commonly performed calculation illustrated the basic concepts. The ancillary cost is, in this case, the cost of raising and servicing an order (the 'purchasing cost') and the simplifying assumption is made that (see Fig. 27.2) the product is used uniformly throughout the year. The total quantity can either be made or bought in one batch, stocked and used from stock, or it can be made or bought as a number of batches, stocked and again drawn from stores. In the first case the average quantity held throughout the year is higher than the average quantity held throughout the year in the second. This means that the storage cost applied to a unit in the first case is higher than the storage cost applied to a unit in the second. Since the total cost is the sum of the

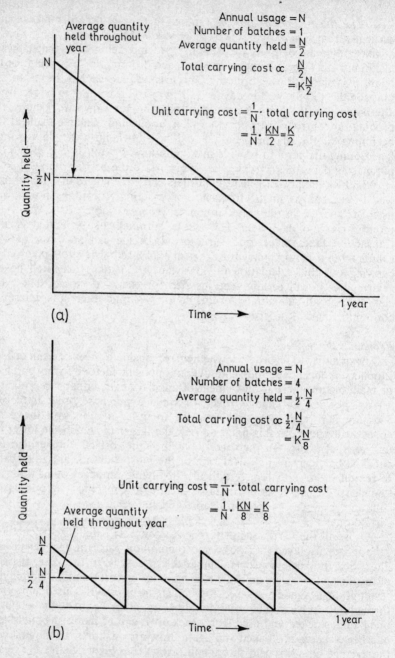

Fig. 27.2. *Variation of Carrying Cost with Batch Size*

initial cost, the carrying cost and the ancillary cost, it is clear that there is an optimum batch size where the total cost is minimum, this being known as the economic batch size.

This result is illustrated in Fig. 27.3, where it is assumed that the unit

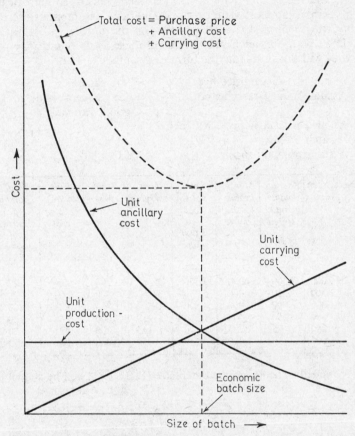

Fig. 27.3. Variation of Total Cost with Batch Size

cost is constant, not being dependent on the size of the batch. The ancillary cost *for each batch* is constant, hence the larger the batch the lower the unit ancillary cost. The carrying cost increases with the quantity held, hence the larger the quantity held—that is, the larger the batch size—the higher the unit carrying cost. These three costs added together will then give the total cost, and will have the shape of the dotted curve which falls to a minimum and then rises again.

The accurate calculation of this economic batch size is difficult, and it has given rise to many analyses. The difficulties arise from the problems concerning the calculation of the carrying cost, since this depends on a number of factors difficult to assess, such as the expected return on invested capital, the cost of storekeeping, the cost of material controlling, wastage, depreciation, insurance, obsolescence, and a number of other factors of varying importance, and from the calculation of the ancillary cost.

The variation of total cost with batch size is illustrated numerically in the following example, where certain simplifying assumptions are made; notably, that neither the factory cost nor the ancillary cost varies in accordance with the batch size. Although these assumptions may not be true, they will not invalidate the form of calculation.

Assume purchase price	= 20p each
Assume annual carrying cost	= 25 per cent value of goods goods stored.
Assume purchasing cost for each batch	= 200p
Assume annual usage	= 5,000.

Number of Batches	Batch size	Average annual quantity stored	Average value of stock	Total value cost for 5,000 units	Unit carrying cost	Total pur- chasing cost	Unit pur- chasing cost	Total cost (purchasing price carrying and pur- chasing costs)
				p	p	p	p	p
1	5,000	2,500	50,000	12,500	2·5	200	0·04	22·54
2	2,500	1,250	25,000	6,250	1·25	400	0·08	21·33
5	1,000	500	10,000	2,500	0·5	1,000	0·2	20·7
10	500	250	5,000	1,250	0·25	2,000	0·4	20·65
20	250	125	2,500	625	0·125	4,000	0·8	20·925
50	100	50	1,000	250	0·05	10,000	2·0	22·05

Algebraically, the economic batch size (E.B.S.) Q^* can be shown to be given by—

$$Q^* = \sqrt{\frac{2SD}{IC}}$$

where—
S = purchasing cost
D = annual usage
I = annual carrying cost as a fraction of the purchase price
C = unit price of the goods being purchased
Using the values given above—

$$C = 20p$$
$$I = 0·25$$
$$S = 200p$$
$$D = 5000$$
$$Q^* = \sqrt{\frac{2 \times 200 \times 5000}{0·25 \times 20}}$$
$$= 632$$

which accords with the arithmetic result obtained above. The change in total cost around the E.B.S. is slow, and no serious increase would result in rounding this value to 650.

Let ordering quantity $= q$

Then, unit purchasing cost $= \dfrac{s}{q}$

i.e. total annual purchasing cost $= \dfrac{sD}{q}$

Average quantity held a year $= \frac{1}{2}q$

∴ annual carrying cost $= \frac{1}{2}q\, I.C$

∴ acquisition cost A $= \dfrac{sD}{q} + \frac{1}{2}q\, I.C$

The results from A being a minimum which occurs when
$$\frac{dA}{dq} = \mathrm{O}, \frac{d^2A}{dq^2}$$
being then positive;
that is, when
$$-\frac{sD}{(Q^*)^2} + \frac{1}{2}q\, I.C. = \mathrm{O}$$
that is—
$$Q^* = \sqrt{\frac{2sD}{I.C}}$$

Note: the above implies that—
1. the unit purchase price is constant;
2. the usage is substantially constant;
3. it is not permitted to be out of stock;
4. orders are fulfilled in one delivery;
5. lead time is constant.

Derivation of the Simple E.B.S. Expression

The Effect of Price-breaks on the E.B.S.

It is not uncommon for a supplier to offer to reduce the unit purchase price if a minimum quantity is purchased ('... if you buy at least 1000 units at a time the price will drop to 19p each ...'). The effect of this change in price—the 'price-break'—can be seen by comparing the *total* cost at the E.B.S. at the existing price level and the *total* cost at the price break level. The total cost curve of Fig. 27.3 takes the form of Fig. 27.4.

Insurance Stock

All the above discussion assumes that both usage and lead time are constant and known, whereas in fact they may both vary. If the usage during the lead time is greater than anticipated, or if the lead time is longer than expected, a stock-out will result—see Fig. 27.3. To safeguard against such an eventuality, an insurance premium is paid in the form of the cost of some 'extra' stock—safety insurance or minimum stock—which exists to absorb unforeseen variations (Fig. 27.4). Clearly, the larger this stock, the greater the cover, but this increase is obtained at the increase in cost of holding the minimum stock. The better the forecast of usage, the tighter the control of lead-time, the smaller the minimum stock to achieve a desired 'cover'. Where it is possible to amalgamate two or more items, it will be found that the resulting minimum stock will be less than the sum of the minimum stocks for the individual items.

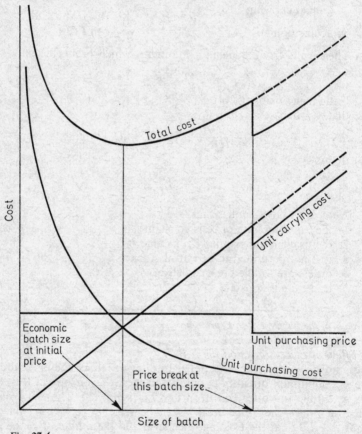

Fig. 27.4

Material Allocation

When a works order is first received, the material requirements are examined, and if necessary material is purchased to fulfil the works order. However, it is sometimes found that when manufacture is due to start

314

(that is, at the dispatch stage) the material is not available, having been used elsewhere.

This situation can be avoided in one of two ways: either by withdrawing the material from stores at the time of receipt of the works order, or by reserving the material for future usage by entries on the stock cards. The first technique, whilst completely safe, can result in excessive long-term stocks and costly storage. By the second method, known as *allocating* (U.S.—*apportioning*) the material is commonly used, and will give flexibility in manufacture and material.

The quantity of material available for general use (that is, the *free* material) is equal to the stock in stores less the stock allocated, and when the free stock falls to, or below, the order level, new material should be purchased, though if manufacturing dates are firmly established the stock controller can sometimes 'borrow' allocated stock to reduce stock holding. This device of borrowing must be employed with discretion, since its abuse can reduce the situation to that which applied when no allocation system is used.

A common source of trouble is the honouring by stores of 'excess material' requisitions (which can arise from a number of causes including scrap, wastage and loss) without reference to the material control department. For example, if an excess material requisition is presented which is greater than the free stock, and this is honoured by the stores, then the result is that the material requirements for at least one allocated job cannot be fulfilled. This situation is difficult to avoid unless the material control department authorizes all requisitions, or the stores and the material control department are geographically very close together. It is sometimes found necessary to insist that all material requisitions, whatever the source, should be authorized by the material control department. On costly and difficult-to-obtain items, this rule should certainly be enforced.

Material Control Documents

There are three major documents in any material control system, namely—

(a) *The material (or stores) requisition*
This is a document which requires the stores department to issue material. It should bear at least the following information (see Fig. 21.3)—

1. Date of origin
2. Originator's signature
3. Cost location
4. Material required, preferably with its code or part numbers
5. Quantity of material required
6. Material issued
7. Quantity of material issued
8. Date issued
9. Issuer's signature
10. Receiver's signature

Depending upon the use to which the requisition is put beyond that of an issuing device, the material requisition can also bear cost information (that is the cost of the material issued) and stock control information. Three copies of a material requisiton are usually needed as a minimum, and are disposed of as follows

The first remains with the originator.
The second and third pass to stores, one then going to the material control and the other to the costing department.

Material requisitions can either be unit requisitions (that is, for one item only) or multiple requisitions (covering a number of items). Unit requisitions allow sorting (for example, into material types or locations) to be carried out easily, and will simplify the problem of dealing with the part issue of material. On the other hand, the multiple requisition will generate fewer pieces of paper but will present difficulties with part issues. The multiple requisition can be the material list itself as prepared in the design department, and this can reduce clerical work and eliminate copying errors. There is on the market a machine which will prepare unit requisitions from material lists, and this has proved useful in many cases. The choice between unit and multiple requisitions is not an easy one, and must be carefully made at the outset since it will be difficult (though not impossible) to alter the decision once taken. Where a computer is used for stock control it can generate and sort requisitions in any manner required, providing of course, that it is so instructed. There is a wide range of stock control packages available.

Excess material requisitions are needed to replace material lost, scrapped or wasted, and these are sometimes coloured differently, or otherwise differentiated, in order to allow them to be sorted easily. Other types of material requisitions may include tool requisitions, gauge requisitions and overhead material requisitions.

(b) The purchase requisition
This is a request to the buyer to purchase material, and may be originated by any department. There is usually a restriction on those signing a purchase requisition (for example, heads of departments only may be allowed to sign them) and the bulk of purchase requisitions should originate from the material control department. These requisitions should bear the following minimum information (see Fig. 27.5)—

1. Date of origin
2. Originator's signature
3. Cost location
4. Material required with full specification
5. Quantity required
6. Date by which it is required

and under no circumstances should the entries be vague: thus the description 'as previously supplied' should not be used, nor should the date of requirement be 'as soon as possible'. These requisitions may be the only information upon which the buyer acts, and he must not be handicapped by lack of information. In some organizations purchase requisitions

PURCHASE REQUISITION					
TO PURCHASING DEPARTMENT *Date*...............................					
Please purchase the following—					
Item	*Material*	*Specification*	*Quantity*	*Charge To*	*Date Req.*
Signed.. *Authorized*............................					
(*Originator*)			(*Dept. Head*)		

Fig. 27.5. Purchase Requisition

involving purchase of capital equipment require to be sanctioned by the board or a nominated director, whilst in others, all requisitions involving spending sums of money greater than a specified amount must be countersigned by designated persons.

(c) *The material control card*

The material control card or stock record card is the central document around which the whole work of the section revolves. It should show stock movement, stock allocation and stock requisitioned, along with such other information (for example, cost of the material) as may be necessary. A material control card is shown in Fig. 27.6, though it is difficult to suggest that any design of card is typical, since each will depend on local circumstances.

The storage of material control cards is, in itself, a matter for some consideration. Modern visible-edge systems, whether in book form or in a cabinet, have much to commend them. With good design the visible-edge card can be turned from a passive record into a positive action-provoking tool. Fundamentally all visible-edge systems are alike, in that cards (or sheets) are stored in such a manner that the bottom strip of each sheet is seen under the sheet immediately above it. These edges will bear information—for example, the description and part/code number of the material concerned—and can also carry movable tags which convey information by colour, by shape, or by location. When a complete set of cards is viewed, the information thus shown by the tags is very effectively presented (see Fig. 27.7.) The advantages of a visible-edge system are so substantial that it would be folly to consider setting up a material control section without thoroughly investigating the various proprietary systems available.

Material control cards which are stored loose—that is, in a box or cabinet from which they can be easily abstracted—are dangerous, since a card can be taken out for some quite legitimate purpose and either incorrectly replaced or mislaid. The resulting disorganization can be enormous, and in the light of the author's experience captive cards only should be used.

Other Material Control Documents

As well as the major documents listed above there are others which are often used, for example—

1. A material return or credit note, which permits unused material to be returned from the manufacturing department to the stores.

2. A material transfer note, which allows material to be transferred from one location to another or from one job to another.

3. A scrap note, which records the scrap generated and permits it to be handed in to the stores in exchange for good material. This usually requires to be countersigned by an inspector.

4. A shortage note, which is issued from the stores to a requisitioner, informing him that material required is not available and citing the action being taken.

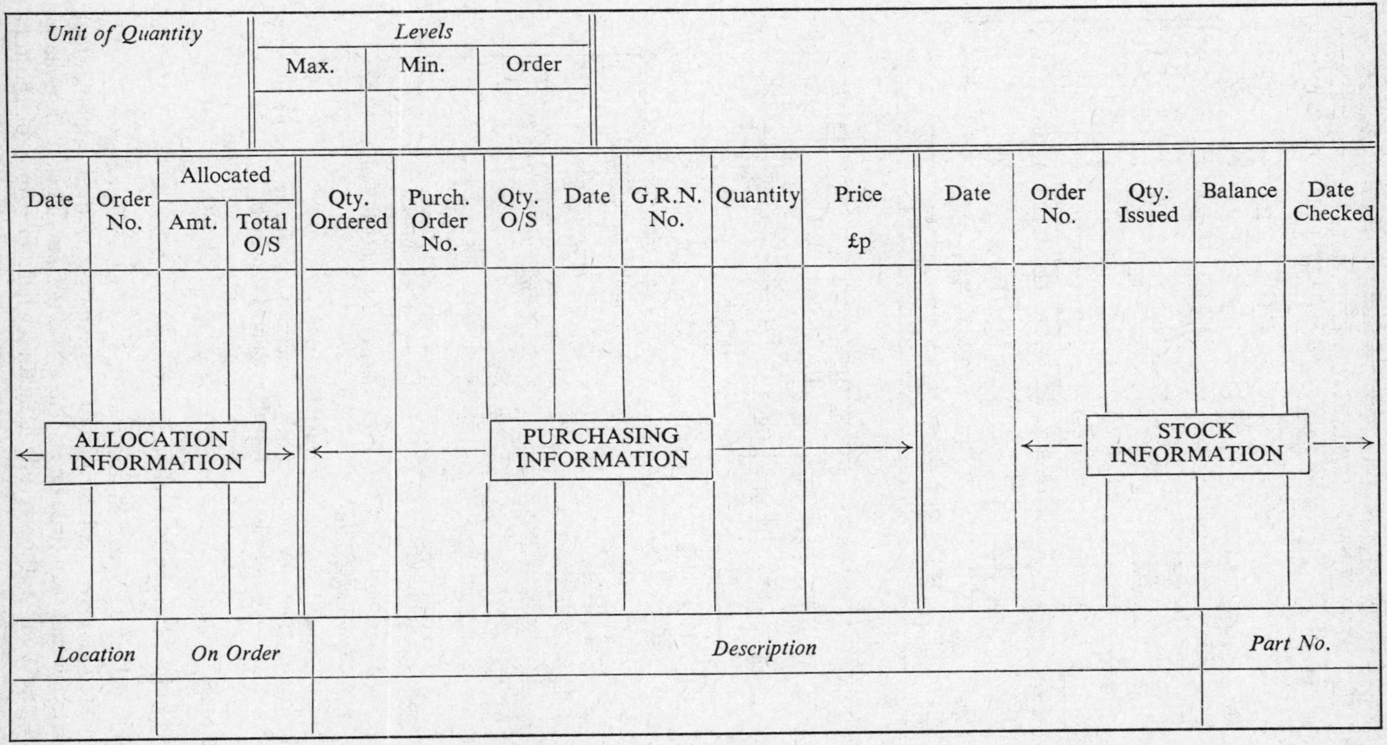

Unit of Quantity

	Levels	
Max.	Min.	Order

ALLOCATION INFORMATION

Date	Order No.	Allocated	
		Amt.	Total O/S

PURCHASING INFORMATION

Qty. Ordered	Purch. Order No.	Qty. O/S	Date	G.R.N. No.	Quantity	Price £p

STOCK INFORMATION

Date	Order No.	Qty. Issued	Balance	Date Checked

Location	On Order	Description	Part No.

Fig. 27.6. *Material Control Card*
(*Note*: This card is meant to be filed with the bottom edge visible)

ORDERED				DELIVERED							
DATE	NUMBER	QUANTITY ORDERED	QUANTITY RECEIVED	DATE	NUMBER	QUANTITY	BALANCE	DATE	NUMBER	QUANTITY	BALANCE
20 6	1/8X		50	50	22 6	1/8X	50	70			
27 6	"		25	25	29 6	"	10	60			
4 7	"		25	25	6 7	"	10	55			
11 7	"		50								

LOCATION: STOCK ROOM BIN NO: 15 CATALOGUE NO: 221A SUPPLIER: BOOTEES LTD.

MAX. 150 MIN. 30 | JAN 20 | FEB 15 | MAR 17 | APR 19 | MAY 27 | JUN 33 | JULY | AUG | SEPT | OCT | NOV | DEC | ARTICLE: BROGUES MENS SIZE 8½

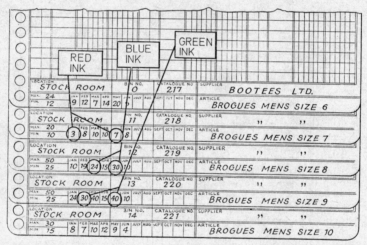

Fig. 27.7. Visible-edge Cards

(*Courtesy of Percy Jones (Twinlock) Ltd.*)

Signalling is shown here by means of coloured inks. It can also be done by adhesive coloured dots or movable coloured metal tags

Carrying out a Material Reduction Programme

The stock valuation figure should include all stock except that which has been declared valueless and 'written off'. Often the so-called valuable stock includes much that is of little or no real worth despite the valuation placed upon it, and your author recalls a factory where one-third of the total stock was worthless due to obsolescence, over-ordering, incorrect ordering and similar causes.

Despite the lack of worth, the storage and 'annoyance' costs may be substantial, and any reduction in stock can have substantial real benefits, some of which are—

1. Holding costs will be reduced.
2. Floor space will be available for manufacture rather than for storage.
3. More cash will be available for use in other ways.
4. Reduction in administration and clerical effort.

The following technique is suggested as one which has been usefully used in carrying out a material reduction programme.

1. Carry out an A–B–C analysis (see p. 426) of the value of stock held against the number of items of stock. This can either be done from the auditor's stock valuation sheets or from the material control cards.
2. From the analysis decide on the A, B and C categories, the A items being those few which represent the bulk of the value, the C items being those many items of trivial value, and the B items being those of moderate value between A and C. *Note*: if there are too many items to handle conveniently, select 100 items *at random*, carry out a Pareto analysis on this sample, and hence determine the A-B-C boundaries. These might appear—

   A items — total value of £100 and over
   B items — total value between £99 and £10
   C items — total value less than £10

3. Examine the 'A' group to determine—

   (*a*) dead items—those which have not been used for two years,
   (*b*) slow moving items—those which have been used in the last two years but have not moved in the last six months,
   (*c*) current items—those used within the last six months.

(*Note*: the definitions of these categories will vary from company to company and will depend upon the technology of the company concerned.)

4. Test the 'dead' items against the following:

   (*a*) can they be used in place of current stock?
   (*b*) can they be transferred into current stock?
   (*c*) can a demand for them be predicted or stimulated?

If the answer to all the above is 'NO', then the items should be written off, and sold or given away. The arguments that they 'will come in useful one day' or that 'we can't afford to get rid of them' are specious and must be resisted vigorously. Particularly frustrating is the 'policy' which limits the value of stock that may be written off in any one financial year, so

321

that—for example—no more than a total of £500 can be written off in a year, whatever, the circumstances. Such a policy is neither useful nor prudent, and serves only to mislead the shareholders.

5. Repeat (4) for slow-moving items.

6. Test the 'current' items against the following—

(a) Is the coverage $\left(= \dfrac{\text{units available}}{\text{average units used/unit time}} \right)$

excessive? If so, then some part of the stock should be treated as 'dead' stock.

(b) Can the unit price be reduced? Try—

    (i) value analysis,

    (ii) work study of the manufacturing methods,

    (iii) alternative suppliers.

(c) Can any item be made common with or inter-changeable with other items? A good coding system is invaluable here (see page 73).

(d) Can the lead time for any item be reduced? The shorter the lead time (that is, the time between the decision to place an order and its subsequent fulfilment) the lower the average value of stock which may be held. It may be that a supplier, hitherto discarded on price, may benefit the purchaser on grounds of a shorter, and more predictable, delivery.

(f) Is the authority to purchase appropriately controlled? Where there are large numbers of orders to be placed, the authority to sign orders is often given to assistant buyers and buying clerks. Item 'A' purchases are often better authorized only by senior members of the organization. The resulting inconvenience in getting such orders signed will, in itself, tend to discourage demands and purchases.

(g) Is the stock-holding reviewed frequently enough? A perpetual inventory (page 339), causing second stock checks of 'A' items can be of assistance here.

7. Repeat the above for 'B' items.

8. To try to carry out the above for 'C' items is usually quite impossible, since the number of items is likely to be extremely large and the rewards obtained small. 'C' items, therefore, should be scrutinized only when stock cards are withdrawn for normal recording purposes. When (7) above is completed the whole process should be STARTED again.

The above procedure will certainly reduce the obesity in the stores, and may even result in some cash inflow from the sale of surplus stock although this should not be considered to be the prime purpose of the programme. On the other hand, supplementing the above by a reduction in stock purchases can result in valuable financial gain, since the savings in cash will be *real* and immediate. A reduction in stock purchases of 5 per cent out of a total of £100,000 will immediately release £5,000, whereas a reduction of 5 per cent in a work content of £100,000 may only result in a saving of £1,000, due to the inability to use less than a complete person, and by a general ability of supervisors to use all the time available on jobs other than direct production jobs.

Material Specification and Numbers

For a control system to be effective, all material should be accurately and unambiguously described; that is, it should be *specified*. The responsibility for making this specification is usually upon the designer, who should be in a position to detail the requirements of his design. This matter has been discussed in detail in Chapter 6. At the same time, all material should be given a number in order that it can be easily and unequivocally referred to. The design of a code numbering system is of great importance to the efficiency of the organization as a whole: here it is only necessary to say that every code number should be *unique*, that is, that it should refer to one type of material only. The importance of the choice of a code numbering system is so great that it is considered in some detail in Chapter 6 and again in Chapter 18.

Further Reading

1. Battersby, A., *A Guide to Stock Control*. Pitman, London 1971. For the British Institute of Management.

An excellent lively work designed to be one 'which can be comfortably absorbed on a railway journey from London to Manchester'. It gives a sound introduction to stock control.

2. Brown, R. G., *Decision Rules for Inventory Management*, Holt, Rinehart and Winston, New York 1967.

An unusual and absorbing book which describes the problems faced by a new O.R. man dealing with the control of stock in a large, multi-plant enterprise. The size of the company is large enough to allow all the usual— and some unusual—problems to be dealt with. The 'human' problems of resistance to change are not ignored. Altogether an outstanding work.

3. Hadley, G. and Whitin, T. M., *Analysis of Inventory Systems*, Prentice-Hall, Englewood Cliffs, N.J., 1963.

A text requiring mathematical understanding of a high order if it is to be fully comprehended. A book for the serious worker.

4. Lockyer, K. G., *Stock Control: A Practical Approach*, Cassell, London 1972.

The author displays 100 stock control cards taken at random from a large inventory and the financial data concerning the company. Using these he develops the theory of stock control, relating it back to reality by way of the cards.

5. Lewis, C. D., *Scientific Inventory Control*, Butterworth, London 1970.

This book is an attempt to bridge the gap between ultra-simple inventory models and sophisticated mathematical treatments. Contains discussions of associated topics often not found in texts on stock control—for example, the properties of some frequency distributions, the methods of generating random numbers, queuing theory, simulation. Includes the only known (by K.G.L.) discussion on Coverage Analysis apart from Murdoch's original paper.

6. Baily, P., *Successful Stock Control by Manual Methods*, Gower Press, 1971.

A practical book designed for the man who wants to do something about stock control in his organization. Written in a somewhat colloquial style, it avoids all but the most elementary mathematics and concentrates on the actual mechanics of running a non-computerized stock control system.

7. Thomas, A. B., *Stock Control in Manufacturing Industries*, Gower Press, 1968.

An excellent book written by a practitioner. Can be read with profit by novice and expert alike.

Chapter 28
Buying

The primary function of a buyer is the obtaining of the right article, at the right time, in the right quantity, and at the right price. He has, however, a number of other duties: he forms the company's 'window on the world' and should provide information on any new products, processes, materials and services. He should also be in a position to advise on probable prices, deliveries, and performance of items under consideration by the design, development and estimating departments. Since purchased material may form a very large proportion of the final selling price of the company's products, buying is an extremely important specialist function which should never be underestimated.

THE RESPONSIBILITY FOR PURCHASING

The organizational location of the buyer will vary from one company to another, but the most commonly found executives to whom the buyer is responsible are—

1. *The Accountant.* It is argued that the buyer is spending the company's money, and, since the control of money is the responsibility of the accountant, then the buyer should report to the accountant. This arrangement will work best when the range of purchases is small and the source of supply limited, as, for example, the polythene tubing used in polythene bag manufacture. In a company making complex equipment, particularly on a batch production basis, this location is probably too remote from the point of production to be effective.

2. *The Managing Director* or the senior executive. Where considerable quantities of material are being bought, particularly of an expensive nature, it is often desirable for purchase negotiations to be carried out at as high a level as possible, since favourable terms can often only be negotiated directly with the managing directors of supplying companies. For this reason many managing directors undertake the purchasing function themselves, or delegate it to some person directly responsible to them.

3. *The Production Manager* or the *Production Controller*. In batch production to customer's order the need for manufacturing resources to be

flexible will often dictate that the buyer be part of the production manager's staff, either directly responsible to the production manager himself or responsible to the production controller, possibly as head of the material control section, where he will undertake duties wider than the buying duties.

Centralization and Localization of Buying

Within a single factory it is now generally accepted that all buying shall be carried out by one department. This avoids the uneconomical purchasing of unnecessary small quantities, irritation of the vendor at having a number of contacts with the company, and the carrying out of a specialist function by non-specialists. In companies with a number of plants, or with a number of autonomous divisions within the same plant, the situation is not so straightforward. Buying can, under these circumstances, either be carried out at one central location for all plants, however widely separated geographically, or by local buying departments, each situated at the plant concerned.

Advantages of Centralization
The advantages of centralized buying are—

1. A *consistent* buying policy;
2. *Maximum* purchasing power in the hands of one person when conducting negotiations with vendors;
3. *Uniform* purchasing records and organization.

Advantages of Decentralized Buying
The advantages of decentralized buying are—

1. *Greater flexibility*: if a centralized buyer is purchasing for a number of plants or divisions he will find it difficult to react rapidly to changes in requirement of individual users.
2. *Close liaison*: a local buyer will be in closer contact with his own manufacturing unit, and will be able to give greater assistance on those 'window on the world' duties mentioned above.
3. *Responsibility*: if the purchasing for a location is not under the control of the senior executive at that location, he cannot be held responsible for the purchase of goods. Since these can vitally affect the overall performance of the location, the executive concerned thus loses responsibility for the output of his department or section; in other words, the division ceases to be autonomous.

As is common with most organizational problems, the most usual situation in widely spread companies or groups of companies is a compromise where both centralized and decentralized buying departments exist together. Each plant or division has a separate purchasing department, whilst a centralized purchasing director or manager has the responsibility for co-ordinating the activities and directing the policies of the local buyers.

Duties of a Buying Department
The usual duties that are assigned to a buying department are—
1. *Finding and approving suppliers.* In this context, suppliers must be taken to include both those who supply goods and those who supply services. This should be done not only by discussions with representatives and examination of catalogues and samples, but also by visits to the suppliers' factories. The approval of the vendor's product is, of course, normally the responsibility of the inspection or design departments, but the buyer should be confident that the source of supply is stable, reliable, and able to fulfil the demands made upon it. Visits to suppliers' factories will not only help to give this assurance but will also allow the buyer to meet, in a direct manner, those people with whom he will be dealing, and build up a spirit of goodwill between the two parties. Used with discretion this goodwill can be of great value in times of difficulty.

Purchasing officers, like all other managers, are becoming increasingly numerous, and are trying to assign quantitative values to the factors which are desirable in a supplier. There are a number of such schemes (*vendor rating, suppliers quality assurance*) and these are discussed later.

2. *Purchasing materials at least cost to the company.* Whilst the quality and quantity of goods may be specified elsewhere, the buyer must purchase these goods at the most advantageous terms. He must be prepared to assist in or lead all discussions on economic batch sizes, and give advice on the imponderables—like anticipated service from the supplier—which can affect decisions on the choice of materials.

Wherever possible, price should be fixed by competitive tender, if possible, by comparison with a target purchase price. It has been pointed out earlier (page 201) that the lowest purchase price may not necessarily be that which is least costly to the purchasing company, since it may attract other costs (rectification, sorting, progressing . . .) which increases the *total* cost of the purchased item. *Any unexpectedly low price should be treated with caution.*

A buyer should provide himself with a list of satisfactory suppliers and should send out as many inquiries as convenient, requesting information on delivery and price; these inquiries being marked most clearly FOR QUOTATION ONLY. Quotations should be examined not only for price but also for such items as delivery charges, discount structure (for example, discounts for prompt payment), tooling charges and any quality or quantity restrictions. The use of the learning curve as a negotiating tool is advocated by some authorities, whilst the practice of incorporating a buyer into a value analysis team is well established and very useful.

3. *Ensuring delivery of goods at the right time.* This will involve contacting suppliers before the material is actually due and seeking assurances that delivery dates will be maintained. A formal 'progress' system should be set up to do this, and a convenient method is to log all delivery requirements in diary form, raising a delivery inquiry two weeks before the material is due, following this up by a further inquiry at a later date to confirm deliveries. It must be realized that deliveries which are too *early*

may form a source of embarrassment, not only because payment may be demanded early, but because excessive space might be occupied. In very large mass-production organizations the delivery date, and indeed time of day, may require to be specified to avoid severe congestion. It is not unknown for goods delivered early to be refused.

When progressing an order, care must be taken to avoid chasing an item which has, in fact, already been delivered. This can only be done by maintaining a close liaison with the Goods Inwards or Receiving Department. A copy of the goods inward note is usefully sent to the buying department in order that deliveries are marked off against the orders.

4. *Warning all concerned if delivieres are not going to be met*. If, as a result of the progressing action mentioned above, it is evident that a delivery date is not going to be met, the production control department *must* be informed in order that work can, if necessary, be re-scheduled.

5. *Verifying invoices* presented by suppliers. This task is sometimes carried out by the buying department, sometimes by the goods inwards department. It is necessary to check that the prices quoted on an invoice agree with those negotiated, and this can be done by a direct comparison with the purchase order if the price is quoted there. If for no other reason, the leaving off of prices on purchase orders is to be avoided, since it restricts the task of verification of invoices to the buying department alone. A further and more real need for verification of invoices arises from the problem of incorrect quantities invoiced, caused by the return of defective material to the supplier, and to help resolve this problem a copy of every rejection note raised by the goods inward inspection department should be passed to the buying department. The recording of these reject notes will also help to build up a picture of the reliability of the supplier, and this may well affect the placing of future orders.

Note: *the cost of verifying invoices can be extremely high, and in the case of low value invoices, quite unjustified. It is as well to consider whether invoices below a fixed figure need to be verified.*

The experience of the Kaiser Aluminum and Chemical Corporation of Oakland, California, is worth quoting in this context. An investigation showed that ' . . . while individual orders of up to $1,000 in value accounted for some 92 per cent of the company's purchase orders, they made up only 8 per cent of the money paid out'. The vast volume of paperwork to release this small quantity of money may be imagined. Kaiser's reaction is brilliant. Each purchase order has a signed blank cheque attached to it, and the vendor is invited to fill in the sum involved when he fulfils the order. Clearly, some safeguards are built in—the cheque may only be paid through the supplier's account, there is a limitation on the sum which can be filled in (each cheque is inscribed NOT VALID FOR MORE THAN $1,000) —but in more than six years of operation the Director of Purchasing reported that out of a total gross outgoing of $195m only one case of fraud had been encountered. Attempts to introduce such a system into the U.K. have, to date, proved abortive since the clearing banks are not prepared to handle the cheques.

6. *Organizing all discussions* with suppliers, both actual and potential. It will be found that departments such as the design department will need to meet suppliers and discuss problems with them, and whilst in many cases the technical departments incorporate the only persons competent to carry out technical discussions with suppliers, these discussions should never take place without the knowledge of the buying department and probably never in the absence of a representative of that department. This will avoid arrangements on delivery and price being made which do not accord with the company's buying policy. In some organizations a firm rule is laid down that all correspondence with suppliers must be signed by a buyer even if it originated elsewhere. This may appear restrictive, but it can save much misunderstanding later on, often at a time when the technical departments have relinquished all interest in the specification and purchase of material.

7. *Speculative buying* is sometimes a duty of the buying department, and implies the purchase of materials or goods not from reasons of immediate need but because it appears that market conditions are particularly favourable. Thus it may seem to the buyer, from his intimate knowledge of the market, that a particular commodity is likely to become difficult to obtain or that its price is likely to rise sharply. Buying in the first case will guard against a manufacturing hold-up, whilst in the second case it may permit material bought cheaply to be resold at a profit. Speculative buying is both difficult and dangerous, and can result in a company carrying extended stocks which are difficult to clear.

8. *Advising on prices* for materials to be used in new or modified designs. This activity can be of substantial value since it may help to decide major policy questions—for example, the feasibility of meeting a marketing requirement on price, or the likely cost of re-equipping a workshop.

9. *Acting as a window-on-the-world.* The buyer's job brings him into continual contact with organizations outside his own, and he can prove a valuable channel of communication whereby news of novel processes, materials, services and equipments are brought to the notice of his colleagues who are most concerned with these matters. In like manner the buyer is often well placed to search out information and his experience at fending off persistent salesmen can avoid considerable waste of time.

---

1. Finding and approving suppliers
2. Purchasing at least cost
3. Ensuring delivery at the right time
4. Warning of delays
5. Verifying invoices
6. Organizing all discussion with suppliers
7. Speculative buying
8. Advising on prices
9. Acting as a window-on-the-world

Duties of a Buying Department

Vendor Rating

Vendor rating schemes are designed to assist the purchasing officer in selecting the most appropriate supplier. Inevitably some sort of ranking must always have been made, but modern schemes attempt to formalize the ranking technique and bring some objectivity to it. Basically all schemes require that some quantitative data is obtained for each supplier on factors such as—

1. Quality
2. Delivery
3. Cost
4. Service and Reliability

The importance of each of the above is not necessarily the same: for example, for some classes of goods quality may be of much greater importance than cost. To account for these differences the above factors may be weighted, so that, for a hypothetical case, the weightings might be—

Factor	Weight
Quality	8
Delivery	6
Cost	4
Service and Reliability	2

Suppliers are then 'scored' for these factors, each score being multiplied by the appropriate weight to give the final factor score. In the crudest possible scoring system the buyer may make a subjective assessment on a 1–5 scale, 5 being the 'excellent' score, 1 being the 'poor' score. The result might then appear as follows—

Supplier A

Factor	Weight	Score	Weighted Score
Quality	8	4	32
Delivery	6	4	24
Cost	4	5	20
Service and Reliability	2	3	6
		Total	82

For a range of possible suppliers this could be combined into a matrix (compare with page 81)—

Factor	Weight	Possible Supplier A		B		C		D	
Quality	8	4	32	3	24	5	40	2	16
Delivery	6	4	24	5	30	2	12	3	18
Cost	4	5	20	2	8	2	8	5	20
Service	2	3	6	5	10	1	2	2	4
Totals			82		72		62		58

Fig. 28.1

Subjective scoring should, of course, be replaced by some objective method if possible. For example, the 'quality' score may be derived from the the number of deliveries rejected by a supplier in the last review period; the 'delivery' score from the number of late deliveries; the 'cost' score from ratio of the price quoted by a supplier to the target purchase price or the lowest obtainable price; and the 'service and reliability' score from a measurement of the number of 'progressing' calls which have to be made.

The Problem of Late Deliveries

The buyer, having placed a purchase order with an approved supplier, is dependent upon that supplier to fulfil his delivery promises. Whilst 'penalty' and 'break' clauses can be written into an order, they are often difficult to enforce, and by the time that it is known that the delivery will be late, it is often too late to renegotiate the order with a new supplier. In an invaluable paper, *Late Deliveries* presented at the Purchasing Officers Association's Annual Conference, September, 1961, Dr. E. N. Hague, then Purchasing Manager for the Shell Petroleum Company Ltd, listed 'Do's' and 'Don'ts' for buyers—

DO—
1. Use clear and complete specifications.
2. Keep demands for 'Rush' delivery to a workable minimum.
3. Keep records of the delivery performance of suppliers.
4. Try to find good alternative suppliers to those whose delivery performances are consistently bad.
5. Keep abreast of suppliers' current range of delivery times.
6. Get to know supplier's policy as regards stocking of raw material.
7. Visit suppliers regularly.
8. Restrict the number of really top level approaches to suppliers with delivery grouses.
9. Consider the elimination of customer's Inspection.
10. Pay suppliers promptly.

DON'T—
1. Nominate a delivery time which is clearly unrealistic.
2. Build in safety factors.
3. Expect 'improved' delivery promises to be met consistently.
4. Give suppliers a ready excuse for late delivery.
5. Expedite suppliers whose delivery promises are consistently kept.
6. Leave finished goods lying around in suppliers' works.

The Purchase Order

The purchase order is a contractual document which may well bind the originating company to a considerable expenditure. It is most important therefore that it should be clear and unambiguous. The following statements—

'Price to be agreed'
'Delivery as soon as possible'
'Of good quality'
'Of normal commercial quality'
'As previously supplied'
'As discussed'

and others of a similar nature should *never* be used, since they are too loose to be useful, and can cause considerable difficulties later when goods are delivered of a quality other than that required, or at a date later than useful.

The purchase order should carry at least the following information—

1. Name and address of originating company.
2. Name and address of receiving company.
3. Identifying number.
4. Quantity of product required.
5. Full description and/or specification of product required.
6. Price agreed between buyer and vendor.
7. Delivery agreed between buyer and vendor.
8. Cost allocation—this for internal use.
9. Delivery instructions—this for internal use.
10. Buyer's signature and standing in company.
11. Company's conditions of business.

The authority to sign purchase orders is usually restricted to one or two persons within the company, and limitations may be imposed as to the amount of expenditure which may be incurred by a signatory: for example, some companies have a rule that orders of value greater than a certain amount must be sanctioned by the board.

It is often convenient to use the back of the buyer's copy of the order as a progress record, and it may then be found desirable to limit the number of items on each order. If, at the same time the items are numbered, then in discussions reference can be made to 'Order number _____, item _____.' This reference is both brief and pointed.

Futures

In some cases orders at an agreed price are placed *now* for delivery *in the future*, the price being paid when the goods are delivered. This form of trading is most commonly met with in the commodity markets where food-stuffs and raw materials change hands. The advantage to the purchaser is that he is insuring a supply of a vital product at a known price, whilst the vendor guarantees a sale, again, at a known price. If either party forecasts the movement of the market incorrectly then he will 'lose' money, but in exchange he has acquired some security. Buying futures differs from speculative buying in that both goods and money change hands *in the future*.

Chapter 29
Storekeeping

For the purposes of this volume the storekeeper will be assumed to be responsible not only for the stores but also for the goods inward or receiving department. This is not invariably so: in some cases it is combined with goods inward inspection and made a part of the inspection department, whilst in others it is part of the purchasing organization or the material control department.

DUTIES OF A GOODS INWARDS DEPARTMENT

All goods entering a factory should pass through a goods inwards department in order that their presence in the plant should be recorded. The duties of this department are—

1. Recording the receipt of (or 'booking in') all goods in a ledger often known as a *goods received* (G.R.) book. This is effectively a simple list of goods recorded as they arrive, and it is not a record of goods received against the order authorizing the goods.

2. Unpacking all goods and checking them against the originating order both for quantity and quality. Whilst the qualitative checks can only be carried out by goods inwards inspection, which is part of the inspection department, the work itself will certainly be geographically located within the receiving area.

3. Returning all defective goods to the suppliers responsible. These should be covered by a *reject note*, giving the reason for the rejection. This note will originate in the goods inwards inspection department, and is either sent off by the goods inwards department with the goods or passed to the purchasing section for onward transmission. In either case it is imperative that a copy of the rejection note is passed to the buyer (see Fig. 29.1).

4. Informing the purchasing and material control departments of the receipt of all goods. This is conveniently done by means of a *goods received note* (G.R.N.), a copy of which can be used to transfer goods to the next location—for example, stores (see Fig. 29.2).

5. Returning all chargeable packing to the supplier.

DAMAGE/SHORTAGE REPORT	Serial No.

To: Carrier

To: Consignor

ORDER NO.............................

With reference to Messrs.........................Advice Note No..........dated......
advising dispatch of the goods detailed below per.....................on..................

☐ the goods have not yet arrived

Enter X in appropriate box

☐ the goods have arrived, but the shortages shown below were found on receipt

☐ the goods have arrived, but the quantities shown below were found damaged on receipt

Vocabulary No.			Description	Quantity Advised	Discrepancy

....

Signature of Storekeeper

Date...............................

N.B. Any correspondence about this report should be sent to the following address and should quote the Serial No. shown above—
Purchasing & Stores Department,
X Co. Ltd,
14 Smith St,
Manchester.

(Reproduced from *Storage and Control of Stock* (Pitmans) by permission of the Author)

Fig. 29.1. Damage/Shortage Report

1. Receiving and recording all deliveries
2. Unpacking and checking against orders
3. Returning defectives
4. Circulating statements of receipts
5. Returning chargeable packing

Usual Duties of a Goods Inwards Department

Every endeavour should be made to clear goods from the goods inwards department on the same day as they are received. Considerable ill-will is generated if it is found that material urgently required is waiting in goods inwards, and since the time spent there does not add to the value of goods but does increase their cost it should be reduced to a minimum. For this reason it is wise when laying out a goods inwards department to provide

GOODS-RECEIVED NOTE			Serial No.		
Date of receipt	Consignor		Consignor's Advice Note No.		
Method of Transport	Type of Packages	No. of Packages	Order No.		
Vocabulary No.	Description	Quantity Received Undamaged	Standard Price	Value	
				Total	
The above stores have been received. Damage/Shortage Report No.................... applies to this consignment.	Signature ...... Date	The above stores are in accordance with the terms of the order as regards quality and are fit for use.		Invoice No.	
The stock record has been posted.	Signature ...... Date	Signature of Inspector .... Date			

(Reproduced from *Storage and Control of Stock* (Pitmans) by permission of the Author)

Fig. 29.2. Goods-received Note

as little storage space as possible, none of which should be of such a design that goods can be inadvertently concealed.

Copies of Purchase Orders and G.R.N.s are usually passed to the Accounts Department where they act as the documents authorizing settlement of the invoices received from the suppliers. Here again it is wise to institute a daily collection procedure to avoid undue delays. Where part deliveries, and part acceptances, occur, care must be taken to inform the Accounting Department, otherwise difficulties over payment can result.

Duties of a Storekeeper

Organizationally the responsibility for the stores may be in the hands of the accountant, the buyer, or the material controller. Furthermore, the duties of the storekeeper also vary greatly with the company concerned: in some organizations the storekeeper is virtually a material controller, keeping comprehensive records and raising all purchase requisitions, whilst in others the storekeeper has no tasks beyond the receiving, storing and issuing of goods. Whatever the organizational situation, care must be taken to give the position its due importance. At the very least, the store-keeper is the custodian of a 'vault' in a 'bank' in which a substantial part of the company's capital is lodged.

It is assumed here that the stores is part of the material control department, and that the duties of the storekeepers are—

1. Receiving and storing in good order and condition all goods including raw materials, purchased parts and components, and partly manufactured items. This may involve a routine handling of material— for example, tins of paint often require to be inverted monthly. Special regulations are in force governing the storage of certain chemicals, spirits, and cellulose paints, and detailed information on this topic should be obtained from the local Factory Inspector.

2. Issuing goods against authorized requisitions only. The storekeeper should never issue material (except for such items as have been declared 'free issue') without a requisition signed by a duly authorized person. A promise by a caller at stores to bring a requisition along later should be disregarded: the storekeeper must regard himself as a cashier in a bank, and should not honour a cheque unless it is presented and signed.

3. Marshalling goods against sets of documents. It is frequently convenient for the storekeeper to assemble together all the materials required for a particular works-order. This material can then either be issued against a summarized material requisition or against a single pack containing all the individual documents. Stores are often provided with special 'job' trolleys on which the marshalled goods are placed for subsequent issue.

4. Maintain such records as may be required of him. This matter is dealt with in more detail later.

5. Carry out any physical stock-taking as necessary. This also is dealt with later.

1. Receiving and storing all goods
2. Issuing goods against authorized requisitions
3. Marshalling goods against sets of documents
4. Maintaining appropriate records
5. Physically checking stock

Usual Duties of a Storekeeper

Card No.	STORES BIN CARD	Part No.		
Description				*Location*
Date	G.R. Note No. or Req. No.	IN	OUT	STOCK

Fig. 29.3. Bin Card

Stores Records

A knowledge of exactly what material is available is essential to the running of the production control department, and accordingly a stock records section is always part of, or very closely associated with, that department. From the records held therein it must be possible at all times to know accurately the stock in stores. Similar records are sometimes maintained in the stores itself in the form of *bin cards*. These are cards placed in the store bin itself recording the movements of stock held in the bin (see Fig. 29.3). In the absence of a properly maintained stock record card the bin card is essential, since it will be the only statement of stock in the company. However, if a stock control department is functioning properly, then the bin card is an unnecessary and confusing device which takes up some considerable time on the part of the storekeeper. It is argued that the bin card is a simple means whereby the stock records can be checked, but this is an admission of weakness which should not be tolerated. A better method of ensuring the accuracy of stock is by carrying out a perpetual inventory, and if this is in being then the stores need not carry bin cards.

Stock-taking

Stock needs to be correctly recorded not only in order that the factory may be run efficiently but also in order that the trading results shall be calculated accurately. When goods are continually being moved in and out of the stocks it is inevitable that inaccuracies creep in, and though a control account held by the costing department might indicate probable errors in total it is clearly necessary to minimize the effect of mistakes. This is normally done by carrying out a *stock-taking*, *stock check* or *inventory*, when a physical count of stock is taken and the results checked against the entries on stock record cards. Errors found are investigated and, if necessary, alterations are made to the records to bring them into line with the actual stock. Stock checks can either be carried out annually (at the end of the company's trading year) or continually throughout the year, a few items being checked each day.

Annual Stock-taking

Even in a small organization the taking of an annual stock is a big undertaking likely to occupy a substantial number of man-hours. For this reason it is imperative that all goods must be immobilized, and it is therefore usual to carry out the annual stock-check over a week-end or during a holiday, when production is not proceeding. To ensure that the whole operation is carried out expeditiously it must be very carefully planned. Instructions to all personnel (many of whom will not normally be associated with the stores) must be issued in writing (see Fig. 29.4) and in as great a detail as possible. Cards or lists of material should be pre-typed, leaving only the minimum clerical work to be done during the stock-taking. All goods in transit (that is, those which have been delivered to goods inwards but have not been passed on to the stores) must be dealt with most carefully. Probably it is better to exclude them from the stock check, and rubber-stamp the subsequent Goods Inwards notes NOT INCLUDED IN STOCK CHECK, but if they are included then the G.I. note should be stamped to that effect.

F. M. COMPANY LIMITED
Annual Stock-taking—19......

To Mr...

(1) The annual stock-taking will take place on Saturday and Sunday, 1st and 2nd October, 19......, starting at 9.00 a.m. each day. Meals will be available in the canteen at 1.00 p.m. and orders must be given for meals to the canteen manageress on Friday, 30th September. Tea will be served at 10.30 a.m. and 3.30 p.m.

(2) No goods may be issued from or into stores, and no movement of part or finished goods may take place between 9.00 p.m. on Friday, 30th September, and 7.00 a.m on Monday, 3rd October.

(3) You will be responsible for counting the stock in bins.................................... to..................................... You will work with Mr.................................... and will use computing scales located at...or weighing scales located at.....................................

(4) When you have checked the items in a bin, you should record your findings on the prepared cards supplied and then affix them to the appropriate bins with adhesive tape. This will then make it obvious which bins have been checked Miss.................................... and Miss .... will be following you to record the figures on your stock cards.

(5) Quantities should be recorded as follows—
        (*a*) in units;
        (*b*) in feet and decimals of a foot;
        (*c*) in pounds and decimals of a pound;
        (*d*) in gallons and decimals of a gallon.
Conversion charts giving decimal equivalents are attached.
Do Not Record in any Quantities Other than the Above.

(6) If you have any questions during stock-taking, please refer to Mr......................
....
....

Fig. 29.4. Instruction for Annual Stock-taking

Perpetual Stock-taking

A perpetual inventory involves much less disorganization and is much simpler to organize than an annual stock-taking. Briefly, each day a number of items are checked so that by the year's end the whole stock will have been counted, fast-moving or very expensive items having been counted two or three times.

One method of organizing a perpetual inventory is as follows—

1. Withdraw all internal stores records (bin cards). This will prevent a storekeeper copying the quantities from the bin cards on to the stock-check lists, a temptation which is great when the storekeeper is hard pressed or

the items very difficult to check. As pointed out above, bin cards serve no useful purpose if the stock record cards are correct.

2. Daily, the material control clerk presents to stores a list of items to be checked. This can be handwritten on a standard form (Fig. 29.5), the part number, description and location being filled in by the stock controller, the storekeeper having only to fill in the quantity found, his signature and the date checked.

3. The storekeeper completes the form and returns it to the material control department each day.

4. The material controller checks the stock found against the record card and immediately causes significant discrepancies to be investigated.

To Stores from Material Control		Date	
PLEASE CHECK THE FOLLOWING			
Part No.	Description	Location	Quantity Found

THE ABOVE QUANTITIES HAVE BEEN CHECKED

Signed.. . Date................................

Fig. 29.5. Request for Stock-check

The stock record card is marked with the date and result of the stock check, and this figure becomes the basis for all future action.

A technique such as the above has the advantage that the choice of item to be checked is in the hands of the material control department, who will be able to ensure that any items requiring special care are checked frequently. If the choice is left to the storekeeper, items which were easy to check might be verified frequently whilst difficult items might be overlooked. In large organizations the checking of stock might be a sufficiently large task to permit the full-time employment of one person. This person (sometimes called a stores auditor) would be a member either of the material control or of the accounts departments, and not a storekeeper. Such an independent check not only has a psychological advantage, it is likely to be acceptable to the company's auditors, who would probably admit the results if incorporated into the company's financial statements.

Advantages of a Perpetual Inventory
1. No dislocation of stores or production.
2. It is cheaper than an annual inventory, since the work is usually part of the stores staff's normal activities and will occupy so little time during a day that it can be carried out during any quiet periods.
3. Results are produced more quickly: during an annual check the comparison of actual with recorded stock may take some considerable time, during which stock movements may confuse the results.
4. Important items can be checked as frequently as desired: stock record cards are likely therefore to be more accurate than in the case of the annual inventory.

Layout and Location of Stores
The criteria for a good layout shown in Chapter 9 are as valid for a store as for any other part of a factory. The following considerations, whilst applying generally, are more important in a stores than elsewhere—
1. The floor loading must be adequate for the most adverse conditions.
2. Stores require to be secure, that is, they should not be capable of being entered by other than stores staff.
3. Weatherproofing must be particularly good—in a production area a leaking roof is immediately observable whilst in a stores it may be so obscured that considerable damage might be done before it is discovered.
4. Special equipment—hoists, lifts, power saws, power guillotines—may need to be shared with other departments.
5. Stores racking will prevent normal movement of air, and temperature distribution can be seriously affected.
6. Gangways need to be wide enough to take any stores trolleys, and must allow articles to be withdrawn from bins and racks, but in general it is not necessary for them to be as wide as production gangways.
7. Items used most frequently should be located nearest the issuing windows.

8. Heavy or bulky items should be stored as low as possible, although the use of truck hoists can allow heavy items to be lifted to heights of 20 feet and over.

9. Shelves and bins should not be so deep as to prevent easy access to the back.

10. A receiving area, where goods can be separated and unpacked prior to dispersal, should be provided.

11. An assembly area where all the parts for a particular job can be assembled before being issued is useful.

12. Computing scales, which should be used wherever possible, must be screened from draughts.

13. A location system enabling the position of any single item to be pinpointed is essential. A simple system is to give a letter reference to each line of bins, and number the bins in each line serially from one end. This reference should be shown on the stock record card, but in addition a location index should be provided in stores.

14. Storing is essentially a volumetric problem, that is, it depends on height as well as floor area. Use of height can be increased by employing some of the modern fork trucks in conjunction with pallets.

Tool Stores

The storage of tools and production aids (apart from expendable tools) is usually done in a store apart from the material stores. The practice of allowing the tools to be stored haphazard in the toolroom is a bad one, involving a great deal of waste of time in searching for tools, and a deterioration in the tools themselves. The following points should be borne in mind—

1. All tools should be stored in a secure place, access to which should be limited only to specified personnel.

2. Tools should be numbered and a tool register kept. Tool numbers can either be logical (i.e. the number has some significance) or they can be arbitrary.

3. Tool numbers should appear on planning layouts and, if any parameter or dimension is governed by the tool rather than by the drawing of the part, on the drawing of the part made with the tool.

4. Tools should only be issued against a valid authorization. This can be a simple tally: each person likely to require tools is issued with a set of tallies bearing his identification. When he requires a tool he hands in the tally, which is put in the tool location itself. In this way clerical work is minimized, whilst the responsibility for the tool is always known. Tools can be placed on a shadow board where the outline of the tool is shown when the tool itself is removed.

5. Tools returned to stores must be checked, and if necessary cleaned, sharpened, or otherwise overhauled, in order that no defective tools are ever issued.

6. Racking should be such that it does not damage the tools stored on it. For this reason wooden or wood-faced racks are often preferred.

7. A good tool crib control system can provide valuable information on the use, quality, and life of tools, and can signal the need for maintenance.

Further Reading
1. Morrison, A., *Storage and Control of Stock*, Pitman, London 1970.
An essentially practical book which describes the office techniques of stock-holding and the physical aspects of storage and handling.

2. England, W. B. and Lewis, H. T., *Modern Procurement Management: Text and Cases*, Irwin, Homewood, Illinois 1970.
The standard U.S. text on this subject.

Section Six   The People

Chapter 30
Personnel Administration

Personnel management can be considered to consist of two parts: one, the supervisory management exerted by the departmental head and his superiors in day-to-day relationships—the leadership exerted by the supervisor; and the other the direction of the conditions of work of the employee. This chapter will be concerned only with the second aspect, which for convenience will be called *Personnel Administration*.

Personnel administration is generally accepted to cover the following activities—

1. Employment
2. Education and Training
3. Industrial Relations
4. Welfare
5. Wages
6. Health and Safety

None of these can be said to be more important than others, although some are more neglected. It should be noted that, in general, the personnel administrator acts in an advisory capacity: as Pigors and Myers point out '... the responsibility for achieving results with members of his work group belongs to the manager, not to the personnel administrator'. This should not be taken to imply that the personnel function is any less important than any of the other support functions: indeed, there is no doubt that with the considerable growth in legislation over the last decade, the tasks of the Personnel Department have become extremely complex. Furthermore, behavioural scientists are daily revealing information concerning the nature of man, and this, allied to the complexity of the task, requires that the personnel function can only be satisfactorily carried out by trained executives of a very high calibre.

NEED FOR A PERSONNEL POLICY

Accepting that personnel administration is an important feature of industrial activity, then as in all other substantial matters, decisions should be made on the basis of a declared policy, not in an arbitrary manner. The importance of this cannot be over-emphasized: a factory where anomalies or distinctions exist will eventually develop internal stresses which can eventually seriously upset productivity. Unless a policy has been carefully considered, anomalies will be extremely difficult to avoid. If the policy has been made public, then the translation of that policy into action is simplified, although it must be realized that the implementing of a personnel policy is made much more difficult if other aspects of management are weak. Goodwill and loyalty can and should be used to overcome difficulties, but they cannot be expected to make up for managerial inefficiencies.

The personnel manager must be actively involved in drawing up and determining this policy. He should be able, by training and inclination, to ensure that the needs of the employees *as people* should carry as much weight as the needs of the company *as a corporation*. As discussed elsewhere in a quite different context (page 50), '. . . all needs are utilitarian to their possessors', and the personnel officer must advise not only on matters such as the number of employees, their recruitment, selection, training and remuneration, but must also be in a position to comment upon human reactions to proposed action.

EMPLOYMENT

This aspect of personnel work covers the obtaining and selecting—in conjunction with departmental supervisors—of new staff, their introduction to the company, and the checking of working conditions to ensure compliance with statutory rules and orders, local bye-laws, trades union agreements and any other appropriate regulations. It is interesting to consider that in many companies where the purchase of a piece of plant worth £100 will be the subject of much deliberation at board level, the recruitment of a new employee will be done on the basis of a five-minute interview, yet the cost of bringing the new employee to a fully useful working condition will be several times greater than the cost of the piece of plant. It is difficult to see why it should be considered that the choice of a new employee—possibly the most complex and unpredictable of organisms—is very much simpler than the choice of a new inert assembly of metal.

The personnel officer should try to ensure that—

1. the need for a new employee has been established;
2. the job has been adequately defined—here he can assist by analysing in appropriate detail the *needs* of the job, and setting them down in a comprehensible manner;
3. appropriate action is taken to locate likely staff. This may involve the use of Employment Exchanges, of advertising or direct 'head-hunting'. Properly kept records will show which channels are most effective in any particular circumstance;
4. useful methods of selecting particular candidates are used. The range of tools here is very wide, from simple five-minute interviews, to 'stress'

348

interviews, from simple aptitude tests to complex psychological investigations. All of these, even the apparently simple interview, require skill in use, and the trained personnel officer should be able to advise on the technique to be used and assist in the actual performance of the selection method. However, again to quote Pigors and Myers, ' . . . the work of the employment department . . . is a supplement to the judgement of line officials and not a substitute for it'.

5. once an employee is engaged, he should be introduced to his work ('inducted') in such a manner that he understands clearly what is required of him, and what he can require of the organization;

6. when an employee leaves, the reasons for his departure are investigated, not with a view to harassing the individual, but in order to resolve any problems. The costs of hiring are substantial, and if labour turnover can be reduced, real savings can be made.

EDUCATION AND TRAINING

All assets waste if untended, and this is probably more true of the human assets of a company than any of the assets usually recorded on a balance sheet. Undoubtedly, there are everywhere human abilities which are untapped, and it is these which in the final analysis determine the success or failure of an enterprise. In a very dramatic way, professional football teams show how human development can be turned to financial benefit: a young player can be 'bought' for £100 and after appropriate training be 'sold' for £100,000 or more.

Throughout industry there is a continual need to educate and train, not only 'on the bench' but at all levels. 'Sitting next to Nelly' is an inefficient way of learning, the student acquiring the bad habits along with the good. A positive training programme should be drawn up and implemented, which should encompass not only a training in manipulative skills but also in academic *and supervisory* skills. Whilst a leader may be born, by training he can be made more useful more rapidly. Moreover, if a potential supervisor can be withdrawn from his immediate tasks for a training period, he can find time to think of the difficulties *and responsibilities* of his new post. This is as true at the works manager's level as at the chargehand level. Too often a supervisor finds himself submerged in day-to-day problems without being able to consider more general problems, and if a training period does no more than allow a 'standing back' it will serve a very useful purpose.

Not only should training be carried on *inside* the factory, but the broader extra-mural training available at technical colleges and polytechnics must be encouraged. Evening classes are extremely cheap, and part-time day classes scarcely more expensive. Many companies allow time off, with payment of fees and book allowances for such courses, believing that the long-term return will be substantial. External courses do have the added advantage over internal courses of allowing students from different companies and industries to exchange ideas—a most salutary experience when it is found that very few problems are special to any one factory. Considerable assistance, both financial and advisory, can be obtained from the appropriate Industry Training Boards.

INDUSTRIAL RELATIONS

The relationships between employer and employee are difficult and delicate, frequently being dependent upon subtle intangibles and the ethos of the company. Too often companies seek to simplify this situation by appointing an Industrial Relations Officer and expecting him to solve all problems. In truth, this relationship is not one which can be avoided. Good industrial relations stem from good personnel policies, and these *must be known and used by all managers at all levels.* The author recalls a company where security of employment was extremely poor—as the founder of the company, a dynamic and forceful entrepreneur, would cheerfully and brutally dismiss 'offending' employees at all levels. This behaviour steadily hardened itself into a 'hire and fire' policy, as managers

Table 30.1. Total Union Membership in the United Kingdom 1892–1964

Year	Labour force (000s)	Annual per cent change in labour force	Total union membership (000s)	Annual per cent change in union membership	Density of membership membership (per cent)
1892	14,125*	—	1,576	—	11·2
1901	15,795	—	2,025	—	12·8
1911	17,555	—	3,139	—	17·9
1921	17,618	—	6,633	—	37·6
1931	19,328	—	4,624	—	23·9
1933	19,498	—	4,392	—	22·5
1938	20,258	—	6,053	—	29·9
1948	20,767	—	9,362	—	45·1
1949	20,818	+0·2	9,318	−0·5	44·8
1950	21,096	+1·3	9,289	−0·3	44·0
1951	21,222	+0·6	9,535	+2·6	44·9
1952	21,322	+0·5	9,588	+0·6	45·0
1953	21,401	+0·4	9,527	−0·6	44·5
1954	21,718	+1·5	9,566	+0·4	44·0
1955	21,990	+1·3	9,738	+1·8	44·3
1956	22,230	+1·1	9,776	+0·4	44·0
1957	22,382	+0·7	9,827	+0·5	43·9
1958	22,346	−0·2	9,636	−1·9	43·1
1959	22,404	+0·3	9,621	−0·2	42·9
1960	22,764	+1·6	9,832	+2·2	43·2
1961	23,037	+1·2	9,893	+0·6	42·9
1962	23,354	+1·4	9,883	−0·1	42·3
1963	23,470	+0·5	9,928	+0·5	42·3
1964	23,616	+0·6	10,065	+1·4	42·6

* This figure relates to 1891.

(*Source*— Research Paper 6, *Trade Union Growth and Recognition,* Royal Commission on Trade Unions and Employers' Association, H.M.S.O., 1967.)

modelled themselves on the founder. The costs of this behaviour were substantial, and in an attempt to reduce them, personnel officers were regularly employed—and as regularly were lost, as they tried to operate a personnel policy in conflict with this extant policy. Quality in industrial relations is like quality in the product—'. . . everybody's business'.

The above having been said, it must also be recognized that the increasing intervention of the State in matters concerning employment, and the growing of the Trades Unions (see Tables 30.1 and 30.2) have made it necessary that at least one executive within the organization should specialize in industrial relations. The executive must be capable of representing the management of the company at any meetings which might take place with either trades unions, works committees, shop stewards committees or other negotiating bodies. This requires a thorough knowledge of all relevant agreements and local customs, and is not a matter which can be easily undertaken, since in some industries the various agreements are most complex and require great study. The situation in a multi-trades factory where a number of trades unions are involved is even more complex. In the United Kingdom the Department of Trade and

Table 30.2. Changing Employment and Density of Union Membership by Industry in the United Kingdom, 1948–1964

Industry	Employees (000s)			Density per cent	
	1948	1964	Per cent change, 1948–1964	1960	Per cent change, 1948–1960
1. Education...	521	1,094	+110	50	−11
2. Professional and business services ...	806	1,268	+57	24	−5
3. Insurance, banking and finance ...	432	637	+48	31	+10
4. Distribution	2,093	3,026	+45	15	−2
5. Paper printing and publishing	472	632	+34	57	+2
6. Gas, Electricity and Water	329	413	+26	51	−9
7. Building	1,375	1,708	+24	37	−6
8. Metals and engineering	3,729	4,537	+21	54	−1
9. Chemicals and allied	447	515	+15	20	+1
10. Food, drink and tobacco	731	842	+15	11	−5
11. Other transport and communications ...	1,221	1,320	+8	75	+2
12. Local government	720	776	+8	84	+16
13. Theatres, cinemas, sports, etc.	238	251	+6	39	+4
14. Furniture, timber, etc.	294	296	+1	37	−4
15. Footwear	116	116	0	63	−1
16. Clothing	498	453	−9	30	−3
17. Textiles other than cotton	708	613	−13	21	−3
18. Cotton	293	228	−22	75	+2
19. National government	717	550	−23	83	+19
20. Coal mining	803	596	−26	89	+10
21. Railways	576	396	−31	84	−5
22. Agriculture, forestry and fishing ...	868	551	−37	27	+5

(*Source*—Research Paper 6, *supra*.)

Industry's Industrial Relations Department can help greatly in quoting the relevant agreements and advising on local customs.

Probably the most important feature of this work is that the personnel officer shall be *seen* to be scrupulously fair. He must present the company's point of view clearly and dispassionately and must not take issue on personal points. Goodwill in industrial negotiations is essential, and any suspicion of underhandedness will result in a loss of confidence which will increase immeasurably the difficulties of later negotiations.

HEALTH AND SAFETY

There are a large number of statutory requirements concerning health and safety which must be observed, and these must be familiar to the personnel department which should bring to the notice of appropriate executives any breaches of these requirements.

It is often convenient to organize the whole personnel department around the first aid department, and it is increasingly common in small factories to find an industrial nurse (who is a State Registered Nurse with additional specialized training in industrial and personnel subjects) engaged to take charge of the personnel department, which includes a first aid section. This arrangement is very satisfactory, since the obvious independence and 'disengagement' of such dedicated persons is clearly seen, and they are generally acceptable to both employees and employers alike.

Safety of the employee is not only a statutory requirement, it is a human obligation. Unfortunately bad safety habits can spring up very easily and it is necessary to observe very closely all potentially dangerous activities. A climate of safety-consciousness must be built up by constant encouragement and propaganda, and in many organizations a special safety officer is appointed whose sole responsibility is the safety of the employees. This function, if carried out thoroughly, can result in a prevention of lost time due to accidents and an avoidance of unnecessary suffering and hardship. Without adequate managerial backing, however, the safety officer will have great difficulty in performing his job, and managements must realize that safety pays, if for no other reason than that industrial injuries lose more working time than any other cause. This matter is of such importance that it is discussed later in a separate chapter.

WELFARE

Under the general heading of welfare work in industry, the personnel officer will usually help in organizing any special sickness benefit schemes, social and recreational facilities, and personal assistance to staff. The attention given to this aspect depends greatly upon company policy, but it can be said that comparatively small expenditures in this field can produce substantial returns in staff loyalty and goodwill. Any personal assistance given, however, should be consistent: help given to one should not be arbitrarily withheld from others. Thus a small loan to one employee which is withheld from another can result in rancour far greater than that arising from the loss of the loan itself. Care must therefore be taken in considering the long-term result of any welfare assistance, and it is important to avoid creating precedents which later would become embarrasing to follow.

The provision of a canteen or restaurant also can be considered under this heading. In a small or medium-sized factory the time spent by staff on running a canteen can often be substantial, and the accountant, for example, can find an unreasonable volume of the work in his office occupied by purely catering problems, while the production manager will find himself embarrassed by having to provide staff to make up for canteen staff who are suddenly absent. For this reason it is becoming usual to find specialist caterers engaged to provide a canteen service. This removes entirely from the factory personnel the problems of catering, and can be most satisfactory provided a wise choice of caterer is made. An elected canteen committee, where grievances can be aired, is a useful safety valve, particularly if the discussions can rise above the 'shortage of sugar' type of complaint.

WAGES

Decisions on wages and wage structures are the responsibility of the board of directors. However, it is in this area of personnel management that the personnel manager must play a leading part in preparing the facts upon which any decisions are based. Fundamentally the problems can be considered to be three in number: (1) the setting up of a logical wage structure; (2) the placing of employees within the structure; (3) the use or disuse of an incentive scheme, and of these the first two will be considered in this section, the third being discussed in the next chapter (Chapter 31). It must be emphasized that the personnel department can act only in an *advisory* capacity on these matters, but if it has built up sufficient goodwill it will be better placed than any other department to be of assistance.

Wages Structure

Within any one homogeneous department it is relatively simple to set up an acceptable wages structure, but when wages are compared between departments the problem becomes much more difficult. How, for example, should the wages of a senior laboratory assistant compare with those of a shorthand typist? Should a line inspector draw more pay than a stock control clerk? To try to achieve some parity between the pay of workers in dissimilar occupations within the same organization it is necessary to refer all jobs to a common base, that is, to place all jobs in a recognized and agreed order of value to the company. Once this has been done, this scale of values can be used as a basis upon which to build a wages structure. Whether, in fact, the scale of values is acceptable to the employer and the employee is a matter for local discussion. At least, the setting up of such a scale can help clarify managerial ideas on the relative worth of various tasks.

Job Evaluation, Grading or Ranking

The setting of tasks in a scale of values is known as job evaluation, grading or ranking, and whilst it appears to the author that job ranking is the best description, since it promises no more than the setting of various jobs in some sort of order, the term job evaluation is most commonly used, and consequently will be employed here. There are a large number of methods of job evaluation, and the choice of one or other must depend upon local circumstances. Reference should be made to the study and report entitled *Job Evaluation*, published by the International Labour Office.

In general, as a first step, all the jobs to be evaluated are considered and a list drawn up of the characteristics of the work which are considered to be important. These characteristics may vary between different types of work, but should be the same for similar occupations (that is, for jobs within a 'job cluster'). It is probably unwise to list too many characteristics or the analysis will become unwieldy. The National Electrical Manufacturers Association (N.E.M.A.) in the United States recognizes four main headings which will cover the majority of occupations, namely SKILL, EFFORT, RESPONSIBILITY and WORKING CONDITIONS. These main headings can then be subdivided into minor or derived characteristics according to the job-cluster concerned. For example, clerical work might be considered under the following headings—

Skill	1. Mental
	2. Manipulative
Effort	1. Mental
	2. Physical
Responsibility	1. Financial
	2. For subordinates
	3. Personal
Working Conditions	1. Surroundings
	2. Monotony
	3. Distractions

Whilst in the same organization the analysis for a worker in a productive department might be—

Skill	1. Experience
	2. Manipulative
	3. Versatility
Effort	1. Physical
	2. Aural
Responsibility	1. Quality of product
	2. Safety of equipment
Working Conditions	1. Surroundings
	2. Noise

For each group of jobs these characteristics are drawn up. The total value of the characteristics is then divided between the various constituents: characteristics of little importance are assigned low values, and those of greater importance high values, so that for the two cases above the values assigned might be—

Clerical			Production		
Skill—		30	Skill—		20
Mental	15		Experience	5	
Manipulative	15		Manipulative	5	
			Versatility	10	
Effort—		30	Effort—		40
Mental	20		Physical	30	
Physical	10		Aural	10	
Responsibility—		30	Responsibility—		20
Financial	10		Quality of Product	10	
Subordinates	5		Safety of Equipment	10	
Personal	15				
Working Conditions—		10	Working Conditions—		20
Surroundings	2		Surroundings	5	
Monotony	3		Noise	15	
Distractions	5				
Total		100	Total		100

Using these scales, a small committee will meet representatives of the various departments, explain the scales and the general idea to them, and invite them to assist in defining and grading the various tasks. These gradings must of course apply to the jobs, not to the individuals doing them, so that it is a comparison between, say, a copy typist, a telephonist, a stock records clerk and a wages clerk, not between Miss A, Miss B, Mrs. C and Miss D. The gradings throughout a department must be carried out by the same group of people in order that consistency is preserved, and it is useful to rate each characteristic of all jobs at once, rather than rate all the characteristics of each job at once. It is also desirable to include amongst the raters representatives of the persons doing the various jobs in order that the less obvious features are not overlooked.

From this a series of definitions, along with a classification in order of value of the various jobs in a department, will be produced. This is done for all departments, and the various departmental classification integrated, usually by finding tasks of comparable value in each department. For example, an analysis may produce ranking as follows—

Dept. A		*Dept. B*	
Job 1	90	Job 1	80
Job 2	80	Job 2	60
Job 3	75	Job 3	50
Job 4	70	Job 4	40
Job 5	60	Job 5	30
Job 6	30	Job 6	10
Job 7	20		

and discussion may reveal that workers are often transferred from Job 1 of department A to Job 5 of department B without loss of efficiency or value. Jobs A.1 and B.5 are thus equated and an integrated table produced—

Job B.1	80
B.2	60
B.3	50
B.4	40
B.5 and A.1	30
A.2	27
A.3	25
A.4	23
A.5	20
B.6 and A.6	10
A.7	7

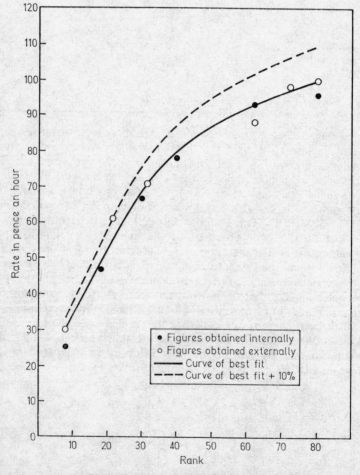

Fig. 30.1. *Relation between Rank and Rate*

This table will then enable comparisons to be made between the values of the various jobs, which in turn could assist in setting up a wage structure. One useful approach would be to investigate local customs, national agreements, employment advertisements and any other source of information, and obtain rates of pay for comparable jobs wherever possible. These can then be graphically represented, relating pay and ranking, the best fitting curve being drawn through the various points obtained and a wages scale produced (see Fig. 30.1) which might read—

Job	Rank	Hourly Rate
		p
B.1	80	50·0
B.2	60	46·0
B.3	50	43·0
B.4	40	40·0
B.5 and A.1	30	35·0
A.2	27	32·0
A.3	25	31·0
A.4	23	28·0
A.5	20	27·0
B.6 and A.6	10	18·0
A.7	7	15·0

This wage scale would thus form the basis of a wages structure— maximum increments at any point might be fixed at 10 per cent greater than basic wage, and these two scales (the basic and the maximum) could define the limits between which rates could be fixed for various tasks.

Job evaluation as outlined above will be useful not only as a method of setting equitable wage rates but also as a means for identifying and defining jobs, thus simplifying the employment, movement and promotion of staff. It is not, as stated above, a method of examining the relative effectiveness of various individuals and placing them within the structure: this is done by a merit rating of the individuals within a department.

Merit Rating

As with job evaluation, a careful study of the job is required, laying down the qualities required of the individuals expected to carry out the job concerned. These should cover only those characteristics which are likely to be of importance to carrying out the job; thus, in a work study engineer 'tact' is a very necessary quality, but in a research physicist it may be of little significance. A typical group of qualities for a development engineer might be—

1. Technical qualification
2. Technical ability
3. Application to the task in hand
4. Originality of thought
5. Co-operativeness
6. Timekeeping
7. Length of service with the company

All members of the company who are development engineers are then compared with each other for the above qualities, and ranked in order of ability. The sum of the rankings would then give a measure of the value of each engineer compared with his immediate colleagues. The value of all qualities is not necessarily the same: 'timekeeping' might be assumed (in the case of development engineers) to have only one-quarter the importance of 'originality of thought' and its contribution to the total would be so placed.

Ranking (or rating) is best carried out by at least two people with whom the group come into close contact. These rate all individuals separately and independently and then come together with a third person—for example, a personnel officer—to discuss the ratings and hence produce a consolidated rating. The method of rating is controversial: numerical systems (for example 1–10) are appealing, but it is the author's experience that raters are loath to use either end of the scale, so that in fact a 1–10 scale becomes a 3–8 scale. A better way probably is by definition, e.g., Outstanding, Excellent, Very Good, Good, Very Fair, Fair, Poor, Bad, Very Bad. The rater then ticks the appropriate description, and at the joint discussion the descriptions are translated into numerical terms. In order to achieve consistency one quality should be rated at a time for all staff being considered by any rater.

Merit ratings should be carried out at least quarterly, and the results made known to the persons concerned. This will have the effect of informing all staff of their progress, and letting them know wherein they are failing and where they are most successful. The quarterly assessment will prevent any distortion occurring due to the exceptional happening; for example, if rating was carried out once only, and that just before pay increments were decided, a particularly serious mistake might colour the whole rating, giving an unreasonably poor result.

Further Reading
1. Probably the most fruitful source of information on practice in the U.K. is H.M.S.O., which publishes numerous short texts, booklets and leaflets on particular aspects of Personnel Administration.

2. *Job Evaluation*, International Labour Office, London 1969.
A sensible discussion of the techniques of job evaluation.

3. *Industrial Relations Handbook*, H.M.S.O., London 1960.

4. Thompson, J. and Rogers, H. R., *Redgrave's Factories, Truck & Shops Acts*, Butterworth, London 1972.
Two invaluable books for any practising U.K. manager.

5. Northcott, C. H., *Personnel Management*, Pitman, London 1968.
Presents a U.K. approach to this subject.

6. Pigors, P. and Myers, C. A., *Personnel Administration*, McGraw-Hill, New York 1969.

The 'Bible' on Personnel Administration. Reflecting U.S. practice and thought, its subject matter reaches far wider than the material of this chapter. A great and wise book.

Chapter 31
Incentive Schemes

One of the most common methods of attempting to increase productivity is by the setting up of a financial incentive or bonus scheme whereby the earnings of a person or group depend upon the output achieved. There is an increasing body of thought which holds that such schemes are not in themselve desirable, and that any benefits which may appear to be derived arise, in fact, from the improvements in managerial methods necessary to run a financial incentive scheme. However, this matter is not in any way resolved, and incentive schemes are found very commonly throughout industry.

NON-FINANCIAL INCENTIVES

Within every organization there must be present a number of non-financial incentives—for example, loyalty to the company or to the supervisor, pride in the product, desire for praise or recognition, or a personal pride in the ability to carry out a task better than anybody else. Such 'emotional' incentives can act very forcibly, and a good leader or manager will always make the maximum possible use of them. Without such appeals a company or factory will lose 'life', the atmosphere will become oppressive, and work will become nothing but drudgery.

Some companies, however, offer tangible benefits as rewards for increases in production. Amongst these are—

1. Extra holidays
2. Greater security
3. Improved status
4. Special working conditions

The use of such incentives requires particular care on the part of the management to avoid any appearance of partiality, and it is often difficult to operate a comprehensive non-financial incentive scheme. The results are probably more long-term than the results of financial bonus schemes, and for this reason both types of scheme are often worked side by side.

FINANCIAL INCENTIVES

It is the financial or wage incentive which is most commonly thought of when incentive schemes are discussed. In these the earnings are related to effort, and such schemes are common at all levels. A managing director's earnings can include a portion dependent upon the turnover of the company, a salesman can earn commission—a bonus on the orders he takes—and an operator can be paid on piece-work. In this chapter, only those wage incentives which can be applied to direct productive labour will be discussed.

Incidence of Financial Incentive Schemes

Astonishingly little evidence is available on the current use of incentive schemes: in 1951 the I.L.O. published *Payment by Results*, and although it was reprinted several times, no new evidence was added to it, so that all the information given therein pre-dates 1950. In 1961, the then Ministry of Labour carried out a nation-wide survey throughout the U.K. on this subject, and published its findings in the *Ministry of Labour Gazette* in September 1961 (see Tables 31.1 and 31.2). In May 1968 the National Board for Prices and Incomes presented a report (Report No. 65, Cmnd. 3627) on *Payment by Results Systems* and again presented some evidence (see Tables 31.3 and 31.4) which was '. . . admittedly fragmentary . . .' Broadly, it would seem that currently about one-third of all direct operators within the U.K. are receiving some proportion of their incomes from financial incentive schemes, and this situation does not appear to be changing rapidly, if at all.

Table 31.1. *The Coverage of Payment by Results Systems*

Date	Men %	Youths %	Women %	Girls %	All Workers %
1961 April	30	22	44	44	33
1957 October	28	22	41	39	31
1955 October	29	23	42	39	32
1953 October	29	22	42	37	32
1951 October	28	22	44	38	32
1949 October	25	20	42	35	29
1947 October	24	20	39	35	28
1938 October	18	21	46	27	25

(*Source—Ministry of Labour Gazette*
September 1961)

Table 31.2. Payment by Time Rates and Systems of Payment by Results

Industry Group	Men (21 years and over)		Youths and Boys		Women (18 years and over)		Girls		All Workers	
	Percentage of Time and Payment by Results Workers in the third pay-week in April, 1961									
	Time	PBR	Time	PBR	Time	PBR	Time	PBR	Time	PBR
Food, drink and tobacco	86	14	89	11	72	28	74	26	80	20
Chemicals and allied industries ...	78	22	94	6	80	20	76	24	79	21
Metal manufacture ...	38	62	59	41	56	44	42	58	41	59
Engineering and electrical goods	54	46	67	33	44	56	41	59	53	47
Shipbuilding and marine engineering	33	67	46	54	76	24	†	†	35	65
Vehicles ...	48	52	49	51	46	54	30	70	48	52
Metal goods not elsewhere specified ...	60	40	70	30	54	46	53	47	59	41
Textiles ...	61	39	75	25	39	61	44	56	49	51
Leather, leather goods and fur... ...	61	39	76	24	70	30	79	21	67	33
Clothing and footwear ...	66	34	68	32	50	50	52	48	53	47
Bricks, pottery, glass, cement, etc.	61	39	69	31	53	47	58	42	60	40
Timber, furniture, etc. ...	73	27	85	15	66	34	73	27	74	26
Paper, printing and publishing ...	83	17	90	10	75	25	78	22	81	19
Other manufacturing industries...	55	45	73	27	49	51	45	55	53	47
All manufacturing industries...	59	41	70	30	53	47	55	45	58	42
Mining and quarrying (except coal)	77	23	89	11	57	43	†	†	77	23
Construction	85	15	93	7	93	7	84	16	86	14

Table 31.2—continued

Industry Group	Men (21 years and over)		Youths and Boys		Women (18 years and over)		Girls		All Workers	
	Percentage of Time and Payment by Results Workers in the third pay-week in April, 1961									
	Time	PBR	Time	PBR	Time	PBR	Time	RBR	Time	PBR
Gas, electricity and water ...	98	2	100	0	100	0	†	†	98	2
Transport and communication (except railways, London Transport and British Road Services) ...	93	7	97	3	98	2	†	†	93	7
Certain miscellaneous services‡ ...	91	9	95	5	75	25	78	22	87	13
Public administration*	98	2	98	2	100	0	100	0	98	2
All the above, including manufacturing industries...	70	30	78	22	56	44	56	44	67	33

† The numbers returned were insufficient to provide a satisfactory basis for the calculation of a general percentage.

‡ Consisting of laundries and dry cleaning, motor repairers and garages, and repair of boots and shoes.

* Industrial employees in national government service have, where possible, been included in the figures for industries such as engineering, shipbuilding, chemicals, printing, construction, transport and communication, and only those employees who could not be assigned to those other industries or services have been included under 'Public administration'.

(*Source—Ministry of Labour Gazette* September 1961)

Table 31.3. Proportion of Adult Male Manual Workers Paid by Results

Industry Sector and Grade	Total Number of Employees covered		Proportion of Number Covered Who Were Paid by Results	
	1964	1967	1964	1967
All Engineering Industries Covered†				
Skilled	551,736	534,952	49·2	46·9
Semi-skilled	504,326	483,175	53·2	52·0
Unskilled	100,527	89,782	21·6	22·9
Total	1,156,589	1,107,909	48·5	47·2

Table 31.3.—continued

Industry Sector and Grade	Total Number of Employees covered		Proportion of Number Covered Who Were Paid by Results	
	1964	1967	1964	1967
Mechanical Engineering				
Skilled	222,601	215,105	48·4	46·2
Semi-skilled	159,040	158,513	54·2	53·6
Unskilled	38,604	35,414	23·2	25·1
Total	420,245	409,032	48·3	47·2
Electrical Engineering				
Skilled	89,855	84,936	41·8	38·1
Semi-skilled	97,908	90,775	57·4	53·8
Unskilled	15,949	14,217	16·6	16·3
Total	203,712	189,928	47·4	44·0
Motor Vehicle Manufacturing				
Skilled	95,469	97,946	49.8	50.0
Semi-skilled	156,488	141,858	46·9	46·3
Unskilled	17,032	13,728	20·6	23·5
Total	268,989	253,532	46·3	46·5
Aircraft Manufacturing and Repairing				
Skilled	66,263	62,402	58·3	54·1
Semi-skilled	28,269	28,224	54·5	53·1
Unskilled	6,620	6,296	14·9	12·7
Total	101,152	96,922	54·4	51·1
Shipbuilding Industry				
Skilled	46,491	50,473	81·8	82·8
Semi-skilled	14,848	14,922	75·2	79·7
Unskilled	12,585	11,992	53·9	61·8
Total	73,924	77,387	75·7	78·9
Chemical Manufacture				
Skilled	17,753	16,600	40·5	43·0
General workers	59,987	59,483	41·2	43·4
Total	77,740	76,083	41·1	43·3
*Iron and Steel Manufacture**				
Skilled	27,881	28,007	79·1	78·1
Semi-skilled	19,208	17,383	78·8	86·9
Process and service workers ...	120,332	107,098	83·1	86·0
Unskilled	22,480	19,018	53·8	62·9
Total	189,891	171,506	78·7	82·2

†This total includes the following four sectors; five other smaller sectors which are also included in the total are not listed.

*'Payment by Results' in shipbuilding and iron and steel includes 'lieu' workers. The figures are not therefore comparable with the other industries shown here, or with the 1961 census.

(*Source—Payment by Results Systems*, N.B.P.I., Cmnd. 3627, 1968)

Table 31.4. Payment by Results and Work Measurement

	(a) No. of manual workers covered	(b) Proportion of (a) paid by results %	(c) Corres- ponding proportion in 1961 %	(d) Proportion of (b) subject to work measure- ment %
Coal				
National Coal Board	349,000	27·8	45	nil
Food Manufacturing				
Food Manufacturers Industrial Group	60,000	33	21	not known
Cocoa, Chocolate and Confectionery Alliance	78,000	75	75	50 to 75
National Seed Crushers' Association	5,700	29	not known	100
*Tobacco**				
Federation of Home and Export Tobacco Manufacturers	14,000	29	higher	100
A major tobacco company outside the Federation	16,000	60	90	100
Chemicals				
Chemical Industries Association Ltd....	85,000	20 to 25	20 to 25	70
A major chemical company outside the Association	61,000	85	71	70
Engineering				
Engineering Employers' Federation ...	1,500,000	50	50	not known
Steel				
Iron and Steel Trades Employers' Association	120,000	90	90	not known
Shipbuilding				
Shipbuilders' and Repairers' National Association	82,000	36	47	not known
Textiles				
The Wool (and Allied) Textile Employers' Council	92,000	70	65	30
U.K. Textile Manufacturers' Association	37,000	57	not known	50
British Spinners' and Doublers' Association	30,000	42	slightly less	66
National Employers' Association of Rayon Yarn Producers	24,000	90	slightly higher	'almost 100'
Association of Jute Spinners and Manufacturers	13,300	60 to 70	not known	not known
British Leavers Lace Manufacturers' Association	1,000	35	35	nil
Cordage and Net Manufacturers' Association	6,000	76	37	61
Footwear				
British Footwear Manufacturers' Federation	48,300	66·7	59·6	42·1
Pottery				
British Pottery Manufacturers' Federation	47,000	55 to 66	54 to 65	10 to 20

Table 31.4.—continued

	(a) No. of manual workers covered	(b) Proportion of (a) paid by results %	(c) Corres- ponding proportion in 1961 %	(d) Proportion of (b) subject to work measure- ment %
Paper Employers' Federation of Papermakers and Boardmakers	62,000	85	65 to 75	50
Rubber Rubber Manufacturing Employers' Association	70,000	71	64	not known
Construction Federation of Civil Engineering Con- tractors	150,000	70	no change	'high'
National Federation of Plumbers and Domestic Heating Engineers ...	25,000	20 to 80	not known	not known
Electricity Electricity Council	150,000	nil	no change	—
Gas Gas Council	73,000	15	5	73
Ports National Association of Port Employ- ers	57,000	over 90	over 90	nil
Clothing Clothing Manufacturers' Federation ...	85,000	75 to 80	slightly less	50
Apparel and Fashion Industry's Asso- ciation	45–50,000	70	no change	33 to 50
Other Manufacturing *Miscellaneous Industries* National Cooperage Federation ...	2,500	93	slightly less	nil

*We directed our enquiry to the Federation of Home and Export Tobacco Manu-
facturers who referred the questions to their individual member firms. The replies from
these firms have been aggregated. The Federation recommended that we contact another
tobacco company who were not members.

(*Source—Payment by Results Systems*,
N.B.P.I. Cmnd. 3627, 1968)

Installation of a Financial-Incentive Scheme

The installation of a financial-incentive scheme must be the culmination of
a great deal of preliminary work, all of which is the work normal in a well-
run factory. An incentive scheme must not be regarded as a substitute for
good management, nor must it be considered the basis upon which good
management is built. An insecurely founded incentive scheme which is
later withdrawn will create such persistent ill-will that subsequent well-
conceived plans will have little chance of success.

The following must be investigated and put into operation before any incentive scheme is installed—

1. *Work Measurement*. Consistency in bonus rates is essential. To achieve this, all rates should be based upon some objective measure of the work content of the job. There is a temptation, particularly when under pressure, for rates to be based upon the selling price. This will not only give rise to inconsistencies, one job 'paying' more than another of equal difficulty; it will also prevent selling prices being altered without a great deal of difficulty. Only when the selling price *accurately* reflects the work content should it be used as a basis for an incentive scheme, and the setting of the selling price itself must then require accurate work measurement. Any work measurement programme will provide both the measurements and/or definition of the task measured. As a result, any subsequent discussions on the rates fixed can refer back to the original conditions which applied at the time of setting the rate and so enable worth-while comparisons to be made. In some organizations it may be necessary to obtain Trade Union agreement to carry out a Work Measurement programme, and this agreement may include a statement of the measurement technique which will be used. Increasingly, one of the PMTS methods is employed in these circumstances, and training shop stewards or other union officials in whichever method is to be used will remove much of the suspicion often felt towards work measurement in general.

2. *Effective Production Control*. Under any circumstances the results of ineffectual production control are serious. Under an incentive wage scheme, the idle time due to absence of material, of drawings, of plant capacity, of tools, of test equipment, will result not only in frustration by the management but by loss of earnings by the operators which can lead to considerable ill-will and a high labour turnover. If the loss of earnings is made up by means of lieu bonuses (that is, bonuses paid for idle time in lieu of the bonuses which would have resulted if the operator had been working) the result will be an increased overhead burden to be borne by the work which is done, and an inducement to create idle time.

3. *Effective Inspection*. A bonus is normally only paid for satisfactory work, defective work being returned to the operator for correction before any payment is made. It is therefore necessary that an acceptable inspection department is in being, one that is impersonal enough to be free from any suggestion of bias. The usual practice is for bonus to be paid only on those items passed by the inspection department, and many bonus cards have a space 'Quantity passed by inspection . . . ' on them from which particulars the bonus can be calculated.

4. *Sound Wages Structure*. To try to use a financial incentive scheme as a means of 'correcting' an unjust wages structure is to court disaster. Not only will the basic inequity remain, the obvious bias in the incentive scheme will create considerable distress.

5. *Training of Wages Staff*. Whatever type of incentive scheme is used, it will inevitably increase the burden upon the administrative staff, and

in particular upon the Wages Department. A very thorough training in the scheme must be given to the wages staff, who will need to be able to—

(*a*) carry out all the calculations, and
(*b*) appreciate all the details of permissible allowances.

Should this not be done, and should the scheme run into administrative difficulties at its inception, it may be discredited and fail. A 'dry run' whereby bonus calculations are made and circulated for several weeks before any bonus payments are made will often help to resolve any difficulties here.

6. *Consultation with Employees.* Before any incentive scheme is installed it is essential that those most directly concerned—the operators who are going to be paid bonus—should be consulted and any proposed scheme thoroughly explained, discussed and if necessary modified. This is not merely common courtesy; it prevents any misunderstandings and ill-feeling later on. It is better to postpone the installation of a scheme if discussions have either not been held or have not reached agreement. Forcing an incentive scheme through against opposition will eventually lead to innumerable difficulties.

---

1. Work Measurement
2. Production Control
3. Inspection
4. Wages Structure
5. Wages Staff
6. Employee Consultation

Points to be Considered before Installing a Financial Incentive Scheme

Safeguards in Incentive Schemes

In order to prevent any unfairness, *or suspicion of unfairness*, to either the employer or the employee, it is usual to write into an incentive scheme a number of safeguarding clauses. These include—

1. *Payment for idle or extra time.* If an employee on bonus is idle he loses the opportunity to earn bonus, and this may substantially affect the wage packet. It is usually accepted as a principle that an operator will not suffer financial loss for reasons attributable to managerial weaknesses, and that idle time due to the operator's fault is borne by the operator. Thus, should an employee be idle because of, say, lack of material due to bad buying, then he would be paid a lieu bonus. On the other hand, if he were idle due to inefficient work on his own part he would be paid only 'time' rate, that is, his basic hourly rate.

If this payment or non-payment for idle or extra time is accepted, then it is necessary for all such time to be recorded, and causes assigned to it. This is often done by setting up an idle time code, listing the usual sources of idle time, and booking time against that code. This time is usually verified by a responsible person (e.g. an inspector, the foreman) and the act of providing an idle and extra time analysis will give useful information upon which other managerial decisions can be based.

2. *Payment for holidays.* When an employee is entitled to a paid holiday, the question of the basis of payment must be resolved. Two alternatives are available: either the payment be at 'day-rate' or 'basic-rate', or some time bonus must be made. Generally the second alternative is adopted, and careful consideration must be given to the method of deriving the time bonus. Consultation with employees is invaluable here.

3. *Payment for incomplete work.* Payment is often required to be made for work which is not complete at the end of the bonus period. If a bonus is paid weekly, and the bonus week ends on a Friday, there may be work partly completed at the end of Friday. In short-cycle time jobs this is of minor consequence, since any loss at the end of one week will be offset by an equivalent gain at the beginning of the next. Moreover, for a task lasting 10 minutes, the error in excluding that job from a 40-hour week is insignificant. In the case of a long time-cycle job, a different situation is created when a task is unfinished at the end of a bonus period, or when a part-finished job is handed over from one operator to another, for example, during annual holidays or when an operator leaves. Some technique is required whereby payment can be made for a partly completed job. This is extremely difficult, and the most usual solution is for an independent person, usually an inspector, to assess the percentage of work complete, any errors resulting being borne by the management. Some companies operate a 'loan' system, whereby part payments on a time-taken rate basis are paid as the job progresses, a reconciliation taking place during the concluding stages of the job.

4. *Ability to change a rate when in error.* Lack of decision in this problem has wrecked many bonus systems. A rate which allows a worker to earn an abnormally high wage (a 'loose' rate) will result in a restriction of output to a level which will provide what is considered by the workers to be a 'fair' wage, whilst a rate which is unachievable (a 'tight' rate) results in frustration. Work-measurement will tend to prevent this, but there will be inevitable errors, particularly at the outset of any scheme. Safeguards should therefore be set up which will enable rates to be adjusted and a common technique is for all rates to be accepted as provisional for the first job, or the first weeks. During this time they can be adjusted without consultation, but thereafter the rate is considered 'established', and can be altered only if there is a change in materials or methods. Fear of rate-cutting is ever present and must be avoided.

5. *Defective work.* If work is defective it is not usual for bonus payment to be made for it, although in some group schemes an allowance is made for the correction of defective work. Safeguards are necessary to ensure that a worker does not achieve high bonus by poor workmanship, and the

quantity 'passed by inspection' is usually the quantity for which bonus is paid. Should the defects arise through causes other than those under the worker's control—for example, poor material or faulty equipment—a lieu bonus is often paid.

6. *Guaranteed week.* It is usual to guarantee to each person covered by a wage incentive scheme a minimum weekly sum of money as wages, whatever the circumstances. This is known as the *guaranteed week* and is extremely common both in the U.K. and the rest of the world. Should a worker's bonus earnings be less than his minimum pay he is said to be 'in debt'. Debts are usually cancelled each week, although in some organizations they are carried forward so that the previous week's debts have to be cleared before any money over the guarantee is paid. This is increasingly rare, and many trades union agreements are in force which have clauses ensuring that debts are not carried over beyond the immediate bonus period.

1. Idle time?
2. Holiday pay?
3. Incomplete work?
4. Error in rate?
5. Defective work?
6. Guaranteed week?

Questions to be Resolved in an Incentive Scheme

Characteristics of Apparently Effective Incentive Schemes

As mentioned above, there is much debate on the total effectiveness of *any* financial incentive and to try to list the characteristics of an effective scheme is to accept the view that such schemes can be effective, a matter about which there is some doubt. However, where schemes are apparently running satisfactorily there are a number of conditions which appear to have been fulfilled.

1. *Intelligibility.* Some schemes are ingenious to the point of obscurity. Should the worker not understand how the scheme operates, there will be a persistent fear that he is being defrauded. 'Justice must not merely be done, it must be seen to be done.'

2. *Administrative simplicity.* To operate a confused or 'clever' scheme can be very costly indeed, and in one company in which the author was employed he remembers with recurrent dismay that he would spend every Friday afternoon checking operators' queries on bonus. The scheme was such that it was barely intelligible, and administratively extremely difficult, so that a query would involve not only tedious calculations, but also cross-referencing to several other departments.

3. *Direct.* The scheme should directly relate effort and reward.

4. *Speedy*. Payment should be made as rapidly as possible after it is earned: some delay is inevitable but this should be kept as short as possible. The holding up of bonus is a considerable source of mistrust.

5. *Adequate*. The reward given shall be sufficiently great to give stimulus, particularly in these days of high income tax. It is often recommended that a 133 performance should earn a bonus of one third of the day rate.

6. *Equitable*. Bonus earnings between workers should be equitable. A potent source of mistrust is the belief that one operator is earning much more than another—that one gets all the 'easy' jobs and another all the 'tight' ones. Often this mistrust is unjustified, and the author recalls that in one company all bonus earnings were calculated, entered into a single book, and this book circulated. This allowed queries to be dealt with, but just as important, it enabled everybody to see the earnings of all his/her colleagues.

1. Intelligible
2. Administratively simple
3. Direct
4. Speedy
5. Adequate
6. Equitable

Characteristics of Apparently Effective Incentive Schemes

Types of Incentive Scheme

There are very many different types of incentive scheme, and the most suitable depends upon many local factors—for example, tradition, type of work, time-cycle and so on. One decision has to be taken at the outset, however: that is, whether a scheme shall apply to an individual or a group. Where the output of any one person depends immediately upon the effort of another, as in a flow line, then a bonus can be calculated only on the output of the group of people concerned. On the other hand, group schemes are sometimes installed even when individual output can be measured. Such a group scheme has the direct advantage of administrative simplicity, and the indirect advantage, often not fully appreciated, that the group can exert considerable pressure upon its less satisfactory members, even expelling those who are 'passengers'. From the management's point of view, in a group scheme it is not possible to derive any figures illustrating the effectiveness of either an individual or a method. This is a substantial loss, and must be well considered before installing a group bonus.

In general all financial incentive schemes operate in the same way: a 'norm' or 'standard' of work is derived, desirably by work measurement, and the operator is given an incentive to achieve this norm. This is done by setting an *allowed time* for a task which is *greater* than the *standard time* by an amount known as the *policy allowance*, see page 165. A *bonus* or *premium* is then paid, the size of which depends upon the *time saved*, that is, the difference between the allowed time and the *time taken*. The differences between various schemes lie in the way in which the bonus is calculated from the time saved, and very many ingenious formulae are available, some simple, some extremely complex, and some where the bonus calculation changes with the level of output. As illustration, three of the most common methods are discussed below. The benefit to management in operating a financial incentive scheme derives, of course, from the fact that unit contribution remains effectively constant whatever the quantity produced, so that the greater the quantity produced, the greater the total contribution.

1. *Piece-work*

The most common, and in many ways the most satisfactory bonus system, is straight piece-work, where a price is assigned to each piece (or item), and the wage paid calculated by multiplying the price by the quantity produced. This can be either a *money* piece-work (in which case each unit has a price of so much) or a *time* piece-work (in which case each unit has an 'allowed time'). The difference between the two approaches is probably best illustrated by an example.

Assume a worker has a guaranteed rate of 50p an hour for a 40-hour week (that is, a guaranteed wage of £20 a week). Under a monetary system he may have a price of 7p an article, and in a 40-hour week he may produce 400 articles. He is then paid 400 × 7p for that week—that is £28. Under a time system for the same article he is allowed a time of 8·4 minutes each, and producing the same quantity he earns 400 × 8·4 minutes' pay, that is 56 hours pay at 50p an hour, which is again £28. In both cases the 'bonus' (i.e. the difference between basic pay and earned pay) is the same, namely £28−£20 = £8. The *money* rate has the advantages of administrative simplicity, clarity, and a constant direct labour cost, whatever the rate paid to the operator. On the other hand the *time* rate will allow savings to be made if an operator of lower rate of pay than originally planned is employed on the job. It also allows changes in basic rate to be made without re-calculating the piece work price.

In both cases above the time taken for the job is the same (namely, 6 minutes each) and if the total earnings are those which it had been expected that the operator would earn, then this time of 6 minutes would be the 'expected time', which coincides with the 'standard time'. Production control calculations must be based on this expected time and not on the allowed time. The allowed time is obtained from the standard time by the addition of a policy factor derived from a managerial decision of the amount of bonus which it is expected that a normal operator will earn. In the case of the example above, it was anticipated that an operator would earn 2·4 minutes every 6 minutes—a bonus of 40 per cent. If the operator had been earning only 'straight time'—that is, earning exactly £20 he would have been said to earn *day-rate*. Had he earned twice that amount (i.e. £40) he would have been said to earn *double time*, so that the earnings under piece-work are linear or 'straight', that is, they increase in direct proportion to the amount of work done once day rate has been passed.

For piece-work by time, the earnings can be written—

Wage = Time allowed × Rate
  = (Time taken + Time saved) Rate
  = Time taken × Rate + Time saved × Rate
and the bonus (or premium) can be considered to be—
Bonus = Time saved × Rate

2. *The Halsey-Weir System*

In the Halsey-Weir system a minimum rate of pay is guaranteed, but above day work a bonus (or premium) is paid, dependent upon the time actually taken to do the job. This premium is calculated from the value of the time saved, and in most schemes this is shared equally between the employer and the employee. This is known as a '50-50' scheme, although other divisions are sometimes used. The wages paid under a 50-50 scheme are given by—

$$\text{Wages} = \text{Time taken} \times \text{Rate} + \tfrac{1}{2}(\text{Time saved} \times \text{Rate})$$

Since Time saved = Time allowed−Time taken, the wages can be calculated—

$$\text{Wages} = \text{Time taken} + \tfrac{1}{2}(\text{Time allowed} - \text{Time taken}) \times \text{Rate}$$

i.e. $$= \frac{\text{Time allowed} + \text{Time taken}}{2} \times \text{Rate}$$

Using the same figures as in the discussion upon piece-work above, wages are calculated as follows—

Time allowed   = 8·4 minutes
Time taken   = 6 minutes (i.e. 400 units in 40 hours)
Rate/minute $= \frac{50}{60} p$

Hence Unit wage $= \frac{6 + 8·4}{2} \times \frac{50}{60} p$

and Total wage $= 400 \times \left[\frac{6 + 8·4}{2} \times \frac{50}{60} \right] p$
    $= £24$

Errors in the setting of the time allowed are not so significant in this system as in straight piece-work.

3. *The Rowan System*

Here again a premium is paid, this time the premium being given by—

$$\frac{\text{Time taken} \times \text{Time saved}}{\text{Time allowed}} \times \text{Rate}$$

so that the wages paid would be given by—

$$\text{Wages} = \text{Time taken} \times \text{Rate} + \frac{\text{Time taken} \times \text{Time saved}}{\text{Time allowed}} \times \text{Rate}$$

$$= \text{Time taken} \times \text{Rate} \left(1 + \frac{\text{Time saved}}{\text{Time allowed}}\right)$$

As before, if—

Time allowed $= 8 \cdot 4$ minutes

Time taken $\quad= 6$ minutes

Rate/minute $\quad= \dfrac{50}{60}$ p

Unit wages $\quad= 6 \times \dfrac{50}{60}\left(1 + \dfrac{2 \cdot 4}{8 \cdot 4}\right)$ p $= \dfrac{45}{7}$ p

and Total wages $= 400 \times \dfrac{45}{7}$ p $= £25 \cdot 7$

The maximum possible wage occurs when the time saved $=$ time allowed, when—

$$\text{Wages} = \text{Time taken} \times \text{Rate} \left(1 + \frac{\text{Time allowed}}{\text{Time allowed}}\right)$$

$$= 2 \times \text{Time taken} \times \text{Rate}$$

$$= 2 \times \text{Day rate}$$

so that under the Rowan system the wage earned is limited to twice the day rate.

The Rowan scheme is very suitable for use when the work measurement is not accurate. It has, however, the disadvantage that the calculation is inherently difficult, and will give rise to suspicion on the part of the operator if he does not clearly understand how his bonus is worked out

Comparisons of the Above Three Schemes

If the time taken is written: $\quad T_T$

the time allowed is written: $\quad T_A$

the time saved is written: $\quad T_S$

and the basic rate is: $\quad R$

then the earnings, for the same period of time are given as follows—

Piece-work Earnings $= T_T \times R + T_S R$

Halsey-Weir Earnings $= T_T \times R + \frac{1}{2}T_S R$

Rowan Earnings $= T_T \times R + \dfrac{T_T}{T_A} \times T_S R$

If earnings start at the same output, then the operation of the three schemes is as shown in Fig. 31.1 and 31.2. Alternatively, if the same bonus is to be paid for the same output (and this can of course only happen at one output), then the three schemes are represented by Fig. 31.3. It can be verified by the reader that the *time allowed* in these three cases is:

Piece-work $\quad T_A = 6$ minutes

Halsey-Weir $\quad T_A = 7 \cdot 2$ minutes

Rowan $\quad T_A = 6 \cdot 4$ minutes

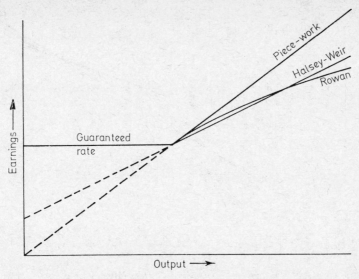

Fig. 31.1 Operator's Earnings under Piece-work, Halsey-Weir and Rowan Schemes, all with Guaranteed Rate

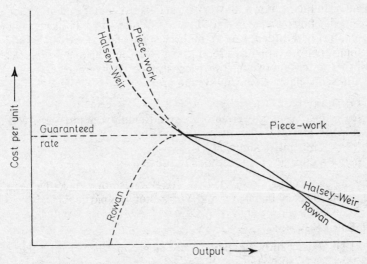

Fig. 31.2. Labour Cost under Piece-work, Halsey-Weir and Rowan Schemes, all with Guaranteed Rate

4. *Measured Day Work*

In the above, and related, schemes, the operator's earnings will vary with output. It may well be that this results in a deliberate control of effort in order that the wage-packet is kept constant, and that changes in method are opposed, or, if operator devised, concealed. To overcome these and other problems, Measured Day Work (MDW) is sometimes

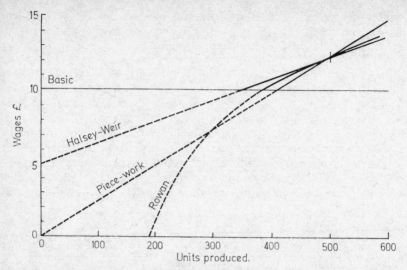

Fig. 31.3. Operator's Earnings under Piece-work, Halsey-Weir and Rowan Schemes, all Adjusted to Give the Same Earnings at one Point

advocated. In this, a 'norm' of work is established, and if operators achieve *or exceed* this norm for an extended period of time, then an increase in pay is automatically awarded. For example, a norm may be set which requires a continuous effort rating of 125, and if this achieved, then an increase of perhaps 30 per cent above the previous basic pay is awarded.

The benefits claimed for this system are:

(*a*) stabilized wages,
(*b*) improved employer/employee and employee/employee relation-ships.
(*c*) administrative simplicity,
(*d*) less opposition to methods improvement.

It must be made clear, however, that MDW does not reduce the need for managerial efficiency in general and Work Study in particular.

Group Bonus Schemes

Any of the above can be adapted to use as group schemes, and there are also a number of special group bonus schemes, amongst them the Priestman scheme and Scanlon Plan.

1. *The Priestman Scheme*

In this scheme all employees are paid a guaranteed basic wage. A figure for total output is then fixed (and agreed) and if the output from the factory exceeds the target by, say, *x* per cent, then all wages are increased by *x* per cent. The problem which arises in this system is in fixing the measure of output. In a single-product factory this is quite straightforward, but in a

376

multi-product factory difficulties arise which are often resolved by assigning a 'points' value to each product, and calculating output and targets in terms of the total number of points produced.

2. *The Scanlon Plan*

Here again, all employees receive a guaranteed basic wage, but the bonus received is calculated from the effective reduction in total labour cost. Some measure—often the ratio of labour cost to total sales value —is adopted as an index of total labour effectiveness. Any reduction in this index (whether from a reduction in labour cost, or an increase in sales value) results in an increase in pay, usually for all employees. In some cases directors and commission-earning salesmen are excluded from participation in the bonus. For example, if a 'norm' of thirty-eight per cent for $\frac{\text{labour cost}}{\text{total sales value}}$ is adopted, and total sales were £100,000, a labour cost of £38,000 would have been considered normal. If, in fact, the labour cost was £34,000, the difference ($=$ £4,000) would be shared amongst the employees as bonus. In some schemes the whole of this 'saving' is used as bonus, in others only part of it—72/25 being not uncommon.

The advantages of this plan are claimed to be that there is very much more worker participation and interest in methods of increasing productivity. Since improvements can come from any source, it is suggested that problems are seen as *joint* problems, and joint efforts are made to solve them. The Scanlon Plan first appeared to have been formalized in the U.S. just previous to World War II, and as yet there is too little experience with the Plan outside the U.S. to judge of its value in different employer/employee climates.

Supervisory Bonus Schemes

The use of bonus schemes for supervisory staff is even more contentious then the use of such schemes for direct labour, as it is often argued that supervisors should not require the spur of a wages incentive. However, many schemes are in current use, some of an extremely complex nature. The simplest and most direct is a bonus which is directly proportional to the algebraic sum of the bonus earnings of the staff under the supervisor's control. This will induce the supervisor to attempt to see that all his staffs are trained to such a pitch that they all earn substantial bonuses. It may have the disadvantages, if safeguards are not imposed, that the supervisor may sacrifice quality for output, that he might raise lieu bonuses too easily, or that he might give direct assistance to an operator to produce more, thus neglecting other supervisory duties. It is probably best to see that supervisory bonus does not form too great a proportion of his wages.

Profit-sharing and Co-Partnership Schemes

Other attempts at 'overall' bonus schemes are those known as *Profit-sharing* or *Co-partnership* schemes. Whilst these are extremely varied, they all have the basic form of a bonus being declared out of profits. This bonus is divided amongst the employees—if in cash, then the scheme is a *profit-sharing* one: if in the form of shares, then it is a *co-partnership* scheme. It will be observed that the Scanlon plan is, under this definition, a form of profit-sharing scheme.

Advantages of a Wage Incentive Scheme

The most usually quoted advantage of a wage incentive scheme is that it increases productivity. This may well be so, particularly if it is a well-designed scheme, although a badly conceived, badly executed scheme will have the reverse effect. There is, no doubt, however, that the increases in productivity can be achieved by other means, principally those of good leadership. There are two other important advantages which accrue and which are rarely appreciated, namely, that an incentive scheme will provide a ready measure of the effectiveness of a department, and that control is easier.

An Incentive as a Yardstick

A well-designed incentive scheme will be such that the bonus paid will be related to overhead recovery. This is not to suggest that bonus is paid only when all the overheads are recovered: political consideration may dictate that bonus is paid at a lower level than this. Nevertheless it can be calculated at what bonus level an individual or a department fully recovers the appropriate overheads. In a stable organization then—that is, one where a budget is being maintained—any department or individual earning above the minimum bonus level can be considered, without any further calculation, to be efficient within the requirements of the organization.

The earning of bonus can also be used as a simple test of efficiency without any considerations of overhead recovery. Even if the bonus scheme is not correctly founded, and the rates used are in error, the amount of bonus earned is an indication of the efficiency of the operator *within the framework in which he is working*. Variations in bonus earnings will similarly indicate variations in efficiency, thus providing an objective measure of progress.

An Incentive Scheme as an Aid to Control

Any production, budget or cost control scheme will depend eventually upon the accurate recording of time. Performance, lost time, labour content, will all require to be expressed in hours of work. Without a bonus scheme it will be found that time recording is slipshod, being regarded as an unimportant task. Once a bonus scheme is in operation, however, it is found that the operator will co-operate very actively in recording, since even without the financial advantage of good bonus, performance is a matter of prestige. Furthermore, social pressure is exerted on indirect staff in order to ensure that—for example—material is issued rapidly from stores, or goods are passed through inspection as soon as possible.

Productivity Agreements

Whilst productivity agreements are not necessarily financial incentive schemes—although they may include them—they are designed to serve the same purpose, namely, increasing productivity. Generally, they involve company-wide agreements in which outmoded working practices are replaced by more effective methods, in return for improvements in pay or conditions. In this way, long-established manning and demarcation traditions have been overthrown, and simpler and more effective structures have been instituted. Inherently the establishing of such an agreement will involve a very considerable investigation into the factors affecting productivity, and lengthy discussions with employees at all levels, the whole process being known as 'productivity bargaining'. When the results of the first agreement of this type were published in 1963, they appeared to be so striking that it was felt that the Productivity Agreement was the long-sought-after panacea which would cure all the ills of British Industry. However, this view has been somewhat modified with the passage of time.

Further Reading
1. Brown, W., *Piecework Abandoned*, Heinemann Educational Books, London 1962.
A powerful argument for the abandoning of piecework. Should be read by all managers who feel that a financial incentive scheme will increase the productivity of their factories.

2. Marriott, R., *Incentive Payment Systems*, Staples Press, London 1969.
The subtitle 'a review of research and opinion' accurately describes this book.

3. *Payment by Results*, International Labour Office, London 1969.
Summarizes the results of surveys carried out internationally.

4. *Wage Incentive Schemes*, H.M.S.O., London 1957.
An excellent short outline of the mechanics of operating various incentive schemes.

5. Lupton, T., *Money for Effort*, H.M.S.O., London 1961.
The summarized results of some field work. Very valuable as it presents data rather than opinion.

6. *Payment by Results Scheme*, H.M.S.O., London 1968. Report No. 65, Cmnd. 3627, 1968.
Whilst this does not discuss, as ref. 4 above does discuss, the mechanics of any particular scheme, it does present the arguments for and against financial incentive schemes, and discusses the effects of such schemes on wages and wage rates.

7. *Productivity Agreements*, H.M.S.O., Report No. 36, Cmnd. 3311, 1967.

8. Owen Smith, E., *Productivity Bargaining: a Case Study in the Steel Industry*, Pan Books, London 1971.
The above two works, read together, will provide a balanced view on productivity agreements.

9. Vroom, V. H., and Deci, E. L. (Ed.), *Management and Motivation*, Penguin, Harmondsworth 1970.
Contains a series of papers on Work Motivation. Extremely useful.

Chapter 32
Safety

THE AVOIDANCE OF INDUSTRIAL ACCIDENTS AND FIRES

Industrial Accidents

Accidents don't just happen, they're caused, and it is the duty of the manager to remove all possible causes of accidents. Spiegelberg (*The Times*, London, 5th May 1971) remarks: ' . . . Estimates (of the cost of industrial accidents) vary between £240m and £900m a year', and the annual reports of the Chief Inspector of Factories show that the number of reported Industrial Accidents is very substantial indeed. Table 32.1 summarizes the accidents reported to the Inspectorate for the last eight years, a 'reported accident' being one which results in an absence from work subject to the Factories' Acts of more than three days. The number of days lost through Industrial Accidents is very much greater than those lost through Industrial Disputes—see Table 32.2. No figures, however, can illustrate the pain and suffering caused by an accident, but a little imagination will suggest the results of a crushed arm . . . or a painful death. On purely economic grounds, therefore, accident prevention is desirable—on humanitarian grounds it is essential.

The Effects of an Accident

Heinrich (see 'Further Reading') has listed some of the sources of cost which derive from an industrial accident. They are summarized here not to provide a 'statement of account' against which management can justify the cost-benefits of any safety policy, but to show the impact of the shock-wave created by an accident. Costs, suggests Heinrich, are generated by—

1. Time lost by injured employee.
2. Time lost by fellow employees who stop work—
   (*a*) from curiosity
   (*b*) from sympathy
   (*c*) to assist
   (*d*) other reasons

Table 32.1. Summary of Reported Accidents

Year	Factory Processes			Construction			Docks and Inland Warehouse			Total		
	Fatal	Non-Fatal	Total	Fatal	Non-Fatal	Total	Fatal	Non-Fatal	Total	Fatal	Non-Fatal	Total
1963	332	167,774	168,106	242	28,106	28,438	36	7,779	7,815	610	203,659	204,269
1964	344	217,606	217,950	271	40,220	40,491	40	10,167	10,207	655	267,993	268,648
1965	358	238,800	239,158	230	44,151	44,381	39	10,139	10,178	627	292,290	293,717
1966	372	240,679	241,051	288	45,319	45,607	41	9,911	9,952	701	295,900	296,610
1967	342	246,716	247,058	197	46,278	46,475	25	10,458	10,483	564	303,452	304,016
1968	359	254,095	254,454	238	46,331	46,569	28	11,379	11,407	625	311,815	312,430
1969	357	266,500	266,857	265	44,305	44,570	27	10,936	10,963	649	321,641	322,390
1970	325	255,682	255,907	203	39,620	39,823	28	8,837	8,865	556	304,039	304,545

(Source—Annual Report of H.M. Chief Inspector of Factories, 1970)

Table 32.2. Comparison of Days Lost due to Industrial Disputes and Industrial Injury

Year	Millions of Days Lost, due to:	
	Industrial Disputes	Industrial Injury
1960	3·0	21
1961	3·0	19
1962	5·8	20
1963	1·7	20
1964	2·0	22
1965	2·9	23
1966	2·4	24
1967	2·8	23
1968	4·7	23
1969	6·9	23
1970	11·0	23

(*Source—Occupational Safety & Health Journal*,
March, 1971.)

3. Time lost by supervision in—
   (*a*) assisting the injured
   (*b*) investigating causes
   (*c*) re-scheduling work
   (*d*) re-training replacement
   (*e*) preparing accident reports
   (*f*) attending enquiries
4. Time spent by first aid staff
5. Damage to equipment
6. Interference to production
7. Payment of compensation
8. Reduced output of the injured employee upon his return
9. Loss of profit due to idle equipment
10. Lowered morale of work-force
11. Non-recovery of overheads by the injured person whilst he is a non-producer

Whilst some of the above can be measured or estimated, 10—lowering of morale—although 'invisible' is potent. The author still recalls with horror an accident which took place when he was first at work. A young girl press-operator 'cheated' a guard with the result that her hand was crushed. A foreman threw the master switch to shut off all machines, and the girl's screams followed by an absolute silence remain vividly in the memory. The whole factory suffered a corporate shock from which it slowly recovered . . . and the girl's hand was lost. No form of accounting can ever 'recover' the distress to the girl and all her colleagues.

Table 32.3. Causes of Fatal Accidents in Factory Processes

Causes	1967	1968	1969	1970
Machinery, other than lifting machinery:				
Prime movers	—	1	—	—
Transmission machinery (transmitting power to machines)	4	3	2	—
Process machinery (during process)	11	16	11	13
During maintenance	5	5	9	1
Moving machine and fixed structure	2	1	3	2
Ejections of parts of articles from machines	11	8	9	8
Materials in motion in machines ...	1	2	2	3
Lifting machinery:				
Jib cranes	14	13	11	9
Overhead travelling cranes	15	11	19	14
Lifts	1	2	3	1
Conveyors	2	6	7	4
Others	3	5	6	15
Lifting tackle	11	4	4	2
Rail transport	17	10	11	11
Non-rail transport:				
Overturning of vehicle	5 ⎫	8 ⎫	7 ⎫	9 ⎫
Collision between vehicles	1 ⎪	1 ⎪	7 ⎪	15 ⎪
Vehicle and fixed structure	15 ⎬38	25 ⎬59	8 ⎬46	17 ⎬73
Run over	16 ⎪	19 ⎪	18 ⎪	15 ⎪
Other	1 ⎭	6 ⎭	6 ⎭	17 ⎭
Fires and explosions	38	65	51	36
Electricity	22	14	18	17
Poisoning, gassing	21	12	12	14
Hand tools	1	—	1	1
Striking against objects	3	1	2	2
Falls of persons:				
On stairs	1 ⎫	— ⎫	3 ⎫	4 ⎫
From ladders	13 ⎪	11 ⎪	12 ⎪	8 ⎪
From stationary vehicles	3 ⎬71	6 ⎬64	5 ⎬71	8 ⎬67
Other falls from heights	46 ⎪	45 ⎪	46 ⎪	42 ⎪
On the flat	8 ⎭	2 ⎭	5 ⎭	5 ⎭
Falls and other movement of objects:				
Collapse of stack of materials ...	11 ⎫	11 ⎫	9 ⎫	6 ⎫
Buried in hopper	— ⎪	4 ⎪	1 ⎪	1 ⎪
Erecting, moving, repairing or dismantling plant	4 ⎬45	18 ⎬49	13 ⎬47	7 ⎬23
During handling operations... ...	8 ⎪	5 ⎪	3 ⎪	3 ⎪
From stationary vehicles	4 ⎪	5 ⎪	6 ⎪	4 ⎪
Other	18 ⎭	6 ⎭	15 ⎭	2 ⎭
Miscellaneous	6	8	12	9
Total	342	359	357	325
Incidence rate per 100,000 persons employed	4·4	4·5	4·5	4·5

(*Source*—Annual Report of H.M. Chief Inspector of Factories, 1970)

384

Types of Accident

Statistics concerning accidents must be treated with caution as only an accident which 'causes disablement for more than three days' is legally notifiable. This does not, however, guarantee that such accidents are reported; in *2000 Accidents* it is noted that in one shop 'only about half of (the injuries leading to three days lost time) . . . were recorded, the rest being recorded as "sickness" or "uncertifiable absence".' Even if the three-day rule were enforceable, it would not necessarily mean that accidents which would generally be regarded as serious were recorded. Creber recounts that ' . . . in the West Midlands a man who had a thumb amputated "as a result of an accident" . . . returned to work the following day . . . '

The team whose work is set out in *2000 Accidents* attempted to observe within 4 different workshops all accidents, both major—those resulting in three or more days lost time—and minor, with the following result—

Department	Minor Accidents	Major Accidents	Period	Ratio: minor/major
Despatch	299	20	12 months	15
Rolling Mill	391	9	12 months	43
Machine Shop	808	15	21 months	54
Light Assembly	823	2	21 months	412

(*Source—2000 Accidents*)

To achieve some comparability between years, the factory Inspectorate present in detail the causes of *fatal* accidents each year—see Table 32.3 and Fig. 32.1, and they also investigate in detail a 5 per cent random sample of reported accidents. Within this investigation, accidents are placed into three broad groups—

Group 1. Severe, including fatalities.

Group 2. Severe in that they resulted in absence of at least 28 days or admission to hospital for in-patient treatment. This group includes a proportion of accidents, particularly strains and sprains, where there is legitimate doubt whether they were caused by a true accident happening at work.

Group 3. Others which did not result in a 28-day absence or admission to hospital as an in-patient.

These groups are analysed with respect to type and site of injury, to industry, to sex of the injured person, and to geographical disposition of factory. The primary cause table is shown below, and all other tables can be obtained from the Annual Report.

Table 32.4. Accidents Analysed by Primary Cause and Injury Group

Primary cause	Group 1	Group 2	Group 3	Total
Machinery	776 (33·1%)	521 (22·2%)	1,048 (44·7%)	2,345
Transport	267 (24·9%)	299 (27·8%)	508 (47·3%)	1,074
Hand tools	167 (16·8%)	221 (22·2%)	608 (61·0%)	996
Falls of persons	510 (22·1%)	682 (29·5%)	1,119 (48·4%)	2,311
Striking against objects ...	168 (12·5%)	373 (27·7%)	805 (59·8%)	1,346
Handling goods	435 (10·7%)	1,153 (28·4%)	2,471 (60·9%)	4,059
Struck by falling object ...	219 (20·9%)	311 (29·6%)	519 (49·5%)	1,049
Not otherwise specified ...	200 (13·7%)	351 (24·0%)	910 (62·3%)	1,461
Total	2,742 (18·7%)	3,911 (26·7%)	7,988 (54·6%)	14,641

(*Source*—Annual Report of H.M. Chief Inspector of Factories, 1970)

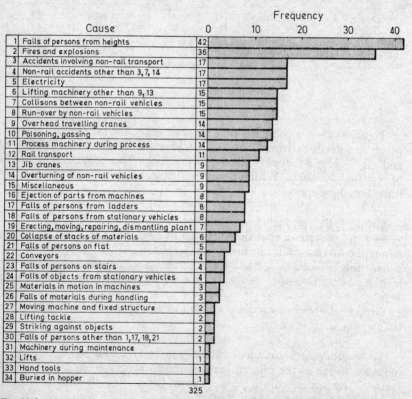

Fig. 32.1

The Responsibility for Safety in a Factory

Broadly, it is the responsibility of the organization to ensure that no person having any business within the organization is exposed to danger. Dangerous parts *must* be fenced, and ' . . . where the duty to fence exists, the obligation is absolute'. The test to determine whether a part is dangerous is not easy, and was enunciated by J. Du Parcq, in 1937, as follows—

' . . . A part of a machine is dangerous if it is a possible cause of injury to anyone acting in a way a human being may be reasonably expected to act in circumstances which may reasonably be expected to occur.'

Later, in 1939, Du Parcq amplified this statement to point out that the behaviour in question is that *which is reasonably foreseeable*, and not necessarily that which is reasonable. Thus, behaviour might be stupid, but if it can be foreseen, and if injury is likely to result from that stupidity, the duty to fence—and fence securely—exists.

Of the 325 fatalities in 1970, 104 cases involved, in the opinion of the Inspector, breaches of the law, 102 by the employer and the other 2 by the deceased. In an attempt to discover where action could have been taken to prevent the accident, the investigating Inspector felt that reasonable precautions could have been taken as follows—

Table 32.5

Reasonable Precautions taken by:	1967	1968	1969	1970
Management only	113	171	110	96
Deceased only	83	41	49	27
Fellow worker only	20	11	20	15
Management and deceased jointly	26	32	67	34
Management and fellow worker	18	9	16	11
Deceased and fellow worker	15	7	11	11
Management, deceased and fellow worker	11	4	24	21
Events unforeseeable, or insufficient evidence for an assessment	56	84	60	110

(*Source*—Annual Report of H.M. Chief Inspector of Factories, 1970)

Fire

The incidence of fire

Fires, like industrial accidents, are rarely experienced by most individuals: on the other hand a fire is likely to affect directly large numbers of people. Both occur through some human frailty (see Table 32.6): both are largely preventable. Regrettably, the incidence of fires appears to be increasing steadily each year (see Table 32.7)—the downturn in 1970 ' . . . is welcome, but there is little reason to suppose that it is anything

Table 32.6. The Main Causes of Fire in Industry and Commerce 1967

Electrical appliances and installations*	3,657
Smoking materials (cigarettes, matches, etc.)	2,161
Children playing with fire	1,936
Oil appliances and installations*	1,168
Mechanical heat and sparks	912
Malicious or intentional ignition	839
Rubbish burning	799
Solid fuel appliances and installations*	607
Gas (town) appliances and installations	550
Chimney or flue, spreading	369
Spontaneous combustion	278

*Misuse and lack of care play a large part in such fires

(*Source—U.K. Fire Statistics 1967*, Joint Fire Research Organization)

other than a temporary respite.' Undoubtedly the true cost of fire damage is much greater than indicated by the totals of Table 32.7, due to the 'shock-wave' effect discussed on pages 381 and 382.

Fire prevention and control

The Fire Protection Association, an association of organizations concerned with the prevention of fires, issues a number of publications designed to assist management in reducing fire risk, and controlling any consequent damage. Amongst their documents is a 'Planning programme for the prevention and control of fire', and the following steps are summarized from part of this.

Organizing against fire is the responsibility of management, and the F.P.A. suggest the following guide lines—

1. Management must accept that a fire prevention policy must be set up *and regularly reviewed.*

2. An estimate should be made of the possible effects of a fire in losing buildings, plant, work-in-progress, workers, customers, plans and records.

3. Identify the fire risks considering sources of ignition, combustible material, and means whereby fire could spread.

4. Estimate the magnitudes of the risks to establish priorities.

5. Establish clear lines of responsibilities for fire prevention.

6. Appoint a fire officer responsible to the Board.

7. Set up a fire protection drill for each department.

8. Set up a programme which will be maintained at appropriate intervals.

Included in the F.P.A. publication is a check-list of 'Good Housekeeping' precautions common to most businesses—see Table 32.8.

As with industrial safety, there is a wealth of information available at little or no cost to assist in reducing the risk of fire. Each Fire Authority in the U.K. has a Fire Prevention Officer who will be delighted to advise on any matter concerning fire hazards: the Fire Protection Association and H.M.S.O. publish many books and pamphlets dealing with all aspects of fire prevention and control.

Table 32.7. Fires in which Estimated Damage was £10,000 or More

Damage in individual fires	1966		1967		1968		1969		1970	
	No. of fires	Damage in all £m	No. of fires	Damage in all £m	No. of fires	Damage in all £m	No. of fires	Damage in all £m	No. of fires	Damage in all £m
£10,000–£100,000	792	24·1	818	25·0	871	24·0	974	29·1	999	30·4
£100,000–£250,000	67	10·4	63	9·4	92	14·6	90	13·6	73	10·8
£250,000–£1,000,000	29	11·6	43	17·0	38	16·3	48	26·3	47	22·6
over £1,000,000	2	2·3	4	5·3	4	6·7	6	9·2	3	6·3
Fires of £10,000 or more	890	48·4	928	56·7	1,005	61·6	1,118	78·2	1,122	70·1
Annual estimated fire damage £m	82·3		90·0		100·0		120·4		110·9	

(Source—Fire Facts and Figures 1970, Fire Protection Association)

Table 32.8. List of Fire Precautions Common to Most Businesses

	Frequency for checking
Doors which may be used for escape purposes unlocked and escape routes unobstructed	Daily at start of business
Fire doors and fire shutters closed	Daily at close-down
All outside doors, windows and other means of access secured against intruders and replaced if broken	,,
Furnaces and boilers safely out	,,
Heating apparatus and mains turned off	,,
Inspection of whole premises—especially storerooms and other parts rarely visited, areas where maintenance staff or contractors' workmen have been engaged—to detect any incipient smouldering fires	,,
Fire detection and alarm systems tested at a specified time (although in some systems testing is required less frequently)	Daily
Free access to hydrants, extinguishers and fire-alarm contact points	,,
Smoking only where permitted; adequate numbers of ashtrays; no smoking during last half hour of working day	,,
Naked lights prohibited	,,
Combustible materials kept well clear of all heaters—including steam pipes; no unauthorized heaters	,,
Combustible materials kept clear of lighting fittings	,,
Glue kettles, crucibles, pressing and soldering irons and similar appliances clear of combustible material and provided with non-combustible stands or holders	,,
Flammable liquids containers closed and away from sources of ignition	,,
Waste-bins, ashtrays and waste-paper baskets emptied at regular intervals and always at end of working day; no unnecessary accumulations of combustible process waste, packing materials or floor sweepings; safe disposal or incineration of waste	,,
Drip trays emptied	,,
Workmen's clothes and overalls kept in special places provided for the purpose away from combustible materials and sources of heat	,,

	Frequency for checking
Electric motors kept clear of all accumulations of material	Daily
Gangways kept unobstructed	,,
Special care with cutting and welding equipment used by maintenance men or contractors	,,
Fire extinguishers and other fire appliances in place and fire buckets filled	Weekly
Fire instructions, fire exit and 'no smoking' notices clearly displayed	,,
Alarms of sprinkler system tested	,,
Sprinkler and fire-detector heads unobstructed by stacked goods or structural modifications	,,
Goods, particularly those on the factory floor, neatly stored so as not to impede fire-fighting	,,
Clear spaces around stacks of stored materials	,,
No non-essential storage in workshop	,,
Flammable liquids and other hazardous goods in workshops—checked to ensure that stocks are kept at minimum	,,
Cupboards, lift shafts, spaces under benches, gratings, conveyor belts and behind radiators kept free of rubbish and dust	Periodically as required (weekly/monthy/quarterly/annually)
Girders and ledges free from dust	
Weeds and grass cut and cuttings removed from around buildings and outdoor storage	,,
Water supply of sprinkler system examined and tested quarterly	,,
Machinery and plant maintenance	,,
Earth leads disconnected, worn cables, broken plugs, overloading and other obvious defects in electrical equipment	,,
Floor drains and scuppers unblocked	,,
Leaks in roof repaired	,,
Gates and fences which might admit children and other intruders made secure	,,
Inspection of fire extinguishers	,,
Maintenance of special extinguishing systems—e.g. dry powder, carbon dioxide	,,
Check of lightning conductors	,,

(Source—The Fire Protection Association's 'Good Housekeeping')

The Reduction of Accidents

Depressingly, the *2000 Accidents* team found that there was a general apathy towards safety, both on the part of management and operators. Frequently danger was accepted as an integral part of the job, and an accident was seen only as a result of carelessness. To quote the report—
'... Two things are required—

(*a*) Management must be induced to take an interest and to look at what is really happening on the shop floor;
(*b*) Workers on the shop floor must be encouraged to feel that something ought to be done ... '

To reduce accidents it is necessary to—

(*a*) *Eliminate the hazard* by good design and layout;
(*b*) *Train* staff in safe behaviour.

Safety in work, like quality in the product, is largely a state of mind, and if an accident is seen as a 'defective', and its causes investigated and eliminated just as the causes of poor quality are investigated and eliminated, then overall safety will improve: safety, like quality, is everyone's business. A great deal of invaluable advice on safety at work is readily obtainable from the Factory Inspectorate and the Royal Society for the Prevention of Accidents. The author's experience as a factory manager is that *invariably* the Factory Inspector is more concerned with positive prevention than in punitive action, and wherever any doubt concerning the safety of a process exists, the Inspectorate has been most helpful.

Further Reading
1. Creber, F., *Safety for Industry*, Royal Society for the Prevention of Accidents, London 1967).
A useful book intended to show how a safety policy may be achieved. Geared to the needs of the training officer, the supervisor and the young worker alike. Contains a wealth of common sense.

2. *Annual Report of H.M. Chief Inspector of Factories*, H.M.S.O., London.
This contains much valuable statistical information and gives an excellent account of that understaffed and overworked group of Civil Servants, the Factory Inspectorate.

3. *Health and Safety at Work*, H.M.S.O., London.
This is a series of booklets effectively setting down codes of safety practice in a wide range of situations. At the time of writing, there are 45 of these booklets and this number is continually increasing. A full list of these and other Government publications can be obtained from—

Her Majesty's Stationery Office,
P.O. Box No. 569,
LONDON, SE1 9NH

4. Powell, P. I., Hale, M., Martin, J. and Simon, M., *2000 Accidents*, National Institute of Industrial Psychology, London 1971.
Probably the most detailed investigation of industrial accidents ever attempted. Four different workshops were observed continuously for at least a year by trained observers who worked normal factory hours. They recorded 2,367 accidents at work along with all the accompanying information on the effects of repetitive work, diurnal distribution of accidents, climatic, noise and personal factors . . . Must be studied by any serious worker in the field of safety.

5. Hearn, R. W. (Ed.), *Industrial Safety Handbook*, McGraw-Hill, London, 1969.
A compendious handbook on the subject.

6. *Accidents*, H.M.S.O., London.
This quarterly publication shows how accidents are caused and how they may be prevented. Each issue describes in detail and with appropriate illustrations, a number of industrial accidents, and shows how they could have been avoided. A depressing picture of man's stupidity emerges.

7. *Fire Facts and Figures*, Fire Protection Association, London.
An annual publication setting down the basic statistics concerning the effects of fire.

8. *Background notes on fire and its control*, Fire Protection Association.
These notes provide a succinct introduction to the whole subject of fire control. It includes notes on the organization of fire services.

9. *F.P.A. Journal*, Fire Protection Association, London.
An invaluable fascinating quarterly journal available from the F.P.A. It regularly includes a 'casebook of major fires' and frequent guides for managers. An essential part of management reading.

10. Thompson, J., and Rogers, H. R., *Redgrave's Factories and Truck and Shop Acts*, Butterworth, London 1972.
A master-work which sets out the Acts and provides commentaries upon them. A serious work to be used seriously, this is not intended to obviate the need for sound legal advice.

Appendices

Appendix 1
Derivation of a Sales Forecast
and Subsequent Budgets

The following example shows how a sales forecast can be prepared in an established organization. The assumption has been made that the net profit can be deduced from the gross profit by using the experience of previous years. This assumption is not strictly valid, but is used to avoid excessive calculations. A budget is necessary to calculate the anticipated profit accurately, and this is done later in this appendix.

THE 'F.M.' FACTORY—

Products	'F.M.' Equipment, 6 types.
Turnover last year	£400,000
Profit last year	£40,000
Requirement	During the year coming to have a turnover of at least £500,000 and a profit of at least £55,000.
General Note	The factory is a manufacturing unit only, producing for a sales department at the parent company. No marketing expenses therefore are involved, but discussions between the F.M. factory and the marketing department are held to determine marketing policy.

Sales forecast
1. *Sales Data*

Equipment	Quantity Sold					Income Last Year	
	Last Year −4	Last Year −3	Last Year −2	Last Year −1	Last Year	Each	Total
						£	£
FM.1	5,000	6,000	7,000	7,000	8,000	3·0	24,000
FM.2	8,000	9,000	10,000	10,000	10,000	6·0	60,000
FM.3	—	10,000	20,000	40,000	60,000	3·0	180,000
FM.4	1,800	1,900	1,800	1,800	1,600	10·0	16,000
FM.5	4,000	4,000	6,000	9,000	10,000	8·0	80,000
FM.6	—	—	2,000	6,000	10,000	4·0	40,000

Total Income £400,000

Market investigations showed that the entry of a new company into the market would make the selling of FM.1 more difficult, and that FM.3 is approaching saturation, which was felt likely to be 100,000 a year. FM.6 is likely to be readily sold in considerably increased quantities.

2. *Initial Forecast*

The initial forecast made by the sales department on the basis of the above figures is as follows—

	Quantity	Income £
FM.1	8,000	24,000
FM.2	11,000	66,000
FM.3	95,000	285,000
FM.4	—	—
FM.5	9,000	72,000
FM.6	13,500	54,000
	Total income	501,000

Production and Cost Data

1. Departmental loading—

Item	Departmental Hours per Product					
	A	B	C	D	E	F
FM.1	0·250	0·125	0·0625	0·0625	0·375	0·125
FM.2	0·227	0·363	0·363	0·136	0·227	0·136
FM.3	0·368	0·368	0·368	0·368	0·368	0·368
FM.4	0·375	0·0265	0·0625	0·4375	0·250	0·625
FM.5	0·222	0·556	0·667	0·667	0·444	0·778
FM.6	0·074	0·592	0·370	0·370	0·444	0·222

2. 'Down' Time and 'Ancillary' Time were calculated as percentages of total running time as follows—

	Department					
	A	B	C	D	E	F
'Down' time	4·7	5·65	5·94	3·13	2·97	4·21
'Ancillary' time	9·40	9·43	5·94	2·08	3·96	8·42

3. Idle times were assumed to be in the same ratios as last year, namely—

(*a*) As a percentage of running time—

Dept.	Per cent
A	26
B	21
C	20
D	$9\frac{1}{2}$
E	30
F	20

(*b*) Analysed according to major assignable causes—

	Percentages of Total Idle Time					
	A	B	C	D	E	F
Waiting material	40	60	50	70	40	60
„ drawings	10	5	10	10	15	10
„ tools	10	10	5	5	15	5
„ work	15	10	5	10	10	5
„ setter	5	5	10	0	10	5
Miscellaneous	20	10	20	5	10	15
Total	100	100	100	100	100	100

Cost analysis per unit last year

	Labour £	Material £
FM.1	0·74	0·50
FM.2	2·00	0·80
FM.3	0·38	1·20
FM.4	2·50	2·50
FM.5	1·06	1·60
FM.6	1·20	1·00

It was anticipated that there would be increases in both labour and material costs during the next year.

Labour Analysis for Initial Forecast

Applying the figures above to the initial forecast, the following results were obtained—

	Departmental Hours						Total Product Hours
	A	B	C	D	E	F	
FM.1	2,000	1,000	500	500	3,000	1,000	8,000
FM.2	2,500	4,000	4,000	1,500	2,500	1,500	16,000
FM.3	35,000	35,000	35,000	35,000	35,000	35,000	210,000
FM.4	—	—	—	—	—	—	—
FM.5	2,000	5,000	6,000	6,000	4,000	7,000	30,000
FM.6	1,000	8,000	5,000	5,000	6,000	3,000	28,000
Total running time	42,500	53,000	50,500	48,000	50,500	47,500	
Estimated down time	2,000	3,000	3,000	1,500	1,500	2,000	
Estimated ancillary time	4,000	5,000	3,000	1,000	2,000	4,000	
Estimated idle time	10,000	11,000	10,000	4,500	15,000	12,500	
Total forecast time	58,500	72,000	66,500	55,000	69,000	66,000	
Total available time	60,000	70,000	65,000	60,000	65,000	65,000	
Overload		2,000	1,500		4,000	1,000	
Underload	1,500			5,000			

Cost Analysis for Initial Forecast

Since the products were already in manufacture, and since records had been kept of material and labour costs, an analysis of costs could be made accurately, allowances being made for anticipated increases in material prices and wage rates. The analysis was—

	Material £	Labour £	Gross Profit £
FM.1	6,080	4,100	13,820
FM.2	22,220	9,020	34,760
FM.3	36,460	117,060	131,480
FM.4	—	—	—
FM.5	9,820	14,760	47,420
FM.6	16,360	13,840	23,800
	90,940	158,780	251,280

Examination of the Initial Forecast

The production analysis showed that the initial forecast produced overloads in four departments (B, C, E and F) and underloads in the remaining departments (A and D). Whilst it was possible that some of the overloading could have been reduced by the reduction in idle time resulting from an increase in volume, the underloading would probably have distorted the cost structure severely by increasing the idle time and thence the overhead rate. On these grounds, therefore, the initial forecast was not acceptable to the production departments.

The cost analysis showed that the total gross profit was £251,280, and a net profit of £55,000 was required. Previous years had shown that the net profit was approximately 21 per cent of gross profit, that is, that a gross profit of at least £262,000 was desirable. On this ground too the initial forecast was unacceptable.

Final Forecast

With the above figures in mind, a second forecast was produced which was again analysed and modified until a final forecast was produced which satisfied the joint requirements of the sales, production and costing departments. The main differences between this and the first forecast were—

1. The selling price of FM.2 was reduced slightly. This product had sold steadily without much variation for the past five years. The sales department felt that a small decrease in price would result in a large increase in sales, so the price of this product was reduced from £6·0 each to £5·6 each, with an estimated increase in sales from 11,000 to 15,000. This gave an increase in gross profit of £6,600, and helped to reduce the underload on departments A, D and E.

2. FM.4 was brought back into the programme, since it helped to increase the gross profit by £3,820, whilst at the same time increasing the load on departments A, D and E.

3. FM.6 was selling very well, and it was decided to increase its selling price by £0·5. This, it was estimated, would reduce the total sold from 13,500 (the figure in the initial forecast) to 12,000. This resulted in an increase in gross profit of £3,400, whilst reducing the total loading through the factory.

The above increased the gross profit to a total of £269,000, which was slightly above the estimated desirable level. At the same time the total load had increased, but the production department estimated that some of this could be overcome by reducing the 'waiting material' and 'waiting work' sources of idle time. This would require an increase in the production control staff, the cost of which would probably offset the apparent gain in net profit due to increased machine utilization. Any further overload would be dealt with by increasing the departmental capacities, a process which would also decrease the net profit due to increases in training costs. No substantial increase in department C was possible due to space limitations, whilst department F had a capacity limited by a piece of equipment whose output could not be increased.

The changes in sales forecast and the reduction in idle time result in three of the six departments (B, C and E) requiring increases in capacity, which were acceptable to the production department. Of the other three departments, two (A and F) had underloads small enough to be ignored, whilst investigations were put in train to see if the surplus labour in department D could be transferred to departments B, C and E.

Final Sales Forecast

	Quantity	Price each £	Income £
FM.1	8,000	3·0	24,000
FM.2	15,000	5·6	84,000
FM.3	95,000	3·0	285,000
FM.4	1,600	10·0	16,000
FM.5	9,000	8·0	72,000
FM.6	12,000	4·5	54,000
			535,000

Labour Analysis

	Departmental Hours					
	A	B	C	D	E	F
FM.1	2,000	1,000	500	500	3,000	1,000
FM.2	3,400	5,460	5,460	2,040	3,400	2,040
FM.3	35,000	35,000	35,000	35,000	35,000	35,000
FM.4	600	100	100	700	400	100
FM.5	2,000	5,000	6,000	6,000	4,000	7,000
FM.6	890	7,100	4,450	4,450	5,340	2,670
Total running time	43,890	53,660	51,510	48,690	51,140	47,810
Estimated down time	2,100	3,000	3,100	1,500	1,500	2,000
Estimated ancillary time	4,200	5,100	3,100	1,000	2,000	4,000
Estimated idle time	9,000	9,500	8,500	4,000	12,000	10,500
Total forecast time	59,190	71,260	66,210	55,190	66,640	64,310
Total available time	60,000	70,000	65,000	60,000	65,000	65,000
Overload		1,260	1,210		1,640	
Underload	810			4,810		690

Cost Analysis

	Material £	Labour £	Gross Profit £
FM.1	6,080	4,100	13,820
FM.2	30,300	12,300	41,400
FM.3	36,460	117,060	131,480
FM.4	4,100	4,100	7,800
FM.5	9,820	14,760	47,410
FM.6	14,544	12,300	27,156
	101,304	164,620	269,076

Factory and Production Management

Note: it is possible to produce a sales forecast using linear programming, and this has been done in Appendix 4.

The Budget

The sales forecast having been agreed, a budget is drawn up, first to show in detail how the required net profit could be obtained, and secondly to provide a set of criteria against which to measure performance. The first step was to determine the organizational structure of the factory; this was laid down by the general manager as follows—

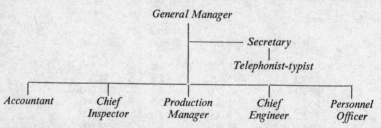

Detailed discussions were then held between the general manager, the accountant, and the departmental supervisors, to determine the staff necessary to produce economically the sales forecast. This produced a series of departmental labour budgets, which were then amalgamated into a general factory budget.

Departmental Budgets

1. *Inspection Department*

The organization required to give the necessary support for the production department was agreed to be as follows—

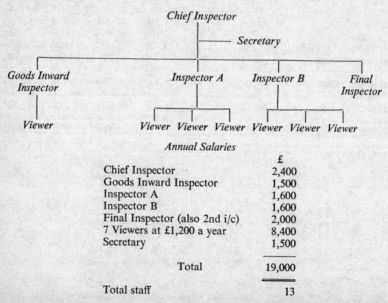

Annual Salaries

	£
Chief Inspector	2,400
Goods Inward Inspector	1,500
Inspector A	1,600
Inspector B	1,600
Final Inspector (also 2nd i/c)	2,000
7 Viewers at £1,200 a year	8,400
Secretary	1,500
Total	19,000
Total staff	13

2. *Accounts Department*
   The organization for this department is forecast to be as follows—

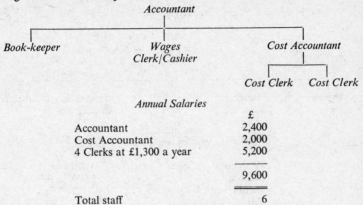

Annual Salaries	
	£
Accountant	2,400
Cost Accountant	2,000
4 Clerks at £1,300 a year	5,200
	9,600
Total staff	6

3. *Personnel Department*

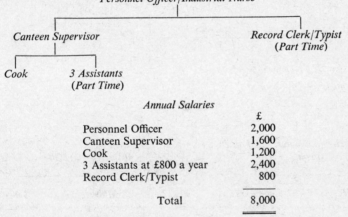

Annual Salaries	
	£
Personnel Officer	2,000
Canteen Supervisor	1,600
Cook	1,200
3 Assistants at £800 a year	2,400
Record Clerk/Typist	800
Total	8,000
Total staff	7

4. *Engineering Department*

Annual Salaries	
	£
Chief Engineer	2,200
Technical Assistant	1,800
Draughtsman	1,800
Total	5,800
Total staff	3

5. *Production Department*
The general organization is as follows—

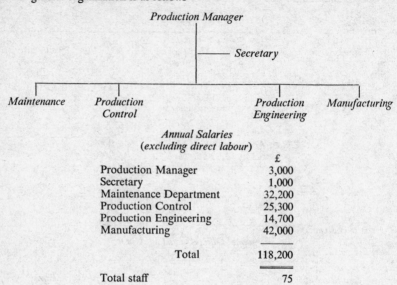

Production Manager

— Secretary

Maintenance — Production Control — Production Engineering — Manufacturing

Annual Salaries
(excluding direct labour)

	£
Production Manager	3,000
Secretary	1,000
Maintenance Department	32,200
Production Control	25,300
Production Engineering	14,700
Manufacturing	42,000
Total	118,200
Total staff	75

Production Department Sub-budgets

1. *Maintenance Department*

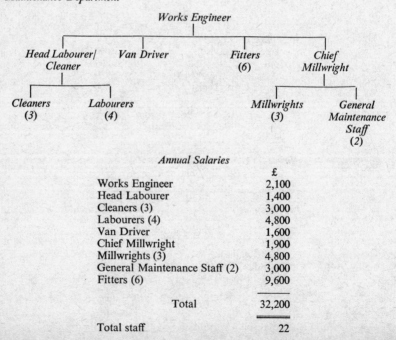

Works Engineer

Head Labourer/Cleaner — Van Driver — Fitters (6) — Chief Millwright

Cleaners (3) — Labourers (4) — Millwrights (3) — General Maintenance Staff (2)

Annual Salaries

	£
Works Engineer	2,100
Head Labourer	1,400
Cleaners (3)	3,000
Labourers (4)	4,800
Van Driver	1,600
Chief Millwright	1,900
Millwrights (3)	4,800
General Maintenance Staff (2)	3,000
Fitters (6)	9,600
Total	32,200
Total staff	22

2. *Production Control Department*

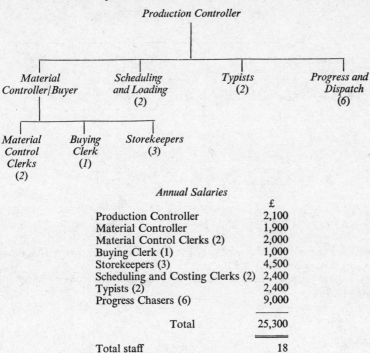

Production Controller

| Material Controller/Buyer | Scheduling and Loading (2) | Typists (2) | Progress and Dispatch (6) |

Material Control Clerks (2) — Buying Clerk (1) — Storekeepers (3)

Annual Salaries

	£
Production Controller	2,100
Material Controller	1,900
Material Control Clerks (2)	2,000
Buying Clerk (1)	1,000
Storekeepers (3)	4,500
Scheduling and Costing Clerks (2)	2,400
Typists (2)	2,400
Progress Chasers (6)	9,000
Total	25,300
Total staff	18

3. *Production Engineering Department*

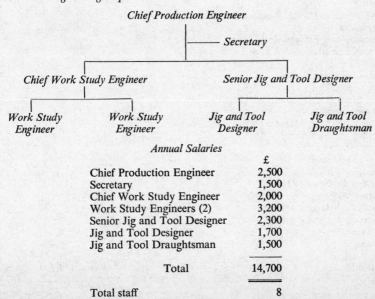

Chief Production Engineer — Secretary

| Chief Work Study Engineer | Senior Jig and Tool Designer |

Work Study Engineer — Work Study Engineer — Jig and Tool Designer — Jig and Tool Draughtsman

Annual Salaries

	£
Chief Production Engineer	2,500
Secretary	1,500
Chief Work Study Engineer	2,000
Work Study Engineers (2)	3,200
Senior Jig and Tool Designer	2,300
Jig and Tool Designer	1,700
Jig and Tool Draughtsman	1,500
Total	14,700
Total staff	8

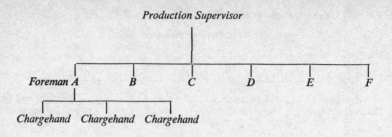

Production Supervisor

Foreman *A*   *B*   *C*   *D*   *E*   *F*

Chargehand *Chargehand* *Chargehand*

Annual Salaries

	£
Supervisor	2,400
Foreman (6)	10,800
Chargehands (18)	28,800
Total	42,000
Total staff	25

Direct labour not itemized above but responsible to the various chargehands totalled 200, at a total wage cost of £164,620.

All the above budgets were consolidated into one general budget along with all other expenses as follows—

General Budget

		£
Rent and Rates		7,000
Repairs and Maintenance (Buildings)		300
Lighting and Power		3,600
Heating		1,000
Small Tools and Tool Maintenance		800
Telephones		1,120
Travelling and Entertaining		640
Canteen Subsidy		400
Welfare		250
Staff Advertising		800
Audit Fee		546
Bank Charges and Interest on Overdraft		380
Cleaning Material		440
Insurances (Plant, Material, Work-in-transit)		500
Printing and Stationery		1,080
Depreciation to Plant		1,000
General Expenses		320
Directors' Fees		1,000
Delivery Expenses (Van)		450
Indirect Wages—		
General Manager and Secretary, etc.	£7,200	
Accounting and Costing	9,600	
Personnel	8,000	
Engineering	5,800	
Inspection	19,000	
Production	118,200	
		167,800

Carried forward

	Brought forward	167,800
Holiday Pay		6,600
National Health Insurance		13,700
Pension Fund Contribution		3,200
Direct Labour		164,620
Direct Material		101,304
	Profit	59,150
	Total	538,000
	Income	538,000

Break-even Chart

Of the items in the General Budget, the following were considered to be fixed, i.e. not dependent upon output—

	£	£
Rent and Rates		7,000
Repairs and Maintenance		300
Lighting and Power		3,600
Heating		1,000
Canteen Subsidy		400
Audit Fee		546
Directors' Fees		1,000
Indirect Wages—		
General Manager, Secretary, etc.	7,200	
Accountant and Cost Accountant	4,400	
Personnel Officer, Canteen Supervisor, and Record Clerk	4,400	
Engineering	5,800	
Chief Inspector	2,400	
Final Inspector	2,000	
Goods Inward Inspector	1,500	
Inspector A	1,600	
Inspector B	1,600	
Production Manager	3,000	
Secretary	1,000	
Maintenance Department	16,000	
Production Control Department	12,000	
Production Engineering	11,700	
Manufacturing Department	13,200	
		87,800
National Health Contributions for above		2,200
Pensions Fund contributions for above		500
	Total	104,346

The budget can thus be recast—

	£
Fixed Costs	104,346
Variable Costs	374,504
Profit	59,150
Total income	538,000

A break-even chart (see Fig. 1) was plotted, from which it was found that the break-even figure was £354,000, and at this level—

	£
Fixed Costs	104,346
Variable Costs	249,654
Total	354,000

Below this figure the factory would run at a loss, whilst above it the factory would run at a profit.

Note: The above B/E calculation is an approximation as it implies that the ratio of fixed costs: variable costs: income is the same for all products. Whilst this is clearly not so, the B/E figure obtained does give a useful bench-mark. Accepting this approximation, the Margin of Safety is given by—

$$\text{Margin of Safety} = \frac{\text{Budgeted income} - \text{B/E income}}{\text{Budgeted income}} \times 100$$

$$= \frac{538 - 354}{538} \times 100$$

$$= 33\%$$

Note: in the above example it has been necessary to quote wage-rates and salaries. These should not be taken to indicate any recommendations as to levels or proportions: all figures quoted are used only to illustrate the method.

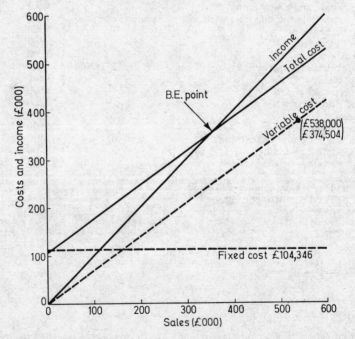

Fig. 1

Appendix 2
Critical Path Analysis

The factory manager, even in a flow-production factory, is frequently concerned with 'one-off' or 'job production' tasks, which will include—

Maintenance programmes.
Overhaul procedures.
Installation of new plant, or processes.
Laying out, or re-laying out, workshops.
Testing equipment or systems.
Designing and making production aids.

For the planning and control of these, and any similar tasks with an identifiable start and finish, Critical Path Analysis can be used.

Critical Path Analysis (C.P.A.) is one form of network analysis, and it is by far the most commonly used. In essence, the activities in any task are represented by *arrows*, and inter-relationships are shown by the positioning of one arrow relative to another. This arrow representation of activities gives rise to the generic name, 'Activity-on-Arrow' (A-on-A) networking. Alternative but closely associated forms represent the activity by a box (or 'node'), and these systems bear the family name, 'Activity-on-Node' (A-on-N) networking. This appendix will discuss C.P.A. extensively, and briefly explain A-on-N systems.

THE BASIC ELEMENTS OF C.P.A.

Every task must have a recognizable beginning and an end in order to be susceptible to C.P.A. planning. These two points in time are represented by two 'nodes' (usually drawn as circles), and the constituent parts of the task (the 'activities') are drawn as arrows located somewhere between the start and the finish nodes. The start and finish of any activity, or group of activities, is also represented by a node circle, and the dependency of one activity upon another is shown by the dependent activity emerging from the node at the head of its preceding activity. These nodes are sometimes called 'events'.

Consider, for example, the problem of moving one piece of plant (X) to a new site, and installing in its place another piece of plant (A). The first step is to define the starting and finishing situations—

Start. The project will be considered to start when the budget for removing and relocating X and A, and obtaining any associated material handling equipment and tools, has been agreed.

Finish. The project will be considered to be completed when X and A are in position, tested and ready to run.

These definitions will then enable two simple arrows to be drawn, as in Fig. 2.

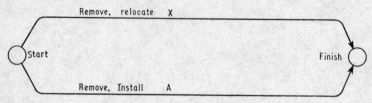

Fig. 2

The 'Remove, relocate X' arrow can be considered to comprise four activities—

> Clear site for X
> Remove X
> Re-install X
> Test X.

Of these, 'clear site' must precede 'Remove X' since X must be placed somewhere once moved. Similarly, it can only be re-installed when removed, and testing must follow re-installation, so that the single arrow would break into a chain of four, as in Fig. 3.

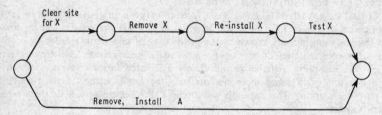

Fig. 3

The 'Remove, install A' activity can be considered to comprise activities—

> Remove A
> Install A
> Test A
> Obtain tools for A
> Obtain associated material handling equipment.

Here again, 'test', 'install' and 'remove' follow each other. However, the act of obtaining tools for A does not depend upon A at all—it can start as soon as the budget is approved, that is, at the START node, but it must be completed before testing can start. The material handling equipment is similarly not dependent upon anything but budget approval (that is, START), and does not influence testing or installation, the only requirement being that it must be available when A is ready to run—that is, by FINISH, so the diagram develops as in Fig. 4.

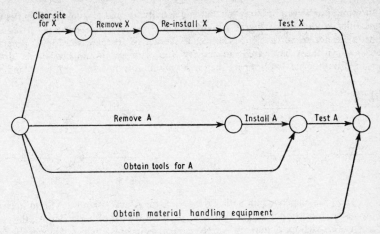

Fig. 4

A closer examination of this diagram indicates that A is installed without its site having been prepared so there is an activity 'Prepare site for A' which is missing. A is going to occupy the site previously used by X and thus the activity 'Prepare site for A' cannot start until X is removed, and it must be complete before A can be installed. See Fig. 5.

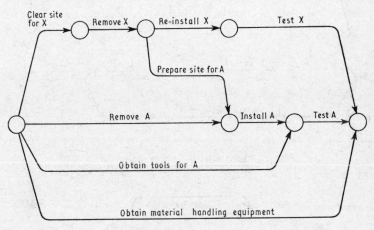

Fig. 5

Dummy Activities
The fundamental convention used in drawing the network is that if one activity must follow another they will be shown as in Fig. 6.

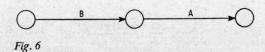

Fig. 6

411

In some situations a 'dummy' or 'dummy activity' is used to avoid ambiguities and illogicalities, a 'dummy' being an activity which *shows only a dependency*—it requires neither time nor resources. For example, if the act of 'Prepare site for A' generates rubbish which must be cleared, an activity 'Cart rubbish' would need to be drawn emerging from the head of 'Prepare site for A', but to draw it as in Fig. 7, would indicate

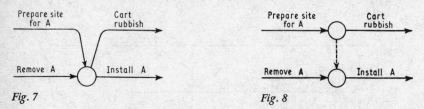

Fig. 7   *Fig. 8*

that 'cart rubbish' depended on both 'Prepare site for A' *and* 'Remove A', and since the rubbish arose from the act of 'preparing the site', not the act of 'removing A', this is an unnecessary restriction. A dummy can be inserted, as in Fig. 8, which removes the false dependency, and shows 'Cart rubbish' depending only upon 'Prepare site for A' and *not* upon 'Remove A'. A dummy is an activity of zero duration, and is usually drawn as a 'broken' arrow. The complete network can be seen in Fig. 9.

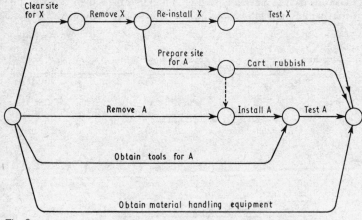

Fig. 9

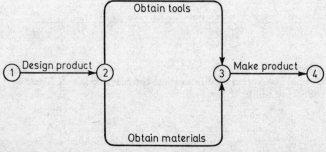

Fig. 10

A dummy may also be needed to remove the ambiguity which arises from two activities having the same start and finish—for example in Fig. 10 two activities ('obtain tools' and 'obtain materials') have the same head and tail nodes. If these nodes are numbered, then both activities have the same head and tail numbers—they are *both* activity 2–3. To release this ambiguity a dummy is inserted at the beginning or end of either activity—see for example Fig. 11.

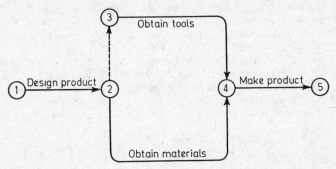

Fig. 11

Activity Times

The network so far shows only the *logic*—that is, the necessary technological requirements—of the project. To this must be added the times required for each activity, and these are shown as subscripts to the activity arrows. Dummy activities require no time, and by convention no subscripts are added to them. Numbers are inserted in the nodes to permit simple reference to the activities. The completed network, with duration times and node numbers is shown in Fig. 12.

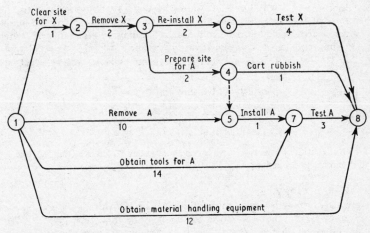

Fig. 12

Analysis of the Network

The total time for the whole task is found by carrying out a *forward pass*, that is, by adding activity times together, starting at the first node. The 'spare' time available in any activity is then deduced from a *backward pass*, when activity times are subtracted in succession from the total project time.

The Forward Pass

In essence, the forward pass determines the earliest times at which activities can start. Assume that the present time is written as Time 0. The earliest time at which any activities emerging from the first node can start is 'now' and this is shown by an E = 0 at event 1.

Note: this does not imply that *all* the activities leaving event 1 *must* start at time 0, but that they *may* start at time 0.

The earliest time at which activity 2–3 may start is $0 + 1 = 1$, hence E = 1 at event 2. The earliest time at which activities 3–4 and 3–6 may start is $1 + 2 = 3$—hence E = 3 at event 3. Events 4 and 6 will both have times E = 5. Activity 5–7 cannot start until activity 4–5 is completed—at times $5 + 0 = 5$—and activity 1–5 is finished—at time $0 + 10 = 10$. To satisfy both activity constraints the later time (10) is necessary, so that E = 10 appears at event 5. By a similar argument the earliest time by which activity 7–8 can start is 14. The total project time will permit all entering activities to finish. Thus—

$$\text{Activity 6–8 can finish by time} \quad 5 + 4 = \;\; 9$$
$$\text{,,} \quad 4–8 \;\text{,,} \quad \text{,,} \quad \text{,,} \quad \text{,,} \quad 5 + 1 = \;\; 6$$
$$\text{,,} \quad 7–8 \;\text{,,} \quad \text{,,} \quad \text{,,} \quad \text{,,} \quad 14 + 3 = 17$$
$$\text{,,} \quad 1–8 \;\text{,,} \quad \text{,,} \quad \text{,,} \quad \text{,,} \quad 0 + 12 = 12$$

and the earliest time which allows *all* these to finish is time 17—hence E = 17 at event 8, so that the total project time is 17.

The Backward Pass

In the backward pass, the latest possible time for the completion of each activity is determined. Assuming that the total project time of 17 is acceptable, then all final activities must be finished by time 17, and an L = 17 is written at the final node. If activity 6–8 must finish by time 17, then activity 3–6 must finish by time $17 - 4 = 13$, and an L = 13 is written at event 6. Similarly, L = 14 will appear at event 7, and L = 13 at event 5. Activity 3–4 must finish by such a time that activity 4–5 finishes at time 13, and activity 4–8 at time 17, so the latest finishing time for activity 3–4 must be time 13. Similarly, activity 2–3 must satisfy activities 3–4 ($13 - 2 = 11$), and 3–6 ($13 - 2 = 11$)—hence L = 11 at event 2. The latest possible time by which all the activities can start is—

$$\text{for activity 1–2 time} \quad 9 - \;\; 1 = 8$$
$$\text{,,} \quad \text{,,} \quad 1–5 \;\text{,,} \quad 13 - 10 = 3$$
$$\text{,,} \quad \text{,,} \quad 1–7 \;\text{,,} \quad 14 - 14 = 0$$
$$\text{,,} \quad \text{,,} \quad 1–8 \;\text{,,} \quad 17 - 12 = 5$$

and for all activities considered together, the smallest of the above, that is, time 0, and L = 0 is entered at event 1.

Calculation of Activity Times

Every activity now has two limiting times associated with it—the earliest starting time, given by E = at its tail node, and the latest finishing time, given by L = at its head node, so that in effect activity $i - j$ is bounded by two times—

$$E_i = \text{the earliest starting time}$$
$$L_j = \text{the latest finishing time}$$

This can be seen in Fig. 14.

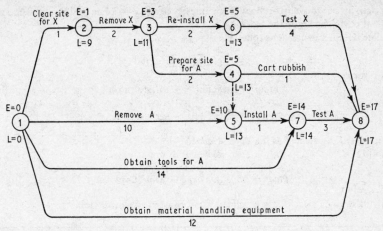

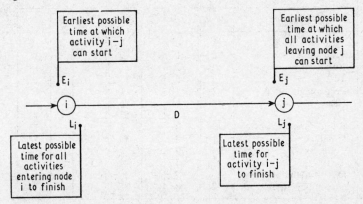

Fig. 13

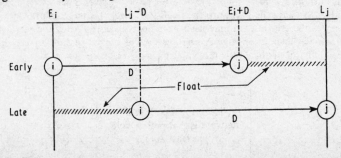

Fig. 14

Knowing the duration D it is possible to carry out the following calculations:

$$E_i + D = \text{the earliest finishing time}$$
$$L_j - D = \text{the latest possible starting time,}$$

or, diagrammatically, as in Fig. 15.

Fig. 15

The activity can thus slip or 'float' from an early position to a late position, the amount of float being shown by the hatching.

The float is calculated as follows—

$$\text{Float} = L_j - E_i - D$$

or in words—

$$\text{Float} = \text{latest finish} - \text{earliest finish}$$

or

$$\text{Float} = \text{latest start} - \text{earliest start}$$

or, if $L_j - E_i$ is defined as the *Time Available*
and D is „ „ „ *Time Required*

$$\textit{Float} = \textit{Time Available} - \textit{Time Required}$$

With these calculations, it is possible to construct the following table:

Nos.	Activity			Start			Finish			Float
	Description	Durn.	Early	S	Late	Early	S	Late	
1–2	Clear site for X	1	0		8	1		9	8
2–3	Remove X	2	1		9	3		11	8
3–6	Re-install X	2	3		11	5		13	8
6–8	Test X	4	5		13	9		17	8
3–4	Prepare site for A	2	3		11	5		13	8
4–8	Clear rubbish	1	5		16	6		17	11
4–5	Dummy	0	5		13	5		13	8
1–5	Remove A	10	0		3	10		13	3
5–7	Install A	1	10		13	11		14	3
1–7	Tools for A	14	0		0	14		14	0
7–8	Test A	3	14		14	17		17	0
1–8	Obtain material handling equipment	12	0		5	12		17	5

Note: The columns headed S refer to scheduled times, and these will be determined later.

In the above table two activities (1–7 and 7–8) have no float, so that any changes in their duration times will affect the total time for the whole project. Hence, these activities are 'critical' in that they determine total time, and the sequence of critical activities is known as the *critical path*. In some situations the project is given a 'target' or 'acceptable' time, and in this case the backward pass will start with this target time. Under these circumstances the critical path may itself have float (*positive* float if the target time is greater than the final E = figure, *negative* float if the target time is less than the final E = figure). Criticality is measured by the size of the float:

> The critical path in a
> network is that path which
> has least float

Reduction of Total Project Time

The total project time can only be reduced by reducing the total length of the critical path. This can be done by using the critical examination technique of the Work Study Engineer (page 152) and/or by changing the logic, that is, changing some of the decisions inherent in the network. It must be remembered that if the reduction in the Critical Path is *greater than* the next lowest value of float, a new Critical Path is created. Thus, if activity 1–7 is reduced by more than 3 units of time—to, say, 10—then the sequence 1–5–7–8 forms a new Critical Path, the original one now becoming non-critical in part.

Representing the Network as a Bar Chart

The network can be translated into a Bar Chart in a number of ways. One method is to 'square' the network as in Fig. 16, and the similarity between this representation of the project and the original arrow diagram is sufficiently great to make a description of a method of drawing unnecessary. In drawing this or any other form of bar chart it is useful to remember that the node numbers effectively describe the logic of the situation, so that any activity whose tail number is M *must* follow *all* activities whose head numbers are M.

The bar chart representation is very useful in three ways:

(*a*) it illustrates the physical meaning of float,
(*b*) it is often more readily understood than the arrow diagram,
(*c*) it can be used to assist in the disposition of the various resources used in the project.

Resource Allocation

In most situations, the resources available are limited, and it is obviously essential to see that the resources required are never greater than those available, as pointed out on page 257. Critical Path Analysis, whilst not resolving this situation uniquely, provides useful assistance in achieving an acceptable solution, since it shows which activities can be 'moved' without increasing the total project time, and also the effect of moving time-limiting activities. In the project so far considered, there are two 'removal' activities:

Activity 2–3	Remove X
Activity 1–5	Remove A

Assume that both of these are going to be carried out by the same gang, then, as drawn in Fig. 16, *two* gangs are required during days 2 and 3, and if only *one* gang is available, then Fig. 16 represents an impossible situation. However, it will be observed that both activities possess float (activity 2–3, 8 days, activity 1–5, 3 days), so that either can be moved. To start activity 2–3 after activity 1–5 has finished would increase the total project time by 1 day, but to start activity 1–5 after activity 2–3 has finished would use up float, but would not increase total time. Hence, the removal gang must carry out the sequence 'Remove X' then 'Remove A'. This would mean that the earliest and latest start and finish times would disappear—the activities concerned would be 'scheduled', the analysis table appearing—

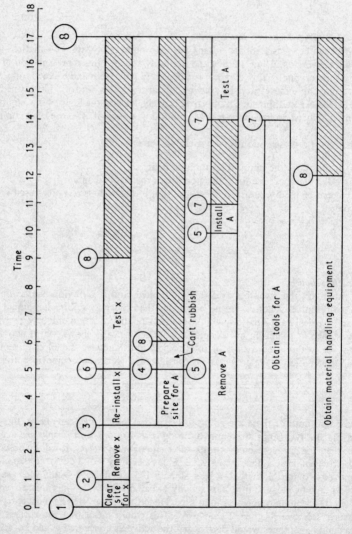

Fig. 16

Nos.	Description	Durn.	Start Early	S	Late	Finish Early	S	Late	Float
1–2	Clear Site for X	1	0	0	9	1	1	9	8 0
2–3	Remove X	2	1	1	8	3	3	11	8 0
3–6	Re-install X	2	3		11	5		13	8
6–8	Test X	4	5		13	9		17	8
3–4	Prepare Site for A	2	3		11	5		13	8
4–8	Clear rubbish	1	5		16	6		17	11
4–5	Dummy	0	5		13	5		13	8
1–5	Remove A	10	0	3	3	10	13	13	3 0
5–7	Install A	1	10	13	13	11	14	14	3 0
1–7	Tools for A	14	0		0	14		14	0
7–8	Test A	3	14		14	17		17	0
1–8	Obtain material handling equipment	12	0		5	12		17	0

This type of manipulation can be very difficult if there are a large number of activities and a large number of resources, as the number of possible 'moves' increases factorially with the number of activities. To allow a systematic procedure to be followed, a set of decision rules must be generated. These rules, which will differ from organization to organization, will not necessarily produce a 'best' or 'optimum' solution, but they will tend to produce 'feasible' or 'workable' solutions in a reasonable time.

Decision Rules for Resource Allocation

All sets of rules depend upon resolving a 'conflict' for resources by means of arbitrary decisions. For example, if two (or more) activities require more resources than are available, a *conflict* is said to exist which is resolved by perhaps, awarding the resources to the activity which has least float, then to the activity which has the next smallest value of float, and so on. If conflict still exists, then resources are awarded to the activity with the greatest work content, and so on, down through a ladder of rules. It is not possible to prove that any one set of rules produces a better answer than any other set, and the rules quoted below, though they have an intuitive appeal, are derived from R. L. Martino's work and are quoted only as an example of one possible set of rules. Other sets may be more appropriate in particular circumstances.

When conflict for resources arises, award resources according to the following rules—

First priority	in order of float
Second ,, ...	,,	work content
Third ,, ...	,,	size of resource
Fourth ,, ...	,,	priority of resource
Fifth ,, ...	,,	latest finish date
Sixth ,, ...	,,	'j' number

Rules for resource allocation following R. L. Martino

The Computer and C.P.A.

Once a network is drawn, a computer can be used to carry out the calculations which are subsequently required. Frequently in a factory situation the effort of preparing the input data will be such that manual calculations are quicker, easier and cheaper. However, if it is necessary to carry out a series of calculations on a network—for example when scarce resources must be allocated—then a computer is invaluable. There are currently a large number of programs both for C.P.A. and A-o-N already available and it is extremely unlikely that a special program will need to be written. Amongst the facilities included in various programs are—

1. *Sorting.* The output can be sorted into any form—by departments—by order of float—by order of start (or finish) time.
2. *Calendar dating.* Calendar dates for the various starts and finishes can be provided.
3. *Resource allocation.* Resources can be allocated to activities in accordance with prescribed rules.
4. *Bar Charting.* The results can be presented in the form of Bar Charts.

Not all the above facilities are available on all programs. The user should choose that program which gives him only the facilities he requires and not one which will generate un-needed output.

Control using C.P.A.

Control upon the progress of a task can be exerted in basically two ways—

(*a*) by using a derived bar chart and marking 'achievement' against 'plan',
(*b*) by inserting into the network the actual activity time and examining the effect upon float.

The detailed working out of either method will be found in any of the more advanced texts. In many cases, the simplest method is to compare actual finish dates with the $L =$ figure on the network. For complex or frequently checked networks a computer re-run ('update') with actual rather than estimated activity times may be appropriate particularly if there is ready access to the computer.

ACTIVITY-ON-NODE NETWORKING

In A-on-N systems, an activity is represented by the node, and the arrow is used to denote only dependency. The subscript to the arrow, in the most commonly used A-on-N system, gives the dependency time—that is, the time which must elapse between the *start* of one activity and the *start* of the next. This eliminates the need for dummy arrows, and simplifies the representation of overlapping activities (see Fig. 17).

The forward and backward passes in A-on-N systems are carried out in precisely the same way as in C.P.A. The result of the forward pass is unchanged—it gives the earliest starting time of the activity. The backward pass, however, gives the LATEST STARTING TIME of the activity, *not* the latest finishing time. The example used earlier in this chapter is shown drawn as an A-on-N network in Fig. 18.

All the manipulations described for conventional C.P.A. can be carried out in A-on-N networking. The main advantage of A-on-N is its freedom from dummies, which newcomers to the subject sometimes find difficult. On the other hand, more arrows are generated, and the diagram may be found to be rather more difficult to read. In practice, neither system appears to have overwhelming advantages, and the choice between them seems largely a personal one. Computer programs to deal with A-on-N are readily available commercially.

SITUATION	C.P.A.	A-o-N.
Activity B depends on Activity A		
Activity C depends on Activities A and B	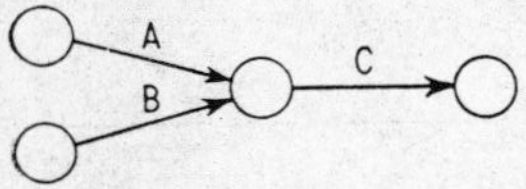	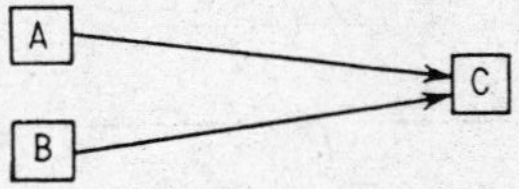
Activities C and D depend on Activities A and B	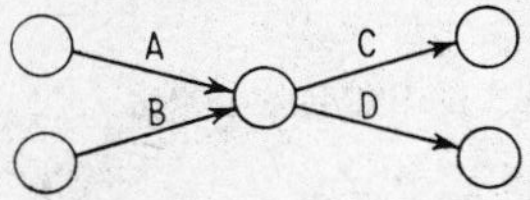	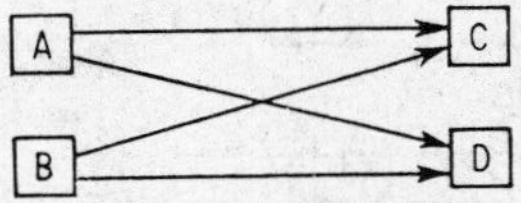
Activity C depends on Activity A; Activity D depends on Activities A and B	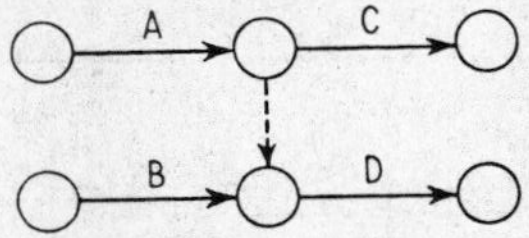	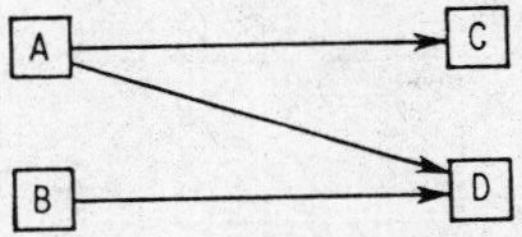
Activity K depends on Activity A; Activity L depends on Activities A and B; Activity M depends on Activities A, B and C	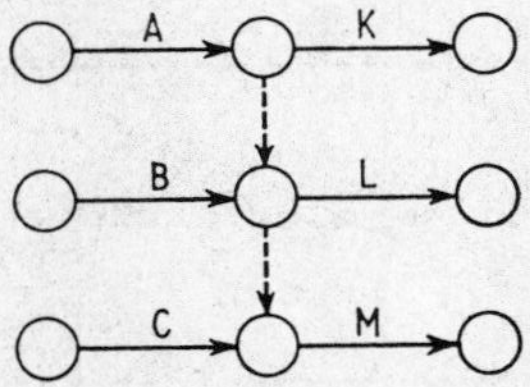	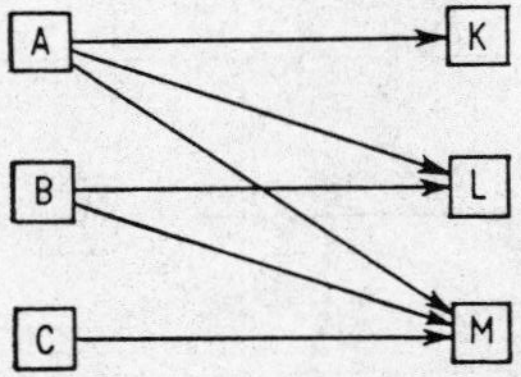

Fig. 17

SITUATION	C.P.A.	A-o-N.
Activity B, which must follow Activity A, may not start until D units of time have elapsed after the completion of A.	A ○──12──○ Delay D ──○ B 15	A 12 ──12 + D── B 15
Activity B must not start until at least R units of time have elapsed after the start of activity A.	○──A 12──○ R-12 ──○ B 15	A 12 ──R── B 15
The interval between the completion of A and the start of B must not exceed X. Note: This is Roy's 'Negative Constraint.'	NOT POSSIBLE	A 12 ──12── B 15 ──(12 + x)──
Activity A and Activity W are both opening activities; Activity A may start at the beginning of the project; Activity W must not start until time T has elapsed after the start of the project.	○──A 12──○ ○ Constraint T ──W 20──○	Start ──0── A 12 Start ──T── W 20

Fig. 17 (cont'd)

SITUATION	C.P.A.	A-o-N.
Activity B can start immediately Activity A is complete.		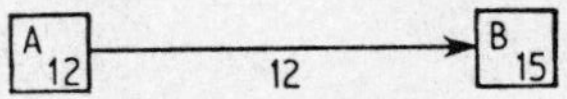
Activity B can start immediately Activity A is complete and Activity C can start when part p of Activity A is complete.	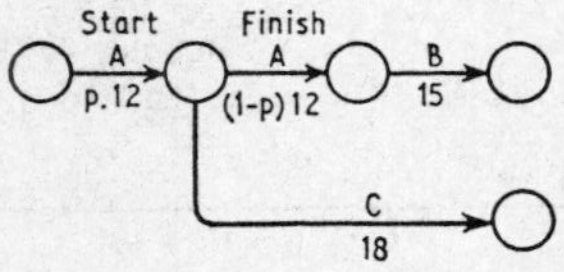	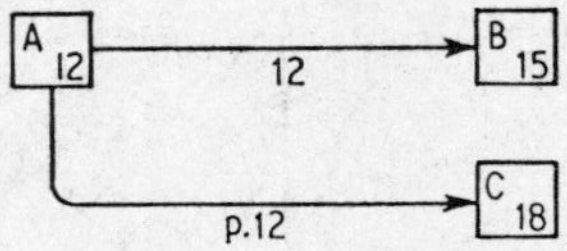
Activity B can start when part p of Activity A is complete; Activity C can start when part r of Activity B is complete; Activity B requires at least s.15 time to finish after the completion of A, and C requires at least v.18 to finish after the completion of B.	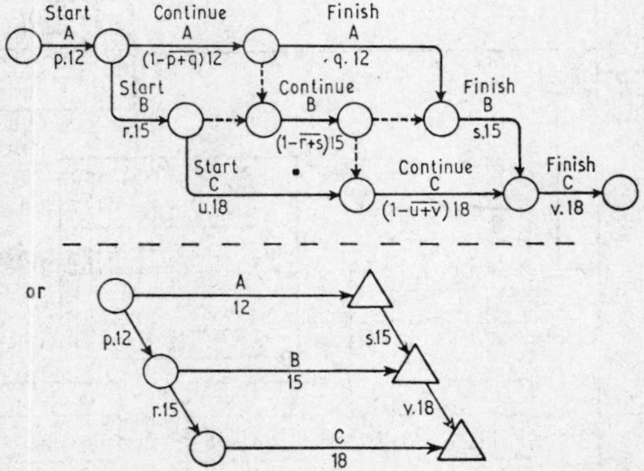	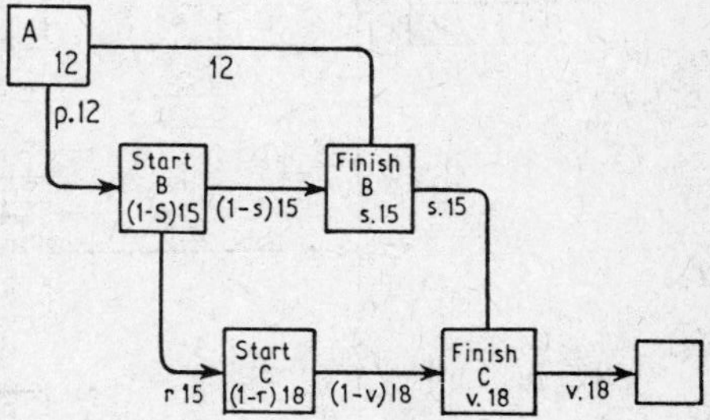

Fig. 17 (cont'd)

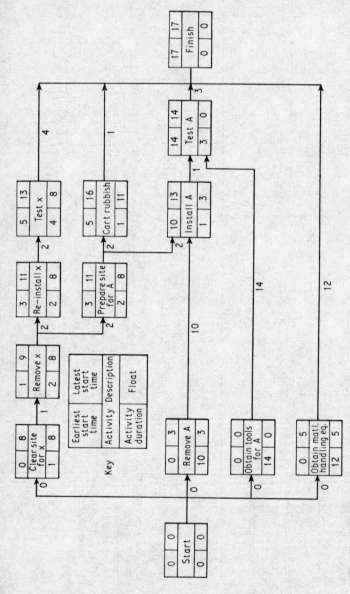

Fig. 18. Activity-on-Node representation of Fig. 12.

Further Reading
1. Lockyer, K. G., *An Introduction to Critical Path Analysis*, Pitman, London 1969. A non-mathematical text, designed to assist those who wish to use Critical Path Analysis.

2. Battersby, A., *Network Analysis for Planning and Scheduling*, Macmillan, London 1970.
The second edition of this book is the definitive work on C.P.A. discussing at length all known forms and manipulations.
Exhaustive bibliographies appear in both the above texts for those who wish to 'try out' C.P.A. for themselves.

3. Lockyer, K. G., *Critical Path Analysis—Problems and Solutions*, Pitman, London 1974.
A series of exercises designed to give practice in all aspects of C.P.A. Solutions appear in the form of diagrams and explanatory notes.

4. Martino, R. L., *Project Management and Control. Volumes I, II, III*, The American Management Association, New York 1964–65.
Dr. Martino's three volumes are, of course, sound. They are also pleasant to read, and take the newcomer to the subject through all the manipulations at a gentle pace.

5. McLaren, K. G. and Buesnel, E. L., *Network Analysis in Project Management*, Cassell, London 1969.
A text based on the authors very wide experience within Unilever. It illustrates very vividly how a network is actually drawn.

6. British Standards 4335. 1972, *Glossary of Terms used in Project Network Techniques*, British Standards Institute.
The purpose of this British Standard glossary is to standardize the terminology and symbols used in project network techniques . . . appendices have also been added to form an interface with related cost measurement, data processing, line of balance and graph theory terminology.

Appendix 3
A – B – C Analysis

One of the most useful analyses which can be carried out on a set of data is the *A–B–C*, *Pareto* or *Lorenz* analysis. The way in which this is done is best shown by means of an example. The income and the contribution from the products sold by an organization are (in appropriate monetary units)—

Product	Income	Contribution	Product	Income	Contribution
T214	102	−11	N204	57	17
N305	4	0	S271	35	10
T114	63	2	T274	20	6
F257	245	42	A079	0	0
P244	217	59	F103	9	3
H121	23	5	W151	42	13
N211	105	24	P215	90	29
B100	43	10	S173	27	9
P218	0	0	H227	62	21
B237	42	10	B166	188	64
A186	579	131	A153	62	21
H132	41	11	N190	59	20
A138	24	7	P191	6	2
B172	0	0	H247	382	133
S284	23	7	A126	6	2
W197	24	7	P229	413	147
A056	0	0	T155	335	121
S107	31	9	F253	19	7
			Totals	3,318	938

Thus, product T214 produces a total income of £102, and a contribution of −£11, N305 a total income of £4 and a contribution of £0, and so on.

Two analyses are possible: income against product range, and contribution against product range. Both are carried out in the same way, and the income against product range analysis will be described in detail.

Step 1. Rank the products in order of descending income, (as in Table 1 below). (*Note* if the data originates from a set of cards, it is most convenient to 'shuffle' the cards into the appropriate ranking. Where there is a large number of items, the sorting is best carried out by computer.)

Table 1. Product-Income Ranking (1)

Rank	Product	Income
1	A186	519
2	P229	413
3	H247	382
4	T155	335
5	F257	245
6	P244	217
7	B166	188
8	N211	105
9	T214	102
10	P215	90
11	T114	63
12	A153	62
13	H227	62
14	N190	59
15	N204	57
16	B100	43
17	B237	42
18	W151	42
19	H132	41
20	S271	35
21	S107	31
22	S173	27
23	A138	24
24	W197	24
25	H121	23
26	S284	23
27	T274	20
28	F253	19
29	F103	9
30	A126	6
31	P191	6
32	N305	4
33	B172	0
34	A079	0
35	P218	0
36	A056	0
	Total	3,318

Step 2. Accumulate the individual incomes (as in Table 2 below).

Table 2. *Product-Income Ranking* (2)

Rank	Product	Income	Accumulated Income
1	A186	519	519
2	P229	413	932
3	H247	382	1,314
4	T155	335	1,649
5	F257	245	1,894
6	P244	217	2,111
7	B166	188	2,299
8	N211	105	2,404
9	T214	102	2,506
10	P215	90	2,596
11	T114	63	2,659
12	A153	62	2,721
13	H227	62	2,783
14	N190	59	2,842
15	N204	57	2,899
16	B100	43	2,942
17	B237	42	2,984
18	W151	42	3,026
19	H132	41	3,067
20	S271	35	3,102
21	S107	31	3,133
22	S173	27	3,160
23	A138	24	3,184
24	W197	24	3,208
25	H121	23	3,231
26	S284	23	3,254
27	T274	20	3,274
28	F253	19	3,293
29	F103	9	3,302
30	A126	6	3,308
31	P191	6	3,314
32	N305	4	3,318
33	B172	0	3,318
34	A079	0	3,318
35	P218	0	3,318
36	A056	0	3,318
	Total	3,318	3,318

Step 3. Divide the total number of items into convenient groups (in the example used, these are groups of 3) and calculate the accumulated percentage of the total range of products represented by each group, and the accumulated percentage of total income represented by each group. The result is shown in Table 3 below.

This table is one form of A–B–C analysis, but it is most usual to represent it graphically (see Fig. 19, below). Table 4 and Fig. 20 (below) show the corresponding product range/contribution analysis.

Table 3. Product-Income Ranking (3)

Percentage of Range	Rank	Product	Income	Accumulated Income	Percentage of Income
	1	A186	519	519	
	2	P229	413	932	
8·3	3	H247	382	1,314	39·6
	4	T155	335	1,649	
	5	F257	245	1,894	
16·6	6	P244	217	2,111	63·5
	7	B166	188	2,299	
	8	N211	105	2,404	
25·0	9	T214	102	2,506	75·4
	10	P215	90	2,596	
	11	T114	63	2,659	
33·3	12	A153	62	2,721	81·5
	13	H227	62	2,783	
	14	N190	59	2,842	
41·6	15	N204	57	2,899	87·2
	16	B100	43	2,942	
50·0	17	B237	42	2,984	
	18	W151	42	3,026	90·5
	19	N132	41	3,067	
	20	S271	35	3,102	
58·3	21	S107	31	3,133	94·3
	22	S173	27	3,160	
	23	A138	24	3,184	
66·6	24	W197	24	3,208	97·5
	25	H121	23	3,231	
	26	S284	23	3,254	
75·0	27	T274	20	3,274	98·5
	28	F253	19	3,293	
	29	F103	9	3,302	
83·3	30	A126	6	3,308	99·0
	31	P191	6	3,314	
	32	N305	4	3,318	
91·6	33	B172	0	3,318	99·5
	34	A079	0	3,318	
	35	P218	0	3,318	
100·0	36	A056	0	3,318	100

Table 4. Product-Contribution Analysis

Percentage of Range	Rank	Product	Contribution	Accumulated Contribution	Percentage of Total Contribution
	1	P229	147		
	2	H247	133	280	
8·3	3	A186	131	411	43·8
	4	T155	121	532	
	5	B166	64	596	
16·6	6	P244	59	655	69·7
	7	F257	42	697	
	8	P215	29	726	
25·0	9	N211	24	750	80·0
	10	H227	21	771	
	11	A153	21	792	
33·3	12	N190	20	812	86·5
	13	N204	17	829	
	14	W151	13	842	
41·6	15	H132	11	853	91·0
	16	B100	10	863	
	17	S271	10	873	
50·0	18	B237	10	883	94·0
	19	S173	9	892	
	20	S107	9	901	
58·3	21	S284	7	908	96·7
	22	A138	7	915	
	23	W197	7	922	
66·6	24	F253	7	929	98·8
	25	T274	6	935	
	26	H121	5	940	
75·0	27	F103	3	943	100·5
	28	P191	2	945	
	29	A126	2	947	
83·3	30	T114	2	949	101
	31	N305	0	949	
	32	P218	0	949	
91·6	33	B172	0	949	101
	34	A056	0	949	
	35	A079	0	949	
100·0	36	T214	−11	938	100
		Total	938	938	100

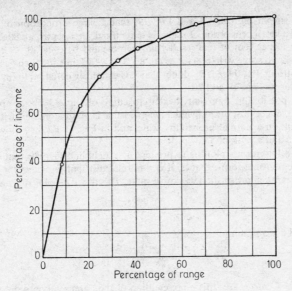

Fig. 19. Range v. Income

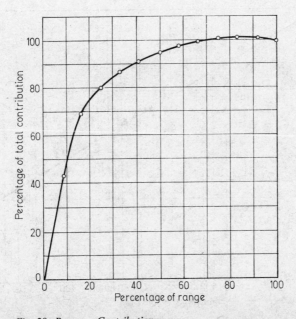

Fig. 20. Range v. Contribution

The result shown by Table 3 and Fig. 19, that a large proportion of income is represented by a small proportion of range, is quite usual. Frequently, an 80/20 relationship is found, 80 per cent of one result being represented by only 20 per cent of the possible causes, and some writers refer to an '80/20 law'. Claims for such generality are probably too strong, but there is no doubt that it is extremely common to find a pattern of results similar to Figs. 19 and 20.

Note: it is possible to represent the Pareto curve of Fig. 19 by an approximate straight line. To effect this, the individual income value is plotted on a logarithmic scale against the rank on a normal probability scale, and in Fig. 21 F257 is shown with its income of £245 and a rank of 5.

The use of a log-normal plotting to produce a straight line suggests that the Pareto curve is of a log-normal form; that is, it is a normal distribution where the logarithm of the variable is taken rather than its simple value. This distribution is represented by—

$$y = \frac{1}{\sigma \sqrt{2\pi}} e^{\frac{-(\log x - \bar{x})^2}{2\sigma^2}} dx$$

c. f. the normal distribution

$$y = \frac{1}{\sigma \sqrt{2\pi}} e^{\frac{-(x - \bar{x})^2}{2\sigma^2}} dx$$

Brown, in *Stock Control*, uses this representation of the Pareto curve to derive a parameter ρ, *the standard ratio*, where $\rho = e^{\sigma}$, and he suggests that measuring ρ gives an indication of the effectiveness of the stock control situation.

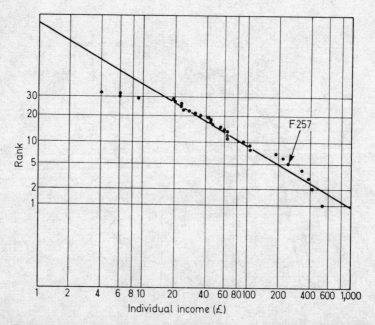

Fig. 21

Deductions from an A–B–C Analysis

Having carried out an A–B–C analysis, it is tempting to draw too many deductions from it. For example, Fig. 19 could suggest that all products from B100 onwards should be discontinued as the income they produce is trivial. This need not necessarily be justified, as some of the products may not have acquired any maturity in the market. Similarly, a high income item may produce a very low contribution, and there may be a good case for discontinuing this item. The A–B–C analysis will help to put problems into perspective: it is a tool to *assist* decision-making, not a 'go-no-go' gauge in itself.

When an A–B–C Analysis can be useful

1. *Production Control.* In a factory making large numbers of batches, an A–B–C analysis will often reveal that detailed control of a few works orders will control the bulk of the work load of the factory.

2. *Material Control.* Analysis of annual usage commonly shows a concentration of value in a comparatively small number of items, so that if there are 10,000 items in stock at any one time, control of 20 per cent of these will effect control of 80 per cent of annual spending. This leads to a stock classification system whereby the first 'slice' is closely controlled, the next 'slice' (say from 20 per cent to 50 per cent of the ranked items) is controlled with less precision, and the remaining 'slice' (from 50 per cent to 100 per cent of the ranked items) is controlled very loosely. These three 'slices' are often known as A Items, B Items and C Items, and it is in the field of material control that the term A–B–C analysis was first used.

3. *Quality Control.* Assigning defectives to causes frequently demonstrates that the bulk of defectives originates from very few causes.

4. *Variety reduction.* This has already been discussed.

5. *Maintenance.* Calculation of time lost due to breakdown against assignable causes after assists in planning a maintenance programme.

Further Reading

1. Juran, J. M., *Managerial Breakthrough*, McGraw-Hill, New York 1965.
Dr. Juran applies the A–B–C technique to a very wide variety of managerial situations

2. Brown, R. G., *Statistical Forecasting for Inventory Control*, McGraw-Hill, New York 1959.
Shows how the log-normal distribution may be used in stock control.

3. Aitchison, J. and Brown, J. A. C., *The Lognormal Distribution*, Cambridge University Press, Monograph No. 5.
The definitive discussion of the mathematics of the log-normal distribution. Not for the reader who is unable to follow a closely reasoned mathematical text.

Appendix 4
Linear Programming

Consider the following problem—

A factory of two departments (A and B) has a product range of three items (I, II and III) which produce unit profits P_I, P_{II}, and P_{III} respectively. The maximum numbers of any of the products which can be sold are known, and there is a limitation on the numbers which can be made since the capacities of the two departments are limited. How many of each product should be made to produce the maximum total profit?

This is typical of the class of problems known as *allocation* problems where limited resources have to be shared between competing needs in order to achieve some desired goal. When some assumptions concerning the relationships between the various items are made, then algorithmic solutions can be found to the problem. In particular, if all the relationships are effectively *linear* then the technique known as *linear programming* (L.P.) is available. In the two product case a graphical solution is readily possible (see inset, pages 440–1) but most real life problems have many more variables than this, and a solution is obtainable only by following a somewhat tedious routine. In practice this routine is rarely carried out manually: there are large numbers of tested computer programs which will follow the routine and produce the desired answer. The difficulty is not in solving the problem, but in expressing it in such a form that it can be readily presented for solution. The purpose of the present appendix is to show how this expression (a 'tableau' or 'matrix') may be made: those interested in the method of solution should refer to one or more of the texts set out under 'Further Reading'.

BASIC L.P. ASSUMPTIONS

There are five necessary assumptions to be made when using L.P. The assumptions may in fact be valid, or be reasonable approximations, or valid over the area of search appropriate to the problem. The assumptions are—

1. that the problem is limited or *constrained*, and these constraints are capable of being expressed in quantitative terms;
2. that there is *choice* or *variation* in the magnitude of the parameters;
3. that the variables are related to the constraints in a linear manner;
4. that there is some quantity which, being related to the variables and the constraints, is required to be optimized; and
5. that the quantity which is to be optimized (the objective function) is related to the variables in a linear manner.

Thus, returning to the opening problem, *assumption 1* requires that the capacities of each department must be known—Department A has a capacity C_A, Department B a capacity C_B. *Assumption 2* requires that the quantities of products I, II and III shall be capable of being chosen in some manner. For example, if the numbers of each product are N_I, N_{II} and N_{III}, then *either* N_I, N_{II}, N_{III} shall be capable of assuming any values, *or* they shall be capable of assuming values between any limits or restrictions. If the work contents of each product are—

for Product:

	I	II	III
in Department: $\{$ A	A_I	A_{II}	A_{III}
B	B_I	B_{II}	B_{III}

then *Assumption 3* implies that—

$$N_I A_I + N_{II} A_{II} + N_{III} A_{III} \leqslant C_A$$
$$\text{and} \quad N_I B_I + N_{II} B_{II} + N_{III} B_{III} \leqslant C_B$$

(Note the linearity in these relationships.)

If the total 'profit' derived from the operation is P_{TOT} and the individual unit 'profits' are P_I, P_{II}, and P_{III}, then *assumptions 4 and 5* state that—

P_{TOT} must be as great as possible and that
$$P_{TOT} = N_I P_I + N_{II} P_{II} + N_{III} P_{III}$$

(Again, note the linearity).

SETTING OUT AN L.P.

1. Determine all the constraints. These may be capacity constraints ('... the capacity of department $X = ...$') and/or quantity constraints ('... the number of Ns produced must exceed ...', or '... the number of Ns produced must be less than ...').

2. Determine the variables, that is, the factors over which control can be exerted.

3. Determine the coefficients by which the variables must be multiplied when ensuring that the constraints are not violated. In the case of a number of products which pass through several departments of limited ('constrained') capacity, these coefficients are the unit departmental work contents of each product.

4. Express the variables in terms of the coefficients and of constraints. Using the symbols above, this would give—

$$N_I A_I + N_{II} A_{II} + N_{III} A_{III} \leqslant C_A$$
$$N_I B_I + N_{II} B_{II} + N_{III} B_{III} \leqslant C_B$$

or if there are constraints $(L_I M_I)$ $(L_{II} M_{II})$ $(L_{III} M_{III})$ on the quantities, then additionally—

$$L_I \leqslant N_I \leqslant M_I$$
$$L_{II} \leqslant N_{II} \leqslant M_{II}$$
$$\text{and} \quad L_{III} \leqslant N_{III} \leqslant M_{III}$$

5. Transform the inequalities of (4) into equalities by introducing balancing terms (*slack variables*)—

$$N_I A_I + N_{II} A_{II} + N_{III} A_{III} + S_A = C_A$$
$$N_I B_I + N_{II} B_{II} + N_{III} B_{III} + S_B = C_B$$

$$N_I + S_{LI} = L_I$$
$$N_I + S_{MI} = M_I$$
$$N_{II} + S_{LII} = L_{II}$$
$$N_{II} + S_{MII} = M_{II}$$
$$N_{III} + S_{LIII} = L_{III}$$
$$N_{III} + S_{MIII} = M_{III}$$

Note that these slack variables represent the unrequired constraints—for example in the above situation S_A and S_B are the spare capacities left in departments A and B respectively when the three products have been made, $S_{LI}, S_{LII}, S_{LIII}$ are the quantities by which the minima L_I, L_{II}, L_{III} are exceeded, and $S_{MI}, S_{MII}, S_{MIII}$ the quantities by which the programmed quantities fall short of the maxima, M_I, M_{II} and M_{III}.

6. Express that which must be optimized ('the objective function') in terms of the variables, that is—

$$N_I\, P_I + N_{II}\, P_{II} + N_{III}\, P_{III} = P_{TOT}$$

7. Assemble all the equations together keeping all the variables in the same columns—

$$
\begin{aligned}
N_I\, A_I + N_{II}\, A_{II} + N_{III}\, A_{III} + S_A &= C_A \\
N_I\, B_I + N_{II}\, B_{II} + N_{III}\, B_{III} \quad + S_B &= C_B \\
N_I \qquad\qquad\qquad\qquad\quad + S_{LI} &= L_I \\
N_I \qquad\qquad\qquad\qquad\qquad\quad + S_{MI} &= M_I \\
N_{II} \qquad\qquad\qquad\qquad\quad + S_{LII} &= L_{II} \\
N_{II} \qquad\qquad\qquad\qquad\qquad\quad + S_{MII} &= M_{II} \\
N_{III} \qquad\qquad\qquad\qquad\quad + S_{LIII} &= L_{III} \\
N_{III} \qquad\qquad\qquad\qquad\qquad\quad + S_{MIII} &= M_{III} \\
N_I\, P_I + N_{II}\, P_{II} + N_{III}\, P_{III} &= P_{TOT}
\end{aligned}
$$

8. Rewrite (7) in the form of a matrix where the column headings are the variables and the rows the equations. Neither the variables nor the equality signs are repeated, and the cells are occupied by the coefficients of the variables in the equations—

N_I	N_{II}	N_{III}	S_A	S_B	S_{LI}	S_{MI}	S_{LII}	S_{MII}	S_{LIII}	S_{MIII}	
A_I	A_{II}	A_{III}	1	0	0	0	0	0	0	0	C_A
B_I	B_{II}	B_{III}	0	1	0	0	0	0	0	0	C_B
1	0	0	0	0	1	0	0	0	0	0	L_I
1	0	0	0	0	0	1	0	0	0	0	M_I
0	1	0	0	0	0	0	1	0	0	0	L_{II}
0	1	0	0	0	0	0	0	1	0	0	M_{II}
0	0	1	0	0	0	0	0	0	1	0	L_{III}
0	0	1	0	0	0	0	0	0	0	1	M_{III}
P_I	P_{II}	P_{III}	0	0	0	0	0	0	0	0	P_{TOT}

(The 0s in the cells arise from the fact that $0 \times S_B = 0$, so that
$N_I\, A_I + N_{II}\, A_{II} + N_{III}\, A_{III} + S_A = C_A$ may be written
$N_I\, A_I + N_{II}\, A_{II} + N_{III}\, A_{III} + 1 \times S_A + 0 \times S_B + 0 \times S_{LI} + 0 \times S_{MI} + 0 \times S_{LII}$
$\qquad\qquad + 0 \times S_{MII} + 0 \times S_{LIII} + 0 \times S_{MIII} = C_A)$

9. The matrix above is the so-called *first tableau* and is the form in which the L.P. is usually presented for subsequent solution, although different computer programs may demand different detailed layouts.

USING L.P.

The usual difficulties in using linear programming arise not from setting out the first tableau, nor from its subsequent manipulation, which can be safely delegated to a computer, but from determining both the constraints and the objective function. In a perfect world both of these should be known; in practice it is often difficult to discover, *in quantitative terms*, the limitations and to isolate the objective function and its constituents. Thus, in a product-mix problem involving—say—20 products and 10 departments it is necessary to know—

(a) the capacities of each department;
(b) the unit work-content of each product in each department;
(c) the unit 'profit' for each product—and here 'profit' means 'contribution', that is, the unit selling price — (unit labour cost + unit material cost).

The determination of all these often presents problems of some magnitude and difficulty. This having been said, it should be pointed out that once a tableau has been set up, changes in the cells can then be made and the effects of uncertainties and inaccuracies quickly estimated.

APPLICATIONS OF LINEAR PROGRAMMING

Within the assumptions set down above, a large number of problems can be solved, and considerable ingenuity is used in translating a problem into L.P. form. Most applications however fall into the following classes—

1. *Product-mix problems.* The example in the previous section is characteristic of this type of problem.

2. *Blending problems.* To produce—say—a furnace charge with given properties, it may be possible to blend together a number of constituents in a variety of ways each of which will produce the required property. Similarly, to make an animal feed-stuff with specific nutritive qualities, various combinations of the basic food-stocks may be used. These blending problems seek to produce a final blend at minimum cost.

3. *Cutting problems.* From a single product, for example, a reel of transformer steel, a number of products may be made by 'cutting' the product. Clearly it is desirable to choose the combination of products which will generate minimum waste, and this choice can be assisted by L.P.

4. *Transportation problems.* Sometimes called *location* or *distribution* problems, this class of problem is concerned with the location of sources and/or sinks of products in such a way that the total transportation costs are minimized. This class of L.P. is capable of being solved by a simpler routine than the previous three problems.

5. *Assignment problems.* Where a number of resources have to be assigned to a number of tasks, each resource being indivisible and capable of only undertaking one task, each task requiring only the whole of one resource, an assignment L.P. routine can be used. This is the simplest of the L.P. routines.

LINEAR PROGRAMMING—A PRODUCT-MIX EXAMPLE

Appendix I deals with the problem of drawing up a budget to meet certain requirements, and a product-mix is derived 'by guess and by God'. An alternative method of solving this product-mix problem is by the use of linear programming, and the data used in Appendix I will be used again here to show how L.P. operates.

The only constraints in this situation are those presented by the capacities of the various departments, as no minimum/maximum sales figures are stipulated. The capacities (page 399) quoted as 'total available' times are—

Departmental Capacities (hours/year)

A	B	C	D	E	F
60,000	70,000	65,000	60,000	65,000	65,000

These times include 'Down', 'Ancillary' and 'Idle' times, and it is necessary to derive a value for the 'running' times, as it is during the actual 'running' of the work-centres that the products producing contributions are made. Clearly, the details of the product-mix will affect all the non-running times and, in the absence of a firm decision concerning the quantities of the products to be made, it is not possible to derive final figures for the lost times. As a first approximation, however, it is probably reasonable to assume that the percentages of lost times are substantially constant for any sensible choice of products and it is known that (page 398) 'Down', 'Ancillary' and 'Idle' times, as percentages of total running time were—

	Department					
	A	B	C	D	E	F
Down time	4·70	5·65	5·94	3·13	2·97	4·21
Ancillary time	9·40	9·43	5·94	2·08	3·96	8·42
Idle time	26·00	21·00	20·00	9·50	30·00	20·00
Total Lost time	40·10	36·08	31·88	14·71	36·93	32·63

or, rounding these totals off—

Department	Lost time
A	40%
B	36%
C	32%
D	15%
E	37%
F	33%

These are percentages of the total running time, and as

$$\text{Running time} + \text{lost time} = \text{total available time}$$

then for Department A—

$$\text{running time} \ (1 + 0.40) = 60,000 \text{ hours}$$
$$\therefore \text{running time} = \frac{60,000}{1.40} \text{ hours} = 43,000 \text{ hours}$$

Similarly, for each of the other Departments—

$$\text{Department B: Running time} = \frac{70,000}{1.36} \text{ hours} = 53,000 \text{ hours}$$

$$\text{Department C: Running time} = \frac{65,000}{1.32} \text{ hours} = 49,200 \text{ hours}$$

$$\text{Department D: Running time} = \frac{60,000}{1.15} \text{ hours} = 52,100 \text{ hours}$$

$$\text{Department E: Running time} = \frac{65,000}{1.37} \text{ hours} = 47,400 \text{ hours}$$

$$\text{Department F: Running time} = \frac{65,000}{1.33} \text{ hours} = 48,800 \text{ hours}$$

The unit times for each product are as given on page 398.

Departments	FM1	FM2	FM3	FM4	FM5	FM6
A	0·250	0·227	0·368	0·375	0·222	0·074
B	0·125	0·363	0·368	0·0625	0·556	0·592
C	0·0625	0·363	0·368	0·0625	0·667	0·370
D	0·0625	0·136	0·368	0·4375	0·667	0·370
E	0·375	0·227	0·368	0·250	0·444	0·444
F	0·125	0·136	0·368	0·625	0·778	0·222

It is required to optimize the contribution, and from page 399 it can be deduced that—

438

Product	Costs in £ Labour	Material	Labour + Material	Selling Price £	Contribution £
FM1	0·74	0·50	1·24	3·00	1·76
FM2	2·00	0·80	2·80	6·00	3·20
FM3	0·38	1·20	1·58	3·00	1·42
FM4	2·50	2·50	5·00	10·00	5·00
FM5	1·06	1·60	2·66	8·00	5·34
FM6	1·20	1·00	2·20	4·00	1·80

Hence, the first tableau is—

	$FM1$	$FM2$	$FM3$	$FM4$	$FM5$	$FM6$	S_A	S_B	S_C	S_D	S_E	S_F	Capacity
A	0·250	0·227	0·368	0·375	0·222	0·074	1	0	0	0	0	0	43,000
B	0·125	0·363	0·368	0·0625	0·556	0·592	0	1	0	0	0	0	53,000
C	0·0625	0·363	0·368	0·0625	0·667	0·370	0	0	1	0	0	0	49,200
D	0·0625	0·136	0·368	0·4375	0·667	0·370	0	0	0	1	0	0	52,100
E	0·375	0·227	0·368	0·250	0·444	0·444	0	0	0	0	1	0	47,400
F	0·125	0·136	0·368	0·625	0·778	0·222	0	0	0	0	0	1	48,800
Contributions	1·76	3·20	1·42	5·00	5·34	1·80							

From this array the product-mix which gives maximum total contribution is derived. This, with the quantities concerned appropriately rounded off, is—

Product	Quantity to be produced	Contribution (£) Unit	Total
FM1	0	1·76	0
FM2	111,000	3·20	355,200
FM3	0	1·42	0
FM4	42,000	5·00	210,000
FM5	9,700	5·34	51,798
FM6	0	1·80	0

Total contribution for all products 616,998

A manual solution of the above matrix is possible, although tedious. More substantial problems require a computer solution, and *given the data* in the matrix the time for the solution would be measured in minutes. The time for the discovery of the data, however, is likely to be very much longer: clearly it will depend upon the control and data collection systems within the organization, but frequently it is found that the derivation of the information is a task of very considerable magnitude.

Further Reading

Linear Programming is discussed in a number of the texts recommended at the end of Chapter 1, (pp. 20–22) in particular Bowman and Fetter (4) and Wild (7). In addition, the following text is also very useful:

Vajda, S., *Planning by Mathematics*, Pitman, London 1969.

This contains a wide range of uses of L.P.

LINEAR PROGRAMMING: A GRAPHICAL SOLUTION TO THE TWO-PRODUCT PROBLEM

The space between the positive cartesian axes Number of Is and Number of IIs contains all the possible combinations of I and II. If upon this space two sets of lines (see Fig. 22) are drawn showing the demand constraints, then the acceptable I–II combinations are enclosed within the resulting rectangle.

The capacity of each department reduces further the I–II space, and Fig. 23 shows the capacity constraint imposed by Department A, whilst Fig. 24 shows all the constraints, both those of demand and those of capacity. The polygon whose boundaries are hatched encloses all those I–II combinations which meet all the constraints.

Any particular level of total contribution can be derived from various combinations of I and II. Each total contribution level will produce a straight line, the values of the I–II pairs represented by points on this straight line generate the same total contribution. Some total contribution level lines are shown in Fig. 25.

The maximum total contribution is obtained when the contribution level line is furthest away from the origin, yet still touching the permissible polygon at some point. This is shown in Fig. 26.

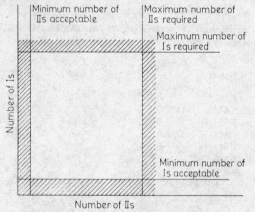

Fig. 22

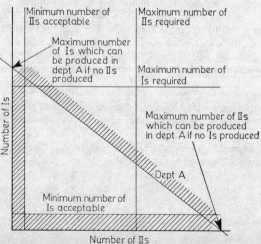

Fig. 23

440

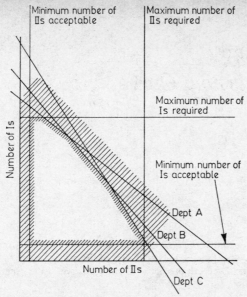

Fig. 24

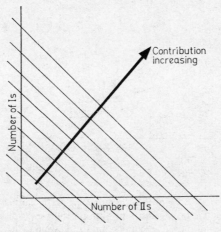

Fig. 25

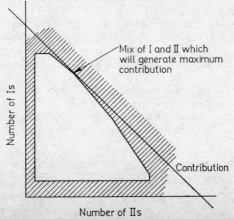

Fig. 26

Appendix 5
The Learning Curve

It is well established that the time taken for an individual to carry out a task will depend upon, amongst other factors, the experience of the operator, and that speed of perform- ance and number of repetitions are related by a curve of the general shape of Fig. 27.

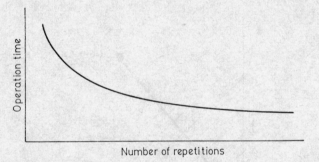

Fig. 27. *Learning Curve*

This curve is the *learning curve* of the operator for a particular task, and some observers claim to have detected noticeable learning even for short-cycle tasks after 1,000 or more repetitions. The slope of the curve at any point would seem to depend upon intelligence, motivation and age.

Organizations, which are groups of individuals, seem also to exhibit the same learning characteristics *but in a more predictable form.* The first observations of this phenomenon were by T. P. Wright in the U.S. aircraft industry, and his findings have been repeated by many later workers. The learning curve for an organization is given by Wright's Law—

For any operation which is repeated, the mean time for the operation will decrease by a fixed fraction as the number of repetitions double.

Wright found that the reduction fraction was 0·8, so that an operation obeying Wright's law would have the following time characteristics—

Time for first operation									100
Mean time for first two			operations	= 100	× 0·8	= 80			
„	„	„	„ four	„ „	= 80	× 0·8	= 64		
„	„	„	„ eight	„	= 64	× 0·8	= 51·2		
„	„	„	„ sixteen	„	= 51·2	× 0·8	= 40·96		

442

and so on, giving the curve of Fig. 28, which is plotted on normal cartesian co-ordinates, or Fig. 29, which is plotted on Log-log co-ordinates.

Later work in fields other than the aircraft industry suggests that the fraction is not necessarily 0·8, and that its value depends upon the proportion of labour which is man-controlled. The following figures were given by Herschmann—

% of labour which is man-controlled	Reduction fraction
75	80
50	85
25	90

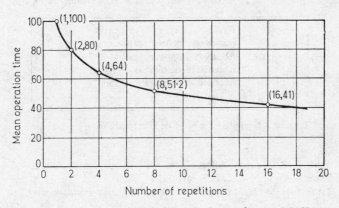

Fig. 28. *Learning curve obeying Wrights' Law* (*reduction fraction 0.8*) (*Linear scales*)

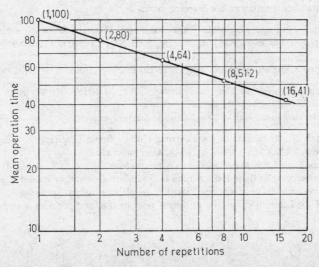

Fig. 29. *Learning curve obeying Wright's Law* (*reduction fraction 0.8*) (*Logarithmic scales*)

Factory and Production Management

Appearance of the Learning Curve

The process of learning by an organization is no more automatic than the process of learning by an individual, and, as with an individual, the most important factor appears to be motivation, which arises from a belief that something can be learnt and that it is desirable that it should be learnt. An organization which believes that it has no need or no room to improve is unlikely to demonstrate any marked learning.

Apart from this apathy, there are other factors which will depress learning—

(*a*) Lack of continuity. If a process is repeated, and then stopped, and then restarted after a time break, the mean time will increase immediately after the time break.

(*b*) Restrictions to output. Some circumstances can give rise to deliberate restrictions in output—for example, the operation of some incentive schemes, the existence of 'cost-plus' pricing, the belief or knowledge that work is coming to an end.

Desire to improve
Ability to improve
Absence of time-breaks
Absence of restricting factors

Factors Affecting Learning in an Organization

Further Reading

1. Wright, T. P., 'Factors Affecting the Cost of Airplanes', *Journal of the Aeronautical Sciences*, Vol. 3, No. 2, February 1936.

The first formal statement of the learning curve phenomenon. A model paper.

2. Hirschmann, W. B., 'Profit from the Learning Curve', *Harvard Business Review*, January-February 1964.

An enthusiastic and very readable article which summarizes much of the evidence for the quantitative nature of the learning curve.

3. United Nations: Economic Commission for Europe, *Effect of Repetition on Buildings Operations and Processes on Site*, Ref: ST/ECE/HOU/14, Sales No. 65 II E/Mim 23.

A very revealing study which brings together evidence from all over the world.

4. Jordan, R., *How to Use the Learning Curve*, Materials Management Institute, London 1965.

A painstaking discussion of the use of the learning curve.

5. Baloff, N., 'Extension of the Learning Curve—Some Empirical Results', *Operational Research Quarterly*, Vol. 22, No. 4, December 1971.

Nicholas Baloff has very much made this subject his own. This paper provides evidence of learning in three labour-intensive industries—automobile assembly, apparel manufacture and the production of large musical instruments. It discusses the basic concept of the learning curve, the problems with its use, and provides a useful bibliography.

Appendix 6
Representative Examination
Questions

The source and date of each question is identified as fully as possible. The initials I.W.M., I.M.E., I.I.A., B.I.M., I.P.E., I.W.S. represent the Institutes (Institutions) of Works Managers, Mechanical Engineers, Industrial Administration, British Institute of Management, Production Engineers and Work Study (now Work Study Practitioners) respectively. S.Q. indicates a 'Specimen Question'. The examination in which the question appeared is not given since, in a number of cases, the same question has been used in a variety of different level examinations. The initials M.R.H. indicate that the questions were provided by Dr. Malcolm Hill, Lecturer at the University of Loughborough.

CHAPTER ONE
INTRODUCTION TO THE PRODUCTION FUNCTION

1. Discuss the differences between the 'objectives' of a company and its 'policies'. Why is it necessary to have well-defined objectives for any organization?

2. 'Sales and Production must co-operate.' How can these functions assist each other?
(*I.W.M.(S.Q.)*)

3. What part would you expect a Works Manager to play in the preparation of a budget, and in what manner would a system of budgetary control help him?
(*I.W.M.(S.Q.)*)

4. The director in charge of manufacturing of a well-known British company has said 'Leadership means deciding where you want to go and then getting people to follow you'. How does this idea affect the action of either—
(*a*) the chief executive;
(*b*) the technical manager;
(*c*) a sales representative;
(*d*) the factory superintendent;
OR
of a company? (*I.M.E.* 1956)

5. 'A clear statement of purpose universally understood is the outstanding guarantee of effective administration.'
Discuss ways in which a 'statement of purpose' can be made universally understood in a manufacturing organization. (*I.W.M.(S.Q.)*)

6. Once a sales forecast in terms of physical units of various products has been prepared, show how this forecast may be translated into the demand it generates for various factors of production. (*University of Aston in Birmingham* 1965)

445

7. Critically examine the relationships between works manager's department and the following—

Development and Design Department;
Sales Department;
Purchasing Department.   (*I.I.A.* 1953)

8. Show by diagram the relationships between the foreman of a production department in an engineering works and the other persons in the organization with whom he is likely to have frequent contact in the course of his duties. Comment briefly on any aspect of these relationships which appear to be important.   (*I.M.E.* 1955)

9. How far can the factory manager's work be assisted by the setting of standards? Illustrate by reference to at least two such standards, and explain the difficulties to be overcome in establishing any such standard.   (*B.I.M.* 1958)

10. What do you consider to be the duties of the Works Manager of an engineering works? If appointed to such a post, to what statistics would you wish to have access, and in what form would you prefer them to be prepared?
(*University of Aston in Birmingham* 1966)

11. An engineering firm engaged in the design, manufacture and selling of scientific instruments employs five hundred people. The works are situated on a trading estate which provides essential services. Control is in the hands of seven full-time working directors.

Sketch an organizational chart suitable for this undertaking and define the duties of the individual working directors, assuming that they are each competent to control a different function of the firm's activities.   (*University of Durham* 1959)

12. 'The principles of management control systems have much in common with certain fundamentals of control engineering theory.'

State the principles of management control systems and comment on the above statement.   (*University of Wales* 1967)

13. Consider a typical engineering firm which requires sales forecasts for the next six months, for the next two years and for the next five years. Give reasons for needing each of these and indicate the methods by which the firm might arrive at some estimate for the three periods.   (*University of Birmingham* 1971)

14. Give your views on the necessity for a company to define and balance basic sub-objectives within its overall production control objective. Identify major sub-objectives and indicate the contribution which techniques can make to the individual and collective effectiveness of achievement.   (*University of Birmingham* 1971)

15. Describe the basic mechanism of a control system. What difficulties would you envisage in setting up a quality control system for a process producing torch reflectors?
(*Portsmouth College of Technology* 1969)

16. You are Works Manager (recently appointed) of a medium sized company manufacturing your own products. There are 15 of these different products currently on offer. Of what value would a sales forecast for next year's requirements be to you and to the company generally?   (*City of Birmingham Polytechnic* 1971)

17. In a manufacturing organization, discuss what implications forecasting has for—
(*a*) the purchasing function, and
(*b*) the design function?

Taking a particular factory of medium size, outline its organizational chart and explain why this may differ from that of a smaller concern.
(*University of Aston in Birmingham* 1971)

18. Define 'Production'.

How and in what ways, will a factory's production target depend on the actions of the Marketing Department?   (*North Staffordshire Polytechnic* 1971)

19. How does a Company's forecasting procedure impinge on the production

planning at shop floor level? *(Sheffield College of Technology* 1968)

20. Discuss the importance of the Sales Forecast as the basis for the manufacturing programme of a business. What are the principal sources of information used in the preparation of the forecast? *(Leeds College of Commerce* 1969)

21. What are the essential features of a control system? Illustrate your answer by reference to Production Control. *(Norwich City College* 1970)

22. Explain what is meant by 'policy'. Show the significance of *four* items that might be included in a statement of the production policy of a company.
(Norwich City College 1971)

CHAPTER 2
CHOICE OF THE PRODUCT

1. A proposal has been made for a novel form of consumer durable. Describe how you would arrange EITHER to validate the proposal OR to carry it through to a successful conclusion. *(University of Aston in Birmingham* 1971)

2. A large well-established firm making domestic cooking ovens has Research, Development and Design teams.

Describe briefly the way in which they would reach a decision on what range they would market in 1970. *(Nottingham Regional College of Technology* 1968)

3. The XYZ Company Ltd has a New Products Committee under the chairmanship of a Director. It has to consider from every aspect proposals for 'new lines', and to make recommendations to the Board.

Name the sections of the business which you think should be represented on the Committee.

Discuss the value of such a committee, and consider the conditions necessary for its successful working. *(Luton College of Technology* 1962)

4. What steps should be taken at the product design stage to provide a wide variety of products for customer choice consistent with manufacturing efficiency? Amplify by describing a product range with which you are familiar. *(M.R.H.)*

5. Describe how a firm should select a correct balance between standardization of product range and diversification. Amplify your answer by reference to any particular products with which you are familiar. *(M.R.H.)*

6. What intra-firm factors influence the products which it manufactures? *(M.R.H.)*

7. In what ways do you consider the products manufactured by automobile firms in 1980 will differ from those currently designed and manufactured? What influences are likely to cause these changes in product design, and what requirements will these place on the automobile and its supplier industries? *(M.R.H.)*

8. Which industries do you consider are subsidized, either directly or indirectly to prevent high unemployment when demand for its products has diminished and is unlikely to return? What alternative products could be produced using the capital and skills within those industries, for which there is high social need? *(M.R.H.)*

CHAPTER 3
CONTROL OF VARIETY

1. In what ways can the systematic allocation of drawing identification numbers facilitate the action of departments other than the drawing office in a firm making a range of petrol and compression ignition engines for universal use? *(I.M.E.* 1956)

2. Discuss the useful scope of standardization (a) of products, (b) of production methods and (c) of management techniques, making some reference to the possible methods of achieving such standardization. *(I.M.E.* 1959)

3. When operating in a buyer's market there is often a strong urge from a sales department for more diversification of the product range. Yet to meet competition by reducing costs, a production department may press for product simplification. Suggest, with examples, how a design department might be able to reconcile these opposing policies.

(I.M.E. 1955)

4. Stress the importance of an adequate classification and coding system of materials and components in a manufacturing organization. Outline a suitable system for coding new materials and comment on the principles upon which the system is based.

(B.I.M. 1958)

5. What do you understand by 'standardization' as applied to products and components? What difficulties of production planning and control arise from the absence of standardization. How would you endeavour to overcome these difficulties?

(I.W.M. (S.Q.))

6. A new company proposes to develop a range of engineering products which will require servicing organization. What steps should be taken to ensure that uneconomic variety will be prevented at all stages of production and distribution?

(Brighton College of Technology 1965)

7. Comment on the problems to be overcome in an engineering factory when standardizing on material sizes and specifications.

(Brighton College of Technology 1967)

8. Of what significance is standardization and simplification to—

(a) Production Manager,

(b) Sales Manager,

(c) Consumer? *(University of Aston in Birmingham* 1966)

9. When operating in a buyer's market there is a strong urge from a Sales Department for more diversification of the product range. To meet competition by reducing costs the Production Department may press for design simplification.

Suggest, with examples, how a Design Department may be able to reconcile these opposing policies. *(University of Aston in Birmingham* 1967)

10. The following statement is issued as company policy—

'The smallest practicable range of machine components must be used to meet the full range of functional requirements.'

Discuss—

(a) The basic engineering standards the designer should consider to implement this policy.

(b) The general implications of the policy. *(University of Wales* 1966)

11. You are Managing Director of a medium sized manufacturing concern producing a wide variety of products, all of which consist of an assembly of several components.

A Management Consultant suggests a programme of variety reduction at finished product, component and bought-in material stages. Write a report, to be distributed to the Production Manager, Sales Manager, Cost Accountant and Production Controller, stressing the need for this. Point out the advantages to be gained by the company as a whole and by individual departments: mention the risks involved and say how these may be kept to a minimum. *(Manchester Polytechnic* 1971)

12. An old established firm manufacturing a wide range of mechanical equipment has adopted a policy of reducing the number and variety of the components used.

Describe methods of assembling data which will assist the management in making the decisions necessary in carrying out the policy. *(University of Birmingham* 1970)

13. Explain how a Company's Standards Department would contribute to the economy of the firm's production operations. *(Slough College of Technology* 1968)

14. 'Simplification (i.e. reduction) of the product range is a constant source of disagreement between the sales and production personnel.'

Discuss this statement quoting the arguments and refutations involved and suggest how a compromise could be achieved. (*Slough College of Technology* 1970)

15. (*a*) What are the benefits of Variety Reduction? Index your answer by briefly ascribing the benefits to the following activities: Sales, Manufacture and Design.

(*b*) Show three methods of achieving Variety Reduction.

(*c*) Display graphically how the product range can be associated with sales revenue.
(*The Polytechnic, London* 1968)

16. You are Works Manager of a company manufacturing consumer goods, and have a variety of 430 different lines. You are confident that the range can be reduced to around 100 lines. Assuming that the Sales Division have done their Market Research and are all in favour of the reduction, what benefits do you anticipate in the following areas of the Manufacturing Division?

(*a*) Methods

(*b*) Stocks and Stores

(*c*) Financial Control

(*d*) Purchasing. (*Norwich City College* 1970)

CHAPTER 4
VALUE ANALYSIS

1. As Works Manager you have been charged with launching value analysis in your company. Draft a memorandum to other departmental managers outlining the purpose of value analysis and indicating your plans for its introduction.
(*Brighton College of Technology* 1968)

2. Discuss the techniques associated with Value Analysis. Illustrate your answer with examples. (*Polytechnic of Central London* 1968)

3. Assuming you were assigned the task of giving a one-day Management Appreciation Seminar on Value Analysis, outline the lecture you would give.
(*Polytechnic of Central London* 1968)

4. Describe the various steps involved in carrying out a value engineering study on a company's product. Particular attention should be given to the sequence of these steps.
(*University of Glasgow* 1967)

5. What is Value Analysis? How is it carried out, and how should the recommendations resulting from Value Analysis be presented to management?
(*University of Aston in Birmingham* 1967)

6. 'Investigation into effective utilization of material can often improve efficiency with a greater monetary saving than the more conventional Work Study investigation.'

(*a*) Discuss the implications of this statement.

(*b*) State with reasons who should be responsible for this task.

(*c*) Outline the procedure you would adopt given this assignment.
(*University of Wales* 1964)

7. 'Value Techniques' are frequently linked with the work of Production Engineers. Explain why this is so and discuss the scope for such techniques in—

(*a*) a company manufacturing a wide variety of automobile accessories in large batches;

(*b*) a firm making a limited range of capital goods which has existed for some years in an area of restricted competition. (*University of Loughborough* 1967)

8. Draw up a Value Analysis checklist of eight items and discuss the practical significances of each. (*University of Birmingham* 1970)

9. Outline the Value Analysis procedure explaining the purposes of each stage. Comment upon the advantages to be gained by V.A. and the major problems likely to

be met by the Value Engineer. Give your views on how these problems should be overcome. (*University of Birmingham* 1971)

10. In your capacity as leader of a value analysis exercise, draw up your report of recommendations to management. You will invent (or remember) appropriate numerical data, but technical detail is not required.

If you wish, you may refer to components A, B, C, etc., and to processes P, Q, R, etc. without necessarily identifying them. (*University of Sheffield* 1971)

11. Describe the methods of value analysis and discuss the components of a value analysis team. (*St. Helens College of Technology* 1971)

12. Describe the procedures of Value Analysis with particular reference to the organization and staffing of the team and the sequence of procedures.

What questions are asked in the 'Investigation' procedure?

(*Nottingham Regional College of Technology* 1968)

13. Compare the techniques of Value Analysis and Work Study, stressing in particular, the Human Relations aspect. (*Slough College of Technology* 1972)

CHAPTER 5
QUALITY OF THE PRODUCT

1. 'Quality Control is not the sole prerogative of the Inspection Function.' Discuss this statement, illustrating your answer with examples.

(*Croydon Technical College* 1968)

2. Discuss the importance of the customer-supplier relationship in the control of quality of products. (*St. Helens Technical College* 1971)

3. Discuss the factors which must be taken into account when decisions are being made concerning the degree of precision to be aimed at in the production of engineering components. Illustrate your answer by reference to some particular engineering product.

(*I.M.E.* 1957)

4. Expenditure on the quality control function in a factory should bear some relation to the avoidable costs which are incurred due to poor quality.

Enumerate and explain a list of items which give rise to avoidable costs in manufacturing operations. (*University of Glasgow* 1965)

5. What effect will the setting of tolerances on any dimension have on the manufacturing cost of an article? What factors need to be considered when setting tolerances?

(*Polytechnic of Central London* 1962)

6. It has been stated that the aim of Quality Control is to achieve the requisite quality of product at minimum cost.

(*a*) How can the costs of achieving the requisite quality be grouped?

(*b*) Which departments should be represented on a Quality Control Committee?

(*c*) Indicate the appropriate lines of action you would expect the Committee to take.

(*Luton College of Technology* 1965)

7. 'The aim of Quality Control is customer satisfaction.' Discuss this statement and indicate the quality factors which have an influence on a manufacturing firm's ability to achieve maximum satisfaction in its customers.

(*Slough College of Technology* 1969)

8. Quality control costs have been classified under four heads: 'prevention, appraisal, internal failure and external failure'. Explain what is meant by each and discuss the contribution that a manufacturing division can make to quality cost reduction.

(*Leeds Polytechnic* 1971)

9. Describe the perception of quality by—

(*a*) the Board of Directors,

(*b*) the Designer, and

(*c*) the Production Operator. (*K.G.L.*)

10. Discuss the proposition that 'all wants are utilitarian to their possessors', paying particular attention to the customer's specification of apparently un-useful properties.
(*K.G.L.*)

11. What is meant by the quality and reliability of an industrial product? Indicate ways in which accountability for product quality and reliability may be allocated within the managerial structure of a manufacturing firm. (*The City University* 1968)

CHAPTER 6
DESIGN OF THE PRODUCT

1. Select some section of the engineering industry with which you are familiar and describe the process of product developments, with particular reference to the sources of new ideas. On whom does the responsibility lie for accepting or rejecting such ideas, and what actions must be taken prior to coming to any decisions? (*I.M.E.* 1957)

2. Discuss the meaning of research, as seen from the viewpoints of an engineering designer. Illustrate, by reference to any engineering product with which you are familiar, how advances in design have been made possible through the application of research methods. (*I.M.E.* 1956)

3. What principles should be considered in creating designs for economic production? To what extent should the production department be allowed to influence the design of a product? (*B.I.M.* 1958)

4. List and explain the need for the information which should be written into a design specification. (*Polytechnic of Central London* 1958)

5. Changes in design during production form one of the biggest difficulties of the production engineer. Draft a procedure classifying changes into various types. Outline the methods you think should be adopted by the planning department to deal with them.
(*I.P.E.* 1958)

6. List the principal stages in the design of an engineering product and suggest a method of organizing the design work, indicating where the responsibility lies at each stage. (*The University of Aston in Birmingham* 1967)

7. Describe a major defect in the design of a product of which you have personal experience. Suggest means of correcting the defect and say what further problems you would expect to result from the implementation of your proposed modification.
(*University of Aston in Birmingham* 1967)

8. 'Thinking cannot be timed.' Discuss this remark with particular reference to the design of a product. (*K.G.L.*)

9. 'Method study should be applied at the design stage.'

Comment on this statement, and quote examples to demonstrate its validity. Explain some of the technical and human problems involved in making the statement true.
(*University of Loughborough* 1968)

10. Write a brief note for your Board of Directors explaining the need for a Research and Development Department in a manufacturing organization. Make recommendations for its organization and its relationship with the Production Departments and with outside research organizations. How much would you recommend your Board to spend on this activity? Discuss points to be considered in determining the level of this activity. (*Croydon Technical College* 1968)

11. Choose an industry with which you are familiar and describe the activities and decisions involved in the introduction of an important new product, from the research and development stage through to marketing launch and bulk production. Discuss the

steps which should be taken to obtain co-operation between the departments involved, and describe briefly how the operation should be planned and controlled.

(*University of Bath* 1971)

12. Consider the organization of a typical research and development department within industry. How is it organized? Why?

(*Medway & Maidstone College of Technology* 1971)

13. Prior to sealing a new product design, what factors should the design function have considered? In most commercial design the problem is to ensure that each factor has been adequately studied. Suggest how this problem can be dealt with.

(*Medway & Maidstone College of Technology* 1971)

14. 'The Design Department is the cradle of manufacturing costs.' Discuss this statement and suggest the contribution that the design department could make towards minimizing production costs. (*Slough College of Technology* 1967)

CHAPTER 7
LOCATION OF THE FACTORY

1. A rapidly expanding engineering firm, occupying rented premises extending to about 30,000 square feet on an industrial estate, is contemplating moving to a new site, four times this size, at the other end of the estate.

List the factors to be considered (*a*) before coming to a decision; (*b*) when drawing up plans for the removal. (*I.M.E.* 1957)

2. Your firm has under consideration the establishment of a branch factory, to employ about 800 people, mainly semi-skilled, to manufacture engineering components. Discuss the advantages of choosing a site on an industrial estate. (*I.M.E.* 1956)

3. Review the factors that must be considered in selecting a site for a proposed factory, indicating clearly for each the sources of the information which will be required.

(*B.I.M.* 1959)

4. A company making light electrical equipment in the London area requires to expand to twice its existing size in the next five years. The present site is incapable of any further expansion and the alternatives for expansion are—

(*a*) to purchase small sites or factories in the same area;

(*b*) to build a single factory away from the London area to cater for the proposed increase in production;

(*c*) to move the factory to another area some 50 miles away where an existing factory is available large enough to continue production on the present scale, together with adjoining land sufficient to allow for expansion.

Comment on the main factors which would be considered by the management when making a decision. (*Brighton College of Technology* 1965)

5. Messrs. A., B. and Company, employing 400 people and manufacturing light engineering products, have been established for 100 years in multi-storey buildings in a crowded district of an industrial town.

Due to the impossibility of further expansion on their present site the Directors have decided to build a new, single storey factory.

(*a*) State the factors to be considered when determining the site of the new factory.

(*b*) Consider in detail the changes likely to be made in materials handling systems and equipment due to the move from multi-storey buildings to a single factory.

(*I.P.E.* 1960)

6. How may the location of a plant affect its profitability? (*K.G.L.*)

7. Discuss the proposition that 'a merger involving the acquisition of additional factories is effectively a plant location problem'. (*K.G.L.*)

8. 'Almost every site imposes restrictions of some kind on the ideal factory layout.' Discuss the implications of this statement. (*University of Edinburgh* 1970)

CHAPTER 8
DESIGN OF THE FACTORY

1. You have been given the responsibility of choosing a new factory premises when there are, within the acceptable location, two types available, i.e. single and multi-storey.
Discuss the merits and demerits of each, and give the reasons for your choice.
(*Polytechnic of Central London* 1956)
2. Compare the relative advantages and disadvantages of single and multi-storey factory design. (*I.W.S.(S.Q.)*)
3. What standard designs of factories are available today? Comment on ways in which these could be improved. (*M.R.H.*)
4. Do you consider that contemporary factory designs adequately consider the problems of pollution (atmospheric, noise and effluent)? If not, how should these designs be improved? (*M.R.H.*)
5. What factors influence the choice of factory design? Amplify your answer by considering likely factory designs for producing:
   (*a*) large pressure vessels
   (*b*) mass produced automobiles
   (*c*) laminated plastics
   (*d*) builder's hardware. (*M.R.H.*)

CHAPTER 9
LAYOUT OF THE FACTORY

1. Sketch and discuss the layout of an engineering works with which you are familiar, and discuss the advantages and disadvantages of this layout for the processes which are being carried on. (*I.M.E.* 1958)
2. What do you understand by 'layout for continuous production'? Discuss the advantages of such a layout, the difficulties that may be encountered in making it work successfully, and methods of overcoming these difficulties. (*I.P.E.* 1952)
3. Explain the advantages of line production in the planning of the work of a new factory. (*I.W.S.*)
4. A decision has to be made to arrange the layout of a factory, either by grouping similar types of machines together in separate sections or by arranging them in sequence for line production.
Give the factors you would consider in order to arrive at a decision and state the advantages and disadvantages of the sequential method of layout. (*I.P.E.* 1953)
5. A factory whose layout has been wisely planned will have many important initial advantages over one whose layout has been badly planned.
State fully the factors you would take into account when planning a factory, and discuss them with particular reference to the general principles which are common to all layout planning. (*I.W.S.(S.Q.)*)
6. Assuming a rectangular site, sketch roughly an appropriate layout for production departments and services, for the manufacture of a lawn-mower in the popular price range which is required at an output of the order of 1,000 per week. (*I.P.E.* 1955)
7. Summarize the various factors which must be considered when deciding the size and location of the stores in a general engineering factory engaged on jobbing work.
(*I.P.E.* 1958)

8. Briefly describe the characteristics of a good factory layout, and indicate an approach to layout problems which attempts to ensure that the new layout possesses these characteristics. *(Portsmouth College of Technology S.Q.)*

9. A company has made a decision to transfer certain products and machines from a process layout production scheme to product layouts. Discuss how the company might have chosen the likely products for manufacture on the product layouts, and the advantages and problems of this type of layout. *(University of Birmingham 1971)*

10. 'Almost every site imposes restrictions of some kind on the ideal factory layout.' Discuss the implications of this statement. *(University of Edinburgh 1970)*

11. You are responsible for the preparation of plans showing the proposed layout of all production equipment and services in a small flow production factory.

(*a*) List the information you would require before proceeding.

(*b*) Assessing the information in (*a*) to be available, how would you proceed to evolve a layout which would provide for the achievement of the production programme? *(Luton College of Technology 1963)*

12. Draw sketches to illustrate the difference between process layout and product layout. Mention any advantages or disadvantages which may be attributed to each type. State briefly the work study techniques which would help to determine the best factory layout. *(Luton College of Technology 1965)*

13. What advantages would you expect from a well laid out factory as opposed to one whose layout has not been planned?

Describe how you would conduct an investigation into the layout of a factory and the handling procedures within the manufacturing area. What areas would you investigate and what questions would you ask? *(Nottingham Regional College of Technology 1968)*

14. In discussing factory layout it is common to speak of 'product layout' and 'process layout'. Explain the relative merits of each and discuss how representative they are of actual practice. *(Leeds Polytechnic 1971)*

15. In planning the re-layout of a factory state how you would ensure that each section is satisfactorily sited for the function it has to perform in relation to all the other sections. *(Slough College of Technology 1972)*

CHAPTER 10
EQUIPMENT

1. Demonstrate with an example how a recommendation to purchase a new piece of engineering equipment giving an improved method of working can be justified in terms of cost. *(I.M.E. 1955)*

2. The manager of a firm engaged on the production of engineering components finds that a bottleneck is being caused by the insufficiency and obsolescence of his milling machines. Discuss the alternative ways by which he might overcome this difficulty. What are the chief points to be considered should he think it advisable to buy new machines? *(I.P.E. 1952)*

3. What factors should be considered when choosing between two different machines? *(Polytechnic of Central London (I.W.S.) 1959)*

4. It is proposed to install a new machine. Give a list of items to be included in the total cost of installation and those to be included in the annual charges. Describe the Discounted Cash Flow technique for allowing for depreciation, explaining why this method may be preferred to any other. *(University of Aston in Birmingham 1966)*

5. Briefly describe what is meant by the time value of money and illustrate your answer by possible uses for all the four uniform series given in the tables of compound discount factors.

The redesign of a machine's control panel will cost £900 for re-wiring and re-layout, but it is estimated that it will pay for itself in the following fashion, allowing for the learning curve and tailing off of the machine's useful life. There is no salvage value obtainable.

Year 1	nil
Year 2	£150
Year 3	£300
Year 4	£450
Year 5	£300
Year 6	£150
Year 7	£75
	£1425

Comment upon the method by which you can estimate a rate of return and say how your calculated figure represents a true statement.
(Tables of Compound Interest Factors provided)   (*University of Birmingham* 1970)

6. Describe some of the problems associated with—
(*a*) estimating,
(*b*) justifying
the cost of a new plant installation.   (*St. Helens College of Technology* 1971)

7. Discuss the factors to be considered in selecting items of plant or processes. To what extent would the factors differ or become more important if the company was in an expansionist phase?   (*Slough College of Technology* 1971)

8. As consultant to the Works Manager of a light engineering factory, you are required to analyse the various factors involved in Plant Selection. What are they?   (*Swansea College of Technology* 1969)

9. A Production Engineer recommends that a certain type of machine tool be purchased for the batch production of a range of components, the production run of which is expected to be 5 years. List and discuss the factors which he would have considered before making a recommendation, and show how his decision affects the factory cost of components produced on the machine.   (*Luton College of Technology* 1962)

CHAPTER 11
MAINTENANCE

1. Outline the duties of the maintenance department of an engineering works with due regard to the planning of the work and the keeping of records.   (*I.M.E.* 1959)

2. State what you understand by the term 'preventive maintenance' as applied to a factory, and describe the features of such a system of maintenance.   (*B.I.M.* 1958)

3. As the newly appointed maintenance superintendent of a flow production factory you find that there has been little organized maintenance of equipment and consequently many breakdowns.
Outline the system of maintenance you would institute to reduce the incidence of breakdowns.   (*Brighton College of Technology* 1965)

4. Present the case for Planned Maintenance and outline the basic elements of a planned maintenance scheme.   (*Portsmouth College of Technology* 1966)

5. What methods are available for improving the productivity of a maintenance department in a manufacturing company?   (*Medway & Maidstone College of Technology* 1971)

6. 100 similar transistor boards are used in a radar system. Boards are replaced

when they fail and may be also replaced as a group. The cost of replacement for single boards is £*b* and for group replacement is £1 per board. Find the values of *b* for which the best policy is to carry out group replacement at 300 hour intervals. Life test data for the boards is as follows—

Age interval (*hours*)	Number of failures
100	0
200	15
300	24
400	25
500	22
600	9
700	5
	100

(*University of Birmingham* 1971)

7. (*a*) What is meant by replacement theory?

Discuss the main factors that require consideration in developing a replacement policy.

(*b*) A manager finds from past records that the costs per year of running an item of plant whose purchase price is £3,000 are as given below—

Year	1	2	3	4	5	6	7	8
Running costs	£500	600	700	900	1150	1400	1700	2000
Resale price	£1500	750	375	185	100	100	100	100

How often should the plant be replaced? (*Slough College of Technology* 1968)

8. Suppose an advertising sign is made up of 5,000 bulbs. Due to constant flashing the life of the bulbs tends to be short. The probability of a bulb failing in its first month is 0·3 and no bulb lasts longer than two months. The cost of replacing bulbs individually is £1·0 per bulb but the cost of replacing all bulbs is £0·4 per bulb. Is it cheaper to replace all bulbs—

(*a*) every month,

(*b*) every other month, with individual replacements if needed, or

(*c*) individually? (*Slough College of Technology* 1970)

9. (*a*) Discuss how the effectiveness of a maintenance department might be improved in a typical large scale engineering organization, which currently practises break-down maintenance only.

(*b*) Discuss what are the problems to be considered before introducing a realistic wage incentive scheme within a maintenance department. (*Norwich City College* 1971)

10. What purpose is served by maintaining plant? Outline the various approaches to plant maintenance and indicate with reasons which approaches you think are likely to become increasingly popular in the future. (*Portsmouth College of Technology* 1969)

CHAPTER 12

BUDGETS AND BUDGETARY CONTROL

1. What is meant by the 'break-even' point? An organization whose fixed costs are £180,000 sells a single product for £2·50 each. The unit material cost is £0·75, whilst the other costs, assumed to be wholly variable are £0·85 a unit. Graphically or otherwise determine—

(*a*) the break-even point;

(*b*) the volume sold which will produce a profit of 10 per cent on the selling price;

(*c*) the effect on the break-even point of a reduction in material cost of 10 per cent.

(Polytechnic of Central London 1962)

2. What are the objectives which would influence you in setting up a system of Budgetary Control? Write short notes about the activities for which you would budget.

(Polytechnic of Central London (I.W.M.) 1962)

3. Marginal costing allied to the employment of the Break-even Chart has particular value in the jobbing undertaking.

(*a*) Give reasons why this should be the case.

(*b*) Outline, for this situation, the method of using—

(i) Marginal costing techniques.

(ii) Break-even Charts and Profit Analysis.

(iii) Budgetary Planning and Control with four-weekly reporting and analysis.

(University of Loughborough 1965)

4. Outline the scope and limitation of controlling a manufacturing concern through its budget. *(I.P.E. 1960)*

5. What is Budgetary Control? Show as fully as possible how this technique is used by management to control expense, and draw up a typical expense budget for a department in your own works. *(I.W.M. (S.Q.))*

6. Define the following terms—

(*a*) (i) Fixed Cost

(ii) Variable Cost

(*b*) A company makes £5,000 profit from selling 10,000 units for £6 each. Its fixed costs are £15,000. What is the break-even point?

(Medway & Maidstone College of Technology 1971)

7. Explain how Budgetary Control can facilitate the delegation of authority and at the same act as an instrument of co-ordination. *(Luton College of Technology 1966)*

8. 'One sign of the good manager is his ability to delegate responsibility, and this is especially true in the area of expenditure control. But if the control expenditure is delegated, as it should be, means must be provided to enable those responsible to exercise control. One such means is the Budget.' (Editorial comment in *The Accountant*, March 1968). Discuss the implications of the above statement in relation to the procedure you would adopt when called upon to install a budgeting system in an organization. Discuss also what further advantages might be obtained if, in addition, a Standard Costing system was installed. *(North Staffordshire Polytechnic 1971)*

9. Outline the main principles on which to base Budgetary Control and explain how you would control the factory budget. *(Leeds College of Commerce 1969)*

10. The following is a summary of the trading results of the Electric Razor Co. for the year ended 31st March 1969, during which 8,000 electric razors were sold.

	£	£
Sales		64,000
Costs		
Material	24,000	
Labour Direct	10,000	
Indirect	4,000	
Other Costs	12,000	
		50,000
Profit		£14,000

You are required to *prepare a summary* of the *expected results* for the *following year*, taking into consideration the matters listed below—

(*a*) the Selling Price of the razor is to be reduced by 50p.

Factory and Production Management

(b) Sales Volume is expected to increase by 10 per cent.

(c) Operatives, the wages of whom are classified as 'direct', are to be paid an incentive bonus of 2½ per cent in order to stimulate production. Indirect labour is not expected to increase during the forthcoming year.

(d) Owing to larger quantities being purchased, suppliers have agreed to grant a discount of 5 per cent on all purchases.

(e) 'Other costs' vary directly with production except to the extent of £2,000 which is considered 'fixed' and a further £500 will arise in the forthcoming year, due to additional rent payable in respect of an extension to the factory.

(f) You are to assume there are no stock or work-in-progress at 31st March 1969.

(Norwich City College 1970)

11. Explain what is meant by Overhead Charges. Discuss the need for a proper allocation of Overhead Charges and explain the factors to be taken into account in making an allocation. (Norwich City College 1970)

12. A manufacturer estimates that the sales of his product at various price levels will be as shown below—

Price per Article £	No. of Articles Sold (thousands)
150	40
140	50
130	60
120	75
110	90
100	100
90	105

The variable costs of the product amount to £50 per article. The fixed costs are £4½ million, but if sales exceed 60,000 the expansion of the productive capacity will increase fixed costs by £200,000.

Show by means of a chart the levels of sales and selling price at which:

(a) a profit begins to be made, and

(b) the maximum profit will be earned. (Norwich City College 1970)

13. The following is a schedule of the expenditure in two departments of a manufacturing business during one year—

(a)

	Department A £	Department B £
Direct Wages	4,690	5,928
Indirect Wages	1,106	894
Toolmakers	528	242
Power Consumed	292	208
Shop Sundries	70	26
Repairs to Plant	281	75
Depreciation of Plant	325	169
Rent and Rates	535	529
Stationery for Manufacturing Departments	32	69
Supervision Salaries	427	642
Storekeeper's Wages	156	110

Divide the overhead expenses of each department into fixed and variable expenses, and show separately the total fixed and variable overhead rates, expressing them as a percentage of direct wages in each case.

(*b*) State briefly the object of distinguishing the fixed from the variable expenses in the above example. (*Norwich City College* 1971)

14. The following figures apply to a manufacturing company—

Annual Sales at 100% effective capacity	£3,600,000
Fixed overhead	£1,100,000
Total variable costs	£2,200,000

It is proposed to increase the capacity by the acquisition of 40 per cent additional space and plant. One result will be to increase fixed overhead by £250,000 per annum.

Plot the foregoing on a single break-even chart, and determine from the chart at what capacity the same profit as before will be produced after the extensions have been made. (*Norwich City College* 1971)

15. The advantages of a budgetary control system are often stressed. However, it would be wrong to assume that these advantages always accrue to an organization which introduces such a system.

Discuss the reasons why these advantages need not necessarily be achieved.
(*Norwich City College* 1971)

16. Explain how Budgetary Control can facilitate the delegation of authority and at the same time act as an instrument of co-ordination.
(*Luton College of Technology* 1966)

CHAPTER 13
TYPES OF PRODUCTION

1. Define and discuss—
(*a*) Job production;
(*b*) Batch production;
(*c*) Flow production;
(*d*) Mass production. (*Polytechnic of Central London (B.I.M.)* 1960)

2. What conditions need to be fulfilled before a flow-production line can be installed, and what are the essential features and advantages of such a production method?
(*Polytechnic of Central London (I.W.S.)* 1959)

3. What is meant by flow, batch and job production? Indicate how each can occur within a single factory.

Sketch a floor plan of a medium sized general engineering factory engaged on batch production, showing the production department, stores and service areas; arrange these so that there is good work flow with a minimum of back tracking.
(*Brighton College of Technology* 1966)

4. Explain the link between demand for a product and the method adopted in its production. Suggest reasons for the trend towards large-scale production, and assess the future prospects for job production. (*I.P.E. (S.Q.)*)

5. The factory of which you are the Production Manager has a process type plant layout in all departments. The quantities of some of the components and assemblies being produced do now, in your opinion, justify a product layout.

Write a report to your General Manager making a case for altering the plant layout in parts of the factory to a product type layout. (*Brighton College of Technology* 1964)

6. Discuss the kinds of problems likely to be encountered when a new production method of involving a number of work stations on a flow line is installed.
(*University of Aston in Birmingham* 1967)

7. Distinguish between the different types of production you might use in a new manufacturing unit. Explain the marketing and production factors you would have in mind in deciding to use one or more types for a product of your choice.
(*Norwich City College* 1971)

8.(*a*) Define the following terms—
 (i) Unit production.
 (ii) Batch production.
 (iii) Flow production.
 (*b*) Outline the main problems encountered in the operation of each of these systems of production, with particular reference to the economic utilization of productive capacity. (*Luton College of Technology* 1963)
 9. Explain what you consider to be the main requirements which must be met to maintain effective Flow Production in a factory. Discuss in what circumstances you consider that this type of production would be most suitable and what advantage you would expect to obtain from its introduction. (*Luton College of Technology* 1966)
 10. Your Managing Director informs you that there is a good chance of obtaining orders which will treble the total quantity that is at present produced, of a certain specific article if we can substantially reduce the unit cost. He then asks you to give the job your earnest attention. How would you tackle this problem? You may choose any manufactured article with which you are familiar, as an example.
(*City of Birmingham Polytechnic* 1971)

CHAPTER 14
WORK STUDY I

1.(*a*) You are assigned the task of establishing a Work Study section in an organization classified as light engineering and manufacturing on small/medium batch size production. Construct a simple organization chart showing the production management functions and discuss the place, size and function of the Work Study section.
 (*b*) Assuming no Work Study personnel are as yet engaged, discuss the policy for recruitment. (*University of Wales* 1965)
 2. Clarify by means of a diagram the connexion between—

Motion Study	Payment by Results
Job Evaluation	Time Study
Standard Cost	Merit Rating
Analytical Estimating	

(*I.M.E.* 1956)
 3. Work Study can be divided into two distinct functions, Method Study and Work Measurement. Describe what is meant by each and describe one work measurement technique in common use. (*Brighton College of Technology* 1965)
 4.(*a*) Write a short account of the range of techniques available for the investigation of task procedures.
 (*b*) Explain the factors which govern the selection of each of these techniques for the examination of productive operations. (*B.I.M.* 1958)
 5. Describe the relationship between Work Study and other industrial engineering functions. (*I.W.S.(S.Q.)*)
 6. Describe in detail, with sketches, one of the recognized charts of method study. Explain the use of this chart. (*P.* (*D.M.S.*) 1967)
 7.(*a*) Describe an application of Method Study in an office (or other non-manufacture situation). It may have been called an Organization and Methods exercise.
 Make clear—
 (i) its objectives,
 (ii) the steps taken,
 (iii) preparation required—by line manager; by whoever did the study,
 (iv) outcome,

and give detailed descriptions and/or sketches to show the technique used for analysing the work.

(b) It has been said that Work Measurement cannot and should not be applied in offices and drawing offices. Comment. (*P.* (*D.M.S.*) 1968)

8. Supposing one of your employees was engaged on a small repetition machining job and you thought his efficiency was lower than it might be. How would you set about improving his efficiency? (*University of Aston in Birmingham* 1966)

9. Discuss (*a*) the functions of an Organization and Methods Section in an office, and (*b*) methods for measuring work in the office. (*Croydon Technical College* 1967)

10. Discuss the need for some critical appraisal of administrative and clerical costs in industrial, commercial and government undertakings and the technical feasibility of measuring clerical work. (*Croydon Technical College* 1969)

11. Explain the considerations to be taken into account when designing a programme of work study assignments. (*University of Aston in Birmingham* 1970)

12. How can the application of work study assist Management in—
(*a*) raising productivity,
(*b*) the planning and control of production? (*University of Edinburgh* 1970)

13. What is a Flow Process Chart? Describe the different types; the symbols used; the kind of information recorded; the kind of questions that should be asked.
(*The Polytechnic, London* 1967)

CHAPTER 15
WORK STUDY II

1.(*a*) Define the term 'Standard Minute' and briefly describe the more common allowances given in Work Standard.

(*b*) On the basis of the following information calculate;
(i) the Operator Performance
(ii) the Pay Performance

Work Value Earned	= 400 S.M.s
Personal Allowance	= 40 S.M.s
Process Allowance	= 50 Mins.
Lost Time	= $\frac{1}{2}$ hour
Clock Hours	= 8 hours.

(*Portsmouth College of Technology* 1966)

2. Show clearly how primary data obtained through Work Measurement can assist management in any TWO of the following fields—
(1) Labour Control
(2) Cost Estimating
(3) Production Control
(4) Application of Incentive Schemes.
Your answer should explain fully how the Work Measurement data is utilized.
(*University of Loughborough* 1965)

3. In 1832 Charles Babbage wrote: 'If the observer stands with his watch in his hand before a person heading a pin, the workman will almost certainly increase his speed, and the estimate will be too large.' What techniques are available to the modern Work Study engineer to overcome this effect when he is finding the standard time for a task?
In your answer you should define any terms used.
(*Polytechnic of Central London* 1962)

4. The design of work methods requires a means of evaluating the extent to which

labour saving devices may be integrated economically. Give your views on, and illustrate, the contribution that a well based system of predetermined motion times can make in this regard. To what extent do you consider that subjectivity in the determination of time standards can be eliminated by the use of a predetermined motion time system?

(University of Birmingham 1970)

5. Define Time Study and list its uses. Evaluate the traditional method of taking a time study on the shop floor by observation and stopwatch. How does this technique compare with the others available for work measurement? Determine the standard time for the assembly of an electric switch from the following data—

Mean observed time for assembly   0·9 min
Rating on the 'hundred' scale   110
Personal allowances   7%   *(University of Birmingham)*

6. Outline the general procedure for a work sampling study to determine the extent of delays and personal time.   *(University of Birmingham 1971)*

7.(*a*) The final operation in manufacture of screws is packing in 1 gross boxes. At standard performance an operator packs 1 gross in 0·40 minutes. If there is a contingency allowance of 10 per cent and a rest allowance of 15 per cent, how many gross of screws are packed in a 5 day 40 hour week, allowing $1\frac{1}{2}$ hours per day for breaks, and how many hours does an operator earn?

(*b*) After packing in 1 gross boxes, the screws are boxed in 100 gross cartons and wired on a machine which suffers stoppages, due to changing wire, stapling boxes, etc., to the equivalent of a 10 per cent contingency. The allowed time for this operation is 2·50 minutes. If there are 20 packers employed working, as previously indicated in (*a*) what is the backlog of work waiting against the machine after 1 week? The machine operates on a 5 day 40 hour week with $1\frac{1}{2}$ hours per day as breaks.

(Derby & District College of Technology 1970)

8.(*a*) List the various Work Measurement techniques and illustrate their application by referring to work with which you are familiar.

(*b*) Describe how you would go about an Activity Sampling study to establish to within ±2 per cent what machine utilization there was in a workshop of ten capstan lathes. There is evidence that suggests that the idle time might well be in the region of 24 per cent.   *(Norwich City College 1970)*

9. Describe what is meant by the following work measurement techniques—
(*a*) time study
(*b*) synthesis
(*c*) activity sampling.
Give examples of work where each technique can be used to advantage.

(Brighton College of Technology 1964)

10. What advantages would you expect from applying work measurement to office work? Describe a method of payment by results suitable for copy typists working in a pool.   *(Brighton College of Technology 1967)*

11. When considering how many store-keepers were required in a factory supply stores, it was decided to adopt activity sampling techniques. Explain how such techniques should be implemented and comment on the possible errors which may occur in assessing the work content of the job.   *(Brighton College of Technology 1967)*

12. Describe fully each of the steps in Time Study procedure required to develop a Standard Time. Give illustrative calculations.   *(I.W.S.(S.Q.))*

13.(*a*) Describe two systems of predetermined motion times.
(*b*) In what ways are these systems most useful?   *(I.W.S.(S.Q.))*

14. Discuss the purposes to which Time Standards may be put in Production Management other than the setting of incentive rates.   *(I.I.A. 1953)*

15. Explain the term 'Standard Minute'. For what purposes are standard times

required in the design and operation of production systems?

(*Portsmouth College of Technology* 1969)

CHAPTER 16
THE WORK PLACE

1. Outline the general concept of Ergonomics and give a considered appraisal of its potential contribution to technological efficiency.   (*University of Birmingham* 1970)

2. 'The design of a display must do more than accurately provide current information about hardware state.' Discuss this statement.   (*University of Birmingham* 1971)

3. Review the potential contribution of ergonomics data and concepts to an area of application of your choice.   (*University of Birmingham* 1971)

4. What factors would you consider when designing a bench top layout for a light assembly job? Explain in detail any principles which you consider are applicable in this kind of job.   (*Luton College of Technology* 1964)

5. Explain what you understand by the term 'Ergonomics'. Describe the application of the principles involved to any factory situation with which you are familiar.

(*Slough College of Technology* 1969)

6. Discuss the use of anthropometric data in workplace design.   (*M.R.H.*)

7. What environmental factors should be considered at the workplace design stage? What information is available on the effect of these factors on worker performance?

(*M.R.H.*)

8. How could Predetermined Motion Time System data assist in workplace design?

(*M.R.H.*)

9. Discuss the layout of controls in relation to the position of the operator and processed workpiece on any machine tool of your choice.   (*M.R.H.*)

CHAPTER 17
MATERIALS HANDLING

1. Discuss *three* types of conveyor with which you are familiar, indicating the situations most appropriate for each.

2. When using package loads, the cost of returning empty pallets or containers may be substantial. Discuss ways in which this cost can be minimized.

3. A reliable estimate has revealed that handling costs might range from 20 to 80 per cent of the total factory wage bill. What ground should be covered by a Materials Handling Survey Team, and what principles should be borne in mind when making recommendations for (*a*) better movement of materials, and (*b*) economical use of equipment?   (*Luton College of Technology* 1965)

4. State the principles to be followed in good materials handling practice. What advantages would you expect Mechanical Handling to have over manual handling and vice versa?   (*Luton College of Technology* 1969)

5. Discuss the likely reasons for the high cost of Materials Handling in a factory. Suggest some of the economic and technical considerations which should be borne in mind when selecting Materials Handling equipment for a multi-storey factory.

(*Luton College of Technology* 1971)

6. Discuss the fundamental principles to be borne in mind when carrying out any materials handling investigation, identifying those to which you would expect to find it most difficult to adhere.   (*Manchester Polytechnic* 1970)

7. Discuss the factors to be considered when dealing with a Materials Handling problem. Outline the effect of the method of production utilized on the type of materials handling problem with which the Works Manager is likely to be faced.

(*Leeds College of Commerce* 1965)

8. You are manager of a medium sized company engaged on batch production. The plant layout was based on the type of work which was being done 30 years ago with additions to the plant over the years placed wherever space could be made available. The type of work done now has changed in character to that of 30 years ago, there has been some additional building. How would you find out your present cost of materials movement? What use would you make of this information? How would you use the information? (*City of Birmingham Polytechnic* 1971)

9. Discuss what economic and technical considerations are involved in selecting Materials Handling equipment for a multi-storey factory.

(*Luton College of Technology* 1964)

10. Examine the likely reasons for the high cost of Materials Handling in a factory. Describe what conditions require to be satisfied if materials handling is to be carried out efficiently. (*Luton College of Technology* 1968)

CHAPTER 18
GROUP TECHNOLOGY

1. What advantages are claimed for the practice of classifying components by shape? Discuss the extent to which such classification may benefit a firm manufacturing on a batch production basis. (*Slough College of Technology* 1970)

2. What is meant by a 'cell' in Group Technology? Assuming that you were in a position to install Group Technology, what factors would you consider in setting up the first cell? (*K.G.L.*)

3. 'Group Technology is all very well, but it must result in under-utilization of plant, and this must increase costs.' Discuss. (*K.G.L.*)

4. The reduction of set-up times, is only one of the benefits of Group Technology. Discuss some of the others. (*K.G.L.*)

5. Discuss the proposition that Group Technology has a profound influence upon the administrative tasks carried out within a factory. (*K.G.L.*)

6. Distinguish between 'component classification' and 'production flow analysis' approaches to the establishment of cells for producing 'families' of similar engineering components. (*M.R.H.*)

7. What steps should be followed when changing the plant layout in a factory from a 'process' to a cell type? (*M.R.H.*)

8. Do you consider that the manufacture of families of components in cells can heighten or diminish the problems of scheduling? (*M.R.H.*)

CHAPTER 19
ESTIMATING AND PLANNING

1. Explain what you understand by a process layout? Show how this document may be laid out and what information it bears. Explain the purpose and use of the different items of information on a process layout. (*I.W.M.(S.Q.)*)

2. In the 'X' Manufacturing Company the 'job order' issued to the foreman of the machine shop states only part number and quantity to be made. What justification is there for giving more comprehensive information than this? (*I.P.E.* 1956)

3. Give the type of information necessary for compiling an operation layout sheet. Illustrate your answer by sketching a simple component having about five machining operations, and draw up a typical operation layout sheet. Discuss the case for the issue of separate tooling information. (*I.P.E.* 1954)

4. Discuss the preparation of a cost estimate for a product with which you are

familiar. Indicate fully the information required before such an estimate can be made.
(Polytechnic of Central London (I.W.S.) 1959)

5. For what purposes may a cost estimate be prepared?

6. What information would you collect and in what form would you collect it if you wished to facilitate the running of the Production Planning Department?
(Polytechnic of Central London (I.W.M.) 1959)

7. What influence, if any, do you consider the planning department should exercise on the design of a part? Give reasons for your opinions based on the consideration of a number of different components. *(University of Aston in Birmingham* 1966)

8. What do you understand by the term 'Process Planning'? Show how the decisions taken by this function connect with the work of—
(*a*) Purchasing Department
(*b*) Production Control Department. *(Portsmouth College of Technology* S.Q.)

9. For what reasons may an estimate of the cost of developing a new product be required? What information is required before such an estimate is attempted? What value may the estimate have to the development engineer?
(Note: 'development' is used here in the sense of the improvement of existing techniques, ideas or systems.) *(Polytechnic of Central London* 1962)

10. Contrast the tasks involved in production planning prior to the start of the first operation in—
(*a*) a jobbing shop manufacturing to order its own specially-designed products,
(*b*) a batch production shop manufacturing a standard range of products for stock, and
(*c*) a batch production shop manufacturing customer-designed products to bulk order and delivery schedule. *(University of Birmingham* 1971)

11. What costs are incurred in 'setting up' or 'preparing' to produce a batch of parts. To what extent does this cost of setting up influence your choice of process?
(Portsmouth College of Technology 1969)

12. Discuss the nature of Process Planning showing its significance to the problems of production control. *(Portsmouth College of Technology* 1969)

13. What do you understand by—
(*a*) Product part lists
(*b*) Operation layout?
Give details of the information which appears on an operation layout.
(Luton College of Technology 1964)

14. With respect to a manufactured part, how far is it possible and desirable to include information about—
(*a*) How to make,
(*b*) How many to make at a time,
(*c*) How long in factory time this quantity takes to make on the document which may be known as the 'process layout', 'operation schedule' or 'planning sheet'?
(University of Aston in Birmingham 1971)

15. In a manufacturing situation what do you understand by the term pre-production planning?
Trace the sequence of procedures and the use made of the information created in the pre-production activities related to a product of your choice.
(Nottingham Regional College of Technology 1968)

16. Discuss the extent to which planning for production justifies being treated as an important function in an enterprise. *(Slough College of Technology* 1971)

17. What costs are incurred in 'setting up' or 'preparing' to produce a batch of parts. To what extent does this cost of setting up influence your choice of process.
(Portsmouth College of Technology 1969)

CHAPTER 20
CONTROL OF QUALITY

1. What conditions could make acceptance sampling appropriate? Define A.Q.L., producer's risk, L.P.T.D. and consumer's risk. Relate these definitions to a typical O.C. curve. Discuss the shape of the average outgoing quality curve. Describe the general structure for double sampling and discuss its advantages and disadvantages.

(University of Birmingham 1971)

2. Acceptance sampling, instead of 100 per cent inspection, might be appropriate under certain conditions provided that managements are willing to take certain risks. Describe these conditions and risks and outline the various types of sampling schemes that are available, together with other information concerning the schemes, that management might consider useful. *(University of Birmingham* 1971)

3. Analyse the factors which determine the location of inspection points in the chain of manufacturing operations. Show how the employment of statistical methods by the inspector may be of value (*a*) to the designer, (*b*) to the production engineer.

(I.M.E. 1956)

4. Illustrate schematically the inspection routine of an engineering concern. Indicate the purpose and distribution of the main documents involved. *(I.M.E.* 1955)

5. How may the principles of Quality Control be applied in a factory? Who should be responsible for maintaining the quality of workmanship? What part does the inspection department play in the scheme? *(I.I.A.* 1951)

6. At what points in manufacture, and for what purposes, are engineering products inspected? Show how a statistical presentation of the inspection records may help to reduce costs. *(I.P.E.* 1952)

7. What benefits would you expect to result from a change to a decentralized system of inspection in a batch production factory? Would there be any disadvantages?

Design an index which reflects the various aspects of product quality and which enables progress towards specified targets to be measured.

(Brighton College of Technology 1968)

8. Comment on the use of single, double and sequential sampling plans of inspection, giving examples of each. *(Brighton College of Technology* 1968)

9. In Quality Control, what is meant by a process being 'in control'? When a process is not in control, what possible causes of variation should be considered?

(The Polytechnic, London 1967)

10.(*a*) Describe the conditions which should exist on a process in order that Statistical Sampling Techniques may be used.

(*b*) List the advantages that S.Q.C. can provide over 100 per cent inspection.

(*c*) Describe with the aid of sketches what control charts are necessary to ensure a process is kept in control.

(*d*) Do the designer's limits have any bearing on the setting up of control charts?

(Norwich City College 1970)

11.(*a*) A manufacturer aims to make electricity bulbs with a mean life of 1,000 hours. He draws a sample of 25 from a batch and tests them. The mean life of the sample bulbs is 990 with a standard deviation of 20 hours. Is the batch up to standard at the 95 per cent confidence level?

(*b*) A manufacturer knows that 10 per cent of a day's production is defective. What is the chance that a customer will accept the output if his plan is to reject all goods if he discovers more than one defective in a random sample of 10 units?

(Norwich City College 1971)

12.(*a*) Discuss under what conditions Statistical Quality Control would be preferred to '100 per cent inspection'.

(*b*) Draw a typical operating characteristic of a sampling plan showing the probability of batch acceptance plotted against the actual percentage defects in the batch, and indicate the zones of acceptance, indecision and rejection.

(*c*) Define the term A.Q.L., and locate a typical value on the operating characteristic.
(*Norwich City College* 1971)

CHAPTER 21
COSTING

1. Describe the methods the cost accountant uses to build up a pre-determined overhead recovery rate. What is the purpose of this rate? Are there any alternatives to full absorption costing? (*Portsmouth College of Technology* 1966)

2. Show how a successful costing procedure can assist a works manager in controlling his labour costs. (*I.I.A.* 1953)

3. Explain what is meant by 'standard cost' and by 'marginal cost'. Show how these costs can be used as a basis for long-term and short-term budgeting.
(*Brighton College of Technology* 1968)

4. Give a brief description of the function and work of the cost accountant. What qualities would you, as a manager, look for in the cost accounting system in your works?
(*I.M.E.* 1958)

5. Assess the benefits that might accrue to production management from the provision of a comprehensive system of cost accounting. Your reply should indicate the sort of information that should be forthcoming and to whom it should be communicated.
(*B.I.M.* 1969)

6.(*a*) Historical or standard costing techniques may be used to arrive at the costs of jobs or processes.

Describe the limitations of the purely historical costing approach and how historical costs are used in a standard costing system.

Outline the requirements for establishing a standard costing system.

(*b*) Calculate the wages variance from the following—

Product data:
Direct Labour—20 standard hours per unit of product
Direct Wages —50p per standard hour

Cost data:
During one month 500 units of the product were produced; 12,000 hours were worked; actual direct labour cost was £6,500. (*University of Birmingham* 1970)

7. 'Accounting information based on absorption costing techniques is not always suitable to use in cost analyses where changes in the volume of production are under consideration.' Explain why this is so; illustrate the answer with reference to the purpose of flexible budgeting and the nature of the accounting data required for cost-volume profit studies. (*University of Birmingham* 1970)

8. Explain what you understand by the objectives and techniques of standard costing. Describe its advantages over a system of historical costing.
(*Slough College of Technology* 1967)

9. Explain what you understand by Marginal Costing. Discuss in which circumstances its use is more appropriate than other methods of costing.
(*Slough College of Technology* 1968)

10. Summarize the nature of—
Absorption Costing, Marginal Costing and Standard Costing.

If a well-run manufacturing company regularly used all three methods, explain the circumstances in which marginal costings are likely to be more important than absorption costings. (*The Polytechnic of Central London* 1970)

11. Explain in detail the significance of Standard Costs as compared with Actual Costs and show how they are applied and what information can be obtained from their application. (*Norwich City College* 1970)

12. 'Costing is an instrument of management control.'
'Costing is nothing more than a detailed analysis of expenditure.'
Reconcile these two statements, quoting examples to illustrate the truth of each.
(*Norwich City College* 1971)

CHAPTER 22
PRODUCTION CONTROL I

1. What are the factors to be considered when organizing a production control system for an engineering factory engaged on a fair variety of work? Consider especially the contingencies which have to be provided for. (*I.M.E.* 1957)

2. When an engineering firm is losing repeat orders from customers due to unreliability in achieving promised delivery dates, what are probable sources of difficulty and how may they be removed? (*I.M.E.* 1956)

3. What arrangements must be made, and information supplied, to enable those in charge of the labour force of an engineering concern to achieve maximum effectiveness of their departments? (*I.M.E.* 1955)

4. Describe a system of machine loading appropriate to a factory manufacturing a product of your own choice. (*B.I.M.* 1958)

5. Describe the work done in the scheduling section of a planning department. What are the symptoms of poor production planning and control, and how would you detect them? (*I.P.E.* 1954)

6. Describe a system of machine loading in a small shop, illustrating your answer with a sketch of a suitable control board. (*I.W.S.(S.Q.)*)

7. Name, and describe the functions of, each of the five main sections of a production control department. (*I.W.S.(S.Q.)*)

8. Describe the principle types of information necessary for efficient production control. (*I.W.S.(S.Q.)*)

9. Discuss the type of activity which you would expect to be performed by a Production Control Department. Illustrate your answer with an Organization Chart.
(*University of Aston in Birmingham* 1967)

10. Explain the objectives and broad principles of effective machine loading. Describe a method of compiling the machine load schedule from the completion of the planning stage.
Explain the effects of 'overload' and 'underload' and state how they may be overcome when they are (*a*) temporary, (*b*) persistent. (*University of Wales* 1966)

11. Give your definition of production control. Briefly describe the major divisions into which this function is split, and indicate how each contributes to the overall objectives. (*Portsmouth College of Technology* S.Q.)

12. Production Control provides a major link between the Production and the Marketing/Sales functions in many organizations. Describe two alternative methods by which this link can be organized and operated. Indicate the type of company and industry for which each alternative would be best suited. Are there any significant weaknesses in either alternative? (*Medway & Maidstone College of Technology* 1970)

13. What information is required from each of—
(*a*) Sales
(*b*) Product design
(*c*) Management

so that Production Control may operate? Give examples of possible shortcomings in this information and explain how Production Control may deal with them.

(University of Aston in Birmingham 1971)

14. 'Production Control is most difficult in batch production type of manufacturing.' Discuss this statement in detail, referring to any techniques that you think are of importance. *(Norwich City College* 1970)

15. Your Personnel Manager, when searching for possible staff reductions, asks 'Just what do the people in each of your Production Control Departments do?' Describe what details you would supply to justify their existence.

(Luton College of Technology 1968)

CHAPTER 23 & 24
PRODUCTION CONTROL II
PRODUCTION CONTROL III

1. A small machine shop has four machines A, B, C and D. Four jobs (W, X, Y, Z) are taken on by this department. The machine time (in hours) and the sequence of operations is shown below—

Job	Operation Sequence				
	1	2	3	4	5
W	C—5	B—3	C—3	B—3	—
X	A—6	C—4	B—5	D—5	A—3
Y	B—3	A—5	C—3	D—4	C—6
Z	D—4	B—5	D—6	A—5	C—3

Assuming an eight-hour working day, and that once an operation has commenced, it may not be stopped (although overnight stops are permitted), compile a suitable loading schedule and thus determine the earliest completion time for each job.

(University of Wales 1967)

2. A bookbinder has a printing press and a binding machine, and 6 different manuscripts to print and bind.

The times required to perform the printing and binding operations are as follows—

	Times (Hours)	
Manuscript	Print	Bind
A	40	90
B	130	110
C	60	100
D	30	70
E	100	40
F	120	20

Determine the order in which the manuscripts should be processed to minimize the elapsed time: and determine the total processing time. *(University of Birmingham* 1971)

3. All the jobs passing through a forge have the same operation layout, described in Column (1) below.

For the next planning period there are five orders, which will be processed as five batches A, B, C, D, E which cannot be split.

The product explosion shows that stages will occupy the durations shown in columns for the batches. Stage capacity will be fully utilized for these durations, which include set-up-and-strike times.

(*a*) Develop and display a schedule for the work, and

(*b*) state how you derived it. Your primary objective is to minimize total through-put time.

(*c*) Suggest secondary objectives which might apply and the modifications to the schedule which they would generate.

Batch Stage Durations (*Hours*)					
Operation Layout (1)	*A*	*B*	*C*	*D*	*E*
Screen for foreign metal in raw material by passing over screening table	1	1	1	1	1
Heat to required temperature in 50 ton electric furnace	4	4	30	6	2
Forge in multiple die automatic hydraulic forge (electronically controlled hopper to maintain temperature of billet batches feeding in)	5	1	4	30	3
Paint to provide temporary preservation for transit to customer	1	1	1	1	1

(*The Polytechnic of Central London* 1970)

4.(*a*) Under what circumstances would you prefer an inventory system which is based on a fixed period to one based on a fixed quantity for re-ordering?

(*b*) There are six jobs, each of which must go through the two machines A and B in the order AB. Processing times in minutes are given in the table below:

	Processing Time	
Job	*Machine A*	*Machine B*
1	30	80
2	120	100
3	50	90
4	20	60
5	90	30
6	110	10

Determine a sequence for the six jobs that will minimize the elapsed time. Illustrate your solution in the form of a bar chart and give the overall elapsed time.

(*c*) A machine shop has six machines A to F. Two jobs must be processed through the shop using these machines. The times spent on each machine and the necessary sequence of the jobs through the shop are given below:

Order	1	2	3	4	5	6
Job I	A–20	C–10	D–10	B–30	E–25	F–15
Job II	A–10	C–30	B–15	D–10	F–15	E–20

In what order should the jobs be done on each of the machines, in order to minimize the total time necessary to finish the jobs? Illustrate your solution with a bar chart. Is your solution optimal? (*University of Manchester Business School* 1970)

CHAPTER 26
PRODUCTION CONTROL V

1. The manager of an engineering firm is anxious to know whether or not production on a certain important job is falling behind schedule. What are the chief means available to him for finding out what the position is, and for determining the causes of any delays which are actually taking place? (*I.M.E.* 1956)

2. Discuss the main advantages and applications of Gantt charts in a factory. Illustrate with a portion of a typical chart. (*I.P.E.* 1957)

3. What are the responsibilities of a progress section? Do you consider the existence of progress 'chasing' reflects bad planning and execution? (*I.W.S.(S.Q.)*)

4. It is suspected that production on a certain important job is falling behind schedule. What are the chief means of finding out whether this is so, and how much the delay is? Suggest some possible causes for the failure to maintain the production programme. (*I.P.E.* 1952)

5. What is the 'dispatch' function in a production control department, and how is this related to the other section of that department?

6. Dispatch is a term often used to describe the production control function which arises after scheduling and before (or during) manufacture.

(*a*) Describe what would be entailed in dispatch of the week's work in a large clothing factory in Leeds where batch production prevails.

(*b*) What are the advantages of centralized dispatching?
(*The Polytechnic of Central London* 1971)

7. Describe a scheme which is intended to control work-in-progress.
(*Luton College of Technology* 1969)

CHAPTER 27
PRODUCTION CONTROL VI

1. Describe the procedure which will enable control to be established over availability of each item of production material in any kind of manufacturing business with which you are familiar. (*I.W.M.(S.Q.)*)

2. What do you understand by the expression 'economic lot size'? State the factors to be considered in calculating it. Of what value is such information for production planning purposes? (*I.W.M.(S.Q.)*)

3. Stock control is now recognized as one of the most important tools of management control. How can this system increase the efficiency of the following sections of the business?

(*a*) Production;
(*b*) Purchasing;
(*c*) Sales;
(*d*) Engineering maintenance;
(*e*) Finance. (*B.I.M.* 1958)

4. What factors influence the fixing of job order quantities in workshops operating under batch production conditions?

How can the most suitable quantity be determined in a particular case?
(*I.P.E.* 1956)

5. What steps should a production manager of a general engineering factory take to overcome delays caused by waiting for materials? (*I.I.A.* 1951)

6. What determines the quantity of material purchased at any one time, assuming that the material is in constant demand?

(*The Polytechnic of Central London* (*I.W.S.*) 1959)

7. What effect do inaccurate stock records have on the operation of a factory? Suggest some of the causes of stock record errors and state how each can be minimized. Why are the auditors of a company interested in the accuracy of stock records?

(*Brighton College of Technology* 1965)

8. Explain the interdependence of re-order level, batch quantity and production time for common or standard parts.

By using values drawn from your own experience demonstrate how this information may be drawn together on key production control documents.

(*University of Aston in Birmingham* 1967)

9. (*a*) By assuming values, demonstrate how stock control methods work.

(*b*) To what categories of Stock would you apply the different methods?

(*c*) Discuss the effect of modern data processing systems on the choice of methods.

(*University of Aston in Birmingham* 1967)

10. What do you understand by Economic Batch Quantity? Describe the area in which this concept may be applied, mentioning any practical difficulties you may envisage. (*Portsmouth College of Technology* (*S.Q.*))

11. Explain the importance of the forecasting function to the engineering industry, giving an outline of the different types of forecast in which a firm in any selected part of the industry would be interested. Using exponential smoothing as one example, give three methods of arriving at an estimate of sales for the next period:

1350   1530   1460   1640

(*University of Birmingham* 1970)

12. What are the essential features of a sound stock control system in modern productive industry? The following figures give three years' monthly demand for one of a group of products. The company's policy is to supply customer's orders as far as possible from finished stock. Recommend a forecasting system suitable for either a manual or computer calculation, and show how your forecast would have compared with actual demand over the years 1969 and 1970.

	1968	1969	1970
Jan	51	41	45
Feb	30	22	63
Mar	58	37	72
Apr	42	33	48
May	33	40	56
June	30	54	48
July	32	54	62
Aug	19	51	61
Sep	27	60	71
Oct	24	33	61
Nov	21	66	80
Dec	42	66	64

Explain how you would use such a system of demand forecasting to help in the scheduling of production and controlling the level of finished stocks. (*University of Bath* 1971)

13. Derive any commonly used formula for determining the optimum order quantity for a good when ordering costs and stockholding costs have to be taken into account Clearly state the assumptions that are made.

Describe the operation of a continuous review stockholding system. Outline the conditions under which the use of more sophisticated purchasing rules than the one you have described are desirable. (*University of Sheffield* 1971)

14. Explain 'minimum stock', 're-order level' and 're-order quantity'. What is their inter-relation? Explain how these quantities are used in a stock control system.
(*Medway & Maidstone College of Technology* 1970)

15. Your Company has, by means of inter-firm comparisons, decided that they have too much capital invested in stocks. You have been chosen to investigate and improve the situation.

Discuss the circumstances that could lead to a high stock investment and describe the steps you would follow in conducting an investigation into this problem.
(*Slough College of Technology* 1971)

16. An electronics company buy in a special component which they use at the rate of 12,000 per annum. Currently the price they pay is 50p per item and the cost of placing an order is £5 per year. The annual stock holding cost is 5p per item.

(*a*) if y = cost and x = order quantity state equations which show the relationship between:
  (i) ordering cost and order quantity
  (ii) holding cost and order quantity
(*b*) Graphically determine the Economic Order Quantity.
(*c*) Their supplier has made an offer to reduce the price to 49p per component if they will purchase 3,000 components each time they place an order. Demonstrate whether or not the company should accept this offer? (*The Polytechnic of Central London* 1970)

17. The term 'Stock Control' covers many kinds of control systems planned to meet the needs of a particular stock problem. Each of the following presents a different kind of stock control problem—
(*a*) Tobacco kiosk
(*b*) Restaurant
(*c*) A warehouse holding 20 different types of lawn mower.
Outline a system of stock control for each of these establishments.
(*North Staffordshire Polytechnic* 1971)

18. One use of stock (raw material, work-in-progress and finished goods) is to 'decouple the supplier—raw material stores—production—warehouse—customer chain'. Explain what is meant by this statement, and hence the uses of stock of the three kinds mentioned. How would you set standards for the work-in-progress inventory, and how would you effect control using these standards?
(*Derby & District College of Technology* 1969)

19. Sales of a non-seasonal industrial product have shown a steady trend over the last three years. Figures for the last 12 months are as follows—

Month	1	2	3	4	5	6	7	8	9	10	11	12
Sales	201	195	210	213	228	218	226	234	228	230	236	230

Show by the exponential smoothing technique, how you might have forecast at the end of month 4 what would be the sales for month 5 and similarly for each month thereafter.

Comment on your choice of smoothing constant.
(*Slough College of Technology* 1972)

20. As a newly appointed Works Manager of a medium sized manufacturing company, you notice that the production processes are frequently stopping due to the non-availability of stocked materials. Discuss what areas you would investigate in order to rectify this situation and explain the possible methods you could use to eliminate this problem. (*Slough College of Technology* 1971)

21. Given the following Time series—

Week No.	Actual Demand
1	52
2	52
3	60
4	81
5	80
6	88
7	100
8	107
9	134
10	124
11	152
12	160
13	170
14	178
15	190

(*a*) calculate the Exponentially Weighted Moving Average, and explain your choice of constant.

(*b*) When would you use the E.W.M.A. and what administrative advantages are there in so doing? (*Norwich City College* 1970)

22. The monthly sales of a particular product have been found as follows—

Year	Month	Sales (£000s)
1969	January	15
	February	17
	March	16
	April	16
	May	18
	June	21
	July	20
	August	22
	September	24
	October	22
	November	26
	December	27

(*a*) Plot the individual monthly sales and cumulative sales since January 1969.

(*b*) Calculate and plot the three monthly moving average.

(*c*) Outline a possible use for moving averages. (*Source—unknown*)

CHAPTER 28
BUYING

1. Describe the work of the purchasing officer of an engineering firm, showing his relationship with other departments within the firm and also with representatives of customers and suppliers. (*I.M.E.* 1956)

2. What are the main objectives of efficient purchasing and what is the scope of the purchasing function within an organization? (*I.W.M.(S.Q.)*)

3. Some industrial firms permit personal contact between the representatives of supplies firms and their own user departments. How far do you consider this practice to be desirable and what general principles do you consider should be observed? (*B.I.M.* 1959)

4. Describe the various methods which a buyer may use to convey to the seller a clear and accurate picture of the item which is required. Give examples where each method may appropriately be used. (*B.I.M.* 1958)

5. Describe a procedure for a manufacturing concern engaged in batch production designed to maintain an efficient supply of raw materials and bought-out parts.

(*B.I.M.* 1959)

6. Draw up a list showing clearly all the information needed on a purchase order, and justify each entry. (*The Polytechnic of Central London (I.W.S.)* 1959)

7. The Board of Directors of a large manufacturing company decide to centralize their purchasing activities.

Describe—

(*a*) The range of activities to be carried out by the new Purchasing Executive.

(*b*) What qualities and qualifications, if any, would you look for in appointing a man to be the Purchasing Executive. (*The Polytechnic of Central London (I.W.M.)* 1962)

8. What are the main advantages of an efficient purchasing organization? To what extent is it necessary for this to form a separate department and what limitations would be incorporated in the terms of reference? (*Croydon Technical College* 1970)

9. In what ways can the Purchasing Department ensure that goods supplied are of suitable quality? (*Croydon Technical College* 1971)

10. What influence does the Purchasing Manager have on the affairs of a company? How far should he be able to act without prior approval and what measures can be used to ensure that the interests of the company are properly safeguarded?

(*Croydon Technical College* 1971)

11. Discuss the importance of the part played by the progressing activity within the supply function and show the need for a high degree of co-ordination between the progressing and buying activities. (*Luton College of Technology* 1961)

12. A company manufacturing control systems needs to purchase small electrical motors and obtains the following quotations from 3 potential suppliers (*A*, *B* and *C*):

A. £6·50/motor for 40 or fewer motors.

B. Fixed charge of £100·00 plus £3·00/motor for 50 or fewer motors.

Fixed charge of £100·00 plus £2·50/motor for more than 50 motors.

C. Fixed charge of £150·00 plus £2·00/motor.

For each supplier, plot on the same paper the cost of purchasing the motors against the quantity ordered. Which supplier should receive the contract if the quantity required is—

(i) 20 motors?

(ii) 40 motors?

(iii) 60 motors?

(iv) 120 motors? (*The Polytechnic of Central London* 1971)

13. A straightforward component may be purchased at the same price from two equally reliable suppliers. Would you purchase the whole of your requirement from one supplier, or would you divide your orders between the two suppliers? (*K.G.L.*)

14. Why is it sometimes useful for a buyer to have a detailed estimate of the costs involved in making a product which he is about to purchase? (*K.G.L.*)

CHAPTER 29
STOREKEEPING

1. Summarize the various factors which must be considered when deciding the size and location of the stores in a general engineering factory engaged on jobbing work.

(*I.P.E.* 1958)

2. Outline the cycle of clerical operations involved when a consignment of material is taken into stock in the material stores of a factory.   (*B.I.M.* 1958)

3. Discrepancies between stock records and physical stocks of components in a stores are causing disruption of production. Explain how discrepancies occur, and state what methods you would consider employing to reduce them.

(*Brighton College of Technology* 1965)

4. Describe the term 'Perpetual Inventory', and list the advantages of this method compared with periodic stock-taking.   (*Croydon Technical College* 1969)

CHAPTER 30
PERSONNEL ADMINISTRATION

1. Discuss the differences between, and the purposes of, Job Evaluation and Merit Rating. Describe how a job evaluation may be carried out.

(*The Polytechnic of Central London* (*I.W.S.*) 1959)

2. You have successfully applied for a post as Works Manager of Messrs. Doright Ltd. Outline the possible structure of the personnel department which you expect to find in the company. Messrs. Doright Ltd consists of a parent works with one branch, employing a total of 3,000 workers, of which 2,500 are employed in the parent works and 500 in the branch factory.   (*I.W.M.* (*S.Q.*))

3. 'The personnel manager holds the key to good relationships within a factory.' Examine this statement and state your reasons for agreeing with or dissenting from it.   (*I.M.E.* 1956)

4. Describe the operation of a scheme of merit rating, applicable to clerical and junior staff workers, with a view to rationalizing their salaries and assessing their worthiness of promotion.

Discuss the likely reactions of the employees to such a scheme.   (*I.P.E* (*S.Q.*))

5. In a recent dispute in the steel industry a suggestion was made to implement a scheme of job evaluation for craft and process workers. Outline a scheme which you consider suitable and discuss its value as a solution to a frequently occurring industrial problem.   (*University of Wales* 1964)

6. State a case justifying the establishment of a personnel department to a director who opposes this action on financial grounds.   (*Luton College of Technology* 1962)

7. What is merit rating? What are the principal methods of doing it, the uses that can be made of it, and the difficulties?   (*The Polytechnic of Central London* 1967)

8. You have been asked to investigate the benefits to be gained from introducing a system of job evaluation into your plant. Write in the form of a short report the advantages and disadvantages you see in the idea.   (*Norwich City College* 1970)

9. The years 1945 to the present have seen the steady increase in the status and function of the Personnel Manager. What are the implications of this development for the Works Manager?   (*Norwich City College* 1970)

10. What advantages would the Works Manager of a medium sized firm expect to gain from the appointment of a Personnel Manager?   (*Norwich City College* 1971)

11. Explain the principle of Job Evaluation. Before applying it, some grades of operators are found to be overpaid and some underpaid. How would you proceed in each case?   (*Luton College of Technology* 1959)

CHAPTER 31
INCENTIVE SCHEMES

1. Describe briefly three methods of payment by results, to be found in the engineer-

ing industry. Explain their relative merits and demerits, and the circumstances under which they may be expected to operate satisfactorily. (*I.M.E.* 1958)

2. State the principles which you consider must be observed when formulating an incentive bonus scheme. (*I.W.S. (S.Q.)*)

3. Assuming that it would be feasible to apply to a productive operation either an individual-centred or a group-centred financial incentive scheme based on rate of output, which would you recommend and why? (*B.I.M.* 1958)

4. Describe and show on a simple diagram the difference between Time Rate, Piece Rate and Premium Bonus schemes of wage payment as they affect the unit labour cost. Give examples and state why time rate and piece rate, respectively, are used in certain industries. (*I.W.M. (S.Q.)*)

5. What desirable conditions need to be present if a scheme for awarding financial incentives is to be successful? What schemes are available other than those involving financial incentives? (*I.W.M. (S.Q.)*)

6. 'Time Study and Incentives are terms which are regarded as synonymous in industry.'

Discuss this statement, giving your views concerning its validity.
(*The Polytechnic of Central London (I.W.M.)* 1959)

7. 'When a company installs a wage incentive plan, it does so with the hope that operating efficiencies will increase.' Discuss the statement with reference to a situation with which you are familiar. (*University of Aston in Birmingham* 1965)

8. What are the advantages of a Measured Day Work System of payment over other systems? (*University of Aston in Birmingham* 1967)

9. What factors influence the choice of a financial incentive scheme based on work measurement?

List the main types of scheme available and outline the particular scheme you would recommend for personnel engaged on engineering maintenance work. Justify your choice. (*University of Loughborough* 1968)

10. It has been said—'The less Production Engineers are involved with financial incentive schemes the better it is for them.'

What are your views on this statement and its implication, bearing in mind the responsibilities of a typical production engineer? (*University of Loughborough* 1967)

11. Discuss the limitations of financial incentives as a means of increasing output and efficiency. Suggest how some of the problems might be overcome.
(*University of Loughborough* 1965)

12. The management of your company is considering introducing either a system of Measured Day Work or a Financial Incentive Scheme and you have been asked to advise on relative merits and demerits of each system. How would you explain these merits and demerits? What are they? (*Luton College of Technology* 1965)

13. Because of a change in product you have been able to introduce mass production methods in the plant and are considering replacing the flat rate system of wage payment by a 'Payments by Results' system. What do you anticipate will be the effect of this on (*a*) women, (*b*) your foremen, and (*c*) indirect workers? (*Norwich City College* 1970)

14.(*a*) With the aid of graphs explain the principles of the 'Straight-Proportional' and 'Rowan' wage incentive schemes. State the type of work for which each one would be most suited.

(*b*) An operator produces a batch of 75 components in 4 hours. If the STANDARD TIME per component is 4 S.M.s, calculate:

(i) Operator performance

(ii) The amount of bonus earned for each of the above incentive schemes.
(*Luton College of Technology* 1964)

CHAPTER 32
SAFETY

1. State a case justifying the establishment of a personnel department to a director who opposes this action on financial grounds.   (*Luton College of Technology* 1962)

2. Give a survey of the following, in so far as they affect the Engineering Industry—
  (i) Education and Training facilities to ensure a suitable supply of skilled labour.
  (ii) The duties of a Safety Officer.   (*Luton College of Technology* 1963)

3. What steps should be taken to protect workers in machine shops from possible skin complaints?   (*M.R.H.*)

4. What are the safety problems arising from industrial noise? What steps are currently taken to reduce these, and what steps are likely to be taken in future?

     (*M.R.H.*)

5. What steps have been taken to improve the safety in working conditions of the drivers of commercial vehicles since the Second World War? What further changes are likely in this area of work?   (*M.R.H.*)

APPENDIX 2
CRITICAL PATH ANALYSIS

1. Explain what is meant by 'critical path scheduling'. Illustrate your answer by means of example where critical path analysis could be used to advantage.

     (*Brighton College of Technology* 1965)

2. The construction of a small petrol filling station involves the following activities—

	Activity	Time
A	Lead Time	7 days
B	Draw plans and estimate materials	4 ,,
C	Clear site	2 ,,
D	Dig foundations	3 ,,
E	Procure sand, cement	3 ,,
F	Lay concrete foundations	4 ,,
G	Procure bricks	3 ,,
H	Procure storage tanks (for underground installation)	21 ,,
I	Build walls	14 ,,
J	Procure roof materials	7 ,,
K	Construct roof	10 ,,
L	Send for electricians	3 ,,
M	Install wiring and connect to electricity supply	7 ,,
N	Send for painters	3 ,,
O	Paint buildings, etc.	10 ,,
P	Procure pumps	14 ,,
Q	Install pumps	3 ,,
R	Clear up	3 ,,

Construct an arrow diagram showing the critical path and hence find the overall time for the complete object. Also determine the 'float' on the non-critical activities.

     (*University of Glasgow* 1965)

3. 'Planning is basically the task of making things happen which would not otherwise occur.' Comment on this statement and indicate the use made of Critical Path Analysis in planning work.   (*Croydon Technical College* 1967)

4. Examine the basic difficulties of planning by conventional systems, e.g.: the GANTT CHART. Explain by use of a simple network the process involved in Critical Path Methods of planning. Discuss their advantages.

     (*Luton College of Technology* 1969)

APPENDIX 3
A—B—C ANALYSIS

1. The following figures relate to the Report of the Census of Production for 19—. Analyse them by means of a Lorenz Curve and explain what it reveals.

Agricultural Machinery and Components

Establishment Nos.	Net Output £(000s)
48	1,406
42	2,263
38	3,699
21	2,836
16	3,152
13	5,032
36	20,385
214	38,773

(*Norwich City College* 1970)

2. The following approximated figures were obtained from the annual order books of two separate engineering companies who reported similar annual turnovers—

Value of order	Company A No. of orders	Company A Total value £	Company B No. of orders	Company B Total value £
Under £5	500	2,000	2,400	10,000
£5–under £10	400	3,000	2,400	20,000
£10–under £20	300	5,000	1,200	20,000
£20–under £50	250	10,000	750	30,000
£50–under £150	160	20,000	75	10,000
Over £150	300	60,000	50	10,000
		100,000		100,000

Compare the order distribution of the two companies by means of Lorenz Curves plotted on the same graph, and comment on your results.

(*Norwich City College* 1971)

APPENDIX 4
LINEAR PROGRAMMING

1. Briefly explain the technique of linear programming.
Explain its uses, quoting examples of the sort of problems it can be used to solve.
A paint manufacturer produces two types of paint, A and B, using the same equipment. The pigment composition of each variety is shown in the table below—

	Paint A	Paint B
Red pigment	3 oz/pint	3 oz/pint
Yellow pigment	2 oz/pint	1 oz/pint
Blue pigment	3 oz/pint	5 oz/pint
Profit per pint	4p	5p

Pigment supplies are restricted by the availability of other plant in the factory and are currently as follows—

Red pigment   12,000 oz/week
Yellow pigment   7,000 oz/week
Blue pigment   15,000 oz/week

What proportions of A and B should be produced to give maximum profit and what is the profit?

Neglect plant time spent in changing from one shade to the other. Paint 'body' need not be taken into account.   (*North Staffordshire Polytechnic* 1971)

2. A businessman intends to diversify his interests in the seaside leisure industry by providing trips for holidaymakers. Two types of boats are available to him—

Type A has a capacity of 120 trips/day.

Type B has a capacity of 48 trips/day.

Market research shows that he can expect to provide 3,600 trips/day.

The manufacturers of Type B boat tell the businessman that they are able to supply him with only 40 boats. Investigation of the local labour situation shows that a total work force of 400 men will be available to man the boats.

Type A requires a crew of 10 and type B a crew of 8.

Type A provides a profit of 3p/trip and Type B provides a profit of 5p/trip. If the businessman wishes to maximize his daily profit what should be the mix of boats which he should purchase? How would his decision be modified if the profit from Type B were to be increased to 7½p/trip?   (*The Polytechnic of Central London* 1971)

3. A manufacturer makes two products A and B, each of which has to be processed in two departments. Processing times, unit and selling prices per item are tabulated below, and the minimal requirement of each product in a standard manufacturing period is also given.

Product	Processing Times in Department 1	Processing Times in Department 2	Selling Prices	Minimal Requirements
A	3	2	10	20
B	3	4	12	15

The capacities of the departments (in the same time-units as processing times) are Dept. 1:–145, and Dept. 2:–150 in a standard manufacturing period. It is assumed that whatever is made in the period can be sold, that the time required in either department to make either product is proportional to the number of the products made, and that the total time requirement in each department may be obtained by summing requirements of the two products separately.

Using graphical methods determine the numbers of each product to make in order to maximize income.

Express as equations or inequalities any functions graphed.

                                        (*The Polytechnic of Central London* 1971)

4. A company is a bulk producer of a single plastic sheet material which sells in two thicknesses. There are two factories set up for production—factory A is of a later design than factory B and was specifically built to produce size 1 economically. However, it is less economic than B for size 2.

Size	Hours/100 pounds Factory A	Factory B
1	0·25	0·40
2	0·35	0·30
Max. machine hours/wk	200	200

If the contribution of size 1 is £40 per 100 pounds and for size 2 is £70 per 100 pounds, how many pounds of each size should the factory produce in order to maximize contribution? (*The Polytechnic of Central London* 1971)

5. A small company makes two products A, B; currently 200 of each per week. It is designed to re-formulate the production policy to improve facility utilization and hence increase profits. Relevant information is—

Product	Raw Material Cost £	Labour Content (hrs)	Inspection Time mins)	Selling Price (£)
A	10	12	10	20
B	8	6	35	14

The labour force consists of 100 assemblers, who are paid 50p per hour worked, up to a maximum of 48 hours, and 4 inspectors, who are available for inspection work for a total of $151\frac{3}{4}$ hours per week. One bought-out component, speakers, is available up to a maximum of 600 per week; one of these components is used in each unit of both products. Fixed overheads are £1,000 per week. The sales function say that a maximum of 600 of either type could be sold weekly.

Using the Simplex Method, or a graphical method, maximize the profit function.

(*Derby & District College of Technology* 1969)

6.(*a*) A manufacturing firm produces two products, Alpha and Omega. Each product has to go through three processes, moulding, drying and baking. Process data is as follows—

	Alpha	Omega	Time Available
Moulding	8 hours	7 hours	112 hours
Drying	6 hours	30 hours	150 hours
Baking	9 hours	27 hours	162 hours

Profit: Alpha–£10 per unit
Omega–£15 per unit

How many of each product should be made to maximize profits?

(*b*) If an additional 27 hours could be made available for the Baking process at a cost of £2 per hour, how much more time should be utilized in that process and what would be the effect on the profit? (*Slough College of Technology* 1972)

7. A company produces two basic products, A and B. Four processes, I, II, III and IV, are involved in both cases, and the times that each product requires in each process is summarized in the table below.

	Product A Time per Unit	Product B Time per Unit	Total Time Available in Process
Process I	15	10	150
II	5	15	75
III	10	10	100
IV	10	5	50

If the unit profit on each product is the same what is the best quantity of each to manufacture in order to make maximum profit?

Over what range of the profit ratio A/B does this answer hold good?

(*Slough College of Technology* 1970)

8. A company produces 2 different models of tape recorder. Both go through the same departments: (i) the assembly section: (ii) the inspection and correction section. There are 1,800 man hours available/week in assembly and 150 man hours/week

available for inspection and correction. The time each recorder spends in each section, the maximum demand per week and the profit on each recorder are shown below.

Recorder	Assembly	Inspection	Maximum demand	Profit per recorder
A	3 hrs.	10 mins.	550	£5
B	2 hrs.	20 mins.	300	£8

The company also buys in speakers for the assembly from an outside supplier. Both A and B use the same speaker and maximum number available per week is 650.

Use a graphical method to obtain the optimum product mix based on maximizing weekly profit. What is this maximum profit?

Write down the mathematical inequalities representing your constraints, definining your symbols.

If the number of products was increased how useful would the graphical method be? Suggest an alternative method of solution in a more complex allocation case.

(*Manchester Polytechnic* 1971)

Index

Group Technology (G.T.), 244
Guaranteed week, 370

Halsey-Weir premium bonus, 373
Health and safety, 352
Highland Park, 147
Hoists, 120, 190
Human engineering, 174

Idle time—
    payment for, 368
    reluctance to book, 237
Illumination, recommended minimum
    service level, 181
Inaccuracy in time recording, reasons
    for, 236
Incentive schemes, 360–80
    and maintenance work, 121
    and production control, 251
Income-contribution chart, 38
Incomplete work, payment for, 369
Indirect labour, control of, 170
Indirect material, 302
Industrial nurse, 352
Industrial relations, 350
Information—
    presentation of, 177
    sources of costing, 235
Information officer, 75
Initiation of production, 207
Inspection, 212–13
    and incentive schemes, 367
    records, 231
Inspection department, responsibilities
    of, 213
Insurance stock, 313
Invoices, verifying, 328
Issuing material, 302

Jig, defined, 210
Job—
    card, 292
    evaluation, 354
    grading, 354
    order, 207
    production, 143
    sheet, 208
    time card, 237

Jobbing, 149
Johnson's two machine algorithm, 262
Juran, J. M., 53, 433

Key operations in preparing layouts, 103
Key points in progress chasing, 294

Labour control, 251
Late deliveries, problem of, 331
Layout—
    advantages of good, 101
    criteria for good, 99
    defined, 96
    displays and controls, 178
    group, 196
    machine, 104
    operation, 208
    preparing a, 102
    process or functional, 97
    produce, flow, sequential, line, 96
    stores, 341
    use of computers in preparing, 105
Lead time, 308
Learning curve, 442–4
Library, 75
Life of—
    factory, 88
    plant, 117
LIFO (Last-in-first-out), 239
Lifting trucks, 190
Lifts—
    floor space occupied by, 93
    in materials handling, 190
Light bulb problem, 122
Lighting, 180
Line—
    balancing, 149
    of balance (L-o-B-), 278–88
    layout, 96
Linear Programming, 434–41
    in location problems, 86
    in setting sales forecasts, 10
Load—
    defined, 258
    example, 401
    package, 190
Loading, 256
Location, 81
Logic (in C.P.A.), 413